Rats, Cats, Rogues, and Heroes

Glimpses of China's Hidden Past

Robert J. Antony

ROWMAN & LITTLEFIELD
Lanham • Boulder • New York • London

Published by Rowman & Littlefield
An imprint of The Rowman & Littlefield Publishing Group, Inc.
4501 Forbes Boulevard, Suite 200, Lanham, Maryland 20706
www.rowman.com

86-90 Paul Street, London EC2A 4NE

Copyright © 2023 by The Rowman & Littlefield Publishing Group, Inc.

Cover: Page from an early twentieth-century register of ancestral rites from the fourth branch of the Cao family, Shanwei village, Leizhou, Guangdong. This page lists various items, such as three piglets, one cock, three hens, six eggs, several types of rice, as well as incense, candles, colored flags, and talismans used in these rites (Source: *Cao sifang zhanbu*, handwritten copy dated 1998; courtesy of the Cao family).

All rights reserved. No part of this book may be reproduced in any form or by any electronic or mechanical means, including information storage and retrieval systems, without written permission from the publisher, except by a reviewer who may quote passages in a review.

British Library Cataloguing in Publication Information Available

Library of Congress Cataloging-in-Publication Data

Names: Antony, Robert J., author.
Title: Rats, cats, rogues, and heroes : glimpses of China's hidden past / Robert J. Antony.
Description: Lanham : Rowman & Littlefield, [2023] | Includes bibliographical references and index.
Identifiers: LCCN 2022034522 (print) | LCCN 2022034523 (ebook) | ISBN 9781538169322 (cloth) | ISBN 9781538169339 (paperback) | ISBN 9781538169346 (epub)
Subjects: LCSH: Criminal anthropology–China. | Outlaws and brigands–China. | Rogues and vagabonds–China. | Gangsters–China. | Prostitutes–China.
Classification: LCC HV7118.5 .A58 2023 (print) | LCC HV7118.5 (ebook) | DDC 364.951–dc23/eng/20220805
LC record available at https://lccn.loc.gov/2022034522
LC ebook record available at https://lccn.loc.gov/2022034523

∞™ The paper used in this publication meets the minimum requirements of American National Standard for Information Sciences—Permanence of Paper for Printed Library Materials, ANSI/NISO Z39.48-1992.

*for all the hidden voices
past, present, and future
that remain to be heard*

Contents

List of Maps, Figures, and Tables viii
Note to Readers x
Prelude. The Illusive Toothless Man 1
Chapter 1. The Underworld of Rivers and Lakes. 20
Chapter 2. Righteous Yang and the Great Comet of 1680. 44
Interlude 1. Pirates into Goddesses 67
Chapter 3. Of Rats, Cats, and Bandits in the Canton Delta 78
Chapter 4. Demons, Gangsters, and Triads. 102
Chapter 5. Religious and Ethnic Unrest in Huizhou. 129
Interlude 2. What Ever Happened to Broken Shoes Chen
    the Fourth? 155
Chapter 6. Identity, Messianism, and Rebellion on the
    Yao Frontier 167
Chapter 7. Water Chicks, Amazons, and Goddesses. 191
Chapter 8. Weizhou Island, Dan Fishers, and the Mysterious
    Third Old Lady. 214
Postlude. China's Culture Wars 229
Afterword 251
Appendixes. 254
Character List 271
Notes. 284
Bibliography 319
Index. 351

List of Maps, Figures, and Tables

Map 1. Early Eighteenth-Century Taiwan   2
Map 2. The Gulf of Tonkin, c. 1680s   45
Map 3. Panyu County, Rat Hill, and Bandit Strongholds, Late Eighteenth and Early Nineteenth Centuries   85
Map 4. Geographic Distribution of Illegal Associations in South China, 1641–1788   106
Map 5. Distribution of Tiandihui, Dachengjiao, and Hakka Areas in Early Nineteenth-Century Guangdong, Jiangxi, and Fujian   130
Map 6. Geographic Scope of Chen Lanjisi's Adventures   156
Map 7. The Hunan-Guangdong-Guangxi Borderland during the Yao Rebellion, 1832   168
Map 8. Distribution of Sanpo Temples on the Guangdong Coast, c. 1850–1900   215
Map 9. Sailing Routes of Fishers between Hong Kong and the Gulf of Tonkin, c. 1930   220

Figure 1. Mao Zedong Astride Little Blue in Northern Shaanxi, 1947   7
Figure 2. Geomantic Locations of Ancestral Tombs in the Cao Family Genealogy, Shanwei Village, Leizhou   13
Figure 3. Heated Argument over Gambling   25
Figure 4. Hooligan Accosting a Young Girl to be His Friend, 1957   39
Figure 5. Contemporary Poster of the Hero Yang Yandi   62
Figure 6. Statues of the Two Mazus in the Zuxi Temple   75
Figure 7. Thatched Hut Beside a Fishpond in Panyu, 2002   81
Figure 8. Ideal Fengshui Model   95
Figure 9. Rat Hill and *Fengshui*   98
Figure 10. All-Purpose Exorcising Charm   114
Figure 11. Triad Altar Showing Common Exorcist Objects   117

LIST OF MAPS, FIGURES, AND TABLES

Figure 12. Sword Wielding Daoist Priests in Taiwan Exorcising Demons, 2002	121
Figure 13. Triad Banner Used by Chen Lanjisi	137
Figure 14. Wu Zixiang's Sect Networks	141
Figure 15. Talisman Used by Wu Wenchun	143
Figure 16. Xu Qianjin's Incantation, 1799	149
Figure 17. Page from the Boluo Chen Family Genealogy, 1833	159
Figure 18. Grave of the Southern Efflorescent King with his Descendant and the Author, 2015	163
Figure 19. A Modern Representation of the Southern Efflorescent King	165
Figure 20. Youling Stockade, c. 1837	174
Figure 21. Yao Stockades and Qing Military Posts in the Lianyang Region, c. 1771	176
Figure 22. Dan Boat Families on the Min River, c. 1910	196
Figure 23. Gateway to the Former "Water Chicks" Anchorage in Macau's Inner Harbor, 2008	199
Figure 24. Side Altar of the Powdered Lady in the Kanggong Temple in Macau, 2019	211
Figure 25. Spirit Medium in Trance with Long Metal Skewer Piercing His Cheeks, Shanwei Village, 2010	223
Figure 26. Chinese Trading Company Venerating Jeff Bezos as the God of Money on Black Friday, November 26, 2021	230
Figure 27. "Ox-Demons and Snake-Spirits" in the Thunder God Procession, Shanwei Village, 2010	233
Figure 28. Light Porn Advertisement for a Female Rock and Dance Performance in Wushi Harbor, Leizhou, 2010	240
Table 1. Backgrounds of the 108 Bandit-Heroes of Liangshan in *Water Margin*	30
Table 2. Temporal Distribution of Illegal Associations in Southeast China, 1641–1788	107

Note to Readers

This book grew out of my discontent with the commonly used sources I found in libraries and archives, which rarely answered all the questions I had about the everyday lives of ordinary Chinese. How did they view their own past and culture? What about their personal experiences, thoughts, and beliefs? How did their understandings of history affect how they acted and how they identified themselves and their community? Was what they said about the past the same as what historians were saying? To answer these and other questions concerning people's historical consciousness I needed to look beyond the libraries and archives to venture outside my comfort zone, to go out into the towns and villages in rural China to talk to the people to collect their stories, folklore, and legends. What I discovered was a world often quite different from what I was reading about in history books. This book is my effort to make sense of that different, hidden world.

Readers should be aware of certain conventions that I use throughout this book. All Chinese names and terms, with only a few exceptions, are rendered in the pinyin system of romanization. In several cases where the characters for Chinese names or terms are unknown, I follow the romanization given in the original text. I have also retained the well-known English renderings for Canton, Hong Kong, Macau, and Amoy, and use the terms Canton delta and Pearl River delta interchangeably. *Italics* are used for non-English words and terms; however, in general, non-English proper names (such as names of people and places, Chinese deities, religious sects, and secret societies) are not italicized. For consistency and convenience I have referred to Han Chinese simply as Chinese unless otherwise noted, and to the secret society known as the Heaven and Earth Society (Tiandihui) and its affiliates as the Triads.

Let me briefly explain how I use certain terms. I use such terms as *ethnicity* or *ethnic group* to indicate specific groups of people who display a sense of self-consciousness and identity as a distinct ethnic group. Folk/folk religion/folk culture are interchangeable with popular/popular religion/popular culture, where I use these terms to merely denote the common religion/culture of people from all walks of life, but especially as expressions of everyday life of ordinary people or commoners (usually rendered as *shuren* or *pingmin* in Chinese). Although there is much scholarly controversy on defining popular religion (a topic that is beyond the scope of this book), for simplicity what I refer to as popular or folk religion is what many scholars today call *minjian zongjiao* (religion among the people). When mentioning religious groups I sometimes use the term *sect* or *cult* without any implied stigmatization. My labeling of these groups as *heterodox* or *unorthodox* were how officials and cultural elites viewed them, but did not represent how participants viewed themselves and their activities. Chinese terms are often ambiguous and difficult to translate precisely into English. For example, the word *wu*, depending on the context, can mean shaman, spirit medium, soothsayer, sorcerer, wizard, and so forth. Terms for female shamans, spirit mediums, sorceresses, and witches include *wunü*, *nüwu*, *wupo*, *shenpo*, *xianpo*, *gepo*, *huapo*, and so forth. I have tried to base my translations on the context in which such terms were used.

In this book a person's age is calculated according to the Chinese system of reckoning in *sui*, that is, the age a person will attain in the current year, not the actual number of months and years that have elapsed since birth. Thus newborns begin at one year old and at the lunar new year another year is added to the person's age. In general, a person who is thirty *sui* is only twenty-nine years old by Western reckoning.

In the notes I use shortened titles for books, articles, and so on. Full citations are in the bibliography. Also in the notes dates to archival documents are given according to the reign year of an emperor in the Chinese lunar calendar as follows: QL 40.10.12, indicating the twelfth day of the tenth lunar month of the fortieth year of the Qianlong reign, and JQ 8.r6.14, indicating the fourteenth day of the sixth intercalary lunar month of the eighth year of the Jiaqing reign ("r" indicates an intercalary lunar month). Similarly I use DG for the Daoguang reign.

Additional resources, mostly illustrations, are available on the book's webpage under the "Features" tab at https://rowman.com/ISBN/9781538169322.

In the text, where indicated, measurements are given in the Chinese style of calculating. Because of fluctuations in the value of money the equivalencies given are only approximations. When taken from Chinese sources references to dollars refer to Spanish silver dollars (*yuan*); however, references to "dollars" in Western sources are more ambiguous.

Note to Readers

Measures and Weights

1 *li* 里 (Chinese mile) = 1,890 feet or 500 meters
1 *mu* 亩 (Chinese hectare) = ⅙ acre
1 *jin* 斤 (catty) = 1.33 pounds
1 *dan* 石 (picul, weight) = 120 *jin*
1 *dou* 斗 (peck) = 316 cubic inches
1 *shi* 石 (picul, dry measure) = 10 *dou* (approx. 3,160 square inches)

Currencies

1 *liang* 两 (tael) = approx. 1.33 ounces of silver
1 *wen* 文 (copper cash) = approx. 0.00125 tael
1 *yuan* 圆 (dollar) = approx. 700 to 1,000 *wen*

Timeline

Ming Dynasty (1368–1644)
    Hongwu Emperor (1368–1398)
    Jianwen Emperor (1398–1402)
    Yongle Emperor (1402–1424)
    Hongxi Emperor (1424–1425)
    Xuande Emperor (1425–1435)
    Zhengtong Emperor (1435–1449 and 1457–1464)
    Jingtai Emperor (1449–1457)
    Chenghua Emperor (1464–1487)
    Hongzhi Emperor (1487–1505)
    Zhengde Emperor (1505–1521)
    Jiajing Emperor (1521–1566)
    Longqing Emperor (1566–1572)
    Wanli Emperor (1572–1620)
    Taichang Emperor (1620)
    Tianqi Emperor (1620–1627)
    Chongzhen Emperor (1627–1644)

Southern Ming (1644–1662)
    Hongguang Emperor (1644–1645)
    Longwu Emperor (1645–1646)
    Shaowu Emperor (1646–1647)
    Yongli Emperor (1646–1662)

Qing Dynasty (1644–1911)
> Shunzhi Emperor (1644–1662)
> Kangxi Emperor (1662–1722)
> Yongzheng Emperor (1723–1736)
> Qianlong Emperor (1736–1796)
> Jiaqing Emperor (1796–1820)
> Daoguang Emperor (1820–1851)
> Xianfeng Emperor (1851–1861)
> Tongzhi Emperor (1861–1875)
> Guangxu Emperor (1875–1908)
> Xuantong Emperor (1908–1912)

Republic of China (1911–present; in Taiwan since 1949)
People's Republic of China (1949–present)
> Mao Zedong (1949–1976)
> Hua Guofeng (1976–1981)
> Deng Xiaoping (1978–1992)
> Hu Yaobang (1981–1987)
> Zhao Ziyang (1987–1989)
> Jiang Zemin (1989–2002)
> Hu Jintao (2002–2012)
> Xi Jinping (2012–present)

Prelude
The Illusive Toothless Man

LET ME BEGIN WITH AN UNFINISHABLE STORY. AT DAYBREAK ON THE twenty-first day of the first lunar month in 1734 a patrolling soldier named Huang Yongxing noticed two flags, one white and the other blue, planted in a paddy field outside the north gate of Zhuluo in Taiwan. The flags were like the ones used in temples and processions. On the white flag was a red circle with the characters "one day" (*yiri*) written inside; above the circle were the characters "Great Ming Fourth Prince Zhu" (*Da Ming Zhu Sitaizi*) and below the circle the characters "North Route Dukes (*guogong*) Chen Zong and Guo Xiushan and Generals (*jiangjun*) Zheng Wei and Guo Quan; South Route Duke Cai Jing and Prime Minister (*chengxiang*) Lai Dengyu."[1] On the blue flag were the characters "Great Ming revive Fourth Prince Zhu, three dukes arise in righteousness" (*Da Ming fuxing Zhu Sitaizi san guogong qiyi*). Huang Yongxing took the flags back to his headquarters and his commanding officer immediately reported the incident to the county magistrate, who afterward told his superiors at the prefecture in Tainan. This set in motion an island-wide manhunt for the suspects and witnesses that continued for several months, but the case appears to never have been fully resolved.

Why did officials make such a fuss about this seemingly innocuous planting of flags in a field outside Zhuluo city? Taiwan only had been incorporated into the Qing Empire in 1683, after the defeat of the separatist regime founded by Zheng Chenggong (better known in the West as Koxinga). The island became a prefecture of Fujian province a year later. In the early eighteenth-century Taiwan was a wild, remote, and sparsely populated frontier composed of numerous aborigine tribes and largely male Han Chinese settlers who were concentrated in the central and southwestern plains between Zhuluo and Fengshan counties (map 1). Officials and soldiers, who were mostly cloistered inside a few walled cities and towns near the coast, were notoriously corrupt and incompetent. Their chief functions were collecting

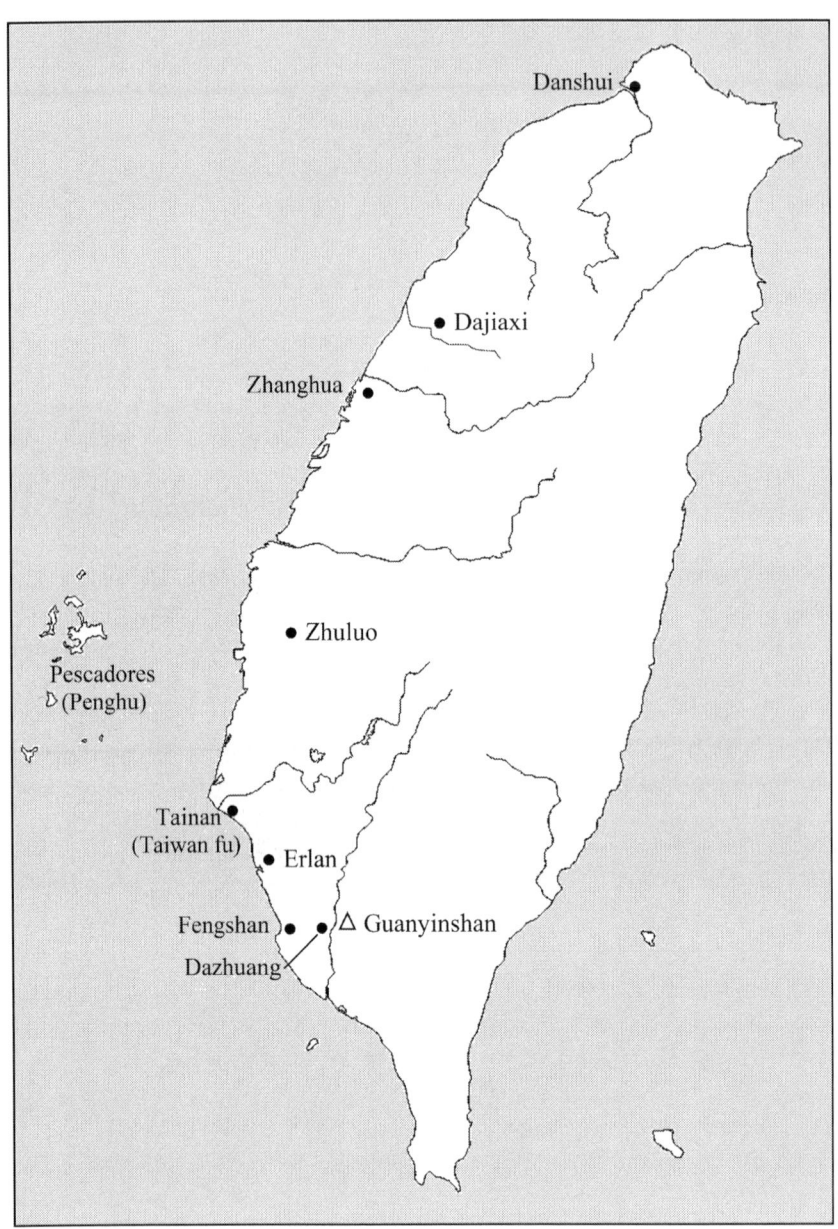

Map 1. Early Eighteenth-Century Taiwan (Source: Created by author).

taxes and reducing conflicts between the aborigines and Chinese pioneers, but in neither case were they very successful. One of these early settlers, a man named Zhu Yigui, was described as a good-for-nothing loafer, someone who eked out a bare subsistence raising ducks in rural Fengshan. Together with several like-minded people, in 1721 Zhu started a revolt that expanded quickly and came to occupy more than a quarter of Taiwan. Because his surname, Zhu, was the same as that of the defunct Ming royal family, the band of insurgents chose him as leader, anticipating that he would be able to rally popular support under the banner of Ming restoration. Although government soldiers crushed the rebellion within a few months, new disturbances erupted a decade later. Aboriginal tribes in the Dajiaxi area revolted in 1731, and a year later a Chinese settler, Wu Fusheng, incited a revolt in Fengshan. In the Zhu Yigui and Wu Fusheng cases, officials reported that both men handed out official titles and produced flags calling for the revival of the Ming dynasty.[2] Thus, when apparently similar flags appeared in Zhuluo only two years later officials were justifiably alarmed.

Within a month after Huang Yongxing first reported the case, soldiers arrested five of the men named on the white flag and brought them to the Zhuluo yamen for questioning. They confessed that they were married and had some property. "We are simple country farmers," they said, "and we dared not put our names on flags and plant them outside the city as bandits." In fact, they suggested, "wicked scoundrels (*jiangun*) did this to damage our reputations and get us in trouble." The magistrate noted that each man was in his seventies and that some appeared crippled or handicapped. Their stories were confirmed by their *baojia* heads and neighbors who were made their guarantors.[3] Suspecting a cover-up, however, the Taiwan circuit intendent, Zhang Sichang, again repeatedly interrogated each prisoner under torture, but their confessions did not change and they were sent home under bond. Investigations continued and a reward of a hundred taels of silver (*liang*) was offered to anyone with new information.

The next break in the case came in the fourth lunar month when Xie Xiyuan, a military degree holder, came forward to report to the commander of the South Route Battalion in Fengshan that a man named Xiao Quan came to his house telling him that at Erlan he came across someone who said he possessed flags that he planned to take to Goddess of Mercy Mountain (Guanyinshan). Xiao Quan was quickly taken into custody and harshly questioned by the Fengshan magistrate. The prisoner testified that on the twenty-eighth day of the third lunar month he ran into an old acquaintance, someone he knew only as the Toothless Man (*wuchifu*), who said that he was going to plant flags at Goddess of Mercy Mountain, and that he would be waiting at the home of Xu Zu in Dazhuang for others to gather. Upon hearing this, the magistrate assembled soldiers and immediately went to Xu Zu's house, but there was no trace of the Toothless Man. Xu Zu was shackled and taken to the county yamen for further questioning. Under torture he confessed that the Toothless Man had come south from Zhuluo to "enlist people as brigands" (*zhaoren weifei*), but Xu Zu did not know where he had gone. Not long afterward soldiers apprehended the Toothless Man, who together with Xiao Quan and Xu Zu were harshly interrogated by the prefect in Tainan. Because each man tried to minimize his own involvement and shift the blame onto others, officials concluded that their testimonies were evasive and inconclusive. After nearly five months of investigations fewer than ten people had been arrested, and we have no further information in the extant records. We do not know the fate of the Toothless Man or others arrested in this case, nor do we know how or if this case was settled.[4]

Who was the Toothless Man? Officials who gathered information on him and others involved in this case had preconceived notions, even paranoia, about an impending revolt. From the government's perspective, as presented in the above documents, the Toothless Man was the ringleader of a rebellious movement that sought to overthrow the Qing and restore the Ming. The Toothless Man and several coconspirators had produced seditious flags that explicitly called for the revival of the Ming dynasty under a rumored Ming scion named the Fourth Prince Zhu. In preparation for the revolt, the would-be rebels had given out official titles to followers as dukes, prime ministers, and generals. Officials believed that the planting of flags was a call to arms in an area of the island, Fengshan and Zhuluo, that was wrought with unrest and resentment against the Qing regime and was ripe for rebellion. Luckily for the state, officials in Taiwan could boast, the revolt was nipped in the bud and never allowed to materialize.

But there are other possibilities regarding the story of the Toothless Man, hinted at in the documents when read between the lines. There is no concrete evidence that he ever intended to overthrow the dynasty; he had neither armies nor weapons. Given the fact that he was the leading suspect in this case, it seems odd that we have no information on the circumstances of his arrest nor do we have even a summary of his confession, unlike the situations of the others who were arrested. We do not even know his real name or where he came from. It is likely that the Toothless Man was a wandering beggar. To many Chinese, beggars symbolized a world turned upside down. They represented utter poverty, filth, vice, and chicanery. In the popular mind, they were associated with ruffians and bandits; they were also likened to ghosts and demons, and therefore intricately linked with sorcery and magic. They were quintessential outsiders, yet individuals who had special powers to work miracles that could help those in need. Begging actually was a common side occupation for Buddhist monks, Daoist priests, shamans, magicians, and other folk religious workers.[5] The making and selling of charms, often in the shape of flags, for protection against diseases or impending apocalypses was a common part of their repertoire. So too was the inclusion on their flags of the names of divine saviors, such as the well-known Fourth Prince Zhu. The placing of flags in open spaces, such as paddy fields, was also a widespread practice in Taiwan and south China; their purpose was to create a protective ritual space by establishing garrisons of spirit soldiers to patrol the periphery of a god's domain. In this scenario, the names on the flags were likely people who had bought protective amulets from the Toothless Man. Goddess of Mercy Mountain was a sacred place dotted with several temples and the Goddess of Mercy herself was an important protective deity often called upon by monks, priests, and spirit mediums in exorcisms.[6]

Unfortunately, we will never know the real intention of the Toothless Man's placement of the flags in a paddy field outside Zhuluo in 1734. Given the sparsity of documents, the evidence is open to several interpretations. Yet it is this ambiguity about the man that intrigues me. His unfinished story provides a glimpse into China's hidden past.

History from the Native's Point of View

What we know about the past is incomplete. We select facts to fit certain purposes and other facts are ignored, silenced, or even misconstrued when they do not fit those purposes. "Distant, intangible, unreliable, lost," writes Natasha Hoare, "our histories ... are at best half-remembered and at worst actively misrepresented."[7] Because history is a puzzle with missing pieces, it is always open to multiple possibilities and conflicting interpretations.

This book is not a conventional history. It is not intended as an account of the political or social developments of late imperial or modern China. Although I deal with the past, my approach is not solely historical, but rather interdisciplinary; I rely heavily on insights from anthropology, folk studies, and literature. As in my previous writings, I engage in what scholars have called history from below or the history of everyday life. Taking my cue from anthropologist Clifford Geertz, I attempt to explore China's past "from the native's point of view."[8] Instead of simply writing about ordinary people, I write this history from the perspective of ordinary people, how they viewed their own lives and behaved as active agents in making their own history. I have tried to reconstruct the past in terms of what people thought and believed and how they acted upon their thoughts and beliefs. What interests me therefore is popular consciousness, especially as expressed in the rituals, sociocultural conventions, language, and complex symbolism of everyday human experiences. Perhaps much of what I write will seem strange and maybe even absurd to Western readers, but it would have made sense to many Chinese living several hundred years ago and even today.[9]

I write with the view that history is subjective. Much of history escapes analysis because it fails to conform to accepted expectations about what is normal and authentic. To uncover the lost mysteries of the past requires imagination and thinking outside the box, as well as relentless interpretation and the conviction that what we write will never be the last word on the subject. According to Hayden White, there is no single correct view of history, but rather "many correct views, each requiring its own style of representation."[10] Because language—both written and oral—is ambiguous it creates the possibilities of numerous understandings and misunderstandings, which exist simultaneously in the same culture and about the same phenomena. While most people believe that the past is important, nonetheless they live "outside history," in the sense that they live with a past different from that constructed by academics. Natives and historians tend to see the past differently and take different paths to arrive at their understanding of the past.[11] My purpose is to recover and explore this outside history.

I chose the title *Rats, Cats, Rogues, and Heroes* because they represent major themes I want to explore in this book, and they are key elements for our interpretation of history from the native's point of view. The rats, cats, and other animals mentioned in this book are symbols that provide social and cultural meanings that help individuals and society make sense of their world in terms that they understand. As Robert Darnton explains, "Ordinary people in everyday life have to find their way through a forest of symbols." People perceive and create reality through symbols that are construed in many complex and often ambiguous ways. Symbols are metaphors that stand for things that they are like but are not.[12] As we will see in chapter 3, rats symbolize poverty, disease, and pilfering, whereas cats symbolize the opposite. While rats can turn into demons, cats possess magical powers

Figure 1. Mao Zedong Astride Little Blue in Northern Shaanxi, 1947 (Source: Wikimedia Commons)

that can scare away demons.[13] The white horse, mentioned in the second interlude, represents purity and loyalty in Buddhism and is usually associated with warrior-heroes and millenarian-saviors in Chinese folk culture. In Daoist rituals and Triad initiations white horses are the standard means of transport for Heavenly messengers.[14] In the sixteenth-century novel *Journey to the West* (*Xiyouji*) the future Tang emperor Li Shimin rode a white horse in battles against the Turks, and much later Mao Zedong rode a white horse, nicknamed "Little Blue" (*xiaoqing*), to victory during the civil war that ended in 1949 (figure 1). Many Chinese know tales of heroes, like Li Shimin and Mao Zedong, riding white horses, so it should not be surprising today to find local heroes like the Southern Efflorescent King to be depicted astride a white steed galloping into battle (see figure 19).[15] According to Roel Sterckx, since ancient times animals have provided Chinese with "a rich thesaurus for the expression of fundamental social, moral, religious, and cosmological ideas."[16] The symbolic meanings of other animals (cocks, dogs, tigers, birds) and objects (flags, jade, iron, comets) are discussed in detail in the following chapters.

Prelude

Rogues occupy a substantial portion of this book, as they exemplify key figures in the history of ordinary people, especially among the working poor. They include rebels, bandits, pirates, thieves, tricksters, soothsayers, beggars, prostitutes, and the like. By and large they were individuals who existed on the fringes of so-called respectable society. Although they likely did not regard themselves as rogues, in official reports they were routinely depicted as a "dangerous class" of "criminals," "hooligans," and "wicked scoundrels." In popular literature and folk culture these men and women often were characterized as denizens of the nebulous underworld of "rivers and lakes" (*jianghu*), a topic I consider in the following chapter. It is quite telling to note that Chinese officials and foreign observers over long stretches of time consistently recounted how difficult it was to clearly distinguish rogues from honest folks. As I have argued elsewhere, the turn to crime was often an important survival strategy to offset abject poverty and rampant discrimination. Most of the individuals convicted of banditry and piracy, in particular, were commoners who occasionally engaged in illicit activities to supplement wages they earned as day laborers, porters, fishers, entertainers, and so forth. They all shared a common sociocultural milieu that coexisted uneasily with that of mainstream society. Because few among them could abide by the Confucian dictum that it was better to go hungry than to steal, in their rough-and-tumble world they often had to adopt lifestyles and values that stood in stark contrast to their more affluent neighbors.[17]

Another important group of people, who generally had low social status and were looked down upon by officials and scholars as charlatans and troublemakers, were the ubiquitous folk religious specialists. Because most Chinese made no distinctions between sacerdotal and temporal activities, religion permeated every aspect of people's everyday lives. To serve the daily needs of the people, China relied on a large range of male and female ritual specialists that included not only the officially registered monks, nuns, and priests, but also shamans, spirit mediums, magicians, wizards, sorcerers, fortune tellers, and geomancers. Nearly every community had a religious specialist who worked out of his or her home or local temple or shrine. Others traveled about the countryside from village to village and from market to market peddling their services and cures, usually earning no more than a subsistence living. These were also the sorts of individuals who frequently played key roles in organizing lay Buddhist sects and secret societies. By and large most of these religious workers came from the lower orders of society and were not held in high esteem within the community social hierarchy.

Nonetheless, they were indispensable local practitioners—doctoring the sick, assuring good harvests, settling disputes, and quieting hungry ghosts. They were both respected and feared by ordinary people because they possessed awesome magic that could bring either benefit or harm.

Women and ethnic groups also played important roles in China's history from below, and when we problematize that history from their point of view we see a different past. As Stevan Harrell has posited, "Civilizers of all sorts have seen peripheral peoples as both erotic and promiscuous in their behavior," perspectives not necessarily consistent with the ways that minorities viewed themselves. He goes on to explain: "Women are thought to epitomize peripheral peoples, since peripheral peoples are in some sense feminine." The sexual metaphor of feminization of peripheral peoples or ethnic minorities was a deliberate act of defining them as subordinate to mainstream Chinese society and culture.[18] While this may be true from the perspective of the civilizing Chinese state, I would argue that the feminization of ethnic minorities could also empower them to become masters of their own destiny. As discussed in chapter 7, ethnic Dan (Tanka) boat women were not only active agents in determining their own fate but also helped feminize China's southern littoral according to their terms.[19] It is therefore no coincidence that several pirate chieftains were women and that the most powerful sea deities were female. Other ethnic groups, such as the Hakka discussed in chapter 5 and the Yao in chapter 6, carved out their own ethnic identities in large measure by resistance and open rebellion against the dominant Han Chinese majority. They also articulated their ethnic consciousness with myths that symbolized their different identities. The Hakka traced their origins to the earliest founders and the cradle of Chinese civilization in the Yellow River basin. The Yao developed a fervent belief that they were descendants of a mystical dragon-dog named Panhu. What was important in defining ethnic identity was the construction of historical consciousness rather than historical truth itself. To realize the history of China's ethnic groups and women we need to uncover their historical voices.[20]

Many of the rogues discussed in this book have been popularized as local heroes. Rebels and outlaws were all potential heroes, especially if they were seen as victims of inequality, injustice, and oppression. For ordinary people heroes were symbolically important: "Although many who have been heroized have been undeserving of celebration, the myth of the good robber who protects and assists his own people is immensely powerful, widespread, and long lasting."[21] Heroes, like deities, were mainly concerned with image and myth, not historical reality. They were superhuman in the sense that they possessed certain qualities that set them apart from ordinary people. There were no clear cut distinctions separating the heroic from the magical. In the popular imagination heroes could be superior humans or gods. According to Robert Ruhlmann, heroes in Chinese art and literature typically embodied the values and ideals of society that inspired imitation and the sorts of positive behavior that could "play a significant role in shaping history." Saviors, who appeared in legends of secret societies and rebel movements, theatrical performances, popular novels, liturgical texts, and folklore, were an important type of hero who alleviated people's suffering and rescued them from wars, natural disasters, and the abuses of authority. Legends that built upon such heroes, prophets, and saviors often became potent forces for social change, as we will see in the cases of Righteous Yang, Broken Shoes Chen the Fourth, and Golden Dragon Zhao examined in the following chapters. Some folk heroes, such as Righteous Yang, Zhang Baozai, Zheng Chenggong, and his sister Zuxi, were even venerated as deities because of their efficacy at succoring the poor and working miracles.[22]

Pieces to the Puzzle

It is no easy task to recover the history of inarticulate and illiterate commoners who left behind few if any records written in their own hand. My central concern therefore has been how to give voice to the silent masses. In writing this book from the native's point of view I have had to rely on a large array of conventional and unconventional sources. Official documents and writings of literate elites were never sufficient; they never answered all my questions and therefore needed to be supplemented with new types of textual, visual, and oral evidence. Over the past thirty years I visited and revisited countless archives and libraries and conducted extensive fieldwork in many out-of-the-way villages and towns looking for missing pieces to the puzzle to retrieve glimpses of China's hidden past. I have tried as much as possible to let my sources speak for themselves, but rarely did they ever speak in one voice. This book is my attempt to make sense of the various and discordant voices I have encountered over these many years.

Most historical studies are derived from documentation written, collected, and preserved by officials and literati. Among these conventional sources the most important ones used in this study are archival records, particularly the judicial reports contained in palace memorials (*zouzhe*) and routine memorials (*tiben*). Written in rather matter-of-fact style by officials for other officials, these documents are raw traces of the past frozen in a moment of time. Despite the inherent biases of government documents, they provide important direct accounts on the activities and lives of ordinary people. "As so often when dealing with official records," Jim Sharpe writes, "they are at their most useful when employed for purposes their compilers would never have dreamt of."[23] They contain much detail on the workings of government and law enforcement at the local level, as well as on the complex routine interactions between communities and the state. When read against the grain, they reveal details of everyday life at the local level through the testimonies of individuals who appeared in courts as witnesses, victims, and suspects. Judicial case records contain countless names of unknown people. The records allow them to speak, to break their silence, even if their words have been transcribed, rewritten, and reinterpreted by yamen clerks and officials. Certainly there are misrepresentations and mistakes, but these records are generally the closest thing we have to hearing the voices of inarticulate commoners from the past.[24] As Arlette Farge succinctly puts it, "The archives always preserve an infinite number of relations to reality."[25]

The judicial archives often include enclosures, such as confessions and material evidence used in criminal prosecutions. Scribes recorded interrogations either in summary or verbatim, frequently in the colloquial language of those being questioned. Often extracted under torture, as we noted in the case of the Toothless Man, confessions inevitably contained complex combinations of both true and false statements that were often contradictory and evasive. To get at the truth, officials were required to gather all the evidence and cross-examine multiple witnesses and suspects; nonetheless when questioned under torture many people simply answered in ways they thought officials wanted to hear. From the evidence, it was not uncommon for the accused to falsely admit guilt or give misleading statements. Although important firsthand sources, confessions must be used with great caution and in combination with other documentation.[26] Even more important than confessions are the confiscated material evidence preserved in judicial cases, such as handbooks, sutras and scriptures, incantations, oaths and pacts, seals, placards, certificates, flags, talismans, and weapons produced by members of secret societies, religious sects, bandit and pirate gangs, and rebel movements. These materials contain invaluable firsthand information, seldom found elsewhere, not only on the organization of these illicit associations and the beliefs of their members, but they also provide crucial insights into the sociocultural mindsets of ordinary people.[27]

As mentioned above, to reach into the hearts and souls of ordinary people we need to dig deeper and explore unconventional sources, those generally unavailable in archives and libraries and therefore underutilized by historians. For the most part these include written, visual, and oral materials that I have collected during fieldwork in rural areas of south China over the past several decades. Observations at local festivals and interviews with villagers were essential to this field research, for helping me get a better understanding of people's daily lives and how they viewed themselves and their past. These sources are widely dispersed in temples, ancestral halls, and private homes; recollected in legends, myths, folklore, song, and drama; and performed in celebrations and rituals.[28]

Some of the most important local documentation are recorded on the largely unpublished steles or stone inscriptions, many of which date from the Ming and Qing dynasties. While literate elites created most steles and therefore expressed their claims to speak for the community, nevertheless they do contain vital information on local society, history, culture, and customs unaccounted for in official documents. Because steles were public documents meant to be seen by everyone, they recorded issues concerning the entire community. They included records on local permits and regulations, litigation, civil service examination success, local defense, building of roads and bridges, temple donations, renovation, and construction, as well as on various aspects of the social and religious life in villages and towns.[29] Occasionally, too, they gave voice to the voiceless. For example, there are several early nineteenth-century steles in the lower Canton delta based on petitions made by illiterate Dan boat people that ensured them of government protection against corrupt officials and soldiers and usurious merchants.[30] In this study I have cited records on stone inscriptions in my discussions about the construction of military posts on the Yao frontier, the conscription of Dan fishers in the government's fight against pirates and Triad rebels, and the creation of sea deity cults along China's southern littoral.

Steles are only one of many unconventional sources representing history from the native's point of view. James Hayes has reviewed more than twenty categories of printed and handwritten village books and manuals—genealogies, almanacs, handbooks on geomancy, divination, and fortune telling, liturgical texts, references on family and social practices, guides for writing contracts and letters, collections of riddles, proverbs, and ballads, illustrated novels and stories, morality books, as well as ephemera such as talismans, notices, placards, posters, broadsides, and so forth. These sources frequently provide counternarratives to official histories. A few examples of the types of village records I have used in this study will suffice. Genealogies are valuable records of family and lineage histories, which include information on members, property holdings, ritual practices, rules and regulations, names of academic and purchased degree holders, and geomantic data on tombs (figure 2). In the second interlude I make extensive use of three Chen family genealogies to discuss the lineage's most famous, or infamous, member, Broken Shoes Chen the Fourth. Talismans were of particular importance in people's daily lives, especially during times of crisis when an abundance of malevolent spirits were particularly active and people sought supernatural

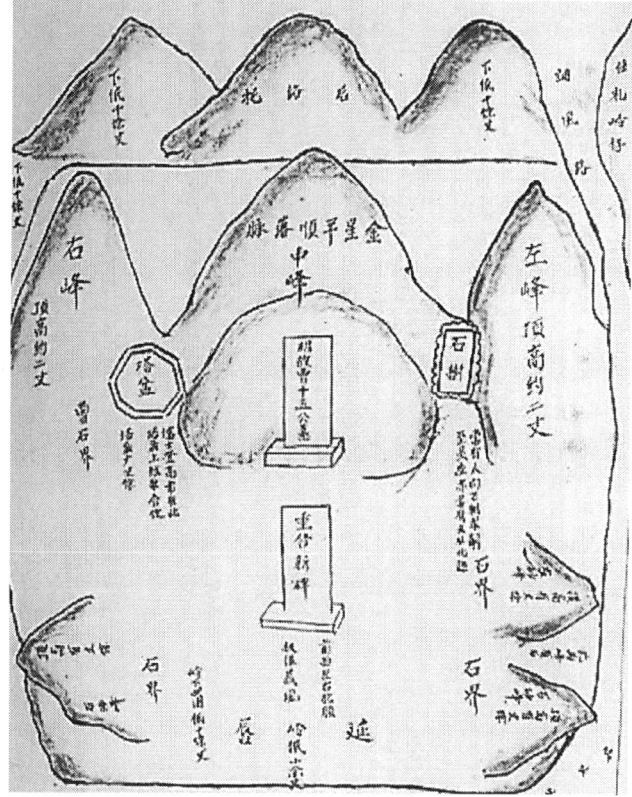

Figure 2. Geomantic Locations of Ancestral Tombs in the Cao Family Genealogy, Shanwei Village, Leizhou (Source: *Cao shi zupu*, 1894)

protection. In south China geomancy (*fengshui*) has always been a ubiquitous practice for siting villages, houses, temples, ancestral halls, and tombs, as well as for guaranteeing protection, health, and good fortune. Illustrated handbooks of charms and geomancy, therefore, were common items in villages and towns, and I have often consulted them in writing this book. Riddles, proverbs, folksongs, and rumors expressed the shared hopes, fears, and concerns of ordinary people otherwise overlooked in traditional historiography. They provide glimpses into the popular imagination, often revealing cynical attitudes of commoners toward the wealthy and powerful in society as well as about Confucian moralism.[31]

Folklore, legends, and myths allow people to use their imagination to take them away from the mundane world. Although contrived and fanciful, many individuals accept these tales at face value as a kind of "popular truth." They are important because they are highly charged with symbolism that gives meaning to human experiences. Their chief value is as insights into the ways ordinary people envision their universe. As folklorist Douglas Cowan explains, myths are a vehicle for explanation, "a cache of symbols lodged in narrative that established a framework of cosmological significance for a particular group of people. They are stories that encode, and, just as importantly, transmit cultural meaning and significance."[32] Because they are meant to be interpretations of the past rather than factual descriptions of the past, folklore, legends, and myths present a different sort of reality and sense of history. Some scholars suggest that much of history might be construed as mythohistory, especially when we consider that fact and fiction are largely relative to place and time. One historian's truth is another's myth. According to Jonathan Friedman, history is very much a "mythical construction, in the sense that it is a representation of the past linked to the establishment of an identity in the present." This is because the past is "constructed according to the conditions and desires of those who produce historical texts in the present."[33] In any case, for this book, folklore, legends, and myths are crucial supplementary sources of historical consciousness that bring to life the imaginations of ordinary people.[34]

Organization of the Book

Following this prelude, I organize this book as a set of linked essays arranged topically into eight chapters, two interludes, and a postlude. While I do discuss other areas and earlier time periods, my focus is southern China—Guangdong, Guangxi, Hunan, Jiangxi, Fujian, and Taiwan—during the

Prelude

late imperial and modern periods, roughly the sixteenth through twentieth centuries.

The first chapter provides the context for what follows by examining the shadowy underworld of "rivers and lakes," a traditional Chinese euphemism for the subaltern culture of knights-errant, bandits, rogues, swindlers, gamblers, beggars, and prostitutes. It is both a real and imagined sociocultural space existing at the fringe of so-called respectable society. Vividly depicted in folklore and vernacular fiction, the denizens of this underworld are best delineated by the stringent laws that the state enacted against them and their activities. Besides the remote bandit lairs secreted away in mountains and marshes, the inns, teahouses, brothels, opium dens, and gambling parlors, which could be found in every market town and city, provided safe refuges for those people persisting on the margins of family and community. Theirs was a social and cultural realm with its own rules, argot, and black markets, interlinked with, yet distinct from, mainstream society.

Chapter 2 is a case study of a little-known but important historical figure known variously as Yang Yandi, Yang Er, and, more colloquially, "Righteous Yang," who lived during the turbulent Ming–Qing transition (1644–1684) on the Sino-Vietnamese water frontier. I begin his story with a discussion of the Great Comet of 1680, seen by rulers and people as an ominous portent of impending disaster that marked either the fall of Righteous Yang or the newly founded dynasty. In that age of chaos and anarchy, it was easy for charismatic individuals like Yang to possess multiple identities and affiliations—as pirate, rebel, and hero. Yang Yandi, who began his outlaw career as a local petty pirate in the 1640s, became the most influential and formidable pirate in the Gulf of Tonkin during the next four decades. At the same time, he also became involved in the anti-Qing resistance movements and for a time collaborated with the Zheng regime in Taiwan. After the latter's decline Yang led several thousand followers back to the gulf where they established bases on Longmen island and later in southern Vietnam. Today Yang is best known locally as an anti-Manchu hero and freedom fighter.

The first interlude continues the narrative of the Ming–Qing transition with an examination of the cult of Zuxi, the purported pirate-rebel, heroine, and younger sister of Zheng Chenggong. Although there is no solid evidence that Zuxi ever existed in actual life, nonetheless for the past three centuries she has been worshipped as a reincarnated sea goddess whom villagers call the "Warrior Mazu." This virtually unknown cult exists only in one small temple in coastal Guangdong. There are several legends about Zuxi, the two

Prelude

most popular ones are that she died in a naval battle fighting the Manchus and alternatively that she was murdered by her brother in order to ensure that she would protect his treasures as a ghost from the afterlife. Based on my fieldwork I explain the possible meanings of the two legends and deification of Zuxi from several perspectives.

I explore the presumably inexplicable connections between rats, cats, and bandits in the Canton delta in chapter 3. In the 1871 gazetteer of Panyu county, Guangdong, the author recorded something that struck me as unusual regarding late eighteenth-century banditry in the border area between Shawan and Jiaotang, two rural districts located near the provincial capital of Canton. For decades gangs of bandits, who occupied a mound known locally as Rat Hill, terrorized villages and markets throughout the delta, while the state seemed helpless in eliminating them. Finally in an act of apparent desperation, in 1780 provincial officials placed a statue of an Iron Cat at Rat Hill in hopes that this would scare away the troublemakers in the area. This chapter takes a close look at the possible meanings of the government's casting of the Iron Cat as well as the nature of persistent banditry in the core Canton delta in the early modern period. My emphasis is on how local officials and villagers in the delta reacted to banditry and explained their past.

The Heaven and Earth Society or Triads was one of many illegal associations that existed in south China in the early modern period. In chapter 4, I investigate the connections between secret societies and Chinese popular religion, and in particular their connections with Chinese demonology and messianism. My purpose is to investigate as best as we can early secret societies from the perspectives and motives of the people who formed or joined them. While officials viewed them as dangerous, seditious organizations aiming to subvert the established political and social order, I argue that Triad leaders and members instead emphasized customary beliefs about the supernatural and/or survival strategies that often involved banditry and racketeering. The Triads, in fact, developed out of a common shared tradition that combined demonological messianic movements and gangsterism, phenomena that frequently utilized blood-covenants that bonded members in solemn brotherhoods.

The next chapter is a case study that follows up on the analysis of the Triads discussed in the previous chapter. In 1802, a major Triad uprising erupted in the mountains of Huizhou prefecture near Canton. Before it was suppressed more than a year later, the disturbances came to involve tens of thousands of people and roughly a quarter of Guangdong province. The areas where the uprising occurred were predominantly Hakka, an ethnic Chinese minority, who came into conflict with the earlier settlers known as Punti. As violence escalated both sides organized their own paramilitary units: Hakka formed Triad groups and Punti formed Ox Head Societies. Significantly too, the Triad groups in Huizhou belonged to a much wider network of secret society and lay Buddhist organizations that spread across the Hakka heartland on the Jiangxi, Fujian, and Guangdong border. In this chapter I address key issues concerning the social, political, and religious contexts and motivations of this Hakka-led rebellion.

The second interlude continues the story of the Hakka-Triad rebellion by taking a closer look at one of the leaders, a man with the unusual name of Broken Shoes Chen the Fourth. According to archival documents he was captured and executed in 1802, soon after the uprising erupted. However, family members and a recent genealogy tell a different story. According to these private accounts Broken Shoes had escaped and fled to the mountains of Lianzhou, where he changed his name and established a new branch of the Chen lineage. His declared descendants today honor him as a hero who went on to fight in other Triad-led uprisings and to establish a short-lived kingdom on the Guangdong-Guangxi border under the name Southern Efflorescent King. This interlude, which traces the story of Broken Shoes as related to me by his descendants in Huizhou and Lianzhou, examines the credibility of his escape and the reasons why he is portrayed as a family and local hero.

Broken Shoes purportedly ended up living in the foothills of the Yao mountains in the borderland of Guangdong, Hunan, and Guangxi provinces, where in 1832 Yao tribes launched a major uprising, discussed in chapter 6. This was a remote area with the largest concentration of Yao people and an area that many of them considered as their sacred homeland. It took the state more than a year to subdue the revolt, which came to involve tens of thousands of Yao insurgents, Chinese bandits, soldiers, mercenaries, and militiamen. In this chapter I address the question of Yao identity, which was imposed by successive imperial regimes on certain highland aborigines in south China who in time also came to view themselves in similar ways. The Yao identified themselves as descendants of a fabled dragon-dog named Panhu who vowed to return to lead his people to a promised land. Given this context, a charismatic Yao Daoist master named Zhao Jinlong (Golden Dragon Zhao) ignited the rebellion in 1832 by mobilizing thousands of followers with claims of being the Yao King and the reincarnation of Panhu, who had come back to earth to lead his people to an earthly paradise in the mountainous Yao frontier. The Panhu myth, I argue, is the key to our understanding of Yao identity, the Yao frontier, and the Yao Rebellion of 1832.

In chapter 7, I take a close look at another ethnic group, the Dan boat women of Guangdong and Fujian. I assert that this southern coastal area was a highly feminized space. The Dan were a seafaring underclass who mostly lived on boats along the coast and river estuaries of south China. Unlike many other places in the world, there were few taboos on women working and living aboard Dan ships. Boat women went to sea as wives and daughters and worked aboard ships as sailors, prostitutes, and pirates. Furthermore, some of the most important sea deities and water sprites in China were female, including the Empress of Heaven, Lady of the Seventh Star, Pissing Woman, and many others. The characterization of a feminine sea space is important as it offers us an alternative approach to understanding China's maritime history, one that moves away from the dominant patriarchal Confucian and terra-centered approaches to Chinese history. Boat women and female pirates represented the most radical departure from the traditional norms of dominant society and culture on shore. They represented a menacing "other" that defied the accepted notions of womanhood, breaking with the established codes of female propriety, virtue, and passivity. Likewise, female sea deities reinforced notions of "otherness" and provided boat women with positive models of womanhood, strength, and defiance in an otherwise male-dominated society.

Building on the discussion about female sea deities in the previous chapter, the last chapter introduces a largely unknown sea goddess with the odd name Third Old Lady (Sanpo). Although her origins are unclear, this obscure deity likely began as a local cult founded by Dan boat people and pirates on Weizhou island in the Gulf of Tonkin. Before her transformation into Sanpo she may have been a water sprite who protected a natural spring on the island. By the middle of the eighteenth century, Sanpo had a growing following among the fisherfolks, seafarers, pirates, and smugglers who frequented Weizhou, and by the end of the century her temples peppered the gulf coast and the Leizhou peninsula. By the start of the following century her temples appeared as far away as the Canton delta. Based largely on unpublished information on stone inscriptions and from fieldwork, in this chapter I argue that fisherfolk and pirates played key roles in the dissemination of the cult from west to east along the Guangdong coast.

The postlude on China's culture wars concludes this book. Many scholars have characterized China's modern period as one of growing integration and homogeneity between elite and popular culture through a process whereby commoners internalized the values and moral principles of dominant society. As this book demonstrates, however, this was not universally the case. Large segments of the population actually had lifestyles, customs, and values that were at odds with the conventions of Confucian or Communist orthodoxy. In this postlude I discuss China's culture wars over folk traditions, beliefs, and ritual practices, gender and sexuality, and multiculturalism and ethnic relations. I argue that because no one side in the culture wars was strong enough to overcome the other, in the long run differences normally were resolved through compromise, accommodation, or tolerance.

This book is my endeavor to present alternative ways of exploring China's culture and history by engaging the native's point of view. While building on previous conventional histories, this study diverges from them to examine in detail the underside of Chinese society and culture in the late imperial and modern eras. My focus is on that group of commoners who existed at the lower end of the social hierarchy, those people belonging to the murky world of "rivers and lakes" (*jianghu*). In writing this book my aim is not to replace standard histories, but rather to offer a different way to look at China's past. When we view China's history through the eyes of ordinary people we see an unfamiliar past, yet one with countless possibilities.

Chapter 1

The Underworld of Rivers and Lakes

Recently in districts in Jiangsu and Zhejiang young rogues, who collude with the wicked sons of gentry families, have been burning incense and swearing blood oaths [of brotherhood]. They openly invite [martial arts] masters to study boxing, tattoo extravagant patterns on both arms, and wear short armored vests down to their waists. Like packs of foxes and dogs, they come and go from tea houses and wine shops; like roaming bees and dancing butterflies, they go wild with women in brothels. Whenever they hear of someone suffering an injustice, they volunteer their services to avenge the wrongs. Street fights and brawls are their obsession; attacking and plundering others is their profession. An inadvertent stare at them can result in broken limbs and even more serious injuries. They call themselves Year Star Gods (Taisui)[1] and their actions thrashings from the sky (dajiang). Lest this evil behavior spread, it must not go unpunished.[2]

*In the last few years quite a few criminal gangs have appeared that are composed of middle-school students and strongly bear the coloration of feudal gangs and black societies. These youngsters imitate the actions of feudal gangs in knight-errant (*wuxia*) fiction, films, and television. They kowtow, take blood oaths, swear brotherhood and sisterhood, place each other in order of precedence, print [secret] signs, make gang rules, fight, brawl, stir up trouble, insult women, lord it over shopping areas, act the local bully, and seriously affect social order.[3]*

ALTHOUGH THESE TWO COMMENTARIES WERE WRITTEN NEARLY THREE centuries apart, nonetheless they are remarkably similar in their depictions of underworld society in both the Qing dynasty and the People's Republic of China (PRC). In the first account, the seventeenth-century scholar-official Huang Liuhong, in his widely read magistrate's handbook, wrote disapprovingly of the gang violence and youth decadence that was enveloping his world. By 1699, the year that Huang published his handbook, the Manchus had recently consolidated their rule over China and the empire was well on its way to economic recovery following the Kangxi emperor's freeing up markets and lifting bans on maritime trade. The second report by China's Ministry of Public Security in 1987 was a candid admission that juvenile gang crime was on the rise in the PRC. Officials noted that with economic reforms and the opening up of the country in the 1980s, there also was a steep increase in money-related crimes—theft, robbery, kidnapping, and swindling—resulting from "contradictions arising from the new socialist commodity economy." Over the decade of the 1980s the number of serious crimes against property more than doubled, and since then gang-related crimes have continued to mount, not only in the more advanced urban and coastal areas but also in the countryside.[4] Both documents are important not only because they link the rise in crime with changes in economic policies, but also because they explain it in terms of a resurgence in the underworld culture of rogues and knights-errant—that nebulous world of "rivers and lakes."

The term "rivers and lakes," which is a literal translation of *jianghu*, has a long history in China. Its usage and meaning evolved over the centuries. Several scholars have pointed out that it originated with the ancient Daoist philosopher Zhuangzi, who used it allegorically as a space outside officialdom and the normative social order. It referred to the lifestyle of disenfranchised and disillusioned hermits who decided to leave society and seek solace living free in nature. Several centuries later, during the Song and later dynasties, *jianghu* came to designate, on the one hand, an imaginary, escapist space among the literary and political elites, and on the other hand, a socialized milieu of misfits and outcasts who fit uneasily in mainstream society. In literature the Ming dynasty novel *Water Margin* (*Shuihu zhuan*) perhaps best exemplifies this unrestrained, subversive *jianghu* culture and society. More recently in China the realm of rivers and lakes has been appropriated by the fantasy worlds of *kungfu* novelists Jin Yong and Gu Long, by cinematographer Zhang Che, by the "cynical realism" of Wang Shuo's hooligan fiction, by underground punk (*pengke*) and hip-hop (*xiha*) musicians, as well as by the underworld street culture of youth gangs, martial arts clubs, and secret societies. *Jianghu* is open to multiple meanings and interpretations. Having a strong historical connection to Chinese culture, literature, and philosophy, the term *jianghu* embodies a much deeper implication than just the literal meaning of rivers and lakes.[5]

Jianghu is both an imagined world and a real social space. It embodies the knights-errant (*youxia*) and tough guys (*haohan*) in fiction and the hooligans (*liumang*) and bare sticks (*guanggun*) in real life. The world of rivers and lakes is not only fantasized but also lived. "The overarching maxim of the *jianghu* is that people are often not what they seem," explain cultural scholars Christopher Rea and Bruce Rusk. For them it refers to "a transitory space of indeterminate geography and fluid identities, a social milieu bounded on one extreme by the order of the state and on the other by the wilds beyond civilization. It is a place of refuge for political exiles, outlaws, martial artists, socially marginal figures, and people hiding from the law."[6] Historian Lu Hanchao adds that it is an idiomatic expression of "a world that diverged from mainstream society, living in an unorthodox way, enjoying adventures far from home, and what can be called the culture of subalterns." It was "a world full of challenges and uncertainties."[7] Avon Boretz, an anthropologist, renders *jianghu* as "a social and symbolic refuge for those at and beyond the margins of family and community: the alienated, discontented, habitually violent, and criminal." He goes on to explain that the term "evokes mobility, fluidity, and movement, life in a shadow society populated by thieves, gamblers, prostitutes, highwaymen, itinerant swordsmen, drifters, and entertainers."[8] It is a marginal culture, one that is in fiction and fact irreverent and unconventional. Its importance is that it offers us an alternate way to look at Chinese history, society, and culture. This chapter explores the space, people, and culture of the underworld of rivers and lakes.

Underworld Geographies

The *jianghu* underworld derived from "the geographical imagination of water as something dangerous and remote."[9] It was the sort of place that "good people" (*liangmin*) were supposed to avoid. In his novel *Playing for Thrills* (1989), Wang Shuo self-reflectively characterized his hooligan youth metaphorically as a flowing river that becomes "a muddy soup."[10] The watery topography of rivers and lakes evoked images of fluidity and movement in a muddled world populated by people existing either permanently or temporarily on or beyond the fringes of conventional society. It also signified an alternative counter-society outside government control and the legitimate economic system.[11] For literary critic Wang Xuetai, *jianghu* referred to any place where marginalized people gathered and operated.[12] It was a liminal and abstruse realm of real and imagined heroes and villains.

As idealized in the popular imagination, the world of rivers and lakes is perhaps best epitomized by the bandit stronghold at Mount Liang (Liangshan), made famous in the novel *Water Margin*. This mountain base became the quintessential outlaw sanctuary and a welcoming refuge for the disenfranchised and anyone fleeing the law. It was at Liangshan that the story's 108 bandit-heroes "gathered in righteousness" to plot their revolt against the corrupt government of the late Song dynasty. According to the literary scholar Song Weijie, Liangshan represented an idealized utopia removed from the injustices of politics and the hierarchy of class society.[13] In fiction it symbolized a utopian safe haven for the downtrodden. It was also a real place tucked away in a remote corner of Shandong province. Bordering on several provinces, Mount Liang was surrounded by vast marshlands that for centuries provided needed sanctuaries outside the reach of the state for bandits, rebels, and other misfits. It remained a viable non-state space well into the seventeenth century when the Qing government established military garrisons nearby and drove the outlaws away. Perpetuating its original idealized and escapist motif, today Liangshan has become a popular tourist attraction, replete with a martial arts school, film studio, and Water Margin Theme Park.[14]

Throughout Chinese history the larger, more permanent bandit gangs and rebel armies tended to gather in remote mountainous areas, such as Liangshan. Bandits and rebels naturally preferred those areas that were outside state control, areas characterized by administrative inefficiency and imprecise jurisdictions. Successive groups of outlaws and dissidents actually used many of the same mountain strongholds for centuries. Between the eighteenth and mid-twentieth centuries, the Great Shiwan Mountains (Shiwan Dashan) on the Guangdong-Guangxi-Vietnam border remained an ungovernable "no-man's-land" for bandits, smugglers, and revolutionaries.[15] In the late 1840s, Hong Xiuquan organized the Taiping Rebellion among downtrodden Hakkas, unemployed miners and charcoal burners, displaced peasants, and bandits, as well as Zhuang and Yao ethnic minorities, in the secluded Thistle Mountains (Zijingshan) in Guangxi province; and in the late 1920s, Mao Zedong organized his first revolutionary army in Jinggangshan on the Hunan-Jiangxi border.[16] But not all bandit lairs were located in remote, underpopulated areas. Rat Hill (Laoshushan), for instance, was a notorious bandit stronghold, lasting intermittently for more than three centuries, situated in the densely populated and commercially rich Canton delta, just within twenty miles of the provincial capital of Canton.[17] Such splotches of territory on China's peripheral borderlands and internal frontiers—areas often labeled "bandit zones" in official records and on maps—provided important spaces where alternative, independent, and self-regulating counter-societies could develop in marked opposition to the state and normative society.

Besides the bandit and rebel strongholds in out-of-the-way mountains, the *jianghu* also existed in both fiction and real life in the tea houses, brothels, gambling parlors, taverns, and less-frequented temples in cities, market towns, and ports. These were places where underworld denizens met, caroused, brawled, and befriended one another. Because drinking liquor—often excessively—was a vital marker of "macho" (*haohan*) manhood, taverns, wine shops, and inns were natural sites for displays of masculinity and male bonding. They were also places where men could socialize and show off their martial prowess and valor.[18] That is why taverns and inns played key roles in *Water Margin*; they were where crooks, prostitutes, and bandits rendezvoused to share information, recruit gang members, sell loot, and devise plans.[19] In Jin Yong's martial arts novels, which were mostly set in China's pre-industrialized past, taverns and teahouses were common backdrops for swashbuckling duels and bloody killings.[20] Wherever there was hard drinking there was almost sure to be gambling, whoring, and fighting—all common pastimes associated with the *jianghu* underworld (figure 3). It is no surprise therefore that officials in late imperial and modern China unceasingly condemned gambling houses, taverns, and brothels as nurseries of vice and banditry.[21]

Taverns, brothels, and gambling dens also were the nodes that interlocked the underworld with mainstream society and culture. With the advent of the commercial economy and increasingly mobile population after the sixteenth century, more and more people from all walks of life took to the road, visiting brothels, gambling halls, and wine shops, and spending nights at inns away from their homes. One such bustling market town was described in *Water Margin* by a tavern-keeper named Shi En:

> *Outside the East Gate of this town [Mengzhou] is a marketplace called Happy Grove. Merchants from Hebei and Shandong all go there to do business. There are dozens of large inns, and twenty or thirty gambling houses and money shops. Since I was a skilled fighter and had eighty or ninety tough ruffians in the prison, I opened a tavern there. All the stores,*

Figure 3. Heated Argument over Gambling (Source: *Renjing huabao*, 1907)

gambling houses, and money shops had to pay me regular tribute. Even singing girls [prostitutes], upon arriving, had to see me first before they could ply their trade. Money kept coming in every day from so many sources. At the end of the month I was usually able to collect two or three hundred ounces of silver.[22]

According to the story Happy Grove was a lively market town—not unlike actual ones—whose many inns, shops, gambling houses, and brothels accommodated untold numbers of outsiders who became prey to rogues like Shi En and other underworld rascals. It should therefore not be surprising that in his *Book of Swindles*—described as a "crooks' playbook"—the late Ming literatus Zhang Yingyu situated most scams in country inns, taverns, and brothels, places where unsuspecting and naive travelers easily fell victims to seasoned con men, prostitutes, and gamblers.[23]

Urban areas, with their labyrinth of streets and alleyways and countless makeshift stalls and night markets, were disputed spaces both in terms of real and imagined associations with everyday violence, pickpocketing, gambling,

CHAPTER I

prostitution, and other vices. Macau's Chinese Bazaar consisted of "a maze of tortuous, narrow streets," many of which remain to this day. The area was extremely overcrowded, with low-rise flophouses and shops all cramped together in haphazard fashion, and since the 1870s, well known for its *fantan* parlors, opium dens, lowbrow brothels, and cheap hotels. By the 1920s Macau had a reputation as one of the world's most notorious "cities of sin," with one visitor commenting: "There is no question that it harbors in its hidden places the riffraff of the world, the drunken ship masters; the flotsam of the sea, the derelicts, and more shameless, beautiful, savage women than any port in the world. It is hell." As historian Jonathan Porter put it: "Macau never lost its notoriety as a seedy, disreputable, and sometimes dangerous place, a refuge for the down-and-out and a haven for smugglers, spies, and other malevolent characters."[24] Wartime Shanghai too had its own "Badlands" in the late 1930s and early 1940s. Located in a contested zone on the outskirts of the foreign settlement, according to one resident, Vanya Oakes, the Badlands was an area "where activities were mainly gambling, opium, and kindred things, with almost nightly shootings thrown in for good measure." It was an ungovernable area where police and politicians connived with gangsters, hooligans, and foreign carpetbaggers, and where gambling, prostitution, and opium consumption thrived. After city ordinances were relaxed in 1941, unlicensed streetwalkers also flooded the area. Racketeers from Canton and foreign gangsters, like the American Lucky Jack Riley, controlled organized crime and vice in the Badlands for nearly a decade.[25] Early modern Chengdu had its Liars' Square (Chehuang ba), near the city's New South Gate, where the so-called river and lake runners (*pao jianghu*)—tricksters, gamblers, fortune tellers, boxers, medicine sellers, and prostitutes—put up stalls or walked the streets hawking bogus goods and dubious services.[26] There would have been few, if any, cities or market towns in China that did not have their own badlands and red light districts.

Two vastly different types of spaces characterized the underworld geographies: one was isolated and sparsely populated (mountain lairs) and the other was bustling and densely populated (urban taverns and inns). The former provided bandits and dissidents with fortified strongholds where they could stockpile food and weapons. They were safe havens where they could unwind and recuperate before undertaking new ventures. The latter were places where various underworld denizens gathered to carouse, get drunk, form gangs, exchange information, sell loot, and make plans. They also were places where the underworld interacted with mainstream society, where crooks, con artists, and prostitutes targeted the so-called good people.

Denizens of the Rivers and Lakes

Although the denizens of the rivers and lakes came from a variety of backgrounds and occupations, nonetheless they shared several common characteristics; most importantly they were usually young, relatively poor, had low social status, and were highly mobile. They were a motley throng of unsubmissive nonconformists who defied the core orthodox values of the state and conventional society. Precariously situated at the bottom rungs of the social order, they existed outside the bounds of the law. Theirs was a world, writes Avon Boretz, "that can exist only beyond the stability and security of village and family and conventional society."[27] They were for the most part individuals who were chronically disadvantaged, marginalized, and criminalized. On the one hand, mainstream society had excluded them because they were disorderly or engaged in shameful activities, and on the other hand, they had cut themselves off from mainstream society by violating the standards of collective behavior by engaging in unlawful or outrageous undertakings. They were street-smart men and women who lived each day by their wits and skills, as well as by outright brute force and ruthlessness.

They have been labeled throughout history as *xia*, *haohan*, *liumang*, and *guanggun*, for the most part interchangeable sociocultural categories of both fictionalized and real underworld characters. In literature, the *xia* (or *youxia*), who are usually rendered as knights-errant, had antecedents in the ancient *shi* or warriors of the Warring States period. Originally the lowest level of aristocrats, those who specialized in martial arts were called *wushi* or *xia*. With the decline of the Warring States period, however, they became socially displaced persons who roamed from one state to another offering their services to local warlords. Over time the *xia* came to be regarded as defiant misfits, as well as heroic bandits and rebels.[28] According to Y. W. Ma, the knights-errant were young men of "atypical prowess," who were exceptionally skilled in the use of arms and hand-to-hand combat.[29] The *haohan*—variously translated as tough guys, macho men, courageous heroes, and more literally as good fellows—always have been closely associated with knights-errant in literature. Both were good at martial arts and had a propensity for violence. "Personal prowess in fighting," W. J. F. Jenner has explained, "is an essential qualification for being accepted as a *haohan*." Rather than being a way of life, *xia* and *haohan* represented ideal types that have continuously influenced people's behavior; up until today they embody a set of values that many youths aspire to attain.[30] As noted in the 1987 Ministry of Public Security report cited at the start of this chapter, officials believed that urban juvenile delinquents emulated the actions of feudal gangs depicted in knights-errant films and novels.

Many of the qualities found in *xia* and *haohan* were also found in the more recent representations of *liumang*, a term that denotes "wandering commoners." While the term *liumang* first appeared in the ancient Qin dynasty designating displaced and homeless people, by the Qing dynasty it came to mean all sorts of troublemakers—hooligans, gangsters, con men, hustlers, vagrants, sexual deviants, and so forth.[31] Although during the turmoil of the first half of the twentieth century, both Nationalists and Communists sought out gangsters and hooligans as allies in their bids for power, after "Liberation" in 1949, rootless, uncontrollable *liumang* became enemies of the new communist state.[32] Despite the many crackdowns against hooliganism, however, the PRC has witnessed a tremendous growth in its floating delinquent population as more and more people have moved from the countryside into the cities. Crimes—especially youth gang crimes—have likewise increased. The hooligan novels and screenplays written by Wang Shuo between the mid 1980s and early 1990s express in contemporary terms the free and unfettered spirit found in the knights-errant literature of the past. According to Geremie Barmé, Wang Shuo's characters are "post-traditional knights-errant."[33] His fiction depicts a cynical realism (*wanshi xianshi*) of the seedy underside of today's youth culture, one that includes unemployed adolescents and young adults, black-marketeers, tricksters, petty thieves, prostitutes, and disenchanted writers and artists. In his novels, especially *Masters of Mischief* (*Wanzhu*, 1987), *Playing for Thrills* (*Wande jiushi xintiao*, 1989), and *No Regrets about Youth* (*Qingchun wuhui*, 1991), his characters are antiheroes—hooligans (*liumang*) and riffraff (*pizi*)—who promote alternative lifestyles that run counter to communist ideology and indoctrination.[34] In post-Deng China, Wang Shuo's hooligans have been transformed into popheroes. Today China's hip-hop singers, such as Zhou Yan, continue to mock communist societal norms while eulogizing hooligans and gangsters in songs like "The Flow of Jianghu" (*Jianghuliu*) and "Gangsta" (*Chaoshehui*).[35]

The rootless rascals or bare sticks (*guanggun*) of the late imperial age were little different from the *liumang* of Republican and Communist China. They were a dangerous floating population of young unmarried males feared by the authorities as the major source of crime, sexual deviance, and social disorder. The word *gun*, which literally means stick or club, infers a rootless loner; in street slang it means penis, thus implying a sexual predator. A Tang dynasty text identified *gun* as "evil village youths" who dressed outrageously, gathered in gangs, and got into fights. Bare sticks were typically wild and restless young men who bullied and terrorized market towns and villages. As "entrepreneurs of violence" they largely depended on belligerence and predation for their livelihoods. They were a ready pool of recruits for bandit gangs, sworn brotherhoods, watchmen, local militia, crop-watching associations, martial arts clubs, and the like. In Ming and Qing literary sources, *guanggun* also referred to any young male who engaged in racketeering, swindling, and extortion. Zhang Yingyu in his *Book of Swindles* characterized petty crooks, hustlers, and tricksters as "sticks" (*gun*). As classic examples of marginal men, who were frequently on the move and in trouble with the law, they lacked steady employment and had little to lose. Such single men were always objects of suspicion and distrust precisely because they were unruly and existed outside the paradigmatic norms of family and community.[36] In recent years, however, the original negative meaning of bare sticks, as rootless ruffians, has become lost on the majority of China's youths, who now only associate the term with an unofficial shopping holiday for singles.[37]

Denizens of the underworld were overwhelmingly of humble birth. The majority were individuals classified as "mean people" (*jianmin*) as well as those who worked in low status occupations. *Jianmin* was a category of servile men and women that included entertainers, yamen runners, prostitutes, gamblers, magicians, social deviants, martial artists, domestic slaves, and certain hereditary groups, such as the Dan boat people of south China, beggars of Suzhou, and the professional musician-dancer families of Shanxi. Although the Yongzheng emperor emancipated many of these pariah groups in a series of edicts between 1723 and 1731, nonetheless they continued to retain debased status in customary practice. According to the information in table 1, on the occupational backgrounds of the 108 bandit-heroes of Liangshan in *Water Margin*, more than 65 percent were itinerants (peddlers, doctors, fishermen, hunters, Daoist priests, swordsmen, entertainers, gamblers) and individuals who worked in mean or low status jobs (butchers, soldiers, jailers, yamen runners). They were mostly unskilled or semiskilled wage laborers whose earnings only provided a bare subsistence. Just to make ends meet, most of them had to keep multiple jobs, both legal and illegal. We might also include ethnic minorities, such as the Yao, Man, Li, and Zhuang, who in the past were not only discriminated against in law and social practice, but also further dehumanized with their ethnic designations transcribed in Chinese characters with dog, pig, and insect radicals.[38]

Table 1. Backgrounds of the 108 Bandit-Heroes of Liangshan in *Water Margin*

Category	Number	Breakdown
Itinerants	24	peddlers, tradesmen, doctors, fishermen, hunters, Daoist priests, entertainers, gamblers, boxers, and swordsmen
Military officers	21	
Gentry and landlords	13	
Career bandits	12	
Petty government workers	11	common soldiers, jailers, yamen runners, and clerks
Village bullies and braggarts	9	
Artisans	8	blacksmiths, tailors, butchers, boat builders, and engravers
Innkeepers	7	
Peasants	2	
Merchants	1	

Source: Jean Chesneaux, "The Modern Relevance of Shui-hu chuan," 13–14.

Because of the emphasis on martial values, swordsmen and boxers were closely associated with *jianghu* culture. While anyone could master martial arts, nevertheless certain sorts of people were more prone to do so. Soldiers, monks, and actors, for example, studied martial arts as part of their regular training. The military officers listed in table 1 were experts in swordsmanship and boxing. In *Water Margin*, Chao Gai was a village guard captain and underworld figure, who devoted himself to perfecting his martial prowess; and in real life, Du Guoxiang, one of the leaders of the Iron Ruler Society (Tiechihui) in late eighteenth-century Fujian, was a cashiered soldier skilled in boxing.[39] Roving monks, who feature in knights-errant novels and movies, in reality did practice martial arts to discipline both body and mind. For example, in Zhang Che's classic 1974 film, *Five Shaolin Masters* (*Shaolin wuzu*), when invading Manchu troops destroyed their temple, five young monks escaped to the south to perfect their own *kungfu* styles before seeking revenge on the alien dynasty. The movie mimicked widespread popular beliefs that five Shaolin monks were the founding ancestors (*wuzu*) of the Triads, a secret society whose avowed purpose (at least according to legend) was to "destroy the Qing and restore the Ming" (*fan Qing fu Ming*). Actually, many martial monks joined the Triads or other illegal organizations. For example, a monk named Daosan, who had trained in boxing since childhood, was a key organizer of the Iron Ruler Society in Fujian in the 1750s.[40] Actors also were generally well grounded in martial arts because such training was essential for their performances. Most of them went through a rigorous training regimen in mastering the techniques of turning somersaults, hand-to-hand combat, and sword play. In fact, in Guangdong there was a prominent tradition linking the martial arts of Canton opera with that of the Shaolin school, considered to be the most demanding of Chinese martial art styles. The operatic actor Li Wenmao, who was a commanding general in the Triad-led Red Turban Revolt of 1854, was a renowned martial arts performer. On and off stage he dressed in a black python robe and black armor in the style of the Three Kingdoms' military hero Zhang Fei.[41]

Although some martial arts masters operated schools in crowded towns or remote mountains, others were itinerants who traveled back and forth to markets and festivals to earn money by performances and teaching students. One well-known member of the "gallant fraternity" of Liangshan was Li Zhong, a freelance martial artist "who put on exhibitions of spears and staves in order to sell medicines" in a market town in Shaanxi province. In 1801 a Triad leader in Fujian named Wu Tao, whom the authorities portrayed as a "knight-errant," put on demonstrations to make money and recruit Triad members; at the end of the nineteenth century the Boxers in Shandong also used exhibitions to solicit contributions and enlist members for their movement. Li Wenmao used his acting talents and martial skills to earn money and attract new recruits for the Red Turban Revolt. Most of Jin Yong's and Gu Long's martial arts novels have featured swashbuckling heroes—many coming from the underclass of monks, orphans, beggars, and bandits—who joined secret societies that battled against corrupt or alien dynasties and foreign invaders. They too used martial exhibitions to enlist pupils and followers.[42]

For marginalized people, like Wu Tao and Li Wenmao, who were shunned and discriminated against by mainstream society, bandit gangs,

CHAPTER 1

sworn brotherhoods, and secret societies provided them with essential social organizations for mutual protection and self-preservation. The lifeblood sustaining these groups was vice and organized crime: gambling, prostitution, extortion, banditry, and piracy.[43] In Jiangsu and Zhejiang in the early Qing, noted Huang Liuhong, youth gangs, calling themselves the "Year Star Gods," swore blood oaths, lorded over neighborhoods, and engaged in street brawls that they euphemistically called "thrashings from the sky."[44] In the suburbs of Canton a local watchman and bully named He Deguang, whom the authorities described as a "notorious rascal" skilled in boxing, led a gang of a hundred bandits—calling their brotherhood the "Hall of Five Conveniences" (Wushuntang)—that terrorized three counties through extortion, kidnapping, robbery, rape, and murder for more than a decade at the end of the eighteenth century.[45] In the late Qing and Republican eras, a secret society known as "Gowned Brothers" (Paoge), operating out of teahouses, theaters, and restaurants, claimed large sections of Chengdu as their turf. By 1947 they ran the city's drug trafficking, gambling, and prostitution rackets.[46]

Despite the many crackdowns there has been a marked resurgence in sworn brotherhoods and secret societies, especially among adolescents and young adults, in post-Liberation China. Street gangs of young Tianjin hooligans in the mid 1950s, who styled themselves with names like "Five Tigers" (*wuhu*) and "Five Rats" (*wushu*), roamed busy commercial neighborhoods, starting fights and pilfering cigarettes.[47] According to the Ministry of Public Security report in 1987, there was a growing problem of teenage hoodlums taking oaths and forming "black societies" to lord over busy shopping areas, where they picked fights, harassed women, and bullied strangers. Reflecting back on his own hooligan youth in Beijing during the Cultural Revolution, in Wang Shuo's 1989 novel *Please Don't Call Me Human* (*Qianwan bie ba wo dangren*), a streetwise pedicab operator and boxing master named Tang Yuanbao swore oaths of brotherhood with a gang of like-minded ruffians. By 2005, Chinese government officials claimed that there were more than 20,000 criminal syndicates and secret societies that controlled an estimated 70 percent of China's entertainment enterprises. Around the same time, in Guangxi province in the city of Baise, for instance, a local thug named Zhou Shounan, who was the general manager of the entertainment department of a major hotel, was also a boss of the Hongxing Society (Hongxingshe), which controlled all entertainment, prostitution, and gambling in the city.[48]

While the world of rivers and lakes was usually depicted in literature, cinema, and hip-hop music, as well as in the real criminal underworld, as a

32

masculine milieu, it also was a feminine milieu.[49] Women appeared as prostitutes, innkeepers, bar maids, beggars, street entertainers, petty thieves, and warriors. As with their male counterparts, none of these backgrounds were mutually exclusive. Most of the females were teenagers and young adults, unmarried, and came from all walks of life. For the most part, these young women did things that so-called respectful society thought they ought not to do. Some acted alone or with other women, while others acted in conjunction with their fathers, brothers, husbands, or lovers. In the real world, female beggars, healers, and streetwalkers wandered alongside, often as accomplices of, male panhandlers, hustlers, pimps, and pickpockets. This underworld female culture is explored in such exposé novels as Mian Mian's *Candy*, published in Beijing in 2000.[50]

In the hands of storytellers and writers, some of these women were transformed into legendary female heroes (*nü yingxiong*); a few were even deified. In fact and fiction, writes Roland Altenburger, these women knights-errant held an "outlaw status and marginal position at the periphery of society, in the alternative sphere of rivers and lakes."[51] In most cases they were depicted as young and beautiful, and expert in both magic and martial arts. Here are a few examples. In *Water Margin*, one of the best-known characters was Big Sister Gu (Gu Dasao), who was a skilled fighter and given much to violence. Also in the novel, the likely inspiration for the swordswoman Hu Sanniang, nicknamed "Ten Feet of Steel" (Yizhangqing), was a real-life female warrior named Yang Miaozhen, who hailed from Shandong in the late Song dynasty. Born into a family of bandits and local strongmen, and trained from childhood in martial arts, she commanded her own army at the age of twenty.[52] Qin Liangyu was a female warrior noted for leading successful campaigns against the Manchus at the end of the Ming dynasty, and Wang Conger, who was an itinerant entertainer, in 1794 commanded a rebel army of about 15,000 and led an uprising in Sichuan province.[53] Two female pirates in south China commanded thousands of male pirates in the early nineteenth century.[54] At the start of the twentieth century, a twenty-year-old prostitute and accomplished martial artist, who proclaimed herself Holy Mother of the Yellow Lotus (Huanglian shengmu), organized a female contingent of the Boxers known as the Red Lanterns Brigade. In 1900 she led roughly 3,000 female boxers, mostly between the ages of twelve and eighteen, to attack the foreign settlements in Tianjin and Beijing. It was said that she possessed magic that could heal wounds with clear water and bring the dead back to life.[55]

Also among the women warriors there were several who were venerated as deities, immortals, and demigods. They all possessed some forms of magic arts—spirit wandering, controlling flying swords, summoning armies out of paper figures, manipulating the weather, and so on. In each of these cases, as in many others, these women mimicked shaman-warriors prior to becoming sanctified. One of the most interesting woman was Tang Saier, who lived in the early fifteenth century and led an unsuccessful uprising against the Ming dynasty under the banner "on behalf of Heaven carry out the way" (*titian xingdao*). Her followers called her Buddha Mother. It was said that she possessed a "demonic book" (*yaoshu*) from which she learned martial arts and the magical ability to travel outside her body. Because she was never captured her real life became entangled with legends enriched with mythical and supernatural elements. In one story she became a reincarnated Moon Goddess named Yue Jun, and in another story an incarnation of the Celestial Wolf Star (Tianlangxing).[56] Other female warrior-divinities included Lady Xian (Xian furen), who, as a chieftain of the Li minority, controlled most of southern Guangdong at the start of the Sui dynasty (581–618); another was Zheng Zuxi, purportedly the sister of the pirate-rebel Zheng Chenggong, and later honored as the Warrior Mazu along the Huizhou coast of Guangdong. Like Tang Saier, Zuxi could also fly to engage her enemies in battle.[57]

THINKING LIKE A *JIANGHU* DENIZEN

Wang Atong was a typical denizen of the rivers and lakes. He hailed from Chaozhou where he was an itinerant medicine man, spirit medium, and fortune teller. Plying his trade, he travelled to many places near and beyond Chaozhou, covering a huge circuit that included Haiyang, Puning, and Jieyang, among other counties in northeastern Guangdong. In 1733 and 1734, as he traveled about the villages and markets, he started making and selling paper amulets and cloth flags that he said could protect people from evil-carrying demons. Local officials said he was a wizard (*wushi*) who was adept at sorcery (*xieshu*). He was assisted by an old woman, his paternal aunt, who not only provided him lodging but was also likely a medium herself. By 1734, he had a sizable following of mostly impoverished tenant farmers, day laborers, tinkerers, and coolies, who banded together under the avowed protection of Wang's wizardry to "rob rich households" (*dajie fuhu*). In a society that had become increasingly polarized between rich and poor, privileged and underprivileged, the turn to banditry was one way that Wang's band hoped to equalize economic and social disparity. Wang likely would have considered his planned actions as righteous and just. But before he could act, the authorities arrested him, his aunt, and most of his followers and charged them with swindling and sedition, the latter being a capital offense.[58]

It is uncertain how Wang Atong got his ideas about robbing the rich and social justice, but it would not be too farfetched to assume he and his followers got their inspirations from oral stories and local dramas. Storytellers and actors, like medicine men and martial artists, were ubiquitous wanderers who routinely travelled about between market towns and villages plying their trades and performing. For most commoners, who were illiterate or at best only partially literate, the stories, legends, and operas that they heard during festivals and at tea houses were their main sources for the lessons of history and moral values.[59] "Fictional characters mirrored actual human beings," explains Charles Holcombe, "and real people then looked up to them for role models." What is more, they "provided a paradigm that gave meaning to their lives and invested them with purpose, courage and nobility."[60] In eighteenth-century Guangdong, storytelling about swashbuckling knights-errant and heroic bandits were common and, in particular, operas based on stories from *Water Margin* were the most popular among Cantonese audiences. Because operas were staged continuously both day and night and often for weeks during festivals, it would have been inconceivable for Wang not to have seen any.[61] We know for a fact that bandits and rebels often whiled away their time recounting events from *Water Margin* and other popular legends, presumably learned from storytellers and plays.[62]

The denizens of river and lakes were noted for their unwritten codes of behavior that emphasized certain Confucian virtues, particularly righteousness (*yi*), loyalty (*zhong*), and filiality (*xiao*)—yet always with a certain twist in their interpretation. Many real life hooligans, bandits, and rebels aspired to be like the heroes in *Water Margin*, who had banded together on Mount Liang in the Hall of Loyalty and Righteousness (*zhongyi tang*) to swear oaths of brotherhood to oppose corruption and dishonesty. The Triads likewise held their initiations in sanctuaries that they named Halls of Loyalty and Righteousness. The Triad organizer Wu Tao, for instance, claimed that young men were attracted to the secret society because its members displayed high degrees of "integrity and righteous spirit." The Boxers called themselves "Righteous Harmonious Fists" (*yihequan*), which, as one member explained, meant "friends get together for their common beliefs in righteousness."[63] Secret society and rebel groups justified their "righteous" actions with the motto "on behalf of Heaven carry out the Way" (*titian xingdao*), which was common Mandate of Heaven terminology and popularized in such novels as *Water Margin*.[64] Yet by invoking Heaven as a higher authority, they declared a self-righteousness that challenged and transcended the emperor's sole authority as intermediary between Heaven and man.[65]

Underworld notions of loyalty and filial piety also diverged from conventional Confucian teachings by transferring emphasis away from the emperor and parents to sworn brothers and gang members. Among martial artists, father–son relationships shifted to master–disciple relationships whereby the master became both teacher and father (*shifu*) and one's fellow disciples became brothers (*xiongdi*). In brotherhoods and gangs, unrelated members also commonly addressed one another as elder and younger brothers. In novels by Jin Yong, Gu Long, and Wang Shuo, duty to one's sworn brothers and friends always took precedents above all else. Confucian vertical loyalties had been skewed into horizontal loyalties. Obviously, *jianghu* codes of behavior significantly modified orthodox Confucian teachings, creating an alternative value system learned from the streets rather than from the classics.[66]

The 108 heroes of Liangshan served as role models for underworld denizens since the Ming dynasty. They were known for their Robin Hood flair—"robbing the rich and aiding the poor" (*jiefu jipin*)—as well as displays of personal honor, selfless generosity, courage, and rough justice. Heroes in fact and fiction were thought to always be willing to use force to protect the weak and stand up for what was right. As Huang Liuhong put it: "Whenever they [youth gangs] hear of someone suffering an injustice, they volunteer their services to avenge the wrongs."[67] In *Water Margin* the bandit-hero Song Jiang was introduced as a noble robber: "He was always making things easy for people, solving their difficulties, settling differences, saving lives. He provided the indigent with funds for coffins and medicines, gave charity to the poor, assisted in emergencies, and helped in cases of hardship."[68] Another Liangshan hero was the avenger Wu Song who thrashed about punishing evildoers and righting wrongs, without once thinking of his own safety. In the first decade of the nineteenth century the Cantonese pirates Zhang Baozai and Zheng Yi Sao had reputations, somewhat deserved, as good outlaws who treated the common people with fairness and justice.[69] In similar fashion the missionary Harry Caldwell described an early twentieth-century Fujian bandit named Dang Gi Ling, who was not only "noted for his courage and zeal" but also for his generosity in helping poor villagers and meting out popular justice.[70] Another colorful early twentieth-century bandit, Bai Lang, better known in Western accounts as "White Wolf," received widespread popular support for dispensing "peasant justice" and redistributing loot among the local populace in north China. According to a local folk song about Bai Lang, "He robs the rich, helps the poor, and delivers Heaven's fate."[71] Of course, in the underworld such noble robbers were few in numbers. It was one thing to hold high ideals and quite another to actually put them into practice. Most bandits and rebels were Janus-faced individuals and at best erratic Robin Hoods.[72]

Denizens of the underworld more often than not expressed values in their actions that ran counter to conventional Confucianism. Stealing, cheating, and brawling were second nature to them. They disregarded the norms of dominant society to make their own rules and to fend for themselves as best they could. This attitude is nicely expressed by the hooligans and riffraff in Wang Shuo's novels, who represent a complete rejection of Confucian notions of social harmony and communist notions of "serving the people"; instead they cared only for themselves and disregarded anyone who got in their way.[73] The underworld valorized violence and getting ahead at any cost. Despite high-sounding claims for avenging wrongs, much of the wanton violence in *Water Margin* and other martial arts fiction was for its own sake and gratuitous, and often was excessive. The hero Wu Song, for instance, in one escapade murdered a woman who stood in his way by viciously cutting off her head with a blunt knife. By the same token, Huang Liuhong related how late seventeenth-century youth gangs went around beating up people for simply giving them "an inadvertent stare." One nineteenth-century missionary described bare sticks as those youths who make "it a sport and a matter of pride to defy the laws and the magistrates, and commit all kinds of crimes. To give and receive wounds with composure; to kill others with the most perfect coolness; and to have no fear of death."[74] Finally, in complete disregard for human values fictional heroes in *Water Margin* and actual bandits, pirates, and rebels at times went to extremes by not only viciously killing victims but also carving them up to eat.[75] From the perspective of officials and the ruling class, *jianghu* values were perverse and unorthodox and therefore a danger to the rest of society.

DENOUNCING "BAD BOOKS" AND "HOOLIGANISM"

In March 1980, in Beijing the Associated Press reported that a man named Xiao Lun wrote to the *China Youth Daily* (*Zhongguo qingnian bao*) complaining how "bad books" corrupted the minds of China's youth and led them astray. "Comrade Editor," he explained, "these books have exerted a very bad influence.... [They] stir up the base passions and flagrantly spread the germs of hooligan mentality." In the 1980s, the *China Youth Daily* was one of the most politically influential newspapers, with a daily circulation of roughly five million. Most of the readers were teenagers and young adults. Xiao Lun's concerns were expressed at the time of one of the many official campaigns against books, movies, and music that the party-state deemed politically dangerous, vulgar, licentious, or morally polluting. In particular, it was a time when the communist government banned martial arts fiction, including those of Jin Yong, as depraved and feudal. "Bad books," the reader continued, "are corrupting young people, encouraging criminal activity and illicit sexual relations." Venting his anger and frustration, Xiao Lun demanded that something be done to stop publication and distribution of such pernicious literature.[76]

Since the 1950s, newspapers and journals published in the PRC have reported countless stories that seem to have confirmed Xiao Lun's fears. There were many reports of young people emulating the heroes in martial arts novels, wearing hooligan-style clothing, running away from home or school to seek out boxing masters, and sinking into debauched and criminal lifestyles (figure 4). In 1950, for example, more than twenty fifth-grade students in Chongqing, Sichuan province, after having been "deeply poisoned" by martial arts stories, formed a sworn brotherhood and ran off to find a martial arts teacher on Mount Huagai in Zhejiang province. In another case that same year four students in Lanzhou, Gansu province, who wanted to learn how to leap from roof to roof and walk on walls, stole money, knives, and swords, and then ran off to look for a master on Mount Emei in Sichuan.[77] In the summer of 1987 (the same year that the Ministry of Public Security published its report cited at the start of this chapter), the *People's Daily* (*Renmin ribao*) recounted a number of incidents of juveniles who had turned to crime after reading pornographic or martial arts stories. The paper reported that "at present many books on murder, sex and superstition are spreading through society." In Beijing alone, a police raid on 967 book stalls revealed that more than half of them sold pornographic or other illegal books and magazines. The report continued: "The surge of bad books and periodicals is a major reason for the new trend that criminals are being younger and younger and their criminal ways are becoming more and more like those of adults." Another news report claimed that forty out of a hundred juvenile delinquents in one unspecified province turned bad because they read books "extolling themes such as murder, pornography and trends going against the Communist Party,

Figure 4. Hooligan Accosting a Young Girl to Be His Friend, 1957 (Source: *China Youth Daily*, February 25, 1957)

the people and socialism."[78] While not backed by scientific evidence, nonetheless, many people and officials believed that bad books had a profound negative impact on some readers, especially younger readers, which would lead them to antisocial, illegal behavior.

Chinese governments, past and present, have reacted by promulgating a large variety of national and local laws and regulations to eliminate the perceived menace of bad books and hooligan behavior. *Water Margin* was one of those bad books condemned by some readers, literati, and officials from time to time. A common saying went, "Let not the young read *Water Margin*; let not the old read *Three Kingdoms*" (*shao bu kan Shuihu lao bu kan Sanguo*). It was feared that young people who read *Water Margin* would be more easily swayed to duplicate the actions portrayed in the novel, which lauded armed

CHAPTER 1

rebellion and made heroes of bandits. Even before the legend was put to paper, in the Yuan dynasty the court banned dramatizations of stories that were later woven into the novel. Although in the early Ming dynasty, many scholars and officials praised *Water Margin* and even supported the building of shrines to honor the story's main hero Song Jiang, in the last decade of the dynasty, as social disorders mounted, the imperial court condemned the novel for its excessive violence, acts of cannibalism, and anti-government sentiment. Despite prohibitions, however, the novel continued to gain in popularity, so much so that in the following Qing dynasty the central government had to issue bans no fewer than four times: 1653, 1774, 1808, and 1851. In 1774, for instance, the Qianlong emperor banned *Water Margin* because of its "vulgar and indecent language" and "pernicious influence on readers." At the end of the dynasty, in 1905, the reformer Liang Qichao criticized the novel because it taught people to become "greenwood heroes" who swore oaths of rebellion. Mao Zedong, who in his youth admired the Liangshan heroes, later in life, in 1975 during the Cultural Revolution, criticized those same heroes as traitors and reactionaries. Recently, the literary critic Liu Zaifu in 2010 deplored *Water Margin* for its "poisonous" influence on the minds of China's youth.[79] Yesterday's heroes all too easily become today's villains.

Also from time to time Chinese governments prohibited certain dramas, films, and music that they deemed immoral, violent, or subversive. The most common reasons given for such bans were that they encouraged extravagance, wastefulness, disorderly conduct, and sexual impropriety. In the Yuan dynasty in 1309, an imperial edict prohibited the public singing of certain "indecent songs" because "they cause the gathering of crowds, congesting of streets and markets, intermingling of men and women, thus not only inducing fights and lawsuits but also leading to other problems." Similarly, a Qing injunction claimed that after watching lascivious operas "sons would run away, sometimes joining troupes and becoming actors, and daughters would long for love and carry on illicit affairs, bringing insult to three generations of their family and inviting calamities upon themselves." In 1813, the Jiaqing emperor prohibited the performances of popular "variety plays" (*zaju*) that featured violence, "least ignorant commoners mistake robbers and gangsters as heroes and model themselves after them." In fact, during the nineteenth century at both the central and local levels of government there were hundreds of prohibitions on operatic performances.[80] In one case, in 1872 the prefect of Guangzhou issued a prohibition banning performances of Cantonese opera because he believed "the local theater only serves to corrupt public morals."[81]

With the advent of films in the early twentieth century, the new Republican government continued to pay close attention to movies deemed indecent and subversive. In the 1920s and 1930s, when cinemas were still being viewed as low class, immoral places, the government tried to ban movies that had "bad influences" on audiences, in particular popular martial arts films that were the rage of the day. After 1949 the Communist Party created an elaborate censorship system that continues to scrutinize cinema, radio, television, and music. In recent years, censorship is most rigid at the points where film and music overlap with youth culture.[82] In 2015, after Xi Jinping came to power, for example, the Chinese Ministry of Culture banned 120 popular punk and hip-hop songs that "jeopardized morality" of young people because they advocated "obscenity, violence, and crime."[83] Three years later the government banned hip-hop musicians and "tattooed performers" (*wenshen yiren*) from appearing on television.[84]

One of the main problems of bad books, drama, and music, from the perspective of the state, was that they encouraged hooliganism. Throughout Chinese history what the authorities variously labeled knights-errant, hooligans, bare sticks, and other similar terms constituted China's dangerous class—impoverished, unmarried, and rootless youths whom they considered to be the main source and symptom of crime, disorder, and rebellion. The ancient legalist philosopher, Han Fei, denounced knights-errant, who went about brandishing swords and stirring up trouble, as a root cause of violence and disorder in society. Ever since the Qin period, in fact, successive dynasties have repeatedly imposed sanctions against what they viewed as hooligan behavior, especially brawling and sexual misconduct.[85] By the late seventeenth century the term "bare sticks" had entered the Qing legal lexicon and increasingly came to include all sorts of unacceptable conduct—swindling, extortion, petty theft, assault, prostitution, rape, and sodomy. The category of bare sticks defined a new class of offenders based on social identity and criminal profiling.[86] Other Qing laws aimed to crackdown on unsavory underworld denizens, such as tricksters, medical quacks, fortune tellers, geomancers, and the like.[87] In 1979 and again in 2005, the PRC promulgated catch-all laws against hooliganism, which the state loosely defined as: "Gathering crowds for brawls, picking quarrels and making trouble, insulting women or carrying out other hooligan activity, and disrupting public order."[88] What Thomas Buoye wrote about the Qing bare sticks laws appears equally relevant to the hooligan laws in the PRC; they both were related "to the social side-effects of an increasingly complex commercialized economy and a highly mobile population."[89]

While the laws aimed to suppress bad books and hooligan behavior, the authorities could never control popular tastes. For many ordinary people in late imperial and modern China, those individuals that the state labeled hooligans and bare sticks were seen as heroes. There has always existed a complex dialectic between acceptable and unacceptable behavior, between legitimate and illegitimate activities, and between heroic knights-errant and lawless hooligans. The state and popular culture has never been able to draw clear distinctions between the two sides. The irony, of course, is that in a society which has worked so diligently to eliminate these bad guys has in the end immortalized many of them as heroes in popular fiction, movies, and songs.

Conclusion

Fiction is not concerned with historical accuracy but rather with the inner truths of the past and present. Undeniably literature has long been used as a source for history writing, as a way to get at veiled realities not always found in facts. Indeed, popular narratives provide an important window into the culture and consciousness of everyday life. As Peter Burke and others have persuasively argued, the typical representation/reality dichotomy we find in most historical studies is no longer tenable as the two realms tend to merge into one another creating an alternate reality.[90] The new history of the everyday must be interdisciplinary, elastic, and built on sources coming not only from official records but also from literature, folklore, legends, myths, anecdotes, and even hearsay.

Certainly some works of fiction, as well as films and operas, are more authentic or truthful than others. The martial arts novels of Jin Yong and Gu Long and the films of Zhang Che, for instance, while mostly set in China's historical past, nonetheless go into great flights of fantasy. They have created an imagined community, a China that neither exists in modern society nor in the past. Yet it is a China that easily fits the popular imagination, especially among young people, who in some cases, as noted earlier, ran off to the mountains seeking martial arts masters to teach them how to fly across rooftops and scale steep walls. In novels, movies, and operas, the mentioning of historic figures, such as Zhang Fei or the Qianlong emperor, helps connect readers and audiences to the real world and allows fiction to be more believable. Creditable fictional characters need to mirror actual people. The swordswoman "Ten Feet of Steal" in *Water Margin* was modeled after the real Song dynasty swordswoman Yang Miaozhen, and the hooligan characters in Wang Shuo's novels were fashioned after himself and his friends during the

Cultural Revolution. In telling and retelling stories, Barend ter Haar explains, what matters is that people "thought that something had happened, and that their experiences were by no means complete inventions without any empirical basis that we could still recognize and accept."[91]

Novels, films, operas, and songs are important because they reveal popular values. They depict real life experiences, a sort of virtual reality of the commonplace. Popular narratives and folktales reflect a perceived sociocultural truth and create tropes that shape how people imagine the world in which they live and influence their actions. In the past most commoners learned about history from storytellers and operas, while today they learn from movies, television, and social media. In real life too the denizens of the underworld are themselves avid consumers of media images of the *jianghu*. Today the underworld of rivers and lakes is no longer confined to the ostracized and marginalized, nor merely to novels, cinema, and music, but rather it has been taken up by all those who have been caught up in two or more dimensions of reality—one physical and the other virtual, one official and the other private, one censored and the other frankly clandestine. They present an alternative vision of the past, one lived and told from the perspective of the underside of society.

CHAPTER 2

Righteous Yang and the Great Comet of 1680

THE MING–QING DYNASTIC TRANSITION BETWEEN 1644 AND 1684 WAS A watershed moment in early modern Chinese history. For the historian Frederic Wakeman, "The fall of Ming and the rise of Qing constitute the most dramatic dynastic transition in Chinese history."[1] Another historian, Lynn Struve, describes this period as a "cataclysm" and "one of the most trying periods in Chinese history."[2] For one eyewitness, Chen Shunxi, it was simply a time of "chaos and abandonment." Chen, who was a local scholar and healer in Wuchuan county in southwestern Guangdong, kept a diary of the things he saw and heard from the 1630s to 1679, the year that he died.[3] In fact, during those forty years between 1644 and 1684 few, if any, local communities escaped the turmoil and devastation of unrelenting wars, banditry, and piracy. While much has been written about the Ming–Qing transition, we know little about the Sino-Vietnamese frontier (map 2) during those chaotic times or about the pirate hero who became known in history and legend as Righteous Yang.

Who was Righteous Yang? How did he fit into the long tradition of maritime piracy on the Sino-Vietnamese water frontier? Why did people consider him a righteous hero? What role did he play in the Ming–Qing transition? What we know about him comes from a mélange of official documents and legends that have circulated over the past several centuries. His real name was Yang Yandi, but he was perhaps better known as Yang the Second (Yang Er), being the second son in his family. Although we do not know when he was born, his family likely hailed from southwestern Guangdong

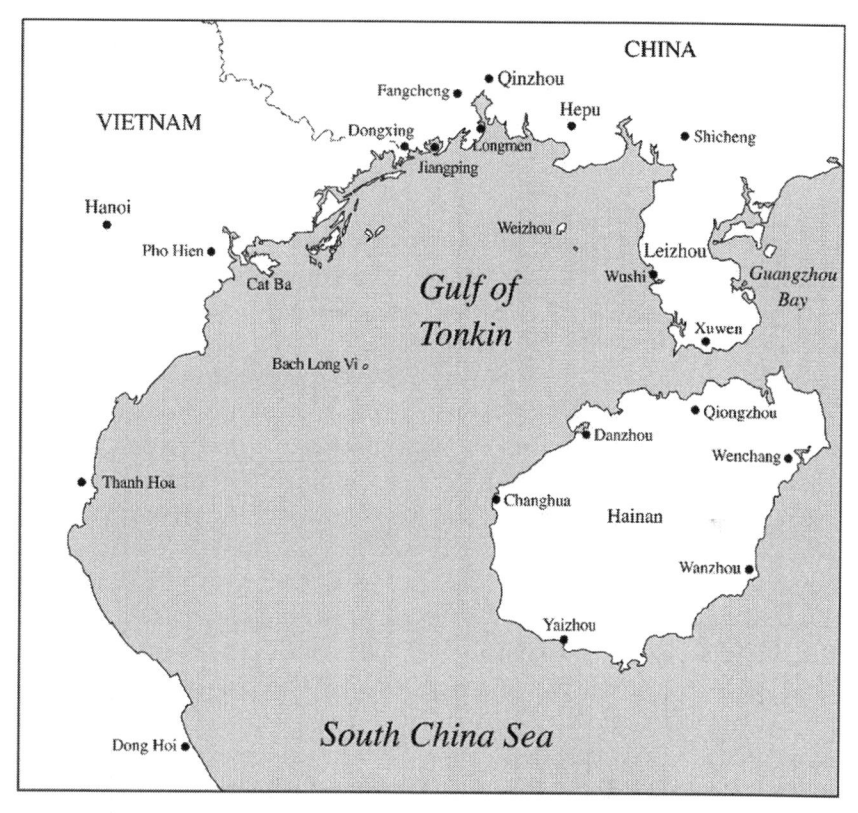

Map 2. The Gulf of Tonkin, c. 1680s (Source: Created by author)

province; some sources mentioned Suixi county on the Leizhou peninsula or in a neighboring county to the east in Maoming, while other sources claimed he was born near Qinzhou, in present-day coastal Guangxi province, or even as far away as Zhejiang province.[4] All these areas claimed him as their native son. During the upheavals of the Ming–Qing transition, Yang was most active in the Gulf of Tonkin in the 1640s to early 1680s, but he also briefly ventured as far away as Fujian and Taiwan in the 1660s and 1670s. In 1682, when the Qing military finally drove away all the pirates from their bases in southwestern coastal China, Yang led about three thousand followers to Vietnam, finally settling at Mỹ Tho in the far south. In 1688 his lieutenant, Huang Jin, assassinated him in an apparent power struggle.[5]

Over the centuries, Yang has been variously labeled as a pirate, rebel, Ming loyalist, and hero. Based on historical writings, legends, and field

Chapter 2

research, this chapter attempts to piece together the story of Yang Yandi and his times in the ill-defined water frontier of the Gulf of Tonkin. I divide this chapter into five sections, each represented by a different Chinese character: omens (*zhao*), chaos (*luan*), pirates (*kou*), rebels (*ni*), and righteousness (*yi*).

Omens

In the Qianlong edition of the *Lienzhou Prefectural Gazetteer*, the compilers described a "baleful star" (*yaoxing*) that appeared in the winter of 1680.[6] It crossed the sky from southeast to northwest and displayed an eerie glowing red head and green tail. As it passed overhead people claimed they heard a great thunderous sound, as if something crashed into the earth. People in Hepu and Qinzhou continued to see this strange comet into the spring of the following year. The scholar-officials who wrote the entry in the gazetteer believed it was an omen (*zhao*) foretelling the end of pirate disturbances in the region. In 1681, indeed, Qing forces overwhelmed the great pirate Yang Yandi, who within a year fled China for southern Vietnam.[7] What the gazetteer writers described was undoubtedly the Great Comet of 1680, also known as Kirch's Comet or sometimes Newton's Comet, which had been seen in the northern skies of Europe between December 1680 and March 1681.[8] The comet must have terrified many people in Europe and in China.

In times of great turmoil and anxiety, as was the Ming–Qing transition, there always appeared excesses of portents and calamities, as well as soothsayers, conjurers, and con men who traveled about offering prognostications and remedies. Omens would have been especially important at this time because people were uncertain about the stability and longevity of the new dynasty, which after all was an alien conquest dynasty that would not consolidate its full control over China until 1684. In fact, local gazetteers and secular writings from southwestern Guangdong recorded an unusually large number of astrological phenomena during the years between 1644 and 1684. Appendix 1 lists the omens, natural disasters, and social unrest in the Gulf of Tonkin region during those years.

Chen Shunxi, in his firsthand account, *A Record of Chaos and Abandonment Seen and Heard*, recorded in vivid detail natural and unnatural occurrences in his home area of Wuchuan and elsewhere in China. He noted a solar eclipse in the third lunar month of 1644, and that it was followed by the sacking of Beijing by the rebel Li Zicheng, the suicide of the Ming emperor, and the arrival of Manchu armies in the north. In the winter of 1652–1653, Chen recorded a comet (*huixing*) in the skies above Guangdong, and in the fifth lunar month of 1659, residents in Qinzhou saw another comet, which (according to the local gazetteer) people believed predicted the demise of piracy in the area. Just a year later, the most powerful pirate at the time, Deng Yao, was defeated and soon afterward executed; but there was also a horrific typhoon followed by a drought and devastating famine in the region. Then again in the tenth lunar month of 1664, Chen witnessed another blazing comet that crossed the night sky, as well as what he described as the intersecting of two stars (*liangri xiangjiao*), a strange astrological event that he observed several times over the next few months. Others also noted the same comet in Lienzhou and Qiongzhou (Hainan) prefectures. In Chen's writings, these sightings presaged not only earthquakes in northern China, torrential rains in Fujian, typhoons in southwestern Guangdong, an earthquake in Gaozhou, and a fire in the walled city of Lienzhou, but also the start of another protracted period of intense violence and chaos involving rebel and Qing armies as well as bandits, pirates, and village militias. The Lienzhou gazetteer recorded yet another comet, seen for three months, in early 1667. After that there was no further mention of comets in the region until the Great Comet of 1680.[9]

Comets, referred to as baleful stars (*xiongxing* or *yaoxing*), were regarded as a category of demons with such names as Year Star or Great Year (Taisui) and Dog of Heaven (Tiangou). They appeared in the skies as rays of bright light with long pointed tails. In the imperial pantheon the Year Star was a powerful protector of armies to whom officials offered sacrifices before every military campaign; but in popular beliefs, the Year Star was a sword-wielding evil spirit, who controlled the weather and human fate. To avoid pestilence and disasters, people called upon Daoist priests and shamans to perform solemn exorcist rituals to appease his fury. The Dog of Heaven was said to take the form of a large shooting star that produced loud thunderous sounds, and when it crashed to earth it left behind what appeared to be dog droppings and blazing fires. In ancient times, people reportedly made human sacrifices to placate the Dog of Heaven. Taken together, while officials considered these baleful stars mostly as protectors and servants of the authorities, the common people regarded them as cruel demons who brought calamities, bloody scourges, cannibalism, and death.[10]

Besides comets, there were other ominous signs cautioning officials and people that things were not the way they were supposed to be. In the fifth lunar month of 1647 there was a blood-red rain in Lin'gao county on Hainan island; in 1654 in Yaizhou county, also on Hainan, a pool of water suddenly

CHAPTER 2

turned red like blood for about ten days; and in 1665 (not long after sighting one of the comets mentioned above) a strange, inexplicable, blood-colored liquid began flowing for three days inside the Haizhu Temple in Canton. In 1653 people in Lin'gao witnessed an odd five-colored vapor or cloud in the sky; in 1659 people in Yaizhou reported seeing a strange white vapor arising from the seashore shooting out rays of lightning and accompanied by thunderous sounds, and in 1666 they again saw the same strange white vapor, but this time it disappeared into the sea. In Lin'gao, Qinzhou, and Fangcheng in early 1668 there were many reports of unusual vapors; in Qinzhou people said there was first a white vapor in the shape of a spear followed a few days later by a black vapor in the shape of three knives, and a month later the moon turned as bright as the sun. Our observer in Wuchuan, Chen Shunxi, reported seeing in 1675 a curious red and white solar halo, which was followed three months later by another wave of violence and bedlam associated with the Rebellion of the Three Feudatories. There were other inauspicious portents: in 1649 hunters in Yaizhou killed a horned female deer; in 1661 a woman in Wuchuan gave birth to a half male, half female baby; and between 1669 and 1673 there were several extraordinary reports of man-eating tigers in the suburbs of both Qinzhou and Wuchuan. In the same year that Qing troops defeated Yang Yandi, in 1681, snow fell in Qinzhou, an extremely rare occurrence.[11]

In traditional China portents, such as the ones mentioned above, were important to everyone from emperor to peasant. As the ancient *Book of Documents (Shujing)* explained, "The king watches the Year Star [for portents]. Ministers and officials watch the moon. The Leader of the Army watches the sun.... The common people watch stars."[12] The trust in portents was predicated on the universal acceptance that man, nature, and the cosmos were so interdependent and intertwined that they operated as a single complex, a harmonious whole. Any disharmonies or irregularities in the cosmic order, evidenced by eclipses, comets, meteorites, blood-colored rain, or abnormal births, were interpreted as divine or supernatural warnings of approaching social disorders or natural catastrophes. The emperor and his officials relied on the correct interpretation of a wide range of celestial and earthly phenomena for the proper running of government as well as to forestall rebellions. The common people were likewise sensitive to omens, not only because they presaged natural or man-made disasters but also reflected the quality of local governance. Rebel leaders, too, looked for portents to rationalize their uprisings.[13] Thus, while everyone trusted in omens, their interpretations by rulers, rebels, and commoners were not necessarily the same. When charismatic figures like Yang Yandi or Deng Yao looked up and saw comets flying across the sky did they interpret them as ominous warnings of their impending fall or did they see something else?

If comets and such were warnings of some imbalance between man, nature, and the cosmos, then natural disasters were signs of supernatural disfavor or punishment. In the Chinese mindset, on the one hand, imbalances in the harmony of the cosmic order produced natural disasters, yet on the other hand, in and of themselves natural disasters were harbingers of other looming disturbances, such as the collapse of a dynasty or a surge in banditry. While rulers liked to blame catastrophes, such as typhoons, floods, droughts, earthquakes, locusts, famines, and epidemics, on social disorders, riots, and rebellions, commoners blamed such phenomena on unscrupulous, corrupt officials, and bad government in general. As one ancient book, the *Luxuriant Dew of the Spring and Autumn Annals* (*Chunqui fanlu*), put it: "When the world is in disorder and the people are perverse, when the will of the ruler is depraved, . . . [then] the transforming power of heaven and earth is impaired and calamities arise."[14] It was common belief that unjust or excessive killings, as in times of war and rampant banditry and piracy, also caused calamities.[15] Indeed, during the Ming–Qing cataclysm soldiers unjustly slaughtered countless numbers of innocent people whom they labeled as bandits, pirates, and rebels.

The people of southwestern Guangdong, therefore, were not surprised by the large numbers of natural disasters between 1644 and 1684; rarely a year passed without a typhoon, flood, or drought, which were often followed by famines and epidemics. All across the region the years 1648 and 1649 were times of floods, droughts, dearth, and disease; people abandoned their homes and fields became unproductive wastelands, and countless numbers of refugees starved to death by the roadsides. Conditions were so bad in some parts of Leizhou, Chen Shunxi wrote, that human flesh was sold in markets. In 1652, the year in which people saw a comet for three months, a series of typhoons, torrential rains, and floods hit Wuchuan, Leizhou, Hepu, and Qinzhou, followed by several more years of famines and epidemics. Between the spring and late summer of 1672, three typhoons, one after the other, devastated a wide stretch of the coast from Wuchuan to Hainan, washing away houses and crops and killing untold numbers of people; besides the typhoon, an earthquake and tidal wave struck the Chengmai coast, causing further deaths and devastation.[16] In the wake of the comet of 1680, over the

CHAPTER 2

following three years the entire Gulf of Tonkin region suffered a series of repeated droughts, famines, and epidemics.[17] By blaming such calamities on the cosmic disruptions caused by bandits, pirates, and rebels, officials justified their own excessive use of force as necessary to restore order and return cosmic balance. For rebel groups, and many commoners, however, natural disasters epitomized a wobbling dynasty and warranted their own "righteous uprisings" (*qiyi*).

In imperial China, the interpretation of extraordinary celestial and natural phenomena were the prerogatives of the state, and anyone caught prognosticating was severely punished. Nonetheless, during the Ming–Qing upheaval—a time of anarchy, carnage, and extreme uncertainties—those individuals officials branded as sorcerers (*yaoren*) appeared throughout China. They claimed to be able to make predictions based on their observations of the heavens, winds, and waters, and to have power to control the forces of nature by summoning spirits and demons. In the autumn of 1664, the same year that a comet was seen crossing the southern sky, Chen Shunxi recorded seeing a man in his fifties, simply referred to as the Sorcerer King (*yaowang*), who traveled throughout Huazhou, Gaozhou, and Dianbai, producing "dragon writings" (*longwen*), disseminating talismans, and handing out official titles of kings and generals. Considered a subversive troublemaker, once Qing officials got wind of his whereabouts, they immediately began a vigilant manhunt and apprehended him soon afterward. Without wasting any time, he and several of his comrades were tried and summarily beaten to death in Gaozhou. One of the presiding officers was the brutal local military commander, Zu Zeqing, whom we will have occasion to mention later.[18] Four years later, in what was apparently an unrelated case, a minor local official in Lienzhou prefecture, who was surnamed Chen, revealed the earthly appearance of the Goddess of Mercy (Guanyin) and a mysterious "sacred book" (*shenshu*). The appearance of the goddess would have presaged an apocalyptic event (such as the fall of the dynasty) and sacred books typically contained prognostications, amulets, and incantations, which could be copied to make charms and certificates to be sold to villagers to protect them from the impending catastrophe. Officials quickly arrested Chen, hastened him off to Canton, where he was thrown into jail and repeatedly interrogated under torture; unable to bear it, he hung himself.[19]

Men like the Sorcerer King were itinerant preachers or medicine men who went about towns and villagers selling cures for all sorts of ailments and amulets that promised protection from an imminent apocalypse.[20] Although officials considered them dangerous and seditious, in local communities they satisfied important social and psychological needs of commoners in times of anxiety and chaos.

Chaos

Our witness, Chen Shunxi, methodically and purposefully juxtaposed extraordinary phenomena (eclipses, comets, vapors), natural disasters (typhoons, floods, droughts), and man-made calamities (wars, banditry, piracy)—to him man, nature, and the cosmos became entwined in a great chaos. The Chinese term *luan* (chaos), however, only approximates the sufferings and losses of several millions of people across China between 1644 and 1684. In southwestern Guangdong, as throughout southern China, those forty years were truly catastrophic. First there were the dynastic wars between the Ming and Qing that continued until the early 1660s. Then between 1661 and 1683 the new Qing rulers instituted a draconian coastal population removal policy, what historians have called the Great Clearance, whereby everyone living on the coast and offshore islands from Shandong to Guangdong were forced to move inland some ten to twenty miles. About the same time, all across south China wars continued with the Rebellion of the Three Feudatories from 1673 to 1681.[21]

Besides these large-scale social disorders, widespread banditry and piracy, urban riots, and peasant and ethnic uprisings assured that carnage and devastation did not cease. The near complete anarchy forced local communities to arm themselves for self-protection against all intruders—Manchu and northern soldiers, pro-Ming bands, deserters, armies of beggars and refugees, and roving gangs of bandits and pirates. Adding to the chaos, as mentioned above, were the numerous famines and epidemics caused by both man and nature, as hundreds of thousands of displaced people died of starvation and exposure. According to Robert Marks, in 1640 Guangdong's population was about nine million, but in 1661 it had been reduced to seven million, a substantial loss of two million people or 22 percent; and by 1650, in southwestern Guangdong as much as 24 percent of the arable land laid in waste.[22] Refugees, who aimlessly roamed the countryside, were easy recruits for bandit gangs and rebel armies.

After the Manchus occupied Beijing in 1644, several Ming loyalist regimes continued to resist the Qing in the south into the 1660s. In 1646, one of the Southern Ming rulers, the Yongli emperor, established his court in Zhaoqing, on the West River, not far from Canton. To dislodge the loyalist forces, the Qing launched two major campaigns to conquer the province, first in 1646 and another in 1649. In the first campaign resistance was weak, as most Ming regulars had already deserted their posts, thereby adding to the increasing numbers of refugees, bandits, and pirates. After Qing troops took Canton in the winter and the Yongli court fled upriver into neighboring Guangxi province, Li Chengdong, the Qing commander, split his army into three routes: Li led the major force to pursue the Yongli emperor into Guangxi, while another force moved up the North River, and the third force, under Xu Guodong, campaigned southwestward into Gaozhou, Leizhou, Lienzhou, and finally Hainan island.[23]

As the Qing armies became overextended, the political and military vacuum that this created in many areas of the province allowed for a further upsurge of riots, uprisings, banditry, and piracy throughout 1647. When the Qing recalled their armies to put down the disturbances in the core Canton delta, several "righteous uprisings" erupted in the southwest in Maoming, Wuchuan, and Suixi counties; in Wuchuan one of the leaders was Deng Yao.[24] Huang Hairu, a Chaozhou pirate who had earlier surrendered to the Qing and was afterward sent to defend Leizhou, also rebelled in the summer of 1647. For about a year he and his pirate-rebels battled with Qing naval forces off the Leizhou and Wuchuan coasts, finally fleeing back to Chaozhou where he died at sea in a storm in 1650.[25] In the meantime, Li Chengdong, the Qing commander in Guangdong, switched sides in 1648, but died during a campaign against his former comrades in the following year. Switching sides, sometimes several times, was quite common during the Ming–Qing wars. Once again, in the interval, Yongli moved his court back to Zhaoqing.[26]

With so many setbacks in Guangdong, in 1649 the Qing court sent a fresh banner army under Shang Kexi to reclaim the province, and in the following year, after a prolonged siege, Canton fell for the second time. What followed was a bloodbath in which soldiers massacred between 60,000 and 100,000 city residents.[27] Again the Yongli emperor retreated with his armies to neighboring Guangxi province. Deng Yao withdrew to the Gulf of Tonkin to Longmen island, which became a base from which over the next decade he launched numerous raiding expeditions throughout the gulf region. His most famous raid was on Qinzhou in 1656, when his band looted the Confucius Temple, making off with a 300-catty bronze incense burner and various other bronze altar pieces, totaling more than 1,500 catties in weight. According to local legend, he melted these down to make weapons to fight the Qing. In 1659 he again attacked Qinzhou but was repulsed, and a year later Shang

Kexi's army drove him out of his stronghold on Longmen island. He fled to Vietnam and soon afterward reportedly shaved his head and became a Buddhist monk. Later he snuck back into China but was apprehended and executed.[28] Remnants of Deng's forces escaped to Hainan where they continued as pirates and insurgents for several more years.[29]

During the Ming–Qing dynastic wars, Longmen and neighboring islands became some of the most notorious retreats for pirates and dissidents. Located at the mouth of the Qin and Yuhong rivers, Longmen served as the chief port of entry for the walled city of Qinzhou. Longmen was on the main coasting route between Vietnam and southern China. According to the early Qing scholar Pan Dinggui, in his *Travel Record of Annan*, published in 1689, Longmen was the "outer door" to Qinzhou, strategically located between Guangdong and Vietnam. Pan described the area, with its many islands, lagoons, and mangrove swamps, as an imposing "sea frontier" and veritable "refuge for pirates."[30] A huge mangrove swamp, called the "Seventy-two Passages" (Qishier jing), with its intricate waterways and dense vegetation, had a deserved reputation as a retreat for pirates and smugglers since at least the eleventh century.[31] From there ships could easily and clandestinely sail eastward toward Hepu and Leizhou or westward toward northern Vietnam, and in either direction the journey took about one day. In the late seventeenth century, in fact, Longmen became the one of the most important centers for anti-Qing resistance in southern China.[32]

Besides Deng Yao there were several other notable pirates and rebels who operated in the Gulf of Tonkin in the 1650s and 1660s. Another Ming loyalist, Du Yonghe, fled to Hainan with his supporters in 1652, and the Leizhou pirate-rebel Wang Zhihan, with more than five thousand followers, repeatedly harassed the Qing military and plundered ships and coastal villages in the region for the next four years. Chen Shangchuan was another Ming loyalist and pirate, who originally hailed from a family of merchants who lived on one of the islands located in the northern corner of Guangzhou Bay in Wuchuan county in southwestern Guangdong. During the turmoil of the Ming–Qing transition, Chen joined the Ming loyalist cause under the Yongli emperor, and soon became associated with Deng Yao and other pirate-rebels on Longmen island. After his defeat in 1681, Chen, together with Yang Yandi and others, fled to southern Vietnam with several thousand followers.[33] Today in Vietnam Chen is venerated as a deified hero who founded the Chinese community at Biên Hòa, located outside modern Ho Chi Minh City (Saigon).

Chapter 2

Over those same years most of southwestern Guangdong was in turmoil as Southern Ming armies under Li Dingguo campaigned in Lienzhou, Gaozhou, Leizhou, and Hainan, and as far eastward as Xinhui county in the Canton delta.[34] During the fighting some areas changed hands several times; for example, Chen Shunxi reported that his native Wuchuan changed hands three times in 1653, four times in 1654, and again four times in 1655.[35] After Qing forces defeated Li Dingguo (in early 1655), many of his troops fled to sea to join Deng Yao and other pirate bands. Between 1655 and 1660 there was not only a noticeable upsurge in piracy across the whole region, but also in uprisings of ethnic "mountain bandits" on Hainan island and in Lingshan county on the rugged Guangdong–Guangxi border. The protracted fighting in the region, accompanied by typhoons, floods, droughts, and locusts, also caused severe food shortages and immense suffering and death that continued into the late 1650s.[36] Between 1661 and 1662, Deng Yao, Wang Zhihan, the Yongli emperor, and a number of others on the Qing most-wanted list had been captured and executed. Effective resistance against the Qing by organized pro-Ming forces was severely hampered in the gulf region.[37]

Although the Qing had virtually defeated the Southern Ming on land by 1661, at sea and on the southern coast Zheng Chenggong and numerous other pirate bands continued to cause serious problems for the new dynasty. In coping with the problems, between 1661 and 1683 the Qing government exacted several sweeping maritime bans and coastal evacuation decrees that forced millions of residents from Shandong to Guangdong to abandon their homes and livelihoods and to move inland anywhere from ten to twenty miles.[38] To implement this Great Clearance soldiers erected barriers, ditches, guard posts, and watch towers to make sure that the area remained clear of all inhabitants. No one was allowed, under pain of death, to live or work inside the evacuation zone or to go out to sea to trade or fish. Because people in Guangdong continued to sneak out to sea, however, in 1664 and again in 1679 the government issued further coastal evacuation orders.[39] Only the Portuguese enclave at Macau and Hainan island did not come under these bans; however, although in Hainan people were allowed to remain in their coastal homes, they were forbidden to set out to sea to trade or fish.[40]

As a result of this draconian policy an estimated 5.3 million hectares (*mu*) of land remained unproductive for more than twenty years. In Wuchuan county alone, for instance, by 1664 roughly 580 villages were abandoned and their fields turned to wastelands. Because several hundreds of thousands of people suddenly lost their homes and no longer had the means of making a living, many became wandering refugees and ready recruits for the ever-increasing numbers of bandit and pirate gangs.[41] The bans were so disruptive to maritime trade and the economy in general, that more than one historian has suggested that it was a major cause of the "Kangxi Depression" between 1661 and 1680.[42] While in some areas the bans were loosened in 1669, it was not until after the Qing had defeated the Zheng regime on Taiwan in 1683 that the policy was completely rescinded.[43]

In the meantime, in the winter of 1673, Wu Sangui, one of the three "pacification princes" in southern China, declared open rebellion against the Qing; this marked the start of the Rebellion of the Three Feudatories, which was not suppressed until 1681.[44] The revolt inaugurated another period of intense political and social instability in south China. In Guangdong, although Shang Kexi, another pacification prince, remained loyal to the new dynasty, his son, Shang Zhixin, simply pushed aside his aged father (who died shortly afterward) and joined Wu's revolt in the spring of 1676. Like so many others, Shang Zhixin would change sides several times during the rebellion. Wu Sangui raised the banner of a new Zhou dynasty and handed out official titles and positions to his supporters.[45] In Gaozhou, between 1675 and 1676, Zu Zeqing abandoned his post as the Qing military commander to accept commissions and seals of office from Wu, first as his "Trustworthy and Imposing General" (*xinwei jiangjun*) and later as the "Marquis who Pacifies the Periphery" (*jingyuan hou*). At the same time military garrisons in Leizhou and Lienzhou also revolted, and Zu Zeqing appointed his henchmen in those areas with both civil and military offices. In 1677, Shang Zhixin shaved his forehead and returned allegiance to the Qing. Once again southwestern Guangdong was in a state of anarchy and chaos, and, as in the 1650s, many areas changed hands several times. Wu Sangui died of dysentery in 1678, and Zu Zeqing was arrested in the following year and sent to Beijing, where he and his entire family were executed in 1680.[46] Also that year, Shang Zhixin, after lingering in a Beijing jail for some time, was allowed to commit suicide, out of respect for his father who had served the dynasty loyally for many years.[47] With the leaders gone, within a year Qing armies had crushed the rebellion.

Because of the chaos and anarchy of the times it is difficult to make clear distinctions between regular Qing or pro-Ming military forces, rebels, bandits, pirates, and local militias. There was, in fact, as Lynn Struve has explained, "a tangled profusion of activities" that blurred identities.[48] Countless numbers of army deserters, from all camps, joined the sizable bandit and pirate bands that were already active in the province. It was not unusual for Southern Ming and Qing armies to collaborate with outlaw groups or even incorporate them into their own forces. As Robert Marks has pointed out, in most cases Ming loyalist troops were not composed of gentry-led forces but instead often contained large contingents of bandits, pirates, and deserters from one army or another.[49] The same was true of the Qing armies fighting in Guangdong. We have noted that the Qing used the pirate Huang Hairu and his forces in the defense of Leizhou in 1647; and during the siege of Canton in 1650, Shang Kexi relied on local pirates to assist in the amphibious attacks on the city. During the Rebellion of the Three Feudatories, things were much worse; Zu Zeqing's army had degenerated into a motley horde of deserters, ruffians, bandits, and pirates. Chen Shunxi described the absolute pandemonium in Wuchuan in 1679, where soldiers, village mercenaries, bandits, and pirates were all fighting one another and indiscriminately pillaging villages and towns.[50]

Village militias (*tuanlian*) were often no better. Many were composed of hired "braves" (*yong*), who were mostly unemployed young juvenile delinquents and local bullies, referred to in the records as "bare sticks" (*guanggun*) or "rotten lads" (*lanzai*). On the pretext of community defense, militias were often organized in fact to settle old scores with rival villages, as was the case in Haikang county in Leizhou. According to a local gentry named Chen Shiqi, near his home there were two villages, one called Taiping (Great Peace) that the Tan family dominated and the other called Xinqiao (New Bridge) that the Feng family dominated. At the start of the Kangxi period (early 1660s), both villages, using the excuse of defense against pirates and bandits, hired braves and formed militias, which in fact, engaged in feuds or "armed affrays" (*xiedou*) with one another.[51] Sometimes, too, local militias took advantage of their numbers to plunder and burn down neighboring, often rival, villages and to kidnap women and children for ransom.[52]

Pirates

Yang Yandi lived his entire adult life during those troubled times, those forty years of extreme chaos and anarchy. During that time he developed a reputation as one of the most daunting pirates (*kou* or *haikou*) in the gulf region. He and his younger brother, Yang San, began their outlaw careers as petty, local pirates (*tudao* or *tuzei*) in the 1650s, or perhaps a decade earlier, carrying out small hit-and-run raids on boats and villages around the Gulf of Tonkin. As Yang Yandi's gang became larger and more formidable his attacks became bolder, and by 1656 he gained the attention of the authorities with his raid on the port town of Tongxi on Hainan island. He not only robbed the trading ships anchored in the harbor but also many shops and homes on shore and killed several merchants who resisted.[53] In 1658, he commanded seven ships and over the next several years he continued his pillaging of ships and looting of towns along the Hainan and Leizhou coasts. In 1661, now with about twenty ships, Yang's gang raided a Li aborigine village at Xiamaling, at the southern tip of Hainan, where they abducted a village leader named Lin Wu and several tens of women and held them for ransom. They also plundered several other coastal towns and villages and kidnapped more than 300 men, women, and children. In 1665, a gang of pirates in thirteen ships, probably associated with the Yang brothers, who were operating from bases on Weizhou and other islands, plundered a Dan anchorage and village on the Chengmai coast of Hainan, killing two people and kidnapping for ransom four others.[54]

During the years between 1656 and 1665, Yang and his brother were mostly involved in raids along the coasts of Hainan island and Leizhou peninsula. In the early 1660s, Yang Yandi probably commanded about a thousand followers, and their attacks were so effective that for a time they upset communication links between Canton and Hainan. Although the sources are unclear on this point, it is likely that at this time the Yang brothers became associated with Deng Yao, Wang Zhihan, and Chen Shangchuan, and that the Yangs also operated from a base on one of the many islands near Longmen. In any case, in 1661 after Qing forces drove Deng Yao from Longmen, Yang Yandi fled to Vietnam to recuperate his losses.[55]

With Deng Yao out of the way, however, Yang Yandi quickly rose to prominence in the Gulf of Tonkin, and for a short time he and his forces reoccupied Longmen, only to be once again driven away by Shang Kexi in 1663. With this loss of the island stronghold for the second time, Yang and his followers scattered. One subordinate, Huang Guolin, led about a thousand men into Guangxi, where they continued to plunder villages and battle with Qing troops until Huang was captured and executed later that same year.[56] The Yang brothers, and several associates, such as Huang Mingbiao and Xian Biao, together with family members and followers, fled to a port called Hải Nha in Vietnam (likely in Hải Dương province) where they received shelter and protection from a local official and strongman named Phan Phú Quốc. He provided them not only with a base from which to launch their expeditions in the gulf region, but also supplied them with provisions, weapons, and ships. When Qing forces were sent there to suppress Yang and his comrades in 1666, Phan Phú Quốc refused to hand over his guests, closed the gates to the city, and fired on the Qing soldiers. Pressured by the Qing court in Beijing, the Vietnamese king in Thăng Long (Hanoi) reluctantly ordered the arrest of Yang and his accomplices.[57]

Forced to flee Vietnam, Yang Yandi escaped to Fujian and Taiwan (in 1666 or 1667) seeking the shelter of the Zheng regime. The next mention of Yang in Chinese sources is ten years later (in 1677), when he left Taiwan with about a thousand men in eighty ships to once again return to the Gulf of Tonkin and retake Longmen island.[58] For the next five years, from his base Yang launched repeated raids on towns and shipping around Qinzhou, Leizhou, and Hainan, and also battled almost continuously with the Qing navy in the region. In 1678, Yang Yandi and another local pirate named Liang Yuhe looted several settlements on the east coast of Leizhou and then blockaded the mouth of the Nandu River, the main entranceway to the upriver ports in the prefectural capital. In the next year, with about forty warships, Yang's band robbed ships in Shiqu harbor and the markets at Senshan and Datie on Hainan's northwest coast. They once again kidnapped women and children for ransom. In 1680–1681, now with about a hundred ships, Yang pillaged Shipai harbor in Lin'gao county, looting, burning, and kidnapping, and then Dongshui harbor and the Chengmai coast, with more looting and kidnapping.[59]

Then in 1681 Qing forces attacked Longmen, finally defeating and driving Yang from his base for the last time. Once again Yang retreated with 3,000 followers in seventy ships to Vietnam, eventually settling in the south in Mỹ Tho in the Mekong delta (about forty-five miles from Saigon), where he and his forces received protection and support from the Nguyễn lords. Yang and his men settled in their new home, engaged in trade, farming, and fishing, as well as the occasional plundering of passing ships. To repay his new lord, Yang helped the Nguyễn consolidate control over southern Vietnam by fighting their Cambodian rivals. Yang died in 1688, when one of his subordinates, a man named Huang Jin, assassinated him.[60]

Rebels

Yang Yandi emerged out of this milieu of chaos in the 1650s as a pirate and rebel leader. But what exactly made him a "rebel" and what was he rebelling against? In the sources, the most frequently used term to indicate rebel or rebelliousness was *ni*, usually seen in such compounds as *nizei* (rebel) and *haini* (sea rebel). Although the term rebellion, at least in English, implies an overt intention to overthrow an established government, this was not the only meaning of the term in imperial China's lexicon. Actually the term *ni* is loaded with several meanings, including outright open attacks against the state and its officials (but not necessarily with the intention to overthrow the government), attempts to assassinate the emperor and the royal family, and to desecrate the royal tombs; it also included treason and the absconding, aiding, and abetting with foreign states and rulers. The first mention of Yang in connection with rebels or rebelliousness that I have discovered was in an entry in the *Veritable Records* (*Shilu*) from 1666, in which Yang was mentioned with several other pirates who were hiding in Vietnam under the protection of a local official and strongman, Phan Phú Quốc, mentioned earlier. Later, in 1678 and thereafter, the *Veritable Records* repeatedly identified him as a sea rebel, beginning with a raid on the administrative city of Qinzhou.[61]

What about Yang Yandi's credentials as an anti-Qing rebel? We can start to answer this question by examining first his associations with other known rebels and second his actual activities. Fundamentally, Yang associated with three anti-Qing rebel camps: Deng Yao on Longmen, the Zheng regime in Taiwan, and Zu Zeqing, a supporter of the Rebellion of the Three Feudatories in southwestern Guangdong. Although several recent writers claim that Yang was a Southern Ming general, and therefore a staunch Ming loyalist, I have not yet found any contemporary evidence that supports this claim. Most sources, however, do mention him as an associate or subordinate of Deng Yao, who is described in the Qing dynasty sources as both a notorious pirate (*haizei* or *haikou*) and rebel (*nizei* or *haini*).[62] We have also noted how Chen Shunxi singled Deng out as one of the leaders of the "righteous uprisings" in 1647 in Gaozhou, which was his home area.[63] Yang Yandi became associated with Deng on Longmen island in the 1650s.

After Deng was defeated and executed, Yang fled first to Vietnam and later to Taiwan, where he and Xian Biao became followers of Zheng Jing, the eldest son and heir of Zheng Chenggong. According to several Republican era and later sources, Zheng Jing commissioned Yang as a general and more than one source claims that he raised the banner to "oppose the Qing and restore the Ming" (*fan Qing fu Ming*),[64] though by this time (1666–1667) the pro-Ming resistance in Guangdong had greatly diminished. Several mainland China scholars suggest that Zheng Jing sent Yang back to the Gulf of Tonkin area to open up a second maritime front to fight the Qing.[65] It is more likely that if Zheng sent Yang back to the gulf it was to protect the important trade and communication routes that linked Taiwan with Vietnam, Cambodia, and Siam.⁶⁶ Another possibility, however, is that Zheng did not send Yang back west, but simply that Yang abandoned the Zheng camp soon after the latter suffered setbacks on the mainland. Unfortunately, for ten years between 1667 and 1677, we have little concrete information on Yang and his activities; these were the crucial years that he was in Taiwan and associated with Zheng Jing.

Other sources, namely the Jiaqing edition of the Leizhou prefectural gazetteer and a book by Du Zhen called *A Record of Campaigns in Guangdong and Fujian* (*Yue Min xunshi jilue*), explained that Yang Yandi and his associates Xie Chang and Liang Yuhe were subordinates of Zu Zeqing, who rebelled against the Qing under Wu Sangui in the 1670s.⁶⁷ However, there is little evidence to substantiate these claims. Nonetheless, Yang's associations with known rebel leaders did not necessarily mean that he took up the loyalist banner to "oppose the Qing and restore the Ming." After all, we must remember that during the Ming–Qing transition, the Southern Ming, the Zheng camp, and later Wu Sangui armies comprised large contingents of bandit and pirate groups, who often used the cloak of legitimacy provided by being associated with a "righteous army" (*yijun*) to continue their nefarious activities.

It is better perhaps to judge Yang Yandi by his actions, as did the Qing government. If Yang was a rebel, then we would expect that he attacked the symbols of Qing authority and power—administrative cities and military instillations—and that he killed Qing officials. In 1663, Yang assailed the military base Baihezhai in Leizhou and killed the commander, Fang Xing, and other officers and soldiers.⁶⁸ For the next two years Yang battled almost continuously with Qing forces under Shang Kexi. In 1666, as previously mentioned, Yang absconded to Vietnam where he "betrayed his country" by receiving shelter and protection from a foreign official. Later, he joined the rebel regime of Zheng Jing in Taiwan, and with his support (perhaps) in 1677, Yang returned to reoccupy Longmen. Once again, Yang and his followers stepped up attacks against Qing forces in the gulf region. In 1677–1679, the Yang brothers and Xie Chang collaborated with Li tribesmen, who were led by Han Youxian, in an uprising on Hainan. While Yang's forces attacked Qiongzhou, Chengmai, and Dingan from the sea, Han Youxian and his followers attacked from land. The Li aborigine disturbances were not suppressed until 1681.⁶⁹ Also during this time, in 1678, we have clear evidence of Yang Yandi as a sea rebel, with his attack on the walled capital of

Qinzhou, although his forces were repulsed by Qing soldiers. The next year Yang's forces captured the important Qing garrison at Hai'an in Leizhou.[70] Finally, in 1680–1681, before retreating to southern Vietnam, Yang attacked and occupied the Qing fort at Haikou, where the Qing commander surrendered to Yang, and afterward Yang plundered the county seat of Chengmai.[71]

We have strong, convincing evidence that Yang and his followers attacked Qing administrative seats and military instillations and killed and wounded a number of Qing civil officials, military officers, and soldiers, which in Qing parlance qualified him as a rebel (*ni*). What is less convincing, however, are the later assertions, first appearing in the Republican era and continuing until today among several scholars, that Yang was an anti-Qing, pro-Ming rebel. There is little actual evidence that Yang was a staunch Ming loyalist. He was most active in the years after 1650, but especially in the 1660s and 1670s; by that time the Southern Ming had been defeated and a Ming restoration only a faded dream. As one scholar put it: "Armies of righteousness were seldom to be seen. People harbored in their hearts the memory of Ming, but nobody started actual warfare."[72] It is perhaps better to think of Yang as one of the many local strongmen to appear in south China at that time. If Yang was a rebel, he was a rebel without a cause. He apparently fought for no purpose other than his own. He was a pragmatist, not an idealist.

Righteousness

If he was a pirate and perhaps a rebel, what made Yang Yandi "righteous"? The Chinese word for "righteousness" is *yi*, which, according to Derk Bodde, "characterizes the conduct of those individuals who are consciously aware of the existence of certain moral standards and obligations, and who strive in their every act to live up to them to the best of their ability."[73] These are lofty ideals that I suspect few people could achieve in real life. But here I will discuss the Yang Yandi of legends, the "righteous hero," as depicted on a modern poster in figure 5. It is impossible to know exactly when people began to call him Righteous Yang (Yang Yi). Although legends about Yang only appeared in written form in the 1930s and 1940s, it is certain that they existed earlier in one form or another in the oral traditions of local communities around Qinzhou and Fangcheng. As several folklorists have demonstrated, storytelling usually exists as an oral tradition long before the tales are put to writing. Actually, most stories about Yang were handed down orally from generation to generation and few were ever written down, even to today. Interestingly, in many cases the villagers I interviewed in January 2010 and July 2011, only

Figure 5. Contemporary Poster of the Hero Yang Yandi (Source: Author's collection)

knew of Yang by the name Righteous Yang (Yang Yi); they were completely unaware that his real name was Yang Yandi.

Stories and yarns about Yang apparently began to be told during his lifetime, or at least soon afterward, and a few were recorded in local gazetteers and anecdotal collections (*biji*). Although most of the early recorded tales (those dating from the Qing period) depict him as a villainous pirate, nonetheless we do have occasional hints about his righteousness, his sense of a higher moral duty. One of the earliest such examples, recorded in the late nineteenth century, comes from Chengmai county, Hainan. In 1681, when Yang's gang attacked his village, Li Chaoqing was sixteen years old; he recounted how Yang and his men badly treated the villagers and abducted his elderly sick father, demanding 300 taels of silver for his ransom. The family did not have such a large amount of money, so being a filial son, of course, Li volunteered to go with the pirates aboard their ship so he could care for his father. Suffering various hardships and humiliations among the pirates, finally when the gang neared the Yangjiang coast, Yang was so impressed with Li's unwavering devotion to his father that the pirate chief released both father and son. Although the story is about a filial son, Li Chaoqing, nonetheless we do get a glimpse of Yang's sense of righteousness and moral obligation.[74] Soon after this incident Yang fled to Vietnam and his legends began to grow.[75]

However, today many of the legends I have read or heard depict Yang as a patriotic rebel, a Ming loyalist, and/or an anti-Qing hero. This tradition first appeared in the Republican period and continues today in historical accounts and in oral tales. It is now impossible to know if these versions of a patriotic Yang were the same as the ones told by storytellers over the previous two centuries. Legends evolve over time and change according to historical circumstances. Nonetheless, this does not mean that in the Qing period the stories about Yang did not portray him as a righteous anti-Qing hero (whether he actually was one or not). After all, throughout the Qing period in south China there was a resilient, mostly clandestine anti-Qing sentiment, epitomized in Triad legends, slogans, and rituals.[76]

The most frequently told tales about Yang Yandi are about how he built a citadel, a palace, and one or more canals near his base on Longmen island. In some stories, Righteous Yang was a Ming general who, after being defeated in the north, retreated with the Southern Ming's Yongli emperor to the south, where Yang ended up building a stronghold near Longmen. Several legends say he was a general in the Zheng regime in Taiwan. In other stories Yang was a self-proclaimed ruler whom locals called King Yang (Yang Wang). In all the legends today Yang is an "oppose the Qing, restore the Ming hero" (*fan Qing fu Ming yingxiong*). The purported ruins of his citadel are known locally as the "King's City" (Wangcheng) or even the "Emperor's City" (Huangcheng).[77]

Legends and rumors abound about imperial treasures being uncovered near the ruins over the past centuries—large ceramic urns filled with copper coins or, in some tales, silver dollars, pieces of jade, ancient bronze mirrors, a solid gold cat figurine, and a book made of gold (*jinshu*). According to one informant, the golden book was found buried beneath a mysterious tree: by the tree when it rained it would not get wet, in the summer it would not get warm, and in the winter it would not get cold. The book was made up of several gold pages with archaic writing on them. Some said the book was actually an imperial edict, awarded to Yang for valorous service to the Ming cause. Others said it was written by Yang himself, who used it to legitimize his claims as king. In another legend, Yang is a powerful warlord and accomplished wizard who used the "dragon writings" in his "golden book" to produce efficacious charms and spells.[78]

At least two actual canals exist, both in the vicinity of Longmen and Fangcheng, which villagers claim were built by Yang. The canal that I saw in 2010 was originally about eight miles in length and, according to one villager, it had been in use up to the time of the Japanese occupation in World War II, when it was being used for clandestine activities against a new wave of foreign invaders. The canal or canals were supposed to have been built when Yang was engaged in a desperate battle for survival against Qing armies. With no way to escape, so one story goes, he built an altar at the highest point in or near his citadel, where he earnestly prayed to the Jade Emperor, the Sea Dragon King, and the Gods of the Mountains and Earth (in other stories he simply prayed to Heaven) for help in creating an escape route. Seeing that Yang fought a righteous cause, that is, against the alien Manchu invaders, the gods took pity on him and at night sent forth an army of celestial soldiers (*tianbing*) to dig out a canal and then brought forth a heavy rain, which allowed him and his men to break out to the sea.[79] In another version of the story, because Yang was a skilled wizard himself, he called down the celestial soldiers and commanded them to build the canal.[80]

Such legends are revealing: taken together they gave Yang credibility as a righteous hero. Yang had magical powers to call down the gods and celestial armies, who were willing to aid him in his righteous cause against alien invaders. The legends also mention buried treasures of silver, gold, and jade, as well as a mysterious golden book. These objects have a double meaning. On the one hand, they can be interpreted as imperial treasures bestowed on Yang by the Southern Ming emperor for his loyal and valorous services. On the other hand, of course, these can be interpreted simply as the booty Yang and his men gathered over many years of raiding expeditions. This, of course, does not make him less a hero in popular imaginations. Yang represented a poor commoner who made good as a righteous pirate hero, perhaps something of a "social bandit" who robbed the rich and powerful to help the poor. Today, in the area said to be the ruins of his citadel, locals have put up a matshed shrine where they venerate a deified Righteous Yang.[81]

Conclusion

Throughout history the Gulf of Tonkin has had a reputation as a "turbulent sea frontier" where piracy, smuggling, and rebellion remained endemic. It was a nebulous water frontier where boundaries and jurisdictions between China and Vietnam were always murky and imprecise. Its remoteness from centers of government and its rugged coastline dotted with countless bays, islands, and mangrove swamps provided ideal geopolitical conditions for illicit activities. Until recently the region remained a hub for pirates who often worked in collusion with local officials on both sides of the border. As late as the 1990s, for instance, pirated vessels frequently showed up in Beihai harbor, where they were repainted, refitted, and renamed, all under the watchful gaze of Chinese military and customs officers who provided protection to the pirates in return for a share of the spoils. Even today, although the pirates have mostly disappeared, the gulf is still an important smuggling zone. In fact, the area retains much of its past rough-and-tumble frontier character.[82]

Piracy played a significant role in the gulf's political, economic, and social history. Politically, various polities sanctioned pirates, gave them official titles, provided them with safe harbors, and outfitted their ships, and in return the pirates provided their supporters with military aid and shares in their prizes. For the Southern Ming and the Zheng regime in Taiwan, the Gulf of Tonkin became a second maritime front in the struggle against the Manchus and an important outlet for trade. In southern Vietnam, pirate-refugees, such as Yang Yandi, were instrumental in securing the Mekong delta for the Nguyễn lords. Economically, throughout the century trade, smuggling, and piracy were usually intermingled and often indistinguishable. Violence was not only a trait of piracy but of trade in general. While many people suffered, others were able to take advantage of and profit from the wars and maritime prohibitions. Socially, piracy allowed many marginal people opportunities to improve their status or at least their own self-images. Political recognition gave some pirate leaders a sense of legitimacy, purpose, and respectability beyond simple pillaging and killing. Yang Yandi developed a reputation as a "righteous" hero.

CHAPTER 2

When he and other Ming loyalists fled to Vietnam in the late seventeenth century, they were quickly transformed from pirates to respectable merchants and prominent social elites, and in some cases even deified.

Yang Yandi emerged simultaneously as both historical figure and legend. For most writers in the Qing dynasty Yang was little more than a violent criminal—a pirate and a rebel. He and others like him were the cause of chaos. Officials manipulated astrological omens—such as comets—claiming that they foretold the defeat of pirates like Yang Yandi. And when he did fall shortly afterward, such omens only served to prove to them that the Qing house held Heaven's mandate and favor. However, by the twentieth century, nationalist writers of the Republican era and later Communist writers as well, depicted Yang as an anti-Qing, pro-Ming hero. For them omens, such as eclipses and comets, presaged social disorders and the fall of dynasties. As the writers of the 1946 Qinzhou gazetteer explained, it was wrong to treat men like Deng Yao and Yang Yandi simply as pirates, as earlier Qing officials had done, because they actually fought a righteous cause against the alien Manchu invaders, and therefore they should be considered patriotic heroes.[83] For common people legends, handed down first orally by storytellers and later written down by folklorists and propagandists, were the stuff of history, and in these versions of the past Yang Yandi became a righteous hero. Heaven favored and aided him, not the Qing, in popular lore.

Yang Yandi, nonetheless, lived in troubled times. He passed his entire adult life during a forty-year period of immense turmoil and lawlessness, truly, as Lynn Struve has written, a cataclysm. It is impossible for us to know how or what Yang felt, thought, or believed. What we do know is that under such trying conditions it was impossible to make clear distinctions between pirate, rebel, or hero. Identities were fuzzy and constantly changing. In fact, the traditional Chinese terms for pirates, bandits, outlaws, and rebels (such as *kou*, *zei*, and *ni*) were themselves inconsistent or contradictory. Although used indiscriminately by officials, such terms were always loaded with negative connotations. It was highly unlikely, however, that Yang viewed or called himself as either a pirate or rebel. Although we cannot know for certain, it would be easy to imagine that he thought of himself as a righteous hero, much the same way as many commoners saw him. When the Great Comet of 1680 appeared Yang was at the height of his power, in command of a battle-hardened navy that ruled over the Gulf of Tonkin; at that moment he may have regarded the comet as an omen for his own success and the demise of the alien Qing dynasty.

Interlude 1

Pirates into Goddesses

About thirty years ago when I started doing fieldwork in south China, I discovered something I had never seen before in the written sources in the Qing archives or local gazetteers. On a tiny island called Dragon's Lair (Longxue) in the Canton delta I came across a grotto and inside was a statue of the pirate Zhang Baozai standing before several spent sticks of incense offerings in a tin can.[1] I was perplexed. Why would anyone worship a pirate? How could Zhang Baozai be a god? Over the following years I found other examples of Chinese pirates who in death were transformed into deities—Yang Yandi in Fangcheng, Chen Shangchuan in Vietnam, Lin Feng in the Philippines, and Zheng Chenggong in Taiwan. There also were other folk stories I heard that seemed even more baffling and incredible. These involved female pirates who became deities in the most uncanny ways. I have uncovered four cases, each involving a spouse or sister of a well-known pirate chieftain—the sister of Wu Ping, the sister of Lin Daoqian, the spouse of Yang Yandi, and the sister of Zheng Chenggong. People began worshipping and sacrificing to them in the expectations of harnessing their fearsome power to secure wealth and protection for themselves, their families, or their communities.[2]

This interlude focuses on the case of Zheng Chenggong's younger sister, Zheng Zuxi. The problem with Zuxi (as with many other deified individuals) is that there is, what historians would say, no documentary evidence that she ever existed as an actual person. She is not mentioned in the Zheng genealogies or other family records, nor in any archives, gazetteers, memoirs, or other historical sources. What we do have, and what we must rely on in telling her story, are legends, anecdotes, hearsay, and the recorded interviews of devotees and villagers who reside close to her temple on the Baishahu coast near the city of Shanwei in Guangdong province (see map 8). Hers was a local cult that never spread beyond a few small isolated villages near her single temple; yet despite the lack of any official recognition her cult has persisted for more than three centuries. To her devotees, it is important to remember, Zuxi is real, as both a person and a goddess. To reconstruct her story we must engage in mythohistory.

HISTORY AND LEGEND

Zheng Chenggong is certainly one of the most famous pirate-heroes in Chinese history. Although not everyone treats him as a pirate, his family background—son of the infamous pirate Zheng Zhilong—and his own actions qualify him as such.[3] Living as he did during the turbulent Ming–Qing transition, it was not easy to make clear distinctions between pirates and rebels or villains and heroes. Individuals like Zheng Chenggong and Yang Yandi, among many others, took advantage of the anarchy of the age to display several identities. With his father in the custody of the Qing government after 1646, the young twenty-two-year-old Chenggong ruthlessly fought family rivals to become the patriarch of his clan and undisputed leader of one of the world's largest commercial conglomerates by 1650. He skillfully used the revenues from maritime trade and plunder to build up his navy to resist the Qing and to forcefully maintain his control of the southern seas. At the same time he also extended his territory from southern Fujian into eastern Guangdong, where he requisitioned grain, levied tribute, and drafted soldiers from the local population. Waving the banner of Ming loyalism, in the spring of 1651 he led a fleet southward ostensibly to aid ailing Southern Ming forces in the Canton delta. Before he could reach his destination, however, his fleet met near disaster with a sudden storm off the Huizhou coast near Baishahu. Soon afterward, receiving urgent news that Manchu troops had attacked his home in Amoy (Xiamen), he aborted his southern campaign and returned immediately to Fujian. With his home base once again secured, Chenggong summarily beheaded his uncle, who had failed in his duty to protect Amoy. Ten years later Zheng Chenggong himself would be dead.[4]

Throughout the southern campaign Zheng's forces had several engagements with the Qing navy, one of which I was told was near Baishahu. The story of the storm that almost destroyed Zheng's fleet is well known among the villagers in this area, having been handed down orally from one generation to the next for hundreds of years. According to local lore Zheng Chenggong had a younger sister named Zuxi, who was an accomplished martial artist and, in some tales, a capable sorceress (*wupo*). Because of her combat skills, she often accompanied her brother on military campaigns, as was the case in 1651. Separated from the rest of the fleet during the storm off Baishahu, she maneuvered her warship between the Zheng forces and the Qing fleet. In the bitter battle that ensued, in some versions of the story, Zuxi used magic to fly across the water to engage in hand-to-hand combat with the Qing forces and to stir up violent winds that wrecked the enemy's ships. However, although she saved the day for Zheng Chenggong, she was struck by a poison arrow and died in her brother's arms two days later, on the twenty-seventh day of the third lunar month (the day that her festival is celebrated). Significant too, like the Empress of Heaven (Tianhou) and so many other goddesses, Zuxi died a youthful unmarried virgin at age twenty. After burying his sister on the northern shores of Baishahu, Zheng Chenggong rushed back to Fujian to drive the Qing army away from Amoy. For the most part this is the story of Zheng Zuxi posted on her temple wall in 2012, a sort of official version that has been sanitized for popular consumption and political correctness. According to this version the Zheng Zuxi Temple was built by local fishers and villagers to honor her as a righteous, self-sacrificing, anti-Qing war hero, just like her brother.[5]

But that is not the only Zuxi legend I heard. The other legend is more visceral; it was told to me by my taxi driver, who grew up in the Baishahu area and knew many stories. He told me this version of the Zuxi legend after we left her temple, adding that this was the original story as understood by most local villagers (not the one posted in the temple). As in the previous version, Zuxi had accompanied her brother on his southern campaign, but in this tale the campaign was more like a piratical raid against ships and coastal villages in which a large amount of booty was collected. During the battle with the Qing navy off Baishahu, Zheng Chenggong received news of the attack on Amoy and so decided to immediately return to Fujian, leaving behind the treasure he had accumulated during this expedition. His sister, Zuxi, however, refused to leave without taking the gold and silver. Chenggong flew into a rage and killed her on the spot. She was buried nearby with the treasure on a small island that became known as Gold Island (Jinyu). My driver also told me a well-known curse associated with this legend: "No one is able to take away the treasure; if anyone takes the treasure they will become sick; and to get well they will have to spend all the gold." In this version Zuxi became a treasure-protecting deity.[6]

INTERLUDE I

What seems odd to me is that three other female pirates all had similar stories: each one also was murdered by a close family member intent on protecting his buried treasure. One story concerns the younger sister of Wu Ping, a notorious sixteenth-century pirate who hailed from Zhaoan, a county in Fujian on the border with Guangdong. According to legend, after Wu Ping occupied Nan'ao island as his base, he built a fortified stronghold where he settled his family and stockpiled weapons and other provisions in preparation for battling the Ming navy and other adversaries. Over many years on the island he had accumulated large amounts of gold and silver, which he stored in eighteen large urns that he buried in secret in eighteen places across the island. In 1565, the Ming court deployed a formidable armada under General Qi Jiguang, with more than 4,000 soldiers—some Nan'ao villagers told me as many as 10,000 soldiers—to annihilate the pirates. In the fierce battle that ensued, with no place to hide, Wu Ping sensed his impending defeat and decided to flee. When his younger sister (whose name we do not know) refused to leave the treasure behind, Wu Ping killed her, chopped her into eighteen pieces, and buried her with his treasure. That very night, soldiers surrounded Wu Ping's compound, but he mysteriously escaped and was nowhere to be found. He soon afterward fled to Vietnam and then disappeared from history. Some people told me that Wu Ping's sister had worked her magic to save him (despite being murdered by him). Today there is a stone statue of Wu Ping's sister located on a small outcropping overlooking the sea. The statue is an image of a young fisher woman, seated on a simple throne, and grasping a double-edged sword in her left hand and a silver ingot in her right hand. By her side is a stack of ingots and a pot for burning sticks of incense. Whenever people visit, they rub their hands on her right hand, the one holding the silver, in hopes that some of her wealth will also rub off on them. People have rubbed her hand and ingot so often that they have turned shiny black. Today Miss Wu (Wu Guniang), as she is locally known, is worshipped as a goddess of wealth.[7]

Lin Daoqian was an associate of Wu Ping, and with the latter's disappearance in the 1560s, Lin expanded his own piratical operations, organizing a huge trading cartel that stretched from south China to Southeast Asia. After a series of naval defeats, he retreated to southern Taiwan in 1563, where he spent the next several years rebuilding his forces. Eventually he fled to Patani in 1578, where he married the ruler's daughter and converted to Islam. He too had a younger sister, Lin Jinlian (or simply Lin Guniang), who is the subject of several legends. In one popular tale, when Lin Daoqian fled

Taiwan his sister stayed behind to guard the treasure that he had hidden in eighteen bins on Dagou Mountain. Later when Jinlian resisted her brother, who wanted to retrieve the treasure, Daoqian murdered and buried her with the bins of gold and silver. She became a mountain spirit (*shanxian*) who has continued to guard the buried treasure, placing a curse on anyone who tries to take it from her. Another, better known legend relates how Lin Guniang committed suicide in Patani after her brother refused to return to his home in Guangdong to take care of their elderly mother. This tale ends with the deification of the filial Lin Guniang and the building of her temple in Patani.[8]

In Yang Yandi's case, he killed his young third wife or, in some stories, his concubine. As we have noted in the previous chapter, according to popular lore, Yang had taken the title of king and had built a walled fortress that people have since called the "King's City" (Wangcheng), where he accumulated a large cache of gold and silver. With the Qing army advancing on his citadel and defeat eminent (this would have been in 1681 or 1682), Yang prepared to flee to Vietnam with his remaining followers. However, his concubine or third wife refused to leave. In a fit of rage Yang killed and buried her by throwing her into a deep well where he had hidden his treasure. In one of the legends, his third wife was transformed into a ghostly bird that local villagers call "Yang Er's Third Wife" (Yang Er Sanpo). Each morning nearby villagers still say that they hear the bird-ghost cry out to curse her wicked husband who murdered her. Up to today people dare not use the land near the ruins of what they believe to have been Yang Yandi's fortress because it is haunted and cursed.[9]

These four legends share several common features. Most importantly in each case the slain females were young (in their twenties) and died violent premature deaths. In three cases the victims were unmarried virgins, thus assuring their chastity and purity, important criteria for deification. According to P. Steven Sangren, only by overcoming their inherent negative, polluting qualities, such as sexual intercourse and childbirth, could women become goddesses.[10] As noted above, among these four female pirates only Yang Er's Third Wife, who was inherently impure by marriage, was not deified; she remained a vengeful ghost. In death these pirate women were transformed into deities (Zheng Zuxi, Wu Guniang, and Lin Guniang), mountain spirits (Lin Jinlian), and vengeful ghosts (Yang Er Sanpo), each one tasked with protecting ill-gained pirate treasures. Their violent deaths were purposeful, based on common folk beliefs that the resulting avenging ghosts would strike out to harm anyone coming near their burial sites, which were also the sites of buried treasure. In each case because the pirate brother or spouse was unable to hold on to or take away his loot by mortal means, he solved the problem by killing a close female relative, who would watch over the treasure from beyond the grave as deities, spirits, or ghosts. In fact, as we have noted above, in three cases there were curses placed on anyone who tampered with the treasure, and according to several of my informants, this was a form of magic that ensured the deceased relative would guard the buried treasure.

From Ghost to Goddess

If Zheng Chenggong did not have a sister named Zuxi and if she was not even an actual person, then how did her story get started? How did the fishers and villagers at Baishahu come to worship Zuxi and build a temple in her honor? Because there is no substantial documentary evidence much of what I will have to say is based on conjecture. What follows is only one of several possible stories, but one I consider to be the most likely, based largely on piecing together bits of historical and anthropological evidence with my fieldnotes from interviews with local villagers who worship at the Zuxi Temple.

Zuxi probably began as a ghost. We know from historical records that in 1651 Zheng Chenggong's navy was caught in a storm off the Baishahu coast and that his forces fought many sea battles with the Qing navy in this region at that time. We also know that it was not unusual for families to accompany Zheng's forces on military campaigns. Undoubtedly the corpses of storm or battle casualties, including women, would have washed up on shore. If this was the case, then whenever villagers found an unidentified corpse, they would first bury it and then erect a ghost altar or shrine to placate an otherwise dangerous spirit.[11] At first it seems Zuxi was a nameless corpse buried in a nameless grave, which only sometime later became identified with her. In fact, several villagers mentioned to me that the site of Zuxi's grave originally had been a "spirit altar" (*shentan*) where people made occasional sacrifices to appease the spirit and to make small, though sometimes inappropriate, requests. Then during the long "forced coastal evacuation policy" that lasted until 1669 in this part of Guangdong, her grave was abandoned and she became, what one informant said, "an old ghost with no one offering [her] sacrifices" (*jiugui wuren si*).[12]

Without offerings and sacrifices, ghosts became vengeful and dangerous demons, and they remained threats to individuals and communities if they were left unattended. Because they tended to lurk near the place of death to avenge themselves upon the living, they became rooted in a specific space as avaricious guardian spirits. Much like bandits, beggars, and prostitutes in real life, ghosts were marginal beings who disrupted the natural order of the cosmos and caused chaos and disorder (*luan*) among humans. It was precisely their inauspicious, premature, and violent deaths that rendered them ruthless, resentful, and dangerous. Yet it also was violence that made ghosts like Zuxi powerful and therefore spiritually efficacious. Indeed, numinous powers (*ling*) were frequently ascribed to people who died violent deaths. Since they were hungry and homeless, ghosts tended to grant the requests, even improper ones, of anyone who worshipped and sacrificed to them. In return for favors, homeless ghosts often required, through spirit mediums or dreams, that individuals or communities build them shrines or temples. Once placated with sacrifices and provided with an abode, spiteful ghosts could be better managed and even manipulated.[13]

According to local sources, the Zuxi Temple was first built in the Yongzheng reign (1722–1735), after the maritime restrictions had been lifted and after Zheng Chenggong had been rehabilitated by the Qing court in 1699.[14] Before that time it would have been unsafe for anyone to openly worship the sister of the well-known pirate-rebel and Ming loyalist, Zheng Chenggong. According to local lore, the building of the temple came about after fishers were caught in a violent storm off Baishahu and only saved by the intercession of a sword-wielding apparition who identified herself as the spirit of Zuxi. After that other seafarers also reported Zuxi performing miracles on their behalf. The previously abandoned ghost had now been identified as Zuxi, and fishers and villagers built a temple in her honor. According to Anne Gerritsen and other scholars, giving ghosts names and identities was not only a way to control them, but also a way to transform ghosts into deities. Only ghosts with recognizable identities, as well as personal histories, became gods.[15] Zuxi had been transformed into a goddess who helped seafarers in distress.

According to a no longer extant stone inscription dated 1809, the temple was renovated in that year, at the height of the great pirate disturbances led by Zhang Baozai and other pirates. Based on a handwritten copy of the inscription, the author was a local gentry named Chen Maosheng, who eulogized Zuxi as a suppressor of pirates and bulwark of the existing sociopolitical order. Chen's inscription not only indicated the rising local popularity of the goddess but it also was an overt attempt to legitimize an otherwise unsanctioned and licentious deity.[16] It is no coincidence, therefore, that the more famous and officially recognized Empress of Heaven also appeared in the Zuxi Temple at this time or perhaps a little earlier, and that the temple became known as the Pavilion of the Two Divinities (Shuangsheng ge). Although never officially recognized by the Qing state, the Zuxi cult and her single temple persisted for another two and half centuries before being demolished during the Cultural Revolution. The stone inscription, a wooden statue of Zuxi, and other religious artifacts were all destroyed at that time. The temple was rebuilt in 1985 and then renovated 1993 as a cultural centerpiece of the Honghai Bay development area. Today, while local devotees continue to worship her as a protective sea deity, Zuxi is honored by the local government as a patriotic anti-Qing female hero.[17]

THE WARRIOR MAZU

At some point after the temple was built in the Yongzheng period Zuxi took on another persona. She became known locally as the Jingang Mazu, meaning the Warrior Mazu. The location of her temple is called the "sacred place of warrior divinities" (*jingang shengdi*), which came from the geomantic attributes of the landscape that I was told made it an ideal site for a temple. The term *jingang*, in fact, refers to the Buddha's warrior attendants or guardians, which derived from ancient Hinduism. Chinese folk religion and culture also have borrowed the term from the former tradition. As noted above, Zuxi was skilled in martial arts, fought alongside her brother in battles against the Qing, and in some stories also was a sorceress who would have been adept at fighting evil spirits. In fact, the most valued relic in the temple is Zuxi's recently discovered double-edged sword, the purported weapon she used in her battle with the Qing navy off Baishahu and the one she also would have used to magically slay demons.[18]

As it turns out, Zuxi is actually one of many female deities labeled as Mazu on the Huizhou coast. In her own temple on the main altar are two statues—one of the Great Mother (Da Ma) and the other of the Second Mother (Er Ma), referring respectively to Lin Moniang (Tianhou) and Zheng Zuxi. Both are worshipped as Mazu (figure 6). In several other temples that I visited in December 2012 in this area, there often were two or more statues of goddesses on the main altars, each one said to be a different, unique Mazu. In the Tianhou Temple in the fishing port of Jiazi there are three Mazus worshipped in the main hall. In another fishing port, the Tianhou Temple in Dade, which dates back to the eleventh century and is near the Zuxi Temple in Baishahu, there are actually five goddesses who are each a different Mazu; they are known locally as the Five Embodied Mazus

(Wushen Mazu)—the first (Da Ma) is Lin Moniang, the second (Er Ma) is Zheng Zuxi, the third (San Ma) is Zhuang Jingyun, the fourth (Si Ma) is Lin Shuxian, and the fifth (Wu Ma) is Mo Mei.[19] In this temple Lin Moniang is the main deity while the others are secondary deities. Except for Lin Moniang, the others are all local deities unknown outside nearby communities. Zhuang Jingyun hailed from the nearby Zhuang Family village, where she

Figure 6. Statues of the Two Mazus in the Zuxi Temple (Source: Photo by author)

was born into a family of famous doctors. Being the only child, she studied medicine with her father and at a young age became a proficient healer in her own right. Before being married, however, she committed suicide after some villagers maliciously accused her of being a witch. Later, after appearing in dreams in which she said that she had ascended into Heaven, Jingyun was admitted into the Dade temple as the third Mazu. Lin Shuxian was also an only child born into a prominent local family. Known for her generosity, her fellow villagers called her a living bodhisattva. On the eve of her marriage, however, she was killed at a ferry crossing, and soon afterward was deified as the fourth Mazu. After a statue of a female deity had washed ashore near the Dade temple, the caretaker had several dreams in which she identified herself as a mountain goddess named Mo Mei (Little Sister Mo), whose upriver temple had been destroyed in a flood. She became the fifth Mazu.[20] There are many more temples in this area that worship multiple Mazus, a fact that my informants believed was unique to Huizhou.

Why were there so many goddesses on the Huizhou coast called Mazu? There are three possible explanations. First, each of the deities labeled Mazu is a manifestation of a single deity. This would be similar to the Christian concept of the Trinity, the idea of one god in three (or in this case multiple) divine beings. The different divinities are distinct, yet of one substance, essence, and nature. Second, the name "Mazu" is a generic term used to designate various female deities in the Huizhou area. Thus, each Mazu has a different name, characteristic, and personality, which makes her unique. And third, the labeling of all these deities as Mazu was a deliberate attempt on the part of devotees to legitimize a local deity by associating her with the state-sanctioned cult of Mazu or Tianhou. In doing so worshippers may have believed that this would have protected the deity (and themselves as worshippers) from being attacked by officials as unorthodox and licentious.

Conclusion

While it may seem strange to us that pirates or criminals could be transformed into gods, this phenomenon was not uncommon in China. Actually, there are a number of cases where not only pirates but also thieves, bandits, gangsters, gamblers, beggars, and prostitutes, despite dubious ethical qualities, were deified.[21] "The formation of Chinese gods," as Mark Meulenbeld has pointed out, "is hardly ever predicated upon an unblemished morality."[22] Those individuals who met unnatural premature deaths became vindictive ghosts who lurked about the sites where they died and in many cases never became deities. In those instances where ghosts changed into gods, such as Zuxi, they often were individuals who exhibited special powers, such as the ability to perform feats of magic or save lives. What was important in this transformation was not their origin but rather their efficaciousness—the fact that they proved themselves responsive to prayers of people in times of need.[23]

The four female pirates discussed in this interlude all met untimely, wrongful, and violent deaths at the hands of close relatives who wanted to harness their unnatural powers as vengeful ghosts to safeguard their treasures. It could not have been long after they had been slain that stories began to circulate locally about buried treasures, haunted gravesites, and the curses of malevolent spirits who guarded them. Yang Yandi's third wife, for instance, remained a malicious ghost who struck out to harm anyone who came near her grave, which was also the location of Yang's buried treasure. Zuxi was deified as a guardian goddess known locally as the Warrior Mazu who guarded her brother's treasure. Deities, especially those of the lower order like Zuxi, who never fully discarded their ghostly qualities, tend to fiercely guard their territory and punish human transgressors. Today local villagers continue to worship Zuxi as a protective sea deity and goddess of wealth, while the local government honors her as a patriotic heroine and role model.

CHAPTER 3

Of Rats, Cats, and Bandits in the Canton Delta

A NUMBER OF YEARS AGO WHEN I WAS DOING RESEARCH ON BANDITS AND secret societies in Qing dynasty Guangdong, and in particular on the Canton delta, I came across a curious entry in the Panyu gazetteer of 1871. The author related how bandits were a particularly serious problem in the border area between Shawan and Jiaotang, two rural districts (*xiang*) located in the vicinity of the provincial capital of Canton. Gangs of bandits occupied a mound known locally as Rat Hill (Laoshushan) and from their lair they would set out in boats on raids to plunder villages and markets along the rivers and coast. In 1780 provincial officials devised a number of measures to suppress the bandits, among these was the erecting of a statue of an Iron Cat in hopes that this would scare away the evildoers in the area.[1] As it turns out, both the persistence of banditry and the placement of the Iron Cat at Rat Hill came about because of Chinese geomancy or *fengshui*.

Although modern readers may find this odd, to most eighteenth-century Chinese, both officials and commoners, the siting of the Iron Cat and the application of *fengshui* was acceptable, normal practice. Based on written historical records, folklore, and fieldwork I conducted in Panyu in 2002 and 2010, this study sketches this curious episode involving bandits, rats, and cats in the midst of the vibrant Canton delta in the early modern period. I divide this chapter into three sections: first is the background about the area and people around Rat Hill; second is a discussion of the bandits and suppression efforts of officials in this troublesome area; and third are my remarks about the symbolic world of banditry, rats, cats, and geomancy.

Of Rats, Cats, and Bandits in the Canton Delta

The Canton Delta and Lineages on the Sands

What today we call the Canton delta developed over a millennium whereby natural and man-made reclamation transformed river marshes into fertile paddy fields, fruit orchards, and fishponds. Before the Ming dynasty, the delta was a boggy expanse of rivers and streams dotted with innumerable hills. Although land reclamation began much earlier, it was only during the Ming and Qing dynasties that reclamation projects became intense and extensive in the delta. The creation of what has become known as the "sands" (*sha*) or "sand fields" (*shatian*), or sometimes referred to as polders, completely transformed the lower delta, physically, politically, economically, and socially. Because of the rich alluvial soil deposited by the rivers, as people moved into the area they began to reclaim and mark off land, building dikes to catch the alluvial sands. According to Nishikawa Kikuko, between 1785 and 1835, more than 300,000 hectares (*mu*) of new polders were registered with the provincial government in Canton. The creation of polders involved large-scale planning and capital, was labor intensive, and took several generations to complete. Atop the hills that dotted the delta people constructed cottages and walled them in for protection against bandits and rival groups that also laid claims to the newly formed sand fields. Over time fortified outposts grew into villages and towns. As competition for the sands became increasingly intense, disputes often erupted into violent clashes and mini-wars.[2]

The Canton delta was (and still is) the core of Guangdong province. The delta was the hub of a vast internal river network that connected the interior to the coast and to the lands beyond China. Although the delta comprised less than a quarter of the total area of the province, by the eighteenth century, in large part due to the expansion of sand fields, it was the most densely populated and commercialized area in Guangdong. According to one estimate, in the early nineteenth century the delta (or more precisely Guangzhou prefecture) had an estimated population of six million people, with a population density of roughly 300 people per square kilometer (or 0.4 square mile), making it the highest in the province and also one of the highest in China. Panyu county had a population of nearly a million inhabitants, mostly farmers who engaged in the highly lucrative commercial crops grown on the polders. Indicative of the high degree of commercialization, the delta as a whole not only had the highest population density but also the largest concentration of markets and pawnshops in Guangdong. By the 1820s, Panyu had about a hundred markets and roughly 220 pawnshops, second only to neighboring Nanhai county.[3]

CHAPTER 3

Closely related to the development and expansion of sand fields was the concomitant development and expansion of lineages. As David Faure has shown, by the late eighteenth century, in fact, lineages had become the basic organizational feature of local society in the Canton delta. Major lineages built ancestral halls, produced genealogies, held land trusts, owned wharfs and shops, and monopolized markets. By belonging to a lineage members gained social status and inalienable rights of settlement that distinguished them from outsiders. Lineage building was closely related to the growth of commercial agriculture and land reclamation. Large lineages actually built up much of their power and wealth through ownership of thousands of hectares of sand fields and domination over thousands of servile tenant farmers and hired workers, who were denied the right to own land or create lineages. By the early twentieth century, powerful lineages owned roughly four-fifths of the arable lands in the delta.[4] The construction of sand fields added not only to the expansion of arable land, but also to increased flooding and to a remarkable growth in lineage feuding over land rights and markets.[5]

Both Shawan and Jiaotang districts were located in the midst of the reclaimed sands. Less than twenty miles from Canton, the market town of Shawan was situated on the edge of the sands: to the north were the older sands dating back to before the sixteenth century, and to the south were the new sands, which were continually expanding ever since that time (see map 3). Shawan was dominated by the "five great surnames," the most powerful landowning lineages in the area. By the late Qing the He was the most prominent lineage with holdings of nearly 60,000 hectares of sand fields in the southeast of the district.[6] Magnate lineages, such as the He, lived in walled towns and built brick mansions with tile roofs, which became important symbols of elite status and ostentatious lifestyles. In the early twentieth century Shawan lineage trusts were collecting annual land rents exceeding 900,000 silver dollars (*yuan*).[7]

As for neighboring Jiaotang district, by the early Ming its river port was the busiest wholesale seafood market in the delta, where day and night Dan fishers came to sell their catches.[8] Wealthy lineages with other interests in Canton and elsewhere in the delta dominated this important market. One of the foremost lineages in Jiaotang was the Qu, which collectively owned several hundreds of hectares of sand fields by the late seventeenth century. Perhaps the lineage's most famous member was the early Qing scholar Qu Dajun, author of *New Discourses on Guangdong*. In the decade before his death in 1696, he enjoyed the life of a gentleman farmer on thirty-seven hectares of sand fields at his ancestral home in Shating village, which he farmed with the help of dozens of hired hands who went to the fields in boats to plant and to harvest.[9]

Tenant farmers and itinerant workers lived precariously in squatter communities that were subordinate to the big lineages. The latter treated these client groups as outsiders, referring to them disdainfully as "sands people" (*shamin*), "lowly households" (*xiahu*), "trivial people" (*ximin*), or "floating twigs" (*shuiliuchai*). The main distinctions between the dominant lineages and the sands people were not based on physical distance but rather on social, economic, and cultural distance. The latter resided on boats and in makeshift thatched huts, much like the one in figure 7, which can still be found in the delta. Sands people generally were poor and illiterate, lacked genealogies, and had no ancestor halls of their own. The dominant lineages denied them the right to permanently settle on or own land, and members of the dominant lineages, of course, did not marry with them. Needless to say, they were looked down upon as being uncivilized and having depraved customs.[10]

Figure 7. Thatched Hut Beside a Fishpond in Panyu, 2002 (Source: Photo by author)

CHAPTER 3

Most of the sands people were originally Dan fisherfolks who had been hired by the powerful lineages to reclaim the sands and do farm work, and then later tentatively settled on the polders in squatter settlements. During the slack seasons they engaged in various menial jobs on shore but at other times continued to go out in boats to fish or ferry passengers around the delta. The men had notorious reputations as bandits and pirates, and the women as prostitutes on the ubiquitous floating brothels that plied the rivers of the delta.[11] During the Ming some of these Dan fishers and subordinate tenant groups, under the protection of local strongmen, defiantly staked out their own claims on several knolls, which they subsequently fortified. Actually over the Ming and Qing periods, as Helen Siu and Liu Zhiwei have shown, many Dan boat people began to move onto shore and thus slowly began a social and cultural transformation from water-borne fishers to land-dwelling peasants. A number of Dan households, in fact, became prominent lineages in the delta; the He of Shawan was likely one of these. Nonetheless, most Dan households continued to live on boats and engage in fishing and ferrying, and as for those who moved ashore, the majority became tenants and hired laborers. In fact, those households labelled as Dan, even after settling on land, remained subservient to the large lineages and have continued to be discriminated against. Even today in this area the Dan are still referred to as "outsiders."[12]

In the fierce competition on the sands lineages had to always be armed and ready to fight. This was the work of watchmen and guardsmen, referred to locally as "sandsmen" (*shafu*), who in the eighteenth and nineteenth centuries regularly patrolled the polders and upheld public order. Powerful lineages hired sandsmen to protect their interests from rival lineages and bandits, as well as to control their tenants and subordinate villages. In Shawan, for example, the He lineage had both a guardsmen unit to maintain public security and a defense corps to patrol the sands.[13] In single surname villages guardsmen were recruited from the poorer members of the lineage and had their headquarters usually in the ancestral hall, but in most other cases they were a motley mixture of sons of tenants and the laboring poor who often had their headquarters in a village temple. The vast majority were bachelors in their twenties and thirties, what one gentry leader in Shunde county called "sands sticks" (*shagun*).[14] In order to perform their duties guardsmen needed to maintain a persona of fierceness and ruthlessness; their victims referred to them as *ngok lo*, a Cantonese insult for evil, cruel, or depraved men. As James Watson has explained, guardsmen were the strong-arm of lineages and belligerent "agents of social control." They were, in many cases, no better than bullies and bandits.[15]

THE BANDITS OF RAT HILL

Since the sixteenth century, both Shawan and Jiaotang had reputations as notorious bandit haunts. So close to Canton, the center of political and economic power, the area remained a thorn in the side of provincial governance and the rule of law for several centuries. This was particularly true in that nebulous area along the border of the two rural districts, an area where political jurisdictions were unclear and gentry and lineage authority was weak. It also was a place with a large number of impoverished villages where people made their livings as tenant farmers, hired laborers, and fishers, the sorts of work that drew little respect and provided meager earnings. In the Ming dynasty because of the persistent problems of bandits and pirates operating out of bases in Jiaotang the government established a deputy magistracy (*xunjiansi*), and later in 1664 following the disturbances of organized gangs of "Dan pirates" led by Li Rong and Zhou Yu, the Qing court established a deputy magistracy in Shawan.[16] Yet as late as the 1930s, there still were reports of bandits in this area. Xie Huoying, for one, commanded more than 200 followers who forcefully occupied sand fields and robbed and extorted protection fees from villagers.[17]

The area was crisscrossed with a maze of creeks and streams and peppered with countless hills, one of which was known locally as Rat Hill, today adjacent to the village of Gold Mountain (Jinshan). As it was situated on the edge of the sand fields and surrounded on three sides by water, boats had easy access to the surrounding counties and to the sea. When officials in the late eighteenth century questioned nearby villagers, they were told that the hill got its name because the heap of rocks resembled a rat.[18] What they did not mention, but everyone knew, was the fact that the name derived from the hordes of bandits who had intermittently occupied the fortified mound for hundreds of years. In traditional Chinese folklore rats have always been identified with bandits.

In 1780 Liang Yaxiang, whom the authorities described as "a brutal and cunning rascal," was the most wanted criminal in Guangdong. A native of Langbian village in Shawan, he had his headquarters at Rat Hill. He had come to the attention of officials a year earlier after the arrest of Mai Yarong (nicknamed "Black Bones") and more than thirty gang members for robberies in several markets in Guishan and Xin'an counties, on the opposite side of the Pearl River. Mai, who had been an outlaw for four years, told officials that he had recently joined Liang Yaxiang's gang in Shawan.[19] In a year-long investigation, headed by the Shawan deputy magistrate (*xunjian*), paid informants and spies gathered information on the names, residences, and movements of the most notorious bandits. Governor-General Bayansan deployed several hundred soldiers from Canton who apprehended Liang and another 400 bandits and harborers. During the trial, it was discovered that Liang had been at-large since 1772, when he was involved in several robberies as a member of Hu Jianglian's gang. After Hu's arrest and execution Liang went into hiding, only to reemerge in 1777 in Shawan as a member of Ling Datourong's gang. Later that same year, with his share of the loot, Liang procured a boat in Dasha village in Shawan and organized his own band that came to number about a hundred men. By 1780 he headed a vast criminal brotherhood that included fifteen gangs which, although operating independently of one another, pooled their loot into a common treasury. Typically gangs of eighty or ninety men would set out from their lairs in boats to plunder villages, markets, and coastal shipping.[20]

The bandits at Rat Hill were able to go undetected for so long because local officials falsified reports and the outlaws received protection from soldiers, runners, and constables, who were all on the payroll of Liang Yaxiang. He paid soldiers at the Shiji guard post (*xun*), who were responsible for checking the comings and goings of boats, "gratuities" of thirty to forty silver dollars each year. In one instance he bribed a soldier named Guo Run, who split his share of the money with his sergeant to ignore Liang's fencing and smuggling operations. In other instances Liang paid twenty silver dollars to soldiers to act as his spies to keep him informed about the plans of officials. Also local bowmen and constables, many of whom were Liang's kinsmen, provided protection to Liang and his gangs.[21]

Although Rat Hill was the most notorious and enduring bandit lair in Panyu, it was not the only one in this area. Actually, there seems to have been an unusually large number of bandit strongholds scattered about in both Shawan and Jiaotang throughout the Qing period, which is surprising given the fact that this area was so close to the provincial capital and in the heart of the prosperous and densely populated Canton delta. This goes against our commonly held notions that bandit gangs were most prevalent in peripheral areas and rare in core areas.[22] As one Panyu official explained at the end of the eighteenth century, there were some 230 villages and roughly 50,000 households in Shawan and Jiaotang, and most of the villages harbored bandits.

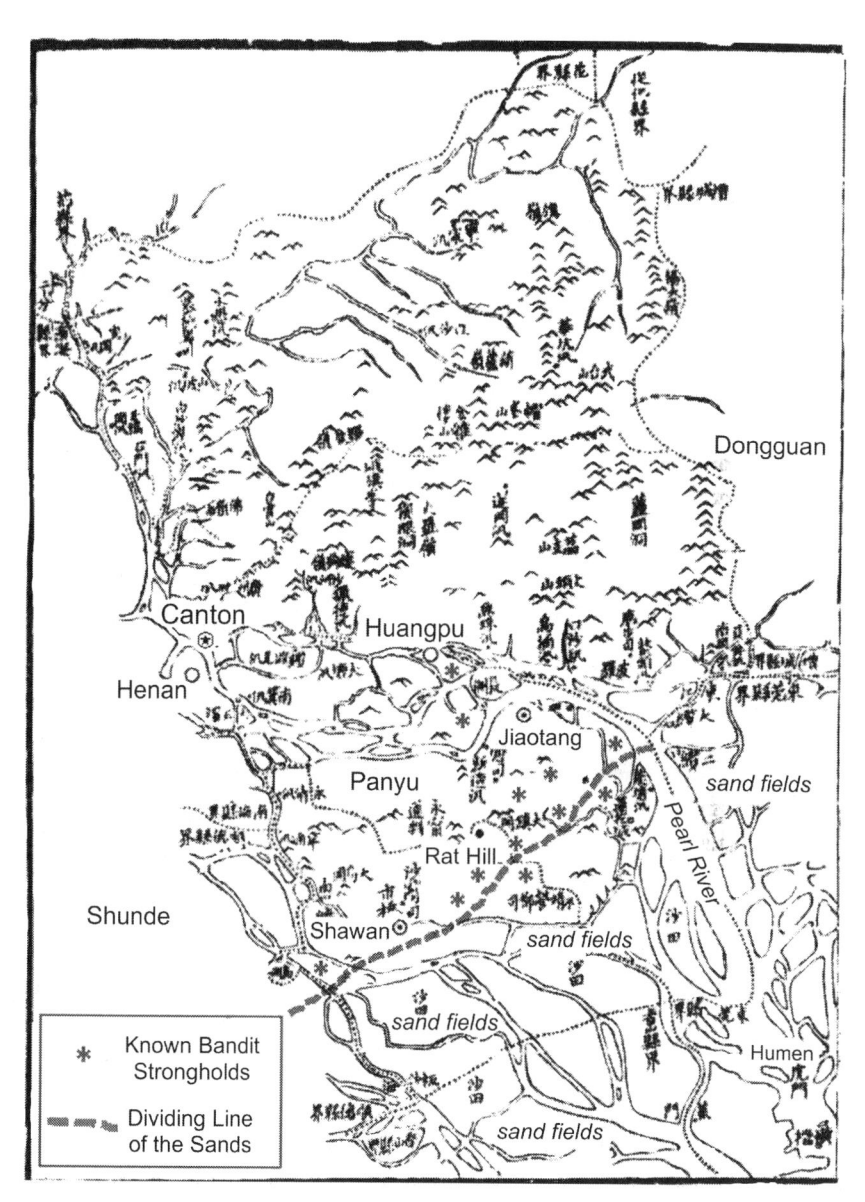

Map 3. Panyu County, Rat Hill, and Bandit Strongholds, Late Eighteenth and Early Nineteenth Centuries (Source: *Panyu xianzhi*, 1871; modified by author)

"Honest people and bandits all mingled together," he lamented.[23] The Qianlong emperor likewise lamented that so many villagers in Shawan and Jiaotang were accustomed to dishonesty and villainy that banditry had become second nature to them.[24]

Based on criminal case records and fieldwork, I have been able to locate twelve bandit strongholds in Shawan and Jiaotang dating from the late eighteenth to early twentieth centuries.[25] Most were situated on hills between the market towns of Shawan and Jiaotang, and also were near the dividing line between the old and new sands (map 3). It is likely that these lairs were in areas of contestation between the great families; several of them were also in areas between administrative jurisdictions. Even though certain strongholds, such as Rat Hill, may have lasted for generations, nonetheless, there was a constant fluctuation in the bandits who occupied them. Leaders, such as Liang Yaxiang and Mai Yarong, may have been permanent fixtures, but gang members came and went with the changing seasons and other employment opportunities.

The vast majority of bandits, in fact, were poor and highly mobile, and they turned to crime mainly as temporary undertakings. Theft and robbery were customary supplements for more legitimate occupations, which even in the best of times were barely adequate for maintaining sustainable livelihoods. Much like the guardsmen mentioned earlier, bandits typically came from the ranks of the laboring poor, a large segment of late imperial China's society that was chronically underemployed and undernourished. For them life was an endless struggle for survival.[26]

From the criminal case records in routine and palace memorials for the years 1765 to 1845, I have information on a total of 183 convicted bandits who were natives of Panyu. Although there are often gaps and missing data in this information, nevertheless, they do provide useful vital statistics on both bandit leaders and followers. As for their occupational backgrounds (total 94 cases), which affords us with the best indicator of their social status, most were hired workers (58 percent), followed by individuals who had aquatic backgrounds: fishers, ferrymen, boatmen, sailors, and grass cutters (21 percent). The remainder were peddlers, porters, watchmen, tenant farmers, and beggars, as well as those simply referred to as poor misfits (*pin bu shoufen*). All were males between the ages of 18 and 66 *sui*. Roughly 80 percent were between 20 and 39 *sui*; the average age was 32 (149 cases). Typically, both bandits and guardsmen were the second, third, or fourth sons born into poor propertyless families. As excess members of a family, they were literally pushed out of their homes and left to fend for themselves as best as they could. Too poor to marry, the majority remained bachelors all their lives. Both bandits and guardsmen were referred to in unflattering terms as "bare sticks," "pugnacious youths" (*dazai*), and "rotten lads" (*lanzai*). Neither bandits nor guardsmen hesitated to use violence and predation to get what they wanted. They were men who had nothing to lose.[27]

Although the criminal case records seldom mentioned the ethnic backgrounds of Panyu bandits and pirates, nonetheless, their descriptions match the typical characteristics of poor, marginalized Dan. Official sources, in fact, routinely depicted Panyu bandits as river bandits (*hefei*) and sea bandits (*haidao*) because they set off on raids on rivers and along the coast in boats. Official documents also specifically pointed out that when bandits—such as Black Bones Mai and Liang Yaxiang—started out on their expeditions, which could last two or three months, they often used the pretext of going out to fish.[28] A term frequently used to describe bandit strongholds in Shawan and Jiaotang also had distinct aquatic implications: *yuansou*, meaning a gathering place or refuge for fish, but also used figuratively as a den for thieves and robbers. Like the Dan who lived precariously on the sands and hillocks, according to one official, bandits were "malicious squatters" living with their families in fortified hilltop villages, such as Rat Hill.[29]

There too was a good bit of collusion between bandits and local notables, though often their associations were indirect and convoluted. As mentioned earlier, there was little distinction between guardsmen hired by great lineages and bandits, as both groups were entrepreneurs of violence and predation. Nie Erkang, a Xinhui county magistrate in the late Qing, described the interconnections between tenants, hired workers, landowners, and bandits on the sands:

> *According to my investigations in the sands, banditry and extortion are frequent. Tenants and hired hands can very well be bandits themselves.... Landlords use them in various ways, some for defense, some for sharing the loot. With the landowners' backing, bandits make pretense of hard work. When opportunities arise, they rob. Other times, they farm. These polders are full of hidden filth and crime, and the landowners are patrons.*[30]

In nearby Panyu, powerful lineages and local bosses frequently recruited or hired boatloads of Dan tenants and hired hands to aggressively encroach on sand fields of rival lineages, who in turn responded in kind. Both sides accused the other as being bandits.[31] Therefore, banditry, in its many forms, was deeply entrenched in local society and only a very thin line separated the good folks from outlaws. Undeniably, there was much fluidity in the Canton delta in the early modern era.

In 1780, once the Qianlong emperor got wind of Liang Yaxiang and other bandits who had been operating in the heart of the Canton delta for a decade, he suspected a massive cover-up and ordered provincial officials to make a thorough investigation and implement new policies to eliminate the outlaws. Over the next three years, with the emperor's approval, Governor-General Bayansan put his plans into operation. First, he replaced the assistant magistrate (*xiancheng*) stationed at the village of Kengtou on the border of Shawan and Jiaotang with an assistant sub-prefect (*tongpan*), with specific duties to carefully oversee the Shawan and Jiaotang deputy magistrates who were charged with investigating and arresting local bandits. Second, he created a "special battalion" (*zhuanying*) of 600 soldiers to replace the discredited Shiji post, and added a number of guard posts, with four to sixteen soldiers each, in trouble spots where bandits were known to gather. Next, he ordered nine new patrol boats assigned to guard the rivers and creeks in the area. Fourth, the Shawan and Jiaotang deputy magistrates were put in charge of registering and overseeing all private boats in the area. Fifth, he required that each year officials had to go to Rat Hill to inspect the area. Next, he proposed a new tougher law to deal specifically with the river bandits operating in the Canton delta. As a final measure, one purportedly prompted by requests of local villagers, Bayansan ordered the casting of an Iron Cat (*tiemao*) weighing several hundred catties to "ward off the evil influences" of bandits who gathered on Rat Hill.[32]

Fengshui and an Iron Cat

Provincial officials ordered that an Iron Cat be cast and placed adjacent to Rat Hill in 1780. Some fifty-six years later, in 1836, the Iron Cat was still watching over the area and officials were still being sent there to conduct inspections. At that time a writer for the *Canton Register* reported a story he had heard about Rat Hill, the Iron Cat, and their connection to geomancy. It is worth quoting in full:

> Hoo, *the* Tungche *of Macao* [Aomen tongzhi], *was ordered by the judge* [anchashi], *on the 22d of the moon [that is, lunar calendar], to go [to] the*

> *neighbourhood of Shaouwan [Shawan] and Keaoutang [Jiaotang], in Pwanyu [Panyu] district, and examine the* Laoushoo-shan,—*old rat's hill. The story is, that several tens of years ago, because this hill was the haunt of robbers, a former judge, who was acquainted with a professor of the* Fungshwuy *art, consulted him on the subject, saying—"This hill is called the 'old Rat's hill.' Now a rat is a cunning beast that is thoroughly versed in all the arts of damaging and destroying; therefore, from this hill also issues forth such a set of men (rats in disposition), who are very expert thieves."—He forthwith ordered a blacksmith to make an iron image of a cat with a great, open mouth, to frighten away the rats, and thenceforth, it is said, the number of thieves was not so great; and since when it has been the custom for the criminal judge himself to visit this hill once year, or to send another officer; and the observance of this custom must not, on any account, be neglected.*[33]

This is the earliest written source I have come across to specifically mention geomancy in connection with Rat Hill and the Iron Cat, but it is not my only source. In 2002 two of my elderly local informants in Jinshan village still remembered the Iron Cat from when they were children. They said that it had been placed on a nearby hill overlooking Rat Hill, a small mound locals appropriately referred to as Cat Hill (Maoshan), for geomantic purposes. They told me that the Iron Cat was hollow and people liked to put coins inside it for good luck. However, in the 1930s, during the turbulent warlord era, "outside" bandits reappeared and stole the Iron Cat with all the money inside. These and other local informants in Panyu also told me stories about *fengshui* and local folklore about rats and cats, some that they knew from personal experience and others they had heard from parents, grandparents, and village elders. It seems that for generation after generation, a rich oral tradition has survived and has been passed down in the area once called Rat Hill.

Symbolic Meanings of Rats and Cats
Rats and cats stand for things that they are not. As metaphors and symbols, their meanings would have been common knowledge among eighteenth-century villagers and literati alike. Though the world of eighteenth-century China was vastly different from our own, the rats and cats that gave symbolic meanings to bandits help us to bridge our mental and cultural world with that of the past. But how do we approach that largely unlettered world of the eighteenth-century Chinese peasant? We get a clue from Robert Darnton,

who wrote that folktales collected in nineteenth-century Europe "provide a rare opportunity to make contact with the illiterate masses who have disappeared into the past without leaving a trace."[34] I believe the same should be true for late imperial China. Folktales provide us an important entry into an invisible history otherwise lost. Although the telling of the stories may not have been the same everywhere, nevertheless Panyu villagers would have been familiar with the common motifs of the shared culture. The symbolic meanings of rats and cats would have been known to everyone.[35]

What then do folktales tell us about rats and cats, and about the symbolic world and mentalité of the people of Panyu? They depict, to quote Darnton again, both "the humanity of animals along with the animality of men."[36] Rats were harbingers of misfortune, disease, and death. People who were duplicitous, treacherous, cunning, sneaky, and mean were likened to rats. To call someone "a son of a rat" (*shuzi*) was an ancient term of abuse. Rats possessed supernatural, occult powers and accordingly they featured predominantly in Chinese demon lore. When rats infested a home, it was an omen of impending poverty for the family. Like human sorcerers, people believed that rats performed black magic by standing on their hind legs to dance and by placing their front paws on their head while whispering spells and curses. Encounters with demonic rats usually led to illness or death. Plague demons were associated with rats, which also transmitted parasites and other vermin; not coincidentally plagues were called "rat epidemics" (*shuyi*).[37] In traditional China rats were also associated with certain illnesses, particularly running sores, ulcers, and abscesses believed to be caused by the poisonous effects of rat saliva. In the ancient *Book of Odes* (*Shijing*) such aliments were designated by the character *shu*, a compound of rat and illness. Folktales were abundant with depictions of rats who used their diabolical powers to transform themselves into other animals and humans. When they took human form it was usually as males, not as females. Rats were known to use magic to seduce young girls and hide them away as brides. Such unions were said to produce monstrous births.[38]

It was also common to relate rats with thieves, robbers, and rogues. A traditional Cantonese riddle puts it nicely: "[Who has a] house of mud with mud doors, [and] children and grandchildren all bandits?—rats" (*niwu nimen tou zaizai sunsun zuozei tou—laoshu*).[39] It was common knowledge that a rat hole (*shuxue*) was another name for a bandit lair, and an archaic term for habitual thieves was *shubei* (literally "generations of rats"), an expression that implied an inherent trait common to the species. Another common phrase was to "pilfer like rats and dogs" (*shuqie goutou*). There was a popular saying that Guangdong had three misfortunes: "too many bandits, too many rats, and too many ants" (*duodao duoshu duoyi*).[40] In one tale from the Tang dynasty, packs of rats disguised as armed highwaymen infested the road near the capital Chang'an; each night these bandits came out to rob and kill travelers, but during daylight they hid away nowhere to be found. Suspecting that these rogues were not human but evil specters, one night a Daoist master, using his mirror and shouting incantations, chased them to their hideout, a huge hole in the earth. Summoning villagers they dug up the hole in which were found hundreds of rats that were immediately slain.[41] Villagers in Panyu told me similar tales.

In the animal kingdom, there was nothing so unalike, indeed so opposed, as rats and cats. In most cultures they were bitter enemies.[42] If rats were thieves then cats were guardians; rats too were much more demonic than cats; symbolically if rats were personified as males, cats were females; and if rats brought plagues and other diseases, cats provided remedies. In the past in south China cats were domesticated not so much as pets, but for more utilitarian purposes—in some places as food but more commonly to protect villages and homes from rats, snakes, and other small predators. The Chinese character for cat depicts an animal in a field of grain (*mao*), undoubtedly protecting the rice from rats. More explicitly, the Song essayist Lu Dian in his antidotal collection *Piya* explained: "When rats harm grain sprouts, cats catch them, thus the word for cat is derived from grain sprouts."[43] In 2013 archaeologists discovered in Shaanxi province the remains of cats dating back more than 5,300 years to the Neolithic Age. Researchers speculate that prehistoric villagers raised cats to keep rats out of their fields and granaries.[44] Much later, the ancient *Book of Rites* (*Lijing*) mentioned a winter festival in which villagers entreated cats to devour field rats by offering sacrifices to cat spirits.[45] Buddhist monasteries kept cats and had granaries with "cat doors," which allowed the felines free access to the interior so as to scare rats away. In my interviews in Panyu in 2002 and 2010, villagers often told me that the main purpose for cats was to catch rats.[46]

In Chinese folk beliefs cats have magical powers and, as in medieval Europe, were closely associated with witchcraft and the occult. Perhaps such beliefs arose because of the cat's ability to see in the dark and to stalk their prey at night. The witching hours after dark were the time when ghosts, demons, and all sorts of spirits lurk about. Night also was the time when rats and bandits were on the prowl; most robberies and thefts, in fact, took place in the three or four hours before dawn.[47] It was believed that cats made scratch marks on the ground to divine their prey (*bushu*), and that by using their abilities of night vision they could put evil spirits to flight. That was why people put the images of cats on amulets.[48] Like European witches, Chinese witches rode on the backs of cats at night. Witches possessed cats with charms, spells, and other tools of magic, thereby inducing them do their bidding.[49] In the Sui dynasty a tale was told of a sorceress known as Madam Gao who conjured up cat specters (*maogui*) with sacrifices and then ordered them to rob and kill people.[50] Even though there are other such tales of demonic cats, most tales involved women who transformed into cat spirits to avenge wrongs done to them in life. A well-known tale involved a Tang dynasty court lady named Xiao Liangdi, whose master and consort had been unjustly and heartlessly put to death by Empress Wu. To carry out her revenge Xiao declared: "I shall become a cat, and Wu shall be changed into a rat, and then I will throttle her in vengeance for the wrong she has done." It was actually common belief in China that humans, at the point of death or soon thereafter, could metamorphose into cat spirits to seek retributive justice by magically sucking out the breath or vital forces (*qi*) of their enemies.[51]

Because of their magical powers cats were a staple ingredient in many folk remedies. All parts of a cat could be used as medicine, but the blood, guts, and bones were especially efficacious. A concoction made from a cat's liver cured malaria and killed parasites that cause consumption. When spells and incantations proved ineffective in curing ailments, one medical treatise recommended that patients kill and burn a cat and then mix the ashes with water to be drunk. Because cats killed and devoured rats, insects, and snakes, it was believed that they were the most appropriate remedy for *gu* poisoning.[52] Bones from a cat's head were thought to be an effective cure for pains in the heart and stomach. For all ailments caused by rats and rat demons the most common cure was to boil a whole cat, preferably a kitten, and for the patient to either drink the liquid or to bathe in it.[53] Cats, obviously, were the perfect foil for rats.

It was not by chance that officials chose to cast an Iron Cat. For centuries in several Panyu villages on the outskirts of Canton people worshipped a guardian cat deity that they called the Venerable Cat (*maolaoye*). At his festival, which was (and still is) celebrated each year on the sixteenth day of the first lunar month, villagers made paper or cloth effigies of local villains and other vile characters that they beseeched the cat god to thrash and destroy.[54] The use of iron was also intentional. Iron symbolized strength, righteousness, determination, and justice. There was a long tradition in China, including the area around Canton, of casting iron statues and iron steles because of the demon-expelling qualities of the metal. Iron was also often used in the construction of pagodas for the same reason. According to Wolfram Eberhard, because iron had a magical quality to it, the very act of casting iron objects "had a quasi-religious significance."[55] In any case, the placing of an Iron Cat at Rat Hill, in a real sense, added a magical or supernatural dimension to official bandit suppression operations. Its symbolic meaning, too, would have been well known to everyone. In terms of sympathetic magic, the Iron Cat was meant to figuratively chase away or kill the rats, which stood for the bandits who burrowed on Rat Hill.

State and Popular Fengshui

How does geomancy relate to the bandits of Rat Hill? During my fieldwork in the summer of 2002 one of my elderly informants explained to me about the vital forces or primordial energy (qi) of *fengshui* in the area. He said that Rat Hill was situated at one end of a "dragon's vein" (*longmai*) that stretched in an undulating fashion across a series of hills and mountains from Rat Hill through Guangdong into Hunan province (he wasn't sure where the other end was located, but only that it was somewhere far away). According to my informant, the bandits were able to last so long in the area—for several centuries he said—because they occupied Rat Hill which controlled the *fengshui* in the area. The Iron Cat, he continued, was supposed to alter the *fengshui*, thereby blocking the vital forces concentrated on Rat Hill that protected the bandits.

The belief in and practice of *fengshui* is ancient. It is intimately related to the well-being of any area, and as such is highly localized yet at the same time interlocked with the wider terrestrial surroundings and cosmic forces. Physical features such as mountains, hills, waterways, and forests all conveyed special geomantic meanings that could be deciphered by *fengshui* masters. This shared symbolic world made the environment meaningful to the local inhabitants of Panyu, influenced their behavior and gave them identity. Chinese believed that *fengshui* affected, for good or for bad, not only individuals and families, but also villages, cities, counties, and provinces. It was taken very seriously and geomancers were frequently called upon to channel cosmic forces to harmonize man and nature. *Fengshui* directly connected customary religion and practices with traditional philosophy and cosmology, thereby linking the worldviews of literati and peasants.

It was the job of geomancers to locate good *fengshui* sites. The optimal site was the "dragon's lair" (*longxue*), that spot with the highest concentration of vital forces (*qi*). To its north should be a mountain, often referred to as the "master dragon mountain" (*zhulongshan*), and beyond that an undulating series of hills and mountains, the "dragon's vein," which ideally extended to the parent mountain, ancestor mountain, and Kunlun Mountains, the legendary dwelling place of the Queen Mother of the West (Xiwangmu) and Daoist immortals. This chain of mountains symbolically represented the lineage structure, and occasionally genealogies described such a pattern connecting the ancestral village with a string of hills and mountains stretching to Kunlun Mountains. *Qi* originates at the top of mountains and gradually flows downward through the dragon's veins to accumulate in the dragon's lair. To the right and left of the dragon's lair should be mountains—the "azure dragon" (*qinglong*) on the east and the "white tiger" (*baihu*) on the west. Together these hills and mountains formed a protective barrier, in the shape of a horseshoe, for the dragon's lair. The south should be open and have meandering rivers or streams, which exit the site at the "water mouth" (*shuikou*); there should also be in the distance low-rising hills, sometimes referred to as the "red phoenix" (*zhufeng*).[56] Figure 8 illustrates this ideal *fengshui* model.

In China nearly every city, town, village, house, and grave were sited using these well-known *fengshui* principles. The city of Canton is a good example. Writing in 1873 Ernest Eitel explained:

> *It is placed in the very angle formed by two chains of hills running in gentle curves toward the Bogue [Humen], where they almost meet each other, forming a complete horse-shoe. The chain of hills known as White Clouds represents the dragon, whilst the undulating ground on the other side of the river forms the white tiger. The most favorable site of Canton is therefore the ground near the north-gates, whence the tiger and dragon run out to the right and left.*[57]

Qu Dajun gave a more detailed explanation: White Cloud Mountain (Baiyunshan), which was some fifteen *li* (about five miles) north of Canton, was the city's "master [dragon] mountain" (*zhushan*). To its left and right stretched a series of interconnected hills interspersed with streams and lakes. From Canton southeastward to Jiaotang there were several hundred *li* of winding hills, all part of the same dragon's vein. At the lower end at the water mouth stood a thirty-meter sandstone hill named Shilishan, which overlooked Humen, the gateway to Canton (see map 3). Its location not only had strategic importance, but also in Qu's mind Shilishan was even more

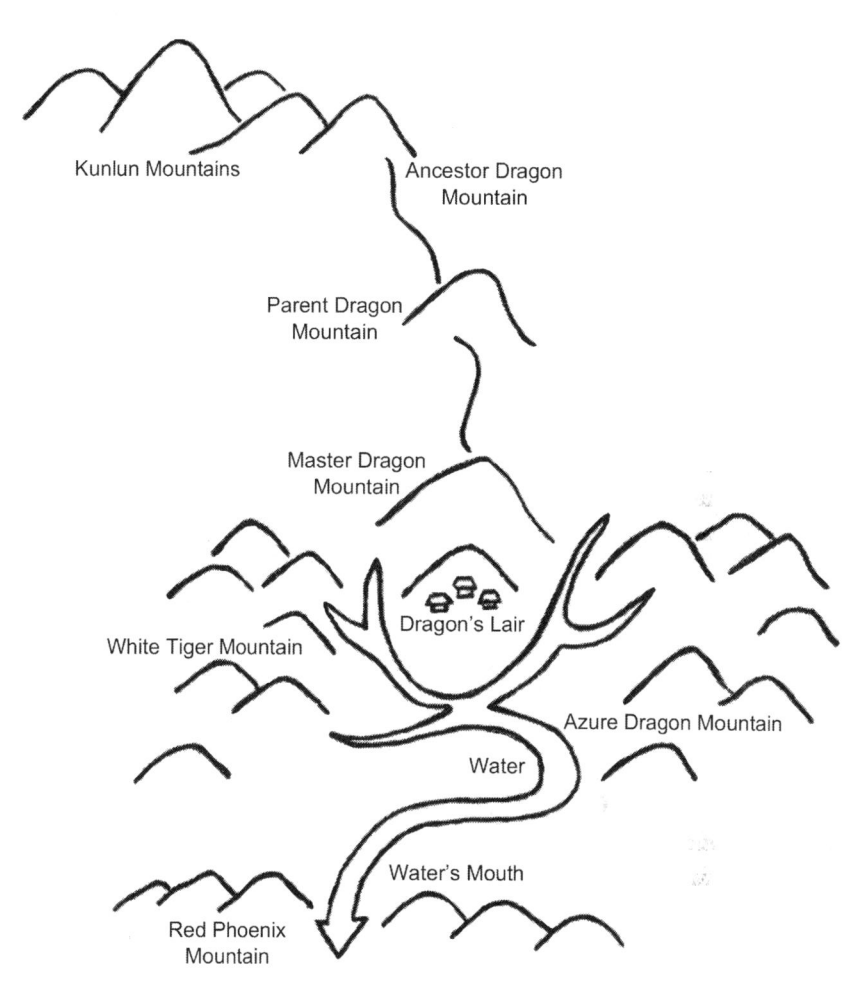

Figure 8. Ideal Fengshui Model (Source: Created by author)

important for the geomantic protection it afforded the city and surrounding areas.[58]

People are not simply passive under the influences of cosmic forces. *Fengshui* can be altered and manipulated. In the Ming dynasty when "unscrupulous scoundrels" began quarrying rocks in Shilishan, wrote Qu Dajun, the mountain's vital force (*shanqi*) and *fengshui* were wounded and calamities befell the area—numerous deaths, mountain slides, collapse of wells and tombs, yellow blood oozing out of the mountain side, appearance of angry ghosts, and so forth. Qu continued, "The mountain spirit screamed in anger," showing great distress. Not only local villages but all of Guangdong was affected. A concerned Wanli emperor (r. 1573–1620) purportedly issued prohibitions against excavating at Shilishan, but rogues continued to clandestinely dig up rocks for "private profiteering." As a countermeasure to protect the area's *fengshui* in 1612, Li Weifeng, a local scholar from Panyu, built the Fulian Pagoda (or Shili Pagoda) on the mountain overlooking Humen's water mouth.[59] Actually the manipulation of *fengshui* was common practice. The construction of pagodas and walls, placement of stone lions, tablets with tigers etched on them, and so-called *fengshui* stones (*shigandang*) were often used to dispel or divert "bad" *fengshui*. Their purposes were solely geomantic: to help assure the well-being and fortune of nearby residents and communities.[60]

Another example of geomantic manipulation comes from neighboring Shunde county, where according to the local oral tradition villagers told a tale that linked rats and geomancy. It was recorded in the late nineteenth century by J. H. Stewart Lockhart as follows:

> *In Sui Pui, in the district of Shuntak [Shunde], Kwangtung Province, there is a monumental gateway in an uninhabited part of the country which is said to resemble in shape a rat-trap. It is related that the crops in the neighbourhood having failed for several seasons in succession, the aid of the geomancers was invoked in order to discover the reason. After carefully considering the surroundings of the place, they found that the hills opposite to where the crops were grown presented the appearance of a rat. This rat, they said, devoured the crops, so they advised the construction of a rat-trap to prevent its depredations. No sooner was the rat-trap erected than the crops yielded grain in abundance.*[61]

As Daniel McMahon has pointed out, intervention took one of two forms: either reshaping the landscape or placing objects in the landscape symbolizing a desired result.[62] In the above case villagers intervened by erecting a giant rat trap symbolizing what they hoped for, the catching of rats that destroyed their crops. The placing of the Iron Cat at Rat Hill was similarly used to symbolically catch or scare away the rats that stood for bandits who were molesting the Canton delta. Symbolic objects—such as the rat trap and the Iron Cat—were placed in strategic locations to strengthen or block geomantic influences.

Not only villagers but also officials and even emperors employed geomancers to locate the best *fengshui* sites for tombs, public buildings, and city walls. Though widely accepted, *fengshui* was never part of the official state cult and officials regarded it with great caution. Aware of the potential threats to political power, imperial governments routinely regulated "unauthentic" geomancy in an attempt to keep it within acceptable bounds.[63] Song Neo-Confucian scholars Cheng Hao and Cheng Yi, who advocated the study of natural phenomena and the proper siting of ancestral tombs, made important contributions to *fengshui* theory, as recorded in their complete works, *Er Cheng quanshu*, compiled in the Ming dynasty. Their writings not only became essential components of subsequent state orthodoxy, but were also adopted by later geomancers seeking to link their theories with mainstream philosophy and metaphysics—and thereby giving themselves a solid claim to legitimacy.[64] The *Ming Code* mentioned geomancy in connection with proper burials and the *Collected Commentaries* on the code listed acceptable practices for locating the dragon's lair, the best place to bury the dead.[65] In both the Ming and Qing dynasties laws stipulated a punishment of eighty blows of the heavy bamboo to individuals who were "led astray by Fung-shui, [and] kept a corpse unburied for longer than a year."[66] In imperial China geomantic theory also was widely used in military planning, especially in the placement of fortifications and defensive walls. Occasionally too officials employed geomancers as advisors during military campaigns against bandits and rebels.[67] Also inevitably at the start of military campaigns, officials sought to locate the ancestral graves of bandit or rebel chiefs in order to desecrate them, and in so doing destroy the *fengshui* that protected the family and ruin their chances of success.[68]

Let us return to Rat Hill and the Iron Cat. As we can see from figure 9, Rat Hill was a good geomantic site, something my local informants told me many times. To the north was Guweishan, the area's master dragon mountain, on the east were Gaogang and Huanggang hills, the azure dragon, and to the west was Cat Hill, the white tiger. Surrounded on three sides by hills and mountains, as well as waterways that have long since disappeared, the dragon's lair at Rat Hill was well protected (and so too were the bandits that occupied the hill). The south opened up to sand fields and in the eighteenth century there would have been a meandering river, exiting at the water mouth. The geomancer shrewdly placed the Iron Cat on Cat Hill, the location of the white tiger, which in Chinese folklore was also closely associated with cats—cats are called "little tigers." Tigers symbolized courage, fierceness, and military

CHAPTER 3

prowess, attributes necessary to defeat bandits.[69] Specifically, the Iron Cat was meant to block the *fengshui* that protected the bandits on Rat Hill.

It is significant that officials when devising pragmatic measures to eliminate bandits at Rat Hill included the use of *fengshui* as an integral part of their plan. There was nothing strange or unusual when officials erected the Iron Cat at Rat Hill. A traditional military strategy, McMahon explains, was a "*fengshui* attack" involving the deliberate "sabotage of the environment to create a geomantic positioning that weakened one's opponent," whether rebel or bandit. The most common sabotage was the placement of symbolic objects—such as the Iron Cat—in strategic spots so as to obstruct the flow of *qi* beneficial to one's enemies.[70]

Given the common knowledge that everyone had about *fengshui*, this would have been an important reason why Liang Yaxiang and other bandits chose Rat Hill as their lair. As long as the bandits occupied Rat Hill they were not only protected but also controlled the benefits of its good geomantic properties. Aside from Rat Hill, the Panyu gazetteer also mentioned an adjacent "Rat Hill village," whose siting undoubtedly would have been chosen according to geomantic principles. It would not be unreasonable to imagine that bandit lairs, like villages or military fortifications, were

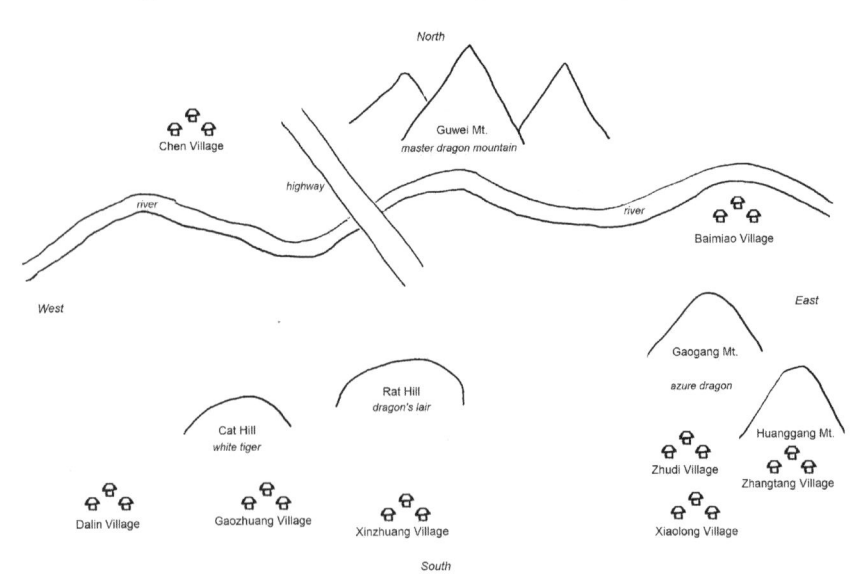

Figure 9. Rat Hill and *Fengshui* (Source: Created by author based on maps drawn by local informants)

specifically positioned by using *fengshui* principles. There is no reason for us to think that bandits thought any differently than villagers. After all, there was close interaction between outlaws and villagers, and as noted earlier one late eighteenth-century official lamented that in Shawan and Jiaotang "honest people and bandits all mingled together." When bandits were not out robbing, they lived and worked among villagers as hired laborers, coolies, and fishermen. They were all cut from the same cloth. Everyone—officials, generals, villagers, and bandits—wanted to harness *fengshui* for their own benefit.

Finally, what about the oral traditions handed down for generations by villagers around Rat Hill? Their stories give voice to the hitherto silenced histories of inarticulate peasants of Panyu. During my interviews in 2002 and 2010 several elder informants provided an alternative narrative to the one given in the documentary sources. Although officials interpreted banditry in terms of social disorder rooted in poverty, poor harvests, and political corruption, eighteenth-century and later villagers may have seen things differently: bandits existed on Rat Hill for hundreds of years because geomantic forces protected them. Simply put, bandits controlled the area because they controlled the *fengshui*. It is not that villagers ignored the sociopolitical explanations of banditry, but rather that they chose to emphasize geomancy as the most suitable reason for the persistence of local bandits. As one informant told me, bandits only returned to the area in the 1930s after a gang had taken away the Iron Cat, thus leaving Rat Hill geomantically unprotected. There is no way that we can be certain about what eighteenth-century Panyu peasants thought, but it is not unreasonable to believe that they thought the same way as my contemporary village informants, especially given the long-standing prevalence of *fengshui* beliefs and practices in the Canton delta. Such a magico-religious justification for banditry tells us much about the hidden worldview of Chinese peasants past and present.

Conclusion

The anthropologist Jack Potter once explained that the villager's world in south China depended upon luck, but that luck could be altered by utilizing the supernatural forces in nature. Peasants believed in a cosmos animated with an impersonal primordial energy (*qi*) that was fundamental to geomantic principles. For villagers *fengshui* was the fundamental source of all luck and efficacy. It offered an amoral explanation of fortune as an alternative to the moral universe of Confucianism and Buddhism. The success or failure of individuals, lineages, and villages all relied on *fengshui*. Therefore, in most

Cantonese villages, he continued, important decisions and actions, whether for an individual or community, had to be adjusted and guided according to geomantic conditions, which determined the prosperity and safety for both present and future generations. Thus geomancy was always used in siting villages, homes, temples, ancestral halls, and graves. *Fengshui* was an omnipresent feature of south China life.[71]

In Panyu banditry too was an ever-present concern that both villagers and officials had to cope with on a regular basis. From archives, gazetteers, and other written records we can glean evidence for the sociopolitical history of banditry in Guangdong. In Shawan and Jiaotang, in particular, there seems to have been an unusually large number of poor marginalized villages—such as the one at Rat Hill—that were friendly with bandits. These villages welcomed or at least tolerated bandits because they provided needy villagers with goods and money as well as protection from overbearing lineages and other predatory groups. Other villages and market towns, those dominated by powerful lineages, and which were often the victims of bandit raids, considered bandits nothing more than vicious rogues deserving harsh punishments. These villages and towns built defensive walls, formed guardsmen units, and often cooperated with officials to capture bandits. Lineage-based guardsmen were also used against rival lineages and to intimidate and control tenants and subordinate villages. All sides accused one another of being bandits.

To dig deeper into the mental and symbolic world of Chinese people in the early modern period we need to get our clues elsewhere, such as from the textual and oral traditions of folklore and geomancy. These are unconventional sources virtually untapped by China historians, but nevertheless provide an important entry point into the otherwise invisible history of illiterate commoners. They are windows to an alternative way of looking at the past. Such sources inform us about how ordinary people made sense of their world, and how they organized reality in their own minds. Peasants used folklore, as Darnton puts it, "to piece together a picture of reality and to show what that picture meant for persons at the bottom of the social order."[72] For Chinese peasants folktales and geomancy helped to explain their world in ways they could easily understand, and to do so in ways that the more conventional sources could never do. Stories about rats and cats revealed an unforgiving, dangerous, and brutal world, much like that of eighteenth-century French peasants. The reality of life for most Chinese villagers was generally capricious and amoral, a far cry from the niceties espoused in Confucian virtues and values. Geomancy offered an alternate system of meaning that explained people's misfortunes—illness, death, poverty, and even banditry. Because *fengshui* could be manipulated to alter luck, it provided a powerful tool individuals could use to cope with unfavorable, adverse circumstances. Geomancy empowered people to take control of their lives.

The utilization of folklore and *fengshui* in historical research is also important in helping us bridge the two worlds of elite and popular culture. How people used folktales and *fengshui* may have differed, nonetheless the stories about rats and cats were common knowledge and what they signified was known to everyone. Similarly, the symbolic meaning of casting an Iron Cat to scare away bandits on Rat Hill was certainly common knowledge. This curious episode of rats, cats, and bandits in a small corner of the Canton delta at the end of the eighteenth century is significant for what it reveals about how villagers, literati, and officials conceptualized their mental and symbolic worlds and acted upon their beliefs.

CHAPTER 4

Demons, Gangsters, and Triads

UNQUESTIONABLY THE MOST FAMOUS CHINESE SECRET SOCIETY WAS THE Heaven and Earth Society (Tiandihui), better known in the West as the Triads.[1] It began sometime during the eighteenth century, most probably either in Guangdong in Huizhou or Chaozhou prefecture or in Fujian in Zhangzhou prefecture. The name "Tiandihui" first appeared in official documents during the Lin Shuangwen Rebellion (1786–1788) in Taiwan. This was the first verifiable Triad rebellion. Officials described the leader of the rebellion, Lin Shuangwen, as a gangster or local bully, who had engaged in a variety of illegal activities ranging from petty theft, gambling, and armed affrays. Lin, however, was not the originator of the Heaven and Earth Society.

A traveling cloth seller named Yan Yan, who had come from Zhangzhou, had transmitted the Triads to Taiwan in 1784. He had been initiated in the previous year by Chen Biao, an itinerant healer from Guangdong, who had taught him the secret codes, hand signals, and lore of the Heaven and Earth Society. Lin Shuangwen was one of several of Yan Yan's disciples. Interestingly, after his arrest in 1788, Yan Yan described the Heaven and Earth Society as a "religious teaching" or "sect" (*jiao*). In his confession he explained that "everyone who enters the society has to establish an incense altar and under crossed swords swear an oath to help out other members of the sect whenever they encounter any trouble." He then went on to describe the rituals and passwords of the society/sect. His confession continues:

> Originally people willingly entered the society to get financial help from other members for weddings and funerals and support if they got into fights. Also if bandits accosted them, as soon as they indicated the secret

signs of the sect, they would not be bothered. What is more, by transmitting the teachings to others they could receive some gratuities.

According to his testimony, the society/sect had been created "in the distant past" in Sichuan province by two people whose surnames were Li and Zhu. Afterward, a certain Ma Jiulong gathered forty-eight Shaolin monks to spread their religious teachings, which also included magical techniques (*fashu*) for dispatching spirit soldiers (*yinbing*). Later, of the original forty-eight monks, only thirteen had survived to spread the teachings everywhere. Yan Yan said that it was Monk Hong Er (also known as Monk Wan, Tixi, or Tuxi) who introduced the Heaven and Earth Society in the 1760s in Guangdong. As Yan Yan explained to his inquisitors, Li, Zhu, and Hong were not only the surnames of key founders of the society but also their names served as secret codes (*anhao*).[2]

INTERPRETING THE EARLY HEAVEN AND EARTH SOCIETY

One of the unresolved debates among historians concerns the origins and nature of the Triads.[3] Following the archival trail left by Yan Yan and others, a number of scholars, particularly Zhuang Jifa and Qin Baoqi, have concluded that the Tiandihui originated in 1761 or 1762 in Huizhou (Guangdong) or Zhangzhou (Fujian). While Qin Baoqi has explained that the Triads arose out of the social and economic contradictions among the laboring poor, Zhuang Jifa has suggested that it originated in the ethnic and lineage feuds (*xiedou*) common throughout southeast China at that time. For them, the Heaven and Earth Society was fundamentally a mutual-aid and self-protection organization.[4] Other scholars, most notably He Zhiqing, while recognizing Tixi as a Triad leader, have insisted that the society was founded much earlier in the Kangxi reign as a rebellious pro-Ming, anti-Manchu organization.[5] And although most current research has debunked such theories, still some scholars maintain that the Tiandihui started in the late Ming dynasty or even that its founders were followers of Zheng Chenggong in Taiwan. They also interpret the secret society in narrow political terms as an anti-Qing organization.[6] Several scholars also have depicted the Triads as being basically secular, even irreligious, in nature.[7] Despite their differences in interpretation, one thing that most of the above-mentioned writers have in common is their attempts at literal interpretations of Tiandihui myths and legends. They each base their arguments, at least in part, by trying to trace the names of places and people in Triad lore to actual historical locations and figures.

Chapter 4

More recently, research by David Ownby and Barend ter Haar has substantially altered previous interpretations. While ter Haar offers no explicit explanation for the origins of the Triads, Ownby suggests that secret societies, including the Triads, had evolved out of two separate and distinct phenomena: the community-based mutual-aid associations (*hui*) and blood-oath brotherhoods. Secret societies only emerged sometime in the 1740s to 1760s when these two types of popular organizations merged for the first time in history. This merger, Ownby tells us, was marked by the appearance of specific names for the various societies, the Tiandihui being one such name. Both Ownby and ter Haar also have rejected the literal interpretation of Triad legends as the basis for historical facts and instead treat them on their own terms as mythology. In doing so they have opened the door to look seriously at Triad rituals and legends as being important to members in creating a community and identity of their own. Significantly too, their findings suggest ways to view the Heaven and Earth Society in terms of popular religion, an approach often ignored by previous scholars.[8]

Following the leads of Ownby and ter Haar, in this chapter I further investigate the connections between Chinese secret societies and popular religion, and in particular ter Haar's interpretation of what he calls the "demonological messianic paradigm." In brief, ter Haar has traced the roots of early Triad rituals and lore back to traditional Daoist exorcist techniques and folk demonology, showing links between several messianic movements and early Triad development. While building on the studies of previous scholars, this chapter attempts to go beyond them to explore secret societies (in the broadest sense) in relation to both popular religion and criminal activities. I link the early Triads, and secret societies in general, to a line of development that emerged out of popular demonological messianic movements and "gangsterism," phenomena in which participants frequently bonded together with blood-covenants (*shaxue jiemeng*).

In this chapter, I am interested in elucidating the context in which the Tiandihui emerged and developed in south China in the eighteenth century. My purpose is to investigate, as best as we can, early illegal associations, including secret societies and messianic groups, from the perspectives and motives of the people who formed or joined them. Of course, these events and movements can be interpreted in different ways depending on the perspective taken. Hence, we can look at them from the official perspective, which invariably emphasized the seditious or criminal nature of these organizations; or we can take the perspectives of the participants or leaders, which emphasized customary beliefs about the supernatural and/or survival strategies that sometimes involved banditry and racketeering. It is dangerous, however, to rely solely on the perspectives and interpretations of officials, because by doing so we run the risk of attributing perceptions and motives to the participants that they did not have. Nevertheless, none of the perspectives are mutually exclusive.

DISTRIBUTION OF ILLEGAL ASSOCIATIONS IN SOUTH CHINA, 1641–1788

My research findings are summarized in appendix 2, which outlines data on more than forty illegal associations in Taiwan, Fujian, and Guangdong between 1641 and 1788. This appendix, however, does not claim to be comprehensive but only suggestive of major trends. I selected these areas because of their direct relevance to the early development of the Triads, other secret societies, and messianic groups. I begin with the Ming–Qing transition in the 1640s and end with the year 1788, which marked the appearance of the Tiandihui in Taiwan during the Lin Shuangwen Rebellion. Roughly half of the cases in the appendix were demonological messianic movements or at least demonstrated certain messianic influences. Just over half of the cases involved associations that purportedly used blood oaths or covenants. While in almost half of the cases groups took specific names, a slightly larger number of groups had no appellations. Officials accused most of the associations of being involved in such activities as banditry, swindling, and/or sedition. In the appendix I have used quote marks on the words "swindling" and "sedition" to indicate that these were labels imposed by Qing officials; it is unlikely that members would have used such terms to describe their activities. This chapter focuses mainly on the cases labeled "messianic" in the appendix.

The geographic distribution of illegal associations in south China (1641–1788) is illustrated in map 4. As the map indicates, these associations were spread throughout much of Guangdong, Fujian, and Taiwan, the centers of Triad power and activities during its formative years. I have not, however, uncovered evidence of illegal associations for this period in southwestern Guangdong (such as the Leizhou peninsula or Hainan island) or in eastern Taiwan (although there was such activity in those areas by the early nineteenth century and likely earlier but undetected by officials). While several illegal associations were located in the peripheral areas of Guangdong and Fujian, the majority of them were located in core areas, particularly the densely populated and highly commercialized prefectures of Chaozhou and Zhangzhou, with a slightly fewer number in Quanzhou and the Canton delta. Although Taiwan was a frontier region during this period, nonetheless, it is important to point out that all the associations on the island were located in the most populated and commercialized areas, namely Zhanghua, Zhuluo, and Fengshan. These were precisely the same areas where Zhu Yigui, Wu Fusheng, and the Toothless Man (discussed in the prelude) were active. Not coincidentally these were areas settled by large numbers of people who came from Zhangzhou, Quanzhou, and Chaozhou on the mainland, and who brought with them their local customs and beliefs. When viewed as a whole, the area with the largest number of messianic incidents, namely Chaozhou, Zhangzhou, and southwestern Taiwan, was one of shared culture, including not only language and religion but also endemic feuds and local violence. Obviously not only peripheral but also core areas were breeding grounds for organizations that the state labelled seditious and dangerous.[9]

Table 2 provides a temporal view of the illegal associations in south China between 1641 and 1788. Most recorded activities occurred in the

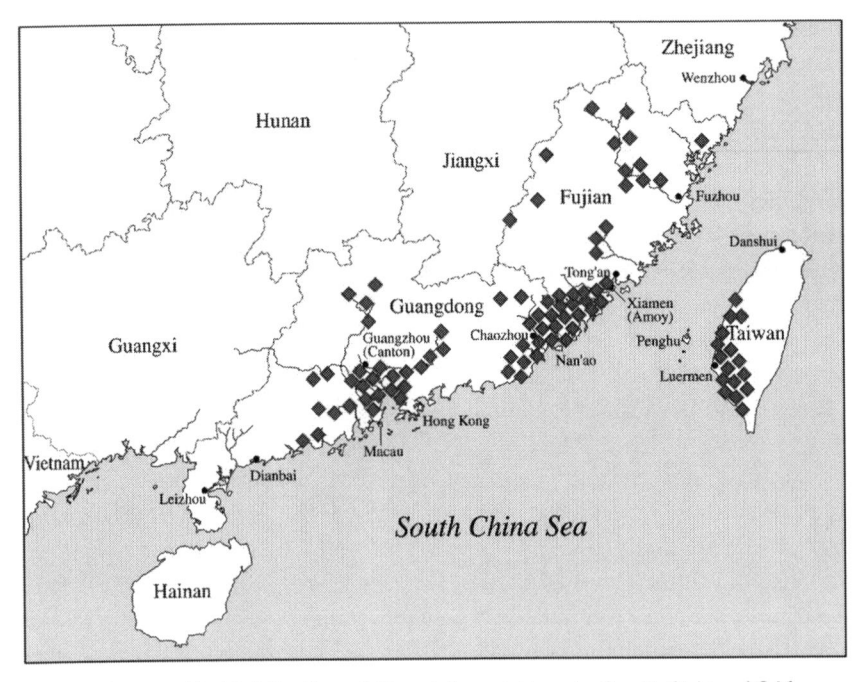

Map 4. Geographic Distribution of Illegal Associations in South China, 1641–1788 (Source: Created by author)

Table 2. Temporal Distribution of Illegal Associations in Southeast China, 1641–1788

Years	Demonic Messianic	Sectarian Messianic	Named Associations	Covenants Blood Oaths
1641–1670	0	1	1	2
1671–1700	1	0	0	1
1701–1730	0	1	6	5
1731–1760	12	2	10	7
1761–1788	5	2	3	9
Totals	18	6	20	24

Source: Robert Antony, "Demons, Gangsters, and Secret Societies in Early Modern China," 76.

years between 1731 and 1788. Not only did many of these associations take specific names—such as the Father and Mother Society (Fumuhui) or Small Knives Society (Xiaodaohui)—but there was also an increase in both demonological messianic and blood-oath activities beginning in the 1730s. Why was there this apparent sudden upsurge? As Rolf Stein has pointed out for an earlier age, demonic cults tended to appear in China during times of decadence and social crisis.[10] The eighteenth century—the so-called High Qing—was, in fact, a time of increasing decadence and instability, as well as of growing anxiety, fierce competition, and violent confrontations. Likely even more important, beginning in the late 1720s both the Yongzheng and later Qianlong emperors took personal interests in the investigation and suppression of so-called heterodox sects and therefore ordered officials to crackdown on their activities, undoubtedly causing a marked increase in the number of prosecutions.[11] Although there were earlier prohibitions, after 1727 the imperial court promulgated several new laws against what it saw as an increase in heretical sects, especially in the southern provinces. In 1747, for instance, the Qianlong emperor issued an imperial edict that condemned the evil customs among the people in Fujian who placed their trust in shamans and magicians who claimed that they could control the forces of nature by summoning spirits and demons.

Even earlier in the 1660s, the government started to enact a series of harsh laws against sworn brotherhoods and secret societies that paralleled those against heretical sects.[12]

INTERPRETING THE DEMONS AND SAVIORS

Demonological messianism was an important type of popular millenarianism. According to Barend ter Haar, rather than needing to change one's lifestyle or even moral behavior, to fight off an impending apocalyptic disaster one simply used Daoist or common exorcist techniques, which called on the aid of various saviors or messiahs, divine armies, and protective amulets. Unlike Buddhist-inspired messianism, vegetarianism and sutra-reading played less important roles in the demonological messianic tradition. In a word, anyone could buy protection from the apocalypse. Furthermore, the demonic messianic movements, as well as secret societies, frequently invoked blood covenants similar to ones used in Daoist exorcist rituals. The beliefs in demons and apocalyptic disasters, of course, were deeply ingrained in China's shared culture.[13]

Although the information in appendix 2 is partial, nevertheless we can make some general statements based on what we do know about those messianic movements. Indeed, there are certain key elements that run through nearly every case labeled messianic in the appendix. What is more, alongside the messianic attributes, most of these same movements also allegedly engaged in various nefarious activities or forms of gangsterism—swindling, extortion, gambling, theft, banditry, murder, and so on.

Demons and the Apocalypse

Messianic movements began with rumors or prophecies of impending eschatological disasters—demons invading this world, plagues and epidemics, wars, barbarian invasions, bandits, floods, fires, locusts, and so forth. Demons were themselves the harbingers and causes of apocalyptic calamities. J. J. M. de Groot explained that in traditional Chinese beliefs demons acted not only alone in causing havoc, but also they frequently banded together "in gangs and hordes, armed, equipped and led by chieftains quite like terrestrial troops and armies." In fact, he continued, "spectral warriors" (*guibing*) and their exploits were key features of China's demonology.[14] Ever since ancient times Chinese have told stories about wars between ghosts and humans, and by the Ming and Qing periods anecdotes about spectral armies and apocalyptic disasters were common tropes in popular culture.[15]

Spirits and demons, who resembled humans and were ruled by "spectral kings" (*guiwang*), resided in a nebulous realm, often said to be in remote barbarian areas beyond the pale of Chinese civilization. The ancient *Classic of Mountains and Seas* (*Shanhaijing*), for instance, described a "ghost kingdom" (*guiguo*) that was inhabited by one-eyed beings with human features and situated among the distant northern regions outside China.[16] This was a region of *yin*, of cold and darkness inhabited by underworld creatures. A sixth-century Daoist work likewise associated barbarians with the forces of darkness, as well as with heterodoxy and licentiousness.[17] The world of ghosts and demons were separated from the world of humans by "specter gates" (*guimen*). During the Tang dynasty and earlier eras, according to the *Old History of the Tang*, one such gate was in the south, at the far extremity of the Chinese empire. Some thirty *li* (about eleven miles) to the south of Beiliu there was a "Specter Gate Pass" (*guimenguan*) marked by two rocks that opened into the malarial regions of Jiaozhi (modern northern Vietnam). It was, therefore, quite natural for Chinese to associate foreign invaders and conquerors—such as the Mongols, Manchus, and later Westerners—with demons and the associated disasters they brought with them as nothing less than apocalyptic.[18]

Divine Armies and Saviors

In each of the messianic cases discussed in this chapter, charismatic leaders appeared who either prophesied about an impending apocalyptic disaster or who took advantage of such rumors already in circulation. They preached that they possessed methods to combat apocalyptic demons and plagues. In some cases they asserted that they themselves were saviors. In 1719 in Fujian, for instance, Xue Youlian said that he could invoke the Bodhisattva (*Pusa*) to descend into his body (*jiangshen*) purportedly to save his followers from the apocalypse. In other cases leaders claimed that they could summon divine armies and saviors to fight demons. In Daoist and customary beliefs, evil-spreading demons had to be battled against and violently destroyed with spirit soldiers (*shenbing* or *yinbing*) by using exorcist rituals. In the Guangdong countryside, in the early and mid-Qing, we have explicit depictions of wizards or male shamans (*nanwu*), who dressed in female clothing and ascended altars to dispatch divine armies to drive away the evil specters lurking in the area.[19]

The five divine armies, called the Five Encampments (*wuying*) in southeastern China, were denoted by five colored flags representing the five directions (north, south, east, west, and center). Divine generals, whose names and titles were often written on their flags, commanded each army. Because of their terrifying demonic qualities, the God of War (Guandi), celestial deities, such as the Year Star God (Taisui), and various local deities were often invoked as divine generals. In 1748, Li Awan, a local Daoist priest from Chaozhou, possessed five colored flags representing spirit armies which he said he could call upon to fight the apocalypse.[20] It is reasonable, too, that the "Five Houses" (*wufang*) in Triad accounts, which were represented by five colored flags, stood for the Five Encampments of divine armies.[21] Such flags could (and still can) be found in rice bushels on temple altars and placed around villages for protection against demonic forces.[22]

Saviors, who always came from some idyllic outside place (often from the west), led and dispatched divine armies to fight demons. Once the demons were defeated a perfect age of "great peace" (*taiping*) would ensue under the rule of a savior. It was common, in fact, for messianic leaders to issue proclamations proclaiming the advent of a new era of great peace. In Daoist teachings, this perfect new world would arise out of the ashes of the old; peace would be born from war and order from disaster. Those who survived the cataclysm were the chosen ones who entered the kingdom of great peace.[23] The message was both messianic and political for it assumed a change of dynasty. According to Triad lore, once the Manchus were destroyed an era of great peace would begin under the rulership of the young Ming prince, Zhu Hongzhu (or Zhu Hongying), who was one of the fabled founders of the society. In mythological terms, during initiations new Triad members would cross a river in a boat to reach the destined Great Peace Market. Not coincidentally, in the earliest extant foundation account (dated 1806), the Shaolin Monastery was purportedly located in the Great Peace Fortress in Great Peace prefecture in Gansu province in western China.[24]

In the eighteenth century, most of the saviors were represented by individuals having the Li or Zhu surnames. Although in early imperial China the Li surname was more commonly used for apocalyptic saviors, in the Qing period the Zhu surname also became quite common. Because there was a popular belief that disasters could be averted by the aid of imperial descendants, saviors were often said to be royal figures, thus the names Li of the Tang dynastic family and Zhu of the Ming dynastic family were popular. The use of the surnames of imperial families also gave legitimacy to messianic movements and bolstered any claims to emperorship.[25] As appendix 2 indicates, one of the most frequently mentioned saviors was named Li Kaihua (or variations such as Li Jiukui, Li Tianbao, and Li Taohong). Other common saviors included Third Prince Zhu (Zhu Santaizi) or Fourth Prince Zhu (Zhu Sitaizi), which used the Ming royal surname. In 1742–1743, in Fujian, one messianic group inscribed the names Li Kaihua and Zhu Son of Heaven (Zhu Tianzi) on a white silk flag; almost a decade earlier in Taiwan the Toothless Man had inscribed the name Fourth Prince Zhu on a blue flag. In the 1750s in one of several incidents in Fengshan county, Taiwan, Zhang Fengjie wrote on banners that Li Kaihua would aid him and his followers in attacking Amoy on the mainland. Taking advantage of a local drought, leaders of the Small Knives Society in southern Fujian in 1742 spread rumors of an impending disaster. They produced banners proclaiming that Li Kaihua would lead five (spirit) armies to drive away demons.[26]

The Heaven and Earth Society, from its very beginnings, espoused various saviors of the Li and Zhu surnames, as well as others. According to Yan Yan, two of the founders of the Triads were surnamed Li and Zhu. There also was a Li Taohong and the familiar Li Kaihua, as well as a Prince Zhu, Zhu Hongde, Zhu Jiutao, and Zhu Hongying; and in a Triad founding myth there was a ten-year-old boy named Zhu Hongzhu, said to be a scion of the Ming dynasty. According to Sasaki Masaya, the name Li Kaihua appeared as early as the Ming dynasty and was deeply imbedded in popular culture.[27] The name Third Prince Zhu, ter Haar suggests, was a takeoff on the popular exorcist deity Santaizi (Third Prince) or Nezha (Nocha), who had the Li surname.[28] As a divine general, Nezha led the central army of divine soldiers, and even today in religious processions he is a popular figure who possesses spirit mediums to combat demons. Such widespread appearances of these specific, well-known saviors over a long period of time and over a large and diverse area of southern China was not the result of simple coincidence but rather of a shared cultural and religious heritage.[29]

Besides their reputed royal heritage, saviors also shared several other distinct characteristics. For one, they were usually young. Because of their strong masculinity, in Chinese traditional beliefs, boys were especially animated with positive *yang* forces. For that reason, male spirit mediums were preferably young men in their late teens and early twenties. In Guangdong in the early Qing period Qu Dajun related how during community exorcisms ritual masters selected small groups of boys aged ten to twelve to accompany them from house to house carrying peach wood amulets and yelling out incantations to expel disease-causing demons. Similarly, in late nineteenth-century Fujian, boys between the ages of eleven and fifteen were employed in religious processions to chant exorcising spells.[30] Saviors also had unusually remarkable personal names, often employing flower or fruit symbolism (such as "peach"), auspicious numbers (such as "nine"), and the color red (*hong*) or its homonym meaning "vast" (*hong*). Red, in particular, has incredibly positive connotations and is efficacious in counteracting evil and averting calamities. For these reasons emperors and Daoist priests used red ink in writing documents and rebels wore red turbans around their heads; it is also why parents in south China tied red thread in the hair of their children. The personal names of saviors were, in general, associated with positive symbols of longevity and life force.[31]

The Li Mei case is instructive. Uncovered by officials in Enping county in Guangdong in 1729, a charismatic preacher named Li Zantao or Li Shixin, but who called himself Li Mei (a name that means "Plum"), appeared that year in the Canton delta, along the West River, and in neighboring Guangxi province, predicting an impending apocalypse of demons and plagues. He had at his command, he asserted, an arsenal of saviors leading (divine) armies. They included the familiar names of Li Kaihua or Li Jiukui, Zhu Santaizi, and Luo Ping, who was associated with another savior known as the Luminous King (Mingwang) and other titles.[32] In one incident from Guangxi officials reported that someone named Li Mei declared that Li Kaihua was his young son, and elsewhere he said that Li Kaihua was a youth of only eight years of age. Li Mei also mentioned other less familiar saviors such as Lord Chu Thunder (Chuzhengong) and Prince Jade Dragon (Yulong taizi). The names Luo Ping and Chuzhengong were written on command flags (*lingqi*), similar to the ones used in Daoist exorcist rituals for commanding spirit armies. Li Mei said that Li Jiukui and other saviors, who were assembling several hundreds of thousands of (spirit) soldiers, resided in the Little Western Heaven (*xiaoxitian*) located to the far southwest in Vietnam, that nebulous region of ghosts and spirits. Zhu Santaizi's army would arrive from Wizard Mountain (Wushan), a name that referred not only to an actual place in Sichuan province but also carried significant magical connotations. At one time or another, Li Mei had told followers that there were divine armies (represented by colored silk or paper flags or placards) in Guangxi, Shanxi, Shaanxi, and Fujian provinces. He also said that one of his associates, a savior-general named Li Tianbao in Guangxi, had "shed his mortal body" and that the Jade Emperor and an immortal named the Second Celestial Lady (Er Xian niangniang) had chosen him to be emperor. People who claimed to be Li Mei (or who used similar names) continued to appear from time to time over a wide area as far away as Yunnan, Guizhou, and Hubei provinces until at least 1743. Interestingly, although over those years several hundreds of people were arrested, there is no record that authorities apprehended anyone with the name Li Mei.[33]

Protective Charms and Magical Techniques
Throughout Chinese history, but especially in times of social and moral anxiety, itinerant healers and priests appeared in towns and countryside selling charms (*fu*) and chanting spells (*zhou*) to cure diseases and ward off calamities believed to have been caused by demons. In 1709 such practices became so rampant and disturbing that the Qing government enacted a new law prohibiting anyone from writing charms and agitating the populace.[34] For most Chinese, however, demonological healing was traditionally the most important type of relief from illnesses and epidemics.[35] Talismans were (and still are) ubiquitous to Chinese culture and could (and still can) be found in temples and homes, as well as in village handbooks and almanacs.[36]

Charms and spells were the chief means used by Daoist priests and other religious practitioners to expel or kill demons, and therefore were indispensable in exorcist rituals. Both were essential to vernacular and classical Daoist rituals, considered being "the most fundamental of cosmic revelations." Talismans were heavenly signs believed to have been handed down from mythical rulers and deities, who, like the ritual specialists, had used them to summon, control, and even punish spirits and demons. Charms were potent because they were contracts between the religious adept and the deities who conferred them.[37] They were written orders sent to the nether world of spirits and, as in the case of the imperial bureaucracy, they bore the impress of official seals. Such seals were necessary for the efficacy of the charm, for, as one magician explained, "a charm without a seal is like an army without a general."[38] Charms were usually stamped or written in some esoteric or archaic script (*zhuanwen*) on yellow (sometimes red or white) silk or paper (sometimes on wood, gold, or jade tablets). Spells were recited over charms to give them potency. Protective amulets were normally worn on the person or hung somewhere in the home or burned and the ashes consumed (often mixed with liquor or tea) or carried in small satchels.[39] Figure 10 depicts an "all-purpose" exorcising charm for expelling from houses all demons that molest and injure people. Note that on the charm spaces are left blank for

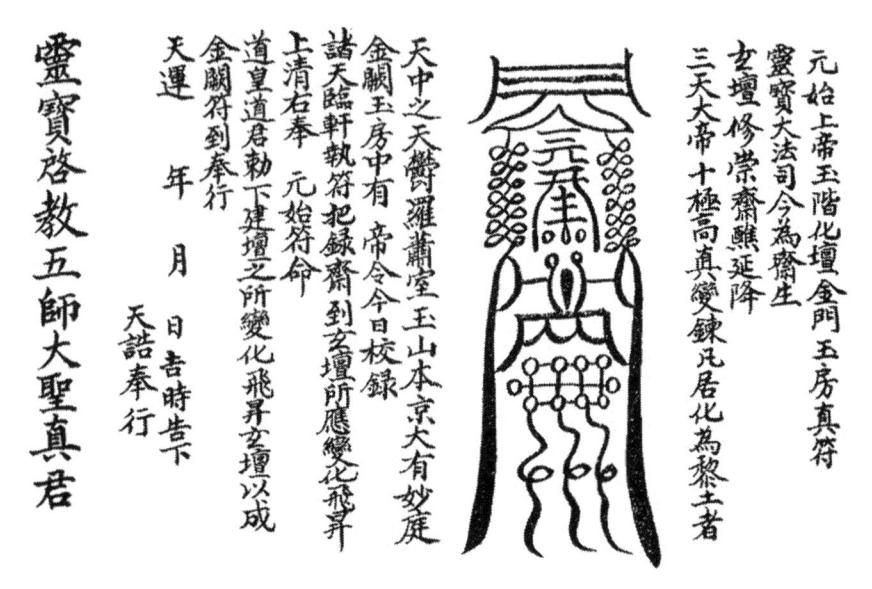

Figure 10. All-Purpose Exorcising Charm (Source: Henry Doré, *Researches into Chinese Superstitions*, 1914–38)

writing in the name of the person for whom the ritual exorcism was performed as well as for the date when it took place.

In the demonological messianic cases discussed in this chapter, individuals used charms and spells as the chief means of protection from demons and eschatological calamities.[40] After warning people of impending catastrophe, preachers like Li Mei, Li Awan, and others promised that no harm would come to anyone who bought their amulets. According to several depositions, Li Mei and his associates produced charms and certificates (*zha*) on yellow silk stamped with a wooden seal in archaic characters with the names of generals and saviors. Spaces were left blank for filling in names and dates. The seal was kept in a special pewter box. The certificate that Li Qisheng had purchased cost three taels of silver. Li Mei had told him to display the certificate at the head of his village to protect himself and his family from (demon) soldiers. Li Mei told Liang Zibin that he needed no weapons but only the amulet for protection. Although the official documents do not mention any predictions of impending apocalypse, the Iron Ruler Society (Tiechihui) case in Fujian between 1736 and 1756 was similar to the Li Mei case. Leaders of the Tiechihui used an "old text" or Heavenly Book (*tianshu*) containing charms and incantations written in the archaic script, which they copied to make seals and certificates that they sold to villagers. These charms were printed on yellow silk and paper with the name Li Kaihua as well as several military titles.[41] When Zhu Ajiang was arrested in 1770, officials found in his possession a seal and a booklet containing charms and spells.[42] The classics, old books with archaic writing, and old seals also were in themselves considered to be effective protective amulets.[43]

During Triad initiations new members were given "certificates" (*yaoping*), often on yellow or red paper or silk, to always be carried on the person for membership identity. These certificates also served members as protective talismans, as depicted in a Tiandihui certificate/charm dated from the early nineteenth century (see figure 15 in chapter 5). Triads also produced amulets for guarding physical health and for "cultivating and regulating the person."[44] During the Lin Shuangwen Rebellion there was the case of Woman Jin who used charms and incantations to cure illnesses among Lin's troops. She reportedly performed exorcistic dances with a sword while beating a drum and chanting spells in order to protect the rebels from the weapons of Qing soldiers.[45] Tiandihui members also used a large variety of hand signals quite similar to the ones used in exorcistic magic. Triad rituals, certificates, amulets, and hand signals, as Ownby has explained, "added a layer of supernatural protection to the more secular protection sought by joining a brotherhood association."[46]

Sometimes door plaques and flags were used as amulets to expel demons and plagues.[47] Perhaps the Toothless Man used flags for these purposes. In 1733 and 1734, Wang Atong in Haiyang county, Guangdong, for instance, claimed to have paper charms that could protect people and cloth flags that could ward off ghosts. On some of the charms were printed the words "Heaven Round National Treasures" (*Tianyuan taibao*).[48] The "national treasures" (*taibao*) in ancient China were considered to be talismans of power and long life that had been miraculously bestowed by Heaven (which traditionally was said to be round).[49] In the mountainous border area between Fujian and Jiangxi in 1767 and 1768, Monk Jueyuan and his band, after foretelling the imminent arrival of brigands, produced flags that they sold to villagers for protection against those bandits.[50] Indeed, it was and still is common for ritual specialists to produce flags and amulets to chase away robbers and to even compel them to return stolen property.[51]

As were Daoist priests and shamans, saviors were often armed with iron or peach wood swords, which usually were said to have been bestowed on them by Heaven, a past emperor, or a famous warrior. In 1770 in Chaozhou prefecture a geomancer named Zhu Ajiang declared that he had received a magic iron sword from Heaven.[52] Iron symbolized strength, determination, and justice, as well as positive *yang* forces. The magnetic properties of iron also infused it with magical properties quite useful in quelling demons.[53] The wood of peach trees likewise had important supernatural qualities useful in exorcist rituals. Because it symbolized vitality, demons feared the peach tree. People in Amoy, for the same reason, wore miniature swords of peach wood as amulets or hung them over the doors of their houses to ward off demons and epidemics.[54]

Besides charms and spells, many of the leaders of the various messianic movements also professed that they or someone close to them had special magical techniques (*fashu*). Li Mei claimed that he possessed magical powers that he could use to summon and command the five divine armies, as well as to excavate hidden treasures of silver buried in the ground in a place called Great Peace (Taiping) in Yangjiang county in Guangdong. He was assisted by an elusive monk named Zhikai, who was his military advisor and who also could use magical arts to stupefy people and exorcise demons. Another associate or savior, Li Tianbao, was said to be able to conjure protective magic with a jade charm that the gods had given to him.[55] Jade, which symbolized Heaven and the emperor and had magical qualities, traditionally had been used in China for good luck, immortality, wisdom, and power, as well as for protection against evil spirits and illnesses. In Fujian in 1752 a Daoist priest named Feng Heng said he could use magic to tell the past and predict the future, as well as invoke the five spirit armies. People who bought charms from Wang Atong said he was a wizard (*wushi*) who was good at magical arts.[56]

Tiandihui initiation rituals normally included a rice bushel and altar containing the usual exorcistic objects—colored flags, swords, scissors, mirrors, rulers, and scales. These items were explicitly mentioned in a Triad initiation in 1802 in Xinhui county, Guangdong.[57] The Triad altar in figure 11 shows these objects, as well as charms, seals, and command flags common in exorcist rituals. In the context of Chinese popular religion, each object had specific functions of expelling demons and providing protection against illnesses and evil. The rice in the bushel, which represented positive rejuvenating powers, commonly was used in divination and exorcism; rice also sometimes represented spirit soldiers. Flags not only symbolized various Triad "lodges" but also spirit armies for combating ghosts. Triad lore spoke of a peach wood sword engraved with dragons, and in at least one early society manual the sword was used ritually to "behead demons."⁵⁸ Scissors, like swords, cut and destroyed demons; and rulers and scales, as instruments of measurement, controlled things. Mirrors, which since antiquity were used to produce "fire from the sun," were instilled with magical powers that could reflect away evil spirits. Even today one can still find mirrors attached to the walls or eaves of houses as "all-efficacious household charms" protecting against malevolent forces.⁵⁹

The rice bushel and altar symbolized the City of Willows (Muyangcheng), which according to ter Haar played a central role in Triad mythology, rituals, and self-identity. The City of Willows was conceived as a refuge and safe haven, a mythical place that occurred both in the underworld geography in popular religion and in messianic traditions. In vernacular Daoist funerary rituals the deceased journeyed through the underworld city before being reborn in the Western Paradise, and in some Ming and Qing millenarian

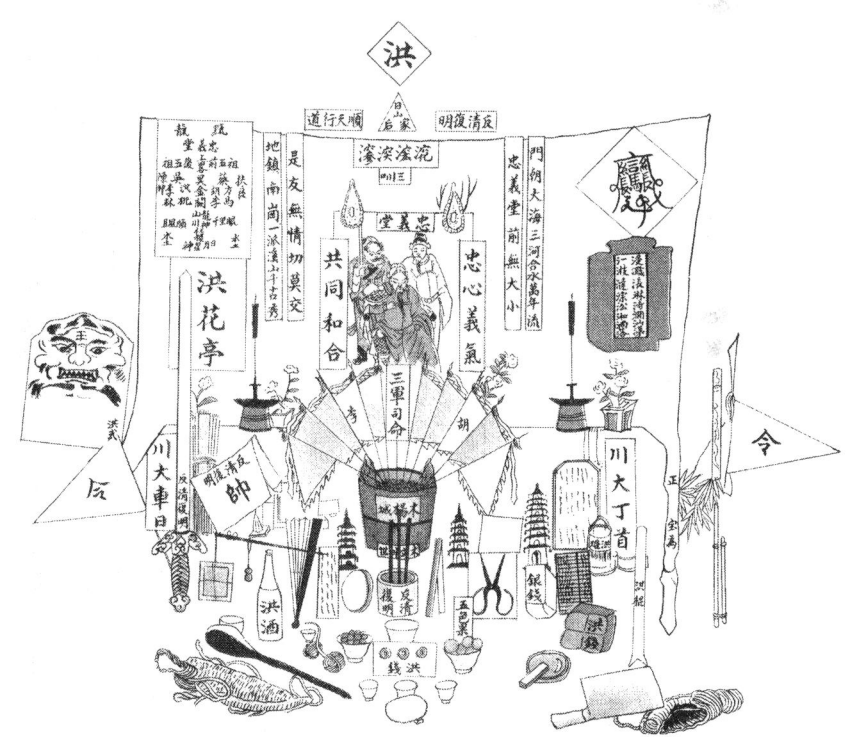

Figure 11. Triad Altar Showing Common Exorcist Objects (Source: Xiao Yishan, *Jindai mimi shehui shiliao*, 1935)

teachings there was a similar idea about a Cloud City (Yuncheng) where believers would be sheltered from apocalyptic disasters. In an even earlier messianic tradition that dates back to the sixth century, when China was plagued by epidemics, famines, and barbarian invasions, such saviors as the Luminous King and Luo Ping, who were later mentioned in Triad lore and rituals, led the chosen believers to gather in a refuge called the City of Willows (Yangcheng or Liucheng). In Triad initiations, new members were symbolically reborn in the City of Willows where all past, present, and future members were protected from harm.[60]

Interpreting Triad Sedition and Gangsterism

The demonological messianic incidents were not politically innocent. In some cases a dynastic change was implied and in other cases it was explicit in their slogans and banners. The seditious propaganda, too, can be viewed in eschatological rather than simply in pure political terms. As ter Haar posits: "Their driving motivation [to rebel] was the threat of apocalyptic disasters, rather than some fundamental dissatisfaction with Qing rule."[61] Triad rhetoric, which was explicitly anti-Manchu, can be viewed, on the one hand, as being politically and ethnically motivated, and on the other hand, as being a conflict with demons. In demonological messianic terms the Manchus, as barbarian invaders, were seen as devastating demons likely to bring about military catastrophes. They were to be fought not only with conventional armies but also with armies of divine soldiers. Significantly, officials noted that in several cases cited here, "rebel" groups had neither actual armaments nor real armies.[62] Li Mei, as noted above, told followers that they did not need weapons. Seldom, in fact, did these cases ever escalate into actual rebellion against the Qing dynasty. In some instances, it is difficult to pinpoint any rebellious intentions even though officials labeled these groups as "seditious."

Imperial Pretensions and Blood Covenants

Although not all messianic incidents purported Ming restoration, several in fact did. The popularity of saviors having the Zhu surname after the collapse of the Ming dynasty was clear reference to the fallen dynasty. In Fujian in 1742–1743, Huang Tianrui and Monk Shanjue produced a white silk banner with the names Orchid Dragon, Zhu Son of Heaven, and Li Kaihua (Lanlong Zhu Tianzi Li Kaihua) written on it. Li Amin told his followers that someone with the surname Zhu, who was a Ming heir, was planning to lead a revolt in 1770 in southern Fujian.[63] The Third Prince Zhu or Fourth Prince

Zhu obviously referred to saviors who were the supposed scions of the Ming royal family.[64] Earlier in Taiwan in 1721, the Zhu Yigui uprising, which also demonstrated certain demonological messianic attributes, called for the "restoration of the Ming."[65] In Triad lore, a Ming scion named Zhu Hongzhu was a purported founder of the society.

Messianic leaders also bolstered their political claims by surrounding themselves with imperial symbols. Saviors with the word "dragon" in their names, the use of yellow silk and paper with writing in red, and precious objects bestowed by Heaven all had clear imperial references and helped to create a sense of legitimacy. Displaying imperial pretensions, Li Mei reportedly wore a yellow robe and rode in a sedan-chair.[66] Du Qi, a leader of the Iron Ruler Society, had a bronze seal and an "old book" with imperial enfeoffments and dragon motifs, which he copied to produce documents on yellow silk.[67] Messianic preachers, as we have noted, claimed to possess various dynastic treasures, including jade tablets, bronze seals, heavenly books, stashes of silver, and celestial swords. Royal treasures were important for guaranteeing the ruling family's custody of the Mandate of Heaven. The appearance of jade charms, such as the one allegedly produced by Li Tianbao (a name that means "Heaven's Treasure"), had traditionally been regarded as portents heralding the rise of a new dynasty.[68] Leaders also produced seals claiming the Mandate of Heaven and new reign titles. Li Mei had banners with the words "[Follow] Heaven and carry out the way" (*tian yu dao xing*) and certificates stamped with the future *guihua* reign year. The Small Knives Society in Fujian and Guangdong in 1742 had banners that proclaimed, "On behalf of Heaven carry out the way" (*titian xingdao*). In Taiwan in 1753 another group included the words "Follow Heaven" (*shuntian*) on its flags.[69] The Triads, of course, had similar slogans (discussed in the next chapter). Leaders also distributed ranks and titles, always an imperial privilege, to their closest followers.

Many illegal associations, both messianic and non-messianic (listed in appendix 2), bonded members with blood oaths and covenants. Such oaths normally consisted of three components: the swearing of an oath or covenant (either written or oral) before a deity, the drinking of a concoction of blood (either of some sacrificial animal or from the participants themselves) mixed with liquor, and a malediction listing specific punishments imposed on transgressors of the oath. Perhaps derived from ancient ideas of human sacrifice, blood oaths were as old as China itself; they were used at one time or another by rulers, statesmen, religious practitioners, and commoners, as well as by bandits, pirates, and rebels.[70] During the Warring States period, according to

Mark Lewis, blood oaths provided a means for elite political and social cohesion following the disintegration of the Shang and early Zhou aristocratic order. At that time, blood rituals involving the killing of a sacrificial animal (usually a sheep) and the drinking of its blood sealed military and diplomatic alliances. Participants performed a solemn ritual calling on the gods and ancestors as witnesses. "Blood was ... sprinkled on the altar to summon the spirits, and the text of the covenant was read. This text included a list of the participants, the terms of the oath, and sometimes a curse upon those who violated the covenant." A covenant master (*mengzhu*) presided over the covenant.[71] Although blood oaths became less important among China's ruling class after the Han dynasty, the practice continued among the lower orders, especially to "sanctify undertakings of great danger."[72] From the Tang dynasty onward there was a surge in the use of blood oaths particularly among the socially marginalized elements of Chinese society who engaged in violent, criminal, messianic, and rebellious activities.[73] That is why under Qing laws on sedition and rebellion members of brotherhoods that had blood oaths were treated more harshly than those that had none.[74]

Also since at least the eleventh century in south China, Daoist priests and shamans used blood oaths in exorcist rituals. In fact, the blood oath between adept and deity was an essential element in exorcisms, without which they would have been futile. In a communal exorcism one or more religious specialists performed a ritual dance while holding swords and flags in their hands (figure 12). Through ritual they summoned the divine generals. As mentioned earlier, the flags of five colors represented the five divine generals of the five directions whose armies helped to exorcise demons. With the sword he fought the demons. Normally too the ritual included a blood covenant between the specialist and the divine generals. The priest drank blood mixed with liquor and offered the same concoction to the divine generals. It was usually the blood of a cock that was offered and used in the covenant. Not coincidentally, cock's blood was traditionally used to cure illnesses caused by demons. The cock and its blood, in fact, were symbols of life itself. According to one source, the blood from a cock's comb "will cure sorcery, drive away evil, and arrest epidemics." Sometimes the blood of the ritual specialist himself was used—human blood being considered even more potent than that of animals.[75]

Triad initiation rituals normally included blood oaths, but they were not the only illegal association to have them. One of the first messianic secret societies to clearly have a blood oath was the Iron Ruler Society in southern

Figure 12. Sword Wielding Daoist Priests in Taiwan Exorcising Demons, 2002 (Source: Shalun, Taiwan, February 2002; photo by author)

Fujian. Although antecedents to the society dated back to 1736 with the God of War Society (Guanshenghui), the first mention of a blood oath ritual was in 1752. Late one night in the fourth lunar month of that year, twelve members had retired to the tiny cloister of Monk Daosan to drink and feast and to initiate several neophytes with prayers, sacrifices, and the swearing of an oath with the blood of a cock. The covenant also included a death curse on anyone breaking the covenant. At an earlier initiation, which took place on the day of the God of War festival (thirteenth day of the fifth lunar month), leaders produced a covenant text and recorded in it the names of more than fifty sworn brothers. As we have noted, they also produced charms or certificates with the name Li Kaihua and the titles of military officials on them.[76] One is immediately struck by the similarity here with the earlier Warring States and later exorcistic blood oath rituals.

Messianic Leaders

Several features immediately stand out when we examine the social backgrounds of leaders of the messianic groups discussed in this chapter. Significantly, the largest number of leaders was itinerant religious practitioners who drifted around from place to place making a living by selling their services and expertise on various religious and medical matters. They were a highly mobile group, who, like itinerant merchants, peddlers, actors, and laborers, traveled from market to market often over long distances. Since ancient times China has known of such men, distinct from Confucian scholars, who were called *fangshi* (necromancers or wizards). They lived close to the common people, spreading their ideas and supporting themselves as diviners, alchemists, astrologers, and healers. After the Han dynasty, because of their association with various banned apocryphal texts and rebellions, they were forced to go underground.[77]

Such folk diviners, geomancers, magicians, spirit mediums, and healers, who were often literate or semi-literate, nonetheless persevered into the Ming, Qing, and our contemporary eras.[78] Li Mei was described as a roving medicine seller and geomancer, who traveled back and forth between Guangdong and Guangxi using several aliases. At one time earlier in his life he had been a common soldier in Dongan county, and he was also described as a magician. Wang Atong was called a wizard who moved about the Chaozhou area between Haiyang, Puning, and Jieyang counties in Guangdong. Li Boju had received his book of amulets from a man named Cao Risheng, who traveled about practicing geomancy and folk medicine.[79]

Often mendicant Buddhist monks and Daoist priests were deeply involved in the cases listed in appendix 2. In 1767 and 1768, Monk Jueyuan led a messianic group, which included a covenant, in the border area between Fujian and Jiangxi. Li Mei said that a certain Monk Zhikai assisted him; Monk Shanjue helped Huang Tianrui, an itinerant tobacco peddler; and the Daoist priest Feng Heng aided Cai Rongzu. According to officials, Li Awan was born into a family of practicing Daoist masters who possessed a "secret book of sorcery."⁸⁰ A purported founder of the Heaven and Earth Society, Tixi, was a monk who reportedly traveled about Fujian, Guangdong, and Sichuan. Because they practiced magic and could summon and control spirits and demons, villagers held such religious practitioners in awe. They were ubiquitous and indispensable components of village life and customs.

In the Ming and Qing periods, monks and priests, who were never a homogeneous group, included not only those belonging to recognized clerical organizations (registered temples and monasteries) but also a great variety of folk religious adepts, such as miracle workers and wandering ascetics. This latter group often lived among the common people and roamed about the countryside where they cured illnesses, told fortunes, practiced magical arts, and spread apocalyptic teachings. In the Ming and Qing periods, there was a tremendous increase in the numbers of itinerant monks and priests, who were in large part "free-lance religious entrepreneurs without any certificate or affiliation to the orthodox institutions." The government and state-sanctioned Buddhist and Daoist establishments considered them dangerous heretics who needed to be controlled and subdued.⁸¹

While many leaders were outsiders, others lived on the margins of village life, and still others were men with some status and property in their local communities. Official records often depicted leaders as bullies, ruffians, and boxing masters. Several depositions described Lin Shuangwen as a local bully, petty thief, and abusive husband.⁸² The Small Knives Society case on the Fujian and Guangdong border in 1742 involved "local bullies" Chen Zuo and He Zhi, as well as two local gentry and a merchant. In another case a decade later, Cai Rongzhu was a lower degree holder (*xiucai*).⁸³ Du Qi, a leader of the Iron Ruler Society, was described as a "good-for-nothing boxer" (*wulai quangun*), and his cousin, Du Guoxiang, was a dismissed soldier and boxing master. Both men traveled around local markets teaching martial arts and recruiting followers. A Buddhist monk named Daosan, who was skilled in martial arts, assisted them. Another leader, Luo Jiaqiu, who came from a lower gentry family, was also a local rogue who practiced boxing and "hung out with riffraff." He Zhi, who helped to organize Lu Mao's brotherhood in 1767, was also a boxing master. So was Li Amin.⁸⁴

One is also struck by several cases in which women took leading, or at least important, roles in instigating or organizing messianic groups. In Fujian in 1748, one of the leaders of the Laoguan zhaihui, a lay vegetarian group associated with the Luo Teaching, was a female spirit medium or shaman (*nüwu*) called Pushao, who predicted the future and claimed that Maitreya

CHAPTER 4

would soon descend to earth to usher in a new world. She was married to Zhu Jinbiao, whom devotees venerated as Maitreya Zhu. Followers honored Pushao by parading her in a sedan-chair, in the same way that deities and spirit mediums were transported in processions. On their flags were the slogans "On behalf of Heaven carry out the revolt" and "Exhort the rich to help the poor."[85] In other incidents, officials named Li Awan's mother as his co-conspirator, and Wang Atong was aided by his paternal aunt. In Jieyang county, Guangdong, between 1770 and 1773, certain members of Lin Ayu's brotherhood were followers of Mrs. Wang, who used amulets and incantations to cure illnesses. Her charms were inscribed with the words "beseech fortune, avoid calamity." Mrs. Wang's remedies were so efficacious that the local people called her "Celestial Matron" (*xianpo*), a name commonly used for female mediums.[86]

Charlatans and Gangsters

Official documents invariably described leaders and followers as rogues (*jianmin*) or some such derogatory term. To officials, messianic preachers were all charlatans, swindlers, and gangsters who duped ignorant villagers out of their money and led them astray. Were such depictions simply biases on the part of officials? In some cases yes but in other cases no. When we closely examine the activities of these groups we get a better insight into their nature. As appendix 2 indicates, these illegal associations were allegedly involved in various nefarious activities. I have used the term "gangsterism" as shorthand for activities that included petty theft, banditry, feuds, gambling, extortion, assault, and murder. Of course, these labels were produced by officials and therefore display inherent biases that we need to keep in mind.

Once again, the Li Mei case is instructive. Late in 1729 officials in Nanhai county near Canton arrested Ou Zaitai, a man claiming to be the brother-in-law of Li Mei and a co-conspirator. In his confession, extracted under torture, he told officials that it was he and Li Mei who had cooked up the whole scheme to make and sell certificates (charms) to "swindle" people. In Enping county Li Mei sold about thirty protective charms and flags within a couple of weeks, collecting anywhere from 1,000 to 3,000 cash (*wen*) apiece. According to Ou, on that one trip alone Li Mei earned more than 20,000 cash, plus three or four taels of silver. Li Mei split up the money with Ou and another two accomplices. At a time when hired laborers earned only 200 to 400 cash per month this was quite a handsome sum of money. Ou also told officials that they had contrived everything to cheat the villagers out of their money. He went on to say that there were no soldiers assembled in Guangxi or elsewhere, and as for the names Li Jiukui, Zhu Santaizi, Chuzhengong, and Monk Zhikai, they too were all unfounded fabrications.[87] To what extent was Li Mei a charlatan is anyone's guess. It is important to reiterate that Ou's confession was taken under torture and therefore he may have merely said what he thought his inquisitors wanted to hear. We must remember too that it was not (and still is not) unusual for religious specialists to collect payments for their services, even large sums. Another important point to bear in mind is that for the people who bought Li Mei's charms and flags, they did believe in his warnings of an impending apocalypse. Demons and plagues were real concerns to most Chinese.

Many individuals, too, explained in their depositions that because of poverty and hardships in making an honest living they formed or joined sworn brotherhoods to engage in theft, robbery, extortion, and swindling.[88] This was the case of the bandits of Rat Hill under Liang Yaxiang (discussed in the previous chapter), who had organized themselves as a sworn brotherhood to engage in criminal activities. Also we have already noted that there was a ready market for spreading rumors of impending disasters and peddling protective charms. But some messianic groups went beyond simple swindling to plan to become bandits and pirates, in some cases expounding slogans of "rob the rich to aid the poor" or some such rallying cry. Although they espoused such high-sounding slogans most individuals or groups were arrested before they could act, and so we will never know their real intentions.[89] But, of course, other groups did act. Wearing red headbands and sashes, members of the Small Knives Society (on the Fujian–Guangdong border) organized to plunder the Zhaoan county seat in 1742. Earlier that year members actually hired an assassin to murder the Zhangpu county magistrate, who had uncovered their brotherhood. At the time of the arrest of Chen Zuo and other leaders, officials discovered two bags of foreign silver, without doubt money they had collected from extortion and selling amulets. Zhang Poliangou (Scarface Dog Zhang), who had joined the Tiandihui in 1781 in Zhaoan county, had opened a gambling parlor in his home in Yunxiao because he was out of work. His abode quickly became a regular meeting place of gamblers, drifters, yamen underlings, and soldiers, as well as petty thieves, robbers, and secret society members. In the early nineteenth century the pirate Wang Zheng reportedly recruited followers by claiming invincibility against the Qing navy by summoning "spirit soldiers" to assist him in battle.[90]

When some messianic groups formed blood-oath brotherhoods ostensibly for self-protection there was little to prevent them from becoming predatory.

Perhaps because they made little money "swindling" villagers by selling their charms, Du Qi proposed that he and his followers become bandits. Everyone agreed and they swore an oath before a deity promising to help and defend one another and to rob people and split the loot among themselves. Du Qi's Tiechihui was composed chiefly of local rogues, yamen runners, and soldiers, all marginal elements of village communities.[91] The Small Knives Society in Taiwan in the 1770s and early 1780s was composed of local thugs (referred to in the sources as *guntu* and *luohanjiao*) who engaged openly in local feuds and gangsterism. In Zhanghua local people referred to them as the "Wangye Small Knives Society" (Wangye xiaodaohui). The Wangye or "Royal Lords" referred to a whole group of demons and deities in Taiwan, who either brought or relieved epidemics. They were therefore both respected and feared. Because of their demonic characteristics and appearances, the term *wangye* was also used colloquially to refer to bandits and ruffians. As Paul Katz has pointed out, "Calling a bandit chief *wangye* proves especially significant, as it implies that in most people's minds holders of that title were not necessarily benevolent."[92] The evidence suggests, too, that this Zhanghua group may have been involved in demonology and exorcist rituals. Not only was Wangye a popular deity used in exorcisms, but this particular group hung out just outside the southwestern gate of the city where the Wangye temple was located, and members swore blood oaths and some carried "double edge swords" (*jian*), like the ones used in exorcist rituals.[93] According to de Groot, the double-edge sword had been used since the first century to exorcise demons and was considered to be the most potent demon-destroying weapon.[94]

Conclusion

The Heaven and Earth Society was but one of many illegal associations that existed in south China in the early modern period. In this chapter, following the leads of Ownby and ter Haar, I have examined the connections between secret societies and Chinese folk religion, and in particular the connections with Chinese demonology and messianism. Embedded in China's rich popular culture, secret society rituals embraced traditional Daoist exorcist techniques and customary demonology. What is more, I have also demonstrated that these secret societies had closer ties with organized crime than they had with rebellious activities. In fact, I argue that the secret societies developed out of a popular milieu that combined the demonological messianic tradition with gangsterism, phenomena that frequently employed blood-covenants that bonded members in quasi-familial brotherhoods.

Demons, Gangsters, and Triads

Most of the people who joined these illegal organizations, and particularly the Triads, lived on the fringes of so-called respectable society. For the most part they were denizens of the "rivers and lakes," discussed in the first chapter. These were the sorts of people—poor, mobile, unattached, and discriminated against—who often turned to gangsterism and predation to survive. They joined illegal associations for support and for protection against both men and demons. Triad members swore solemn blood oaths before the gods pledging to help one another in debt and in fights. Yan Yan explained that people joined the Heaven and Earth Society for many reasons, including earning money by transmitting the secret codes, argot, and hand signals to new members (what officials routinely labeled as "swindling"). A fortune teller surnamed Chen, who was active spreading the Triads in Guangdong at the turn of the nineteenth century, always tried to attract new followers by telling them that as members they could benefit not only by receiving help in times of trouble but also by taking advantage of their numbers to rob villages and to share in the loot.[95]

Let me end with a final anecdote concerning a messianic leader named Yang Daohua from Linhong in Guangdong, who claimed to possess a magical sword that could slay everyone within a radius of twenty miles. After gathering a group of villagers from his home community he led an armed uprising, which attacked the granary, markets, and government posts in the area. Yang and his band killed seven people and absconded with a sizable amount of official funds before being apprehended by the authorities. Although similar to the other cases mentioned above, what is striking about this incident is the fact that it did not occur in the eighteenth century but rather in the summer of 1957.[96] Despite the repeated attacks on popular "superstitions" by the Communist government since 1949, numerous similar cases have been reported throughout China in recent years. As one Chinese newspaper editorial in 1982 explained:

> *In the past few years, there have been indications of a revival of reactionary superstitious sects and secret societies in some places. In some areas, scoundrels and counterrevolutionaries have appeared, claiming to be "emperors" or the "Jade Emperor" descended to earth.*[97]

As in the past, wizards and charlatans continue to appear from time to time in China's vast countryside gathering bands of followers by offering protection from dangers in both the seen and unseen worlds of men and

CHAPTER 4

spirits. Charismatic leaders offered protection as well as opportunities for predation. In gathering his band, Yang Daohua relied on traditional, time-honored methods of recruitment. Indeed, he could never have gathered a following had what he been preaching not been deeply embedded in Chinese popular culture and consciousness. Clearly traditional beliefs in demons and apocalyptic calamities are still alive and flourishing in today's China.

CHAPTER 5

Religious and Ethnic Unrest in Huizhou

IN THE MOUNTAINS OF HUIZHOU PREFECTURE IN GUANGDONG PROVINCE IN 1802, Hakka communities banded together to form secret societies that rose up in revolt. As a marginalized ethnic minority, the Hakkas organized themselves for mutual-aid and self-protection in secret societies, usually labeled as the Heaven and Earth Society (Tiandihui) or Triads.[1] This was the first major Triad rebellion in Guangdong and its second major rebellion in Chinese history. Before the uprising was suppressed more than a year later, the disturbances came to involve tens of thousands of people and roughly a quarter of Guangdong province. Significant, too, was that Triad groups in Huizhou forged links with a much wider network of secret society and sectarian organizations (in this case, the Dachengjiao) that spread across the Hakka heartland on the Jiangxi, Fujian, and Guangdong border (map 5). Oddly enough, this important uprising and its wider connections have received little attention from scholars.

This chapter, based on extant historical records and field research carried out by the author, takes an interdisciplinary approach, incorporating historical and anthropological methodologies, to examine the roots and nature of this important uprising. The archival materials are the most valuable written sources on the revolt, providing a depth of understanding that is virtually unobtainable from any other available written sources. These records include summaries, often quite detailed, of testimonies and confessions, as well as minute descriptions of military campaigns and judicial procedures. The fieldwork, which I conducted in the summer of 2002 in Boluo and spring of 2011 in Huidong, was essential to my research as it has revealed important information on the uprising and local conditions that are unavailable from

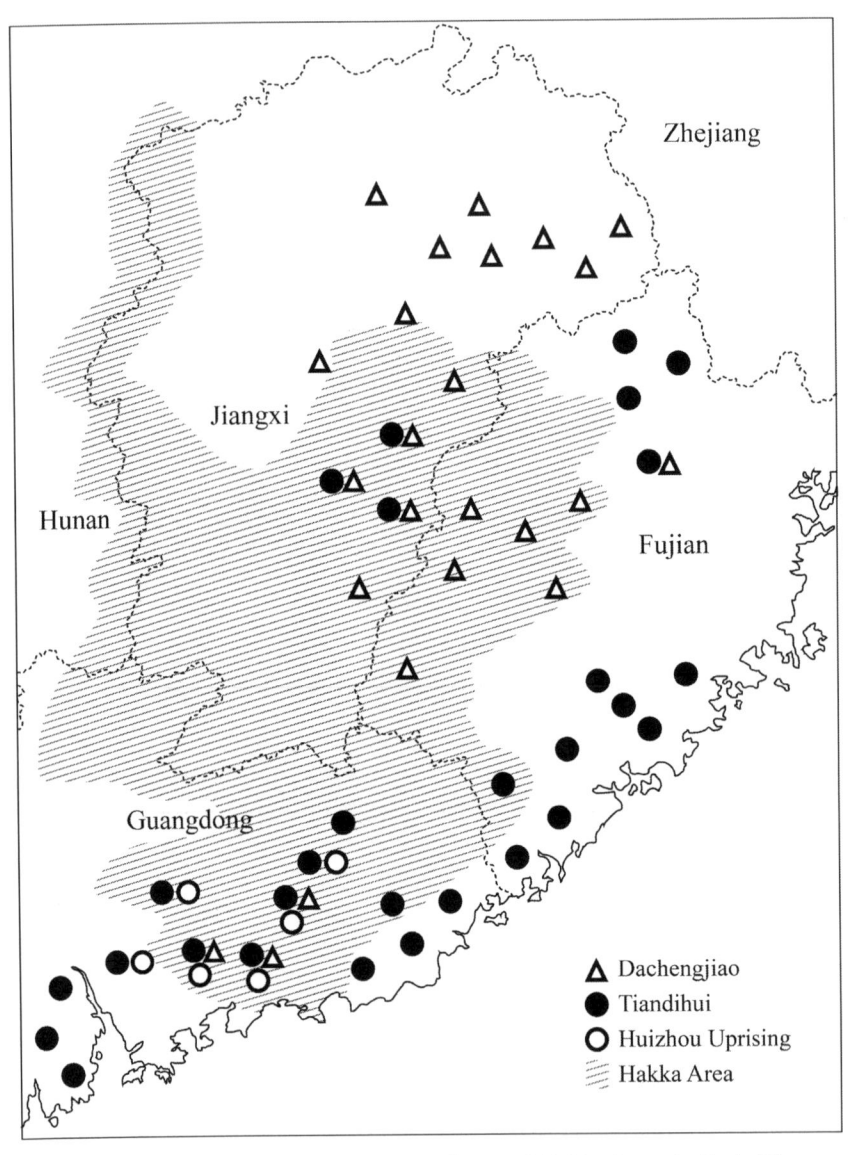

Map 5. Distribution of Tiandihui, Dachengjiao, and Hakka Areas in Early Nineteenth-Century Guangdong, Jiangxi, and Fujian (Source: Created by author)

official written sources. I was able not only to visit the actual sites of the Triad uprising, including several "ruins" of Triad stockades deep in the mountains, but more importantly I was able to interview descendants of Chen Lanjisi, the Hakka rebel leader in Boluo county, and also make a copy of the Chen family's informative 1833 genealogy, as well as to collect other epigraphic materials.

I address several important questions concerning the Hakka-Triad uprising of 1802. Those few scholars who have touched on this uprising see it as a secret society rebellion that aimed to overthrow the Qing dynasty. Is that assessment correct or were there other perhaps deeper objectives? What were the chief motives of the Hakka insurgents? Was the uprising a sudden aberration or was it a manifestation of longstanding social polarizations and ethnic conflicts in the region? Another important, but neglected, aspect of the uprising concerns the Tiandihui's connections with sectarian groups, usually incorrectly labeled as White Lotus in the sources, which practiced vegetarianism and recited sutras. Who were these sutra-chanting vegetarians and what role did they play in the uprising? In answering these questions, this chapter is divided into four sections. First, I put the uprising in the larger historical context with discussions about the Huizhou area, the Hakka settlers, and the conflicts between the Hakka and Punti before 1802. Next, I examine the Triad uprising in Huizhou in 1802–1803. This is followed by a section on the relationships between the Triads and popular religion, with a focus on the connections between the Triad and lay Buddhists groups in the Hakka heartland on the Jiangxi, Guangdong, and Fujian borders. The last section explores Triad and Dachengjiao slogans and teachings in light of the popular culture of south China, extending the discussion from the previous chapter.

Hakka-Punti Ethnic Strife

Long before 1802 the Huizhou area already had a reputation as a hotbed of armed feuds and dissidence. Huizhou prefecture is a mountainous area with generally poor soil and low agricultural yields. It was also an area prone to natural disasters: floods, pestilence, droughts, famines, and occasionally earthquakes. A major geographical feature of the region, the Luofu Mountains (Luofushan), had for centuries been the home of Buddhist and Daoist ascetics, as well as bandits and dissidents of all sorts. Although poor and underdeveloped, Huizhou was strategically located on the East River, which linked the prefectural capital with Canton to the west and Jiangxi province upriver to the north.

CHAPTER 5

Huizhou prefecture supported a mixed population with diverse customs and languages. The politically and economically dominant group was called Punti, or native residents, who claimed to be descendants of the earliest Han Chinese settlers in Guangdong and who were mostly Cantonese speakers. They also laid claim to the best lands and operated the largest number of markets. The Hakkas, literally "guest people" (*kemin*), had begun moving into Huizhou prefecture in large numbers probably in the mid sixteenth century and settled in the less arable hilly areas where they farmed indigo, made charcoal, and worked mines. The term "Hakka" (*kejia*) began to appear in written records in 1687 in Yongan county and by the early eighteenth century was in common use in the Huizhou and surrounding areas. Hakkas who settled in Guishan and Yongan counties mostly came from nearby Xingning and Changle counties, as well as from Wuping and Anyuan on the Jiangxi-Fujian border; they were predominantly miners. Those that migrated to Boluo were mostly from Xingning and Changle and engaged chiefly in indigo farming. Most Hakkas, however, did not own the lands where they lived and worked, and they had to pay rent to absentee Punti landlords who often lived in market towns and cities. In the late Qing period, an estimated 80 percent of the population in Boluo were tenants and itinerant laborers. Punti looked down upon the Hakkas, referring to them derogatorily as ruffians and brutes. In Dongguan county, for example, locals called the Hakkas *ngai-lou*, a Cantonese term of abuse meaning vagrant. The character *ngai*, in fact, was written with the dog radical "to give emphasis to the native view of the Hakkas as subhuman."[2] The term "guest people" itself was a constant reminder of their permanent status as outsiders.

By the eighteenth century, the Hakkas, like other Chinese, were feeling the pressure of increased population and so continued in even greater numbers to move into Huizhou and other areas occupied or claimed by the Punti. Once a Hakka community was formed it tended to grow rapidly as more newcomers, mostly relatives and friends from the same overcrowded home areas, arrived and settled. For example, Jiaoziwo village in Boluo was first settled in the sixteenth century by the Xie family, Hakkas from northern Guangdong on the border with Jiangxi; in the mid eighteenth century a new wave of Hakka settlers of the Chen, Wang, Wu, Huang, Lian, Wen, and He surnames relocated in the same area. Indicative of its isolation as late as the 1980s the village had a population of only 220 people. Chashan village, situated in Boluo on the mountainous border with Longmen county, was settled during the turbulent Ming–Qing transition by members of the Qiu family from Fujian; then in the late seventeenth century a branch of Chen Lanjisi's family settled there. Villagers withstood the harsh environment to sustain a subsistence living growing tea, peanuts, sweet potatoes, and vegetables.[3] From the perspective of Punti landlords, the Hakka migrants were like "swarms of ants and bees." By the early nineteenth century, the majority of the population in Boluo and Yongan were Hakkas.[4]

As newcomers to the area Hakka settlers generally lacked strong lineages and therefore they formed their own communal organizations based on native-place and language.[5] At first encouraged by local officials, Hakkas in Huizhou in the early seventeenth century organized villages into community pacts or alliances (*xiangyue*). Originally intended by officials to restrain the Hakkas and incorporate them more fully into the state's orthodox political culture, according to historian Sow-Theng Leong, instead the *xiangyue* system "actually encouraged ethnic solidarity and mobilization," which in turn "facilitated extralocal organization for interethnic conflict."[6] In the 1640s, for example, several thousand Hakka miners in Boluo county organized themselves into a Xing-Chang Pact (*yue*), referring to the two counties of Xingning and Changle where they had originated. Within a short time they had become so strong that they refused to pay rents and taxes.[7] By the 1750s numerous other Hakka strongholds had also organized themselves into intervillage alliances that defied landlords and officials. In Zengcheng, for instance, Hakkas formed multi-surname pacts consisting of anywhere from ten to several hundred villages. Over the next century, as rivalries and conflicts with native Punti and local officials mounted, Hakka settlers increasingly organized themselves into fortified villages defended by paramilitary units.[8]

Punti, too, had organized their villages and market towns into alliances, constructed fortified villages, and formed militia units. In Yongan most Punti communities were protected with walls, and in Boluo in the Qianlong period 48 percent of the 461 villages listed in the gazetteer had the word *wei*, *zhai*, or *bao* in their name, terms that indicated walled communities.[9] In Yongan in the early nineteenth century the Punti had thirty-seven multi-village alliances. The Fenghuang alliance, for instance, which was headquartered in the market town of the same name, was led by a military degree holder named Gan Runchang and a local scholar named Huang Tongruo. During the time of the Triad disturbances the alliance organized a militia of several hundred local volunteers and hired mercenaries and constructed fortifications and watchtowers.[10] Throughout the areas in Huizhou where the uprising erupted,

CHAPTER 5

Punti organized Ox Head Societies (Niutouhui) with the avowed purpose to protect their families and property from "Hakka bandits" (*kezei*). Oxen, which were quite scarce and thus valuable commodities in mountain areas, were favorite targets of bandits, and in fact, there was a long tradition of cattle theft allegedly perpetrated by Hakkas in Yongan, Guishan, and Boluo. Nonetheless, it should be noted that the Punti were likewise accused of stealing Hakka crops and cattle.[11]

Actually almost as soon as Hakkas moved into Huizhou prefecture, tensions and conflicts flared up between them and the Punti. Local gazetteers frequently described the Hakkas as wild and belligerent, and in fact, no better than thieving rogues.[12] In the late Ming, thousands of Hakka migrants in Guishan engaged in illegal zinc and lead mining. Because the same mountainous areas where they settled and mined were also notorious bandit strongholds, the Hakkas were routinely associated with outlaws.[13] Following a severe famine in 1624 in Boluo county, Hakka settlers, described in the official records as roving bandits (*liuzei*) and vagabonds (*liumin*), rose up to plunder Punti granaries in several markets and towns. The disturbances continued on and off until the spring of 1630. In the previous autumn fighting had erupted after gangs of Hakka indigo farmers and charcoal burners from Fujian, who had moved into the foothills of the Luofu Mountains, plundered Punti villages and kidnapped for ransom more than three hundred people.[14]

Fighting never ceased between the Hakka and Punti, and in fact intensified over the next century. In the 1640s, roving bandits, vagabonds, and Hakkas, who were mostly displaced people due to the chaos and anarchy of the Ming–Qing dynastic wars, built mountain lairs in Luofushan, Chashan, Yashan, Qingxishan, Tianzizhang, and other isolated areas on the borders between Boluo, Zengcheng, and Yongan.[15] Even after the wars ended and the Qing government had consolidated its rule over all of China in the 1680s, these same mountain areas remained troublesome bandit and rebel nests.[16] The largest disturbance occurred between 1752 and 1753. A local gentry and fortune teller named Wang Liangchen from Chashan, after organizing a sworn brotherhood and disseminating seditious books, certificates, seals, and white banners to his followers, started an uprising in Indigo Mountain (Lanfenshan) in Zengcheng that spread into Dongguan, Boluo, and Guishan, the same areas that fifty years later the Triads would stage their revolt. According to official reports Wang claimed to possess talismans and magical powers whereby he could summon spirit soldiers (*shenbing*) and messianic saviors, such as Li Kaihua and Zhu Hongzhuo, as discussed in the previous chapter.

According to one report, the rebels were poor riffraff (*wulai guntu*) who robbed grain from wealthy households. Most of the followers were indigo farmers and miners, and therefore most likely Hakkas. When soldiers from Canton were sent to suppress them, the rebels fled back to their old nests in the mountains.[17]

During the next several decades local officials in Huizhou repeatedly reported Hakka and Punti villages forming paramilitary units and hiring gangs of trained mercenaries, who armed themselves with swords and fowling pieces to engage in armed feuds (*xiedou*) with one another.[18] Also the years between 1781 and 1796 witnessed an unusually large number of floods followed by famines; and as the costs of food rose so too did the numbers of roving vagabonds and bandits.[19] Thus most of the individuals involved in the 1802 uprising grew up and reached maturity in an atmosphere of almost constant—seemingly perpetual—ethnic violence, internecine conflict, and natural disasters. For many local residents the upheaval must have seemed apocalyptic. On the eve of the Triad uprising the situation in Huizhou prefecture was already very tense and belligerent; local society had become severely polarized and dysfunctional.

THE TRIAD UPRISING IN 1802

By the start of the nineteenth century several Triad groups were already operating in Guangdong, particularly in the Chaozhou and Huizhou areas. In fact, one of the earliest leaders, a man named Chen Biao, came from Huizhou. In the early 1780s, and perhaps earlier, he was involved in the establishment of several Triad cells in Zhangzhou in southern Fujian and possibly also in Huizhou.[20] Officials estimated that at the time of the uprising 80 to 90 percent of the Triad members in Huizhou were Hakkas.[21] By 1803, besides the Triad groups in Huizhou, there were other groups spread across the coastal areas of Guangdong.[22]

The disturbances in Huizhou that started in 1802 came to involve several thousand, and perhaps as many as ten thousand, "society bandits" (*huifei*), as they were labeled in official reports. The Huizhou Triads first came to the attention of Guangdong officials in the summer of 1802, when Governor-General Jueluo Jiqing received information that people in Renshan village in Guishan county had organized a Tiandihui cell and were planning a revolt.[23] Jiqing personally led several hundred soldiers from the Canton garrison to Huizhou to investigate, where he discovered that Triad activities were much more widespread than first reported by local officials. He ordered a crackdown and soon afterward the Guishan magistrate, Fu Bilai, arrested nearly a hundred Tiandihui members, and local Punti militiamen also apprehended an additional hundred society bandits, who were subsequently handed over to the authorities. Another 190 Triad members surrendered to local officials, also handing over weapons and sixty cloth banners. Getting word about the arrests, the remaining members fled into the mountains to hide.[24]

Cai Buyun was one of the men arrested. He was a native of Zhangpu county in Fujian and had some time earlier arrived in Guishan seeking work. During his interrogation he confessed to being one of the original Triad leaders in Guishan. On May 12, 1802, he said, Chen Yaben, a Guishan native, visited him at his home, and as they talked about their hardships and troubles, Chen suggested that they organize a Triad cell to rob Punti villages and markets. Afterward both men quickly recruited another sixteen like-minded men who gathered four days later at Chen's home to be initiated. Each man was given a five-colored cloth banner on which were written the words "follow Heaven to carry out the way" (*shuntian xingdao*), which they were to keep on their person as a secret identification and membership registration. Chen Yaben took the title Great King (*dawang*) and Cai Buyun took the title Great Marshal (*dayuanshuai*); other initiates were also given titles as generals and commanders. Next they all returned to their homes in Renshan, Baimanghua, Pingshan, and elsewhere, where they recruited more followers and prepared weapons for raids on Punti villages and markets. Before they could act, however, they were discovered by the authorities and arrests were made. After a hasty trial in Huizhou, Cai Buyun and another twenty-three men were summarily executed; another seventy-five followers were sentenced to exile in Xinjiang.[25] Chen Yaben, who had fled into hiding, was soon afterward arrested and also summarily executed.[26]

Other society members escaped into neighboring Boluo and Yongan counties where they joined forces with existing Triad groups. By late summer there already were thousands of Triad members spread across Guishan, Boluo, and Yongan counties, as well as new reports of groups in Lufeng, Dongguan, Zengcheng, Longmen, Xiangshan, and other nearby counties. A twenty-six-year-old man with the curious name Broken Shoes Chen the Fourth (Chen Lanjisi) was the Triad leader in Boluo, which became the epicenter of the uprising. He came from a prominent local Hakka family, but one that had seen better times.[27] Broken Shoes had begun organizing his association in the summer of 1801, or perhaps as early as 1799, and had several thousand followers by the summer of 1802. After receiving word of the arrests in Guishan and perhaps anticipating trouble from the local authorities, he led his followers and their families into a remote and inaccessible refuge known locally as Goat Dung Mountain (Yangshishan),[28] where they had previously prepared stockades, stored food, procured gunpowder, and made weapons; he made his headquarters in a large hollow called Luoxiying. Broken Shoes also produced several banners with the familiar phrase *shuntian xingdao* and gave followers pieces of red cloth to bind around their heads. Figure 13 depicts one of the extant banners preserved in the First Historical Archives in Beijing. On the

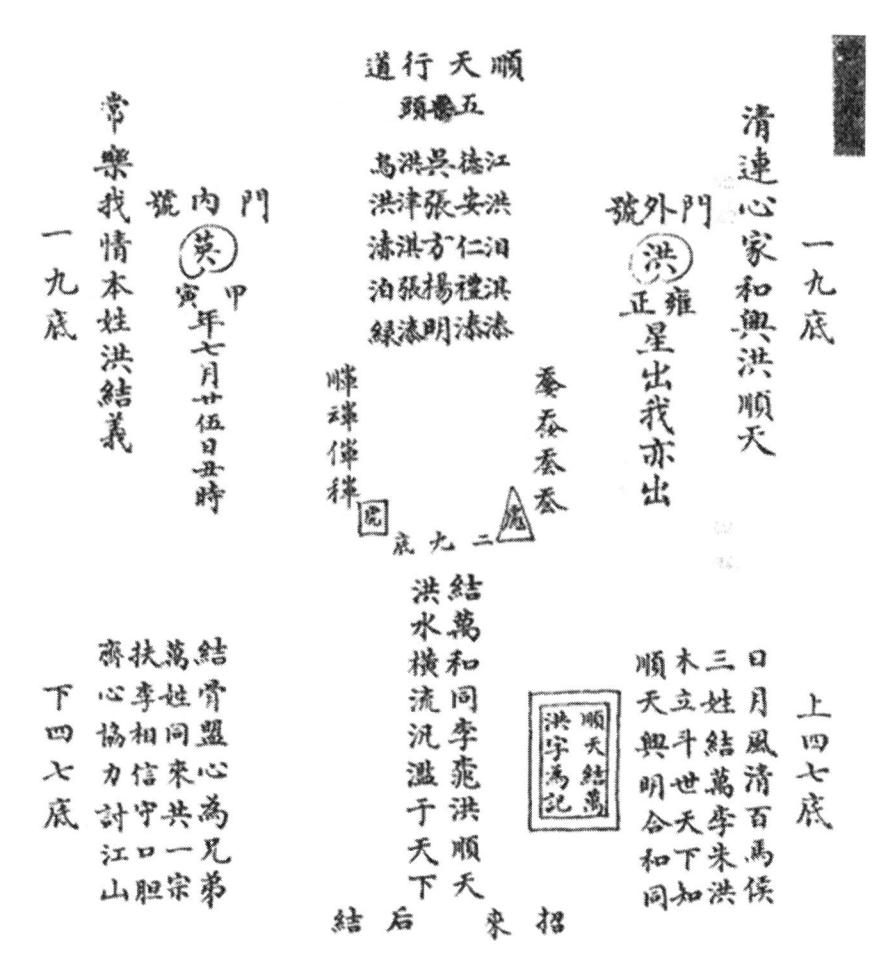

Figure 13. Triad Banner Used by Chen Lanjisi (Source: First Historical Archives, Beijing)

eighth day of the eighth lunar month (September 4), considered an auspicious day, he made sacrifices to his banners (*jiqi*), donned yellow robes, and took the title Great King. He bestowed on his seventy-year-old father, Chen Shizhuang, the title Venerable Great King (*laodawang*), who likewise put on yellow robes. Chen Lanjisi also gave ranks and titles to more than twenty of his closest and most loyal followers. For a month he and his men continually descended from their mountain stronghold to raid Punti villages and markets in the nearby lowlands. Soldiers reported the capture of Broken Shoes in October 1802 in the foothills of Luofu Mountains. Other followers fled elsewhere in Guangdong, where they continued to cause unrest for another year.[29]

In the meantime, the uprising had spread into Yongan county, where disturbances lingered on into the winter of 1803. There the uprising had been provoked by a Punti-led Ox Head Society and local officials. Hearing about the disturbances in Boluo, one of the leaders of the Ox Head Society, Lan Xiuwen, decided to act first. He gathered his men and arrested Wen Dengyuan, a local Triad leader, and then turned him over to the county magistrate. Unfortunately, Wen Dengyuan died in custody shortly afterward. Then Zeng Qinghao, Lai Dongbao, Guan Yuelong, and other Triad leaders assembled their groups in their mountain stockades in a safe haven called Tianzizhang where they offered a human sacrifice (undoubtedly a captured Punti villager) to their banners and soon afterward began attacking Ox Head Society villages and markets in Qingxi, Huangtang, Zhongpuwei, and elsewhere. According to the local gazetteer, no Punti villages were spared. Jiqing now called up several thousand additional troops who were sent to the scene to suppress the uprising, and Punti communities also organized militia and hired local mercenaries to protect their homes and fight "Hakka bandits." By winter the situation in the Tiandihui stockades had become desperate; pressed on all sides by soldiers and militia and running out of food and supplies, insurgents broke through the blockade to pillage lowland areas or to flee elsewhere. Fighting spread to neighboring Xingning, Zengcheng, Dongguan, Lianping, Longmen, and Longchuan counties.[30]

The fighting had been most devastating in Boluo and Yongan, where mopping up operations involving soldiers and militia continued for more than a year. In late 1802, Nayancheng, the special commissioner sent by the Jiaqing emperor to investigate the uprising, reported that some 160 villages and markets in Boluo and more than eighty in Yongan had been looted and burned by Triad bandits. Even more Hakka villages and stockades had been destroyed. The number of people killed—Hakka, Punti, and soldiers—remains unknown, but could have reached tens of thousands. The destruction of crops and disruption of people's livelihoods had been so great that the emperor approved tax relief for three years in both counties. Although local and provincial officials pursued a pacification policy that encouraged Triad members who had surrendered to return home and rebuild their villages, it would be another ten years before many of them felt safe enough to do so. A large number of Hakka refugees, in fact, never returned home but scattered and resettled elsewhere in Guangdong, Hunan, and Guangxi.[31] While hundreds of officers and Punti militia leaders received rewards for valorous service during the fighting, other officials were reprimanded and punished for negligence in handling the suppression of the uprising. Governor-General Jiqing, who was dismissed from office and ordered back to Beijing to stand trial for malfeasance and recklessness in dealing with the disturbances, returned to Canton in disgrace where he committed suicide.[32]

Although the Huizhou Triads displayed various seditious slogans, banners, and seals, and their leaders took such titles as Great King and Great Marshall, nonetheless, it is significant that they never targeted government military instillations or county seats, the most conspicuous symbols of Qing authority in the countryside. Instead their uprising aimed against their longtime Punti rivals, attacking their villages and markets. In other words, the strife was a more intensified version of the ongoing conflicts and feuds between Hakka and Punti. The 1802 Triad uprising was, much like the earlier Lin Shuangwen uprising in Taiwan, a local disturbance that escalated into a major social disorder. Both in Huizhou and in Taiwan, the Tiandihui rebels only began their uprisings after being provoked by officials and local rival groups. As one banner carried into battle by Yongan Triad members proclaimed: "Officials compel the good people [to rebel]" (*guanbi liangmin*).[33]

Triad-Sectarian Networks

An important but neglected aspect of the Hakka-Triad uprising in Huizhou was its connections with sectarian groups associated with the Great Vehicle Teaching (Dachengjiao). In the late Ming and Qing periods in the mountainous border area of Guangdong, Fujian, and Jiangxi there were numerous lay Buddhist groups, usually associated with the Luo Teaching (Luojiao), organized around vegetarian halls with a large number of different names, such as Goddess of Mercy Vegetarian Hall (Guanyin zhaitang), Old Official Vegetarian Hall (Laoguan zhaitang), Great Vehicle Vegetarian Hall

(Dacheng zhaitang), and the like.[34] Many of the Hakka families who participated in the 1802 uprising, including Chen Lanjisi's family, had migrated from this tri-border area to Huizhou several generations earlier; it would have been natural for them to have taken their homeland customs and beliefs with them.[35]

Many lay Buddhist groups practiced vegetarianism, recited sutras, and believed in the Buddha of the Future (Maitreya); some groups professed millenarian beliefs that Qing officials condemned as seditious.[36] This was particularly true in the predominantly Hakka area bordering Jiangxi and Fujian, which had a long tradition of Buddhist sectarianism and sectarian disturbances. In 1724 and again in 1729, for instance, the emperor complained to the governor of Jiangxi about the rapid spread of "heretic sects" (*xiejiao*) that congregated at night and conferred bogus ranks and titles on their adherents. Then between 1747 and 1749, officials uncovered a series of lay Buddhist groups, associated with the Luo Teaching and Maitreyan eschatology, in the rugged borderlands between Fujian, Jiangxi, Guangdong, and Hunan, which were also accused of planning uprisings over this vast area.[37] Most lay Buddhist groups, however, never became involved in millenarian uprisings, even though the government repeatedly prosecuted them as seditious organizations.

In some cases, including Huizhou to be discussed below, Triad cells had close connections with sectarian groups, even sharing in one another's ritual practices and organizational structures. Between 1782 and 1806, a lay Buddhist sect referred to as the Great Vehicle Teaching (Dachengjiao, as well as Dacheng Luojiao, Wupanjiao, and Laomujiao, and so forth) was active in the Jiangxi, Fujian, and Guangdong border area—the Hakka homeland. Besides lay preachers, Buddhist monks and a network of itinerant barbers, who were mostly Hakkas, played key roles in the spread of the teaching throughout this and other regions. One of the leaders was a man named Li Lingkui, who came from Jianning county in Fujian and had opened a shop in Nanchang, the capital of Jiangxi. At some point in his career he also had purchased a minor civil service degree, whereby he joined the ranks of the local gentry elite. In 1782 he took Wu Zixiang as his teacher.[38] He instructed his disciple to practice vegetarianism and recite particular scriptures in order to avoid catastrophes and to cure illnesses. Li Lingkui also bought from his teacher lay Buddhist scriptures, including *Scripture on the Great Precepts of the Great Vehicle* (*Dacheng dajie jing*) and *Scripture on the Roots of Benevolence* (*Enben jing*). Later that same year he returned to his home in Fujian, where he copied the scriptures and propagated the teaching, earning for himself

Religious and Ethnic Unrest in Huizhou

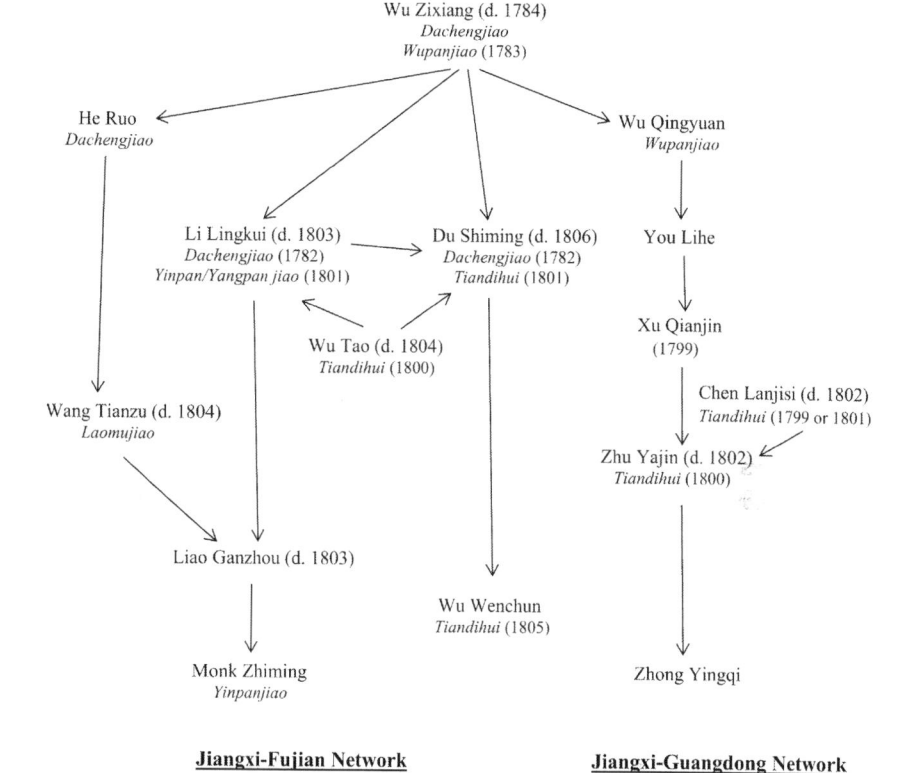

```
                    Wu Zixiang (d. 1784)
                       Dachengjiao
                      Wupanjiao (1783)

He Ruo                                              Wu Qingyuan
Dachengjiao                                          Wupanjiao

        Li Lingkui (d. 1803)    Du Shiming (d. 1806)    You Lihe
        Dachengjiao (1782)       Dachengjiao (1782)
        Yinpan/Yangpan jiao (1801)  Tiandihui (1801)
                                                      Xu Qianjin
                    Wu Tao (d. 1804)                    (1799)
                    Tiandihui (1800)
                                              Chen Lanjisi (d. 1802)
                                              Tiandihui (1799 or 1801)
Wang Tianzu (d. 1804)
    Laomujiao                                 Zhu Yajin (d. 1802)
                                               Tiandihui (1800)

        Liao Ganzhou (d. 1803)
                                Wu Wenchun
                                Tiandihui (1805)
            Monk Zhiming                        Zhong Yingqi
             Yinpanjiao

         Jiangxi-Fujian Network        Jiangxi-Guangdong Network
```

Figure 14. Wu Zixiang's Sect Networks (Source: Created by author)

more than fifty silver dollars from disciples.[39] Figure 14 summarizes two of Wu Zixiang's Dachengjiao networks, one in Jiangxi-Fujian and the other in Jiangxi-Guangdong between 1782 and 1806.

In 1801, Li Lingkui and several acquaintances joined the Tiandihui in Chongan county under a man named Wu Tao, a martial artist who officials depicted as a "knight-errant" (*haoxia*). The neophytes each gave Wu one silver dollar and accepted him as their teacher; in return Wu taught them the secret codes and hand signals and told them that by joining the Tiandihui they could avoid being harassed during their travels. Li Lingkui now added the Triad teachings to his repertoire, initiating hundreds of followers over the next several years. Those that followed the Triad tradition belonged to the Yangpan Teaching and those who followed the sectarian tradition by chanting sutras and practicing vegetarianism belonged to the Yinpan Teaching.

CHAPTER 5

The latter group was given white turbans to wear. Nonetheless, despite the two labels both groups were closely interconnected and clear distinctions between them are hard to make. In 1803, Li Lingkui, who foretold an impending apocalypse, proclaimed himself to be the reincarnation of a Tang dynasty emperor and prepared to lead his followers in revolt. He was, however, arrested and executed before he could act.[40]

Undeterred by the setback, one of his disciples, Liao Ganzhou, made sacrifices to a banner and rose in revolt in Shicheng county, Jiangxi, in the tenth lunar month (November 1803). Just prior to the revolt, Liao took Wang Tianzu, who was a follower of Wu Zixiang, as his teacher. Wang claimed to be the reincarnated Maitreya and said he foresaw an approaching cataclysm. He taught his followers to eat vegetarian diets and chant sutras to avoid calamities. Afterward, Liao gathered about 1,500 adherents who wore white turbans emblazoned with red crosses (likely as amulets). They were assisted by several Buddhist monks who also helped recruit followers who they instructed in reciting sutras and practicing vegetarianism, as well as disseminating protective charms. Also teachers and disciples maintained contacts with one another, frequently over long distances, by sending letters (*jixin*).[41]

Although Liao Ganzhou and his group were quickly crushed, yet another disciple, Du Shiming, who claimed to have an associate (or savior) named Zhu Hongzhu, who he said was a descendent of the Ming royal family, attempted a new uprising in 1806, but was arrested before he could start. On his banners were written the familiar names Li Kaihua and that of another (royal) savior named Zhu Qigui. One of Du's disciples, a thirty-seven-year-old drifter named Wu Wenchun, confessed that when he was initiated into the Triads, Du Shiming told him that there were two groups, vegetarians and meat-eaters, and that he had followers in several provinces as far away as Shandong ready to rise up. Wu was then given three amulets: the first one was to be pasted on the house gate when the (spirit) soldiers arrived "so that it would be known that I was of the same teaching (*jiao*) and would not be killed or injured" (figure 15); the second talisman, which he was instructed to draw on cloth, was to be wrapped around his head; and the third one was a silver tally that he was told to wear on his waist as a form of identification. There also was a banner with the four characters *shuntian xingdao*. When the fighting started he was told to paste a "water-mouth charm" (*shuikoufu*) at the entrance to the village so that villagers would not be harmed during the fighting. Du Shiming had told Wu that by following these exorcist measures

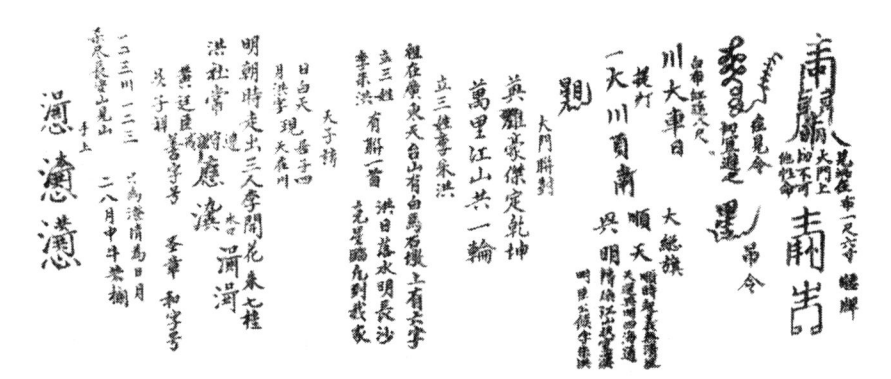

Figure 15. Talisman Used by Wu Wenchun (Source: First Historical Archives, Beijing)

he would be protected from the impending cataclysm. It was understood that those without such protective amulets would perish.[42]

While Li Lingkui and his followers were organizing in Jiangxi and Fujian, another branch of the Dachengjiao (also referred to as Wupanjiao) had spread into Guangdong (see figure 14). About three years before the Huizhou uprising erupted an itinerant peddler named Xu Qianjin, who was a native of Boluo, had transmitted the same, or quite similar, lay Buddhist teachings into his home area. He had learned the teachings from an acquaintance, You Lihe, who had a shop that sold herbal medicines in Xincheng county in Jiangxi. You Lihe told his friend that by being a vegetarian and reciting scriptures he could avoid calamities and also become rich (presumably by recruiting his own disciples). They afterward went to visit You Lihe's master, Wu Qingyuan, in Guixi county, Jiangxi. Significantly, Wu Qingyuan was the nephew and disciple of Wu Zixiang, who, as mentioned earlier, was one of the most important patriarchs of the Dachengjiao tradition.[43] Xu Qianjin took Wu Qingyuan as his teacher and bought from him a copy of a scripture (although not specifically mentioned, it was likely either *Enben jing* or *Dacheng dajie jing*) for one silver dollar. Later Xu made copies of the scriptures and distributed them among his followers. He personally recruited more than forty followers in Boluo, where he taught them to recite scriptures and practice vegetarianism to cure illnesses and to avoid an impending apocalypse.[44]

Although we do not know if Xu Qianjin became a Triad member, in 1800 and 1801, a number of his disciples, in particular Zhu Yajin, joined Triad cells in Boluo and other nearby counties, thereby bringing with them

Xu's sectarian teachings, including a belief in an impending apocalypse. Official reports described Zhu Yajin as a lay preacher who practiced vegetarianism and distributed "heretic teachings" among the Triads in Chen Lanjisi's camp.[45] Similar to the above mentioned Triad-Dachengjiao groups in Fujian and Jiangxi, those in Huizhou were also divided into two groups. In Boluo one group, which recited Buddhist scriptures and were vegetarians, wore white turbans; according to the Chen family genealogy, they "gathered at night to secretly practice sorcery." Other members wore red turbans and apparently did not follow a vegetarian diet.[46] According to the Daoguang edition of the Yongan gazetteer, "In the ninth lunar month [of 1802], Guan Yuelong and Lai Dongbao gathered their motley throng in Yongan. Guan Yuelong formed an Adding Brothers Society and his followers wore red headbands as their distinctive mark, while Lai Dongbao formed a White Lotus [group] and his followers wore white headbands as their distinctive mark."[47] Huizhou Tiandihui leaders also disseminated to their followers talismans (*fu*), wood seals (*muyin*), bamboo placards (*zhupai*), certificates (*zhao*), banners (*qi*), memorials (*biaowen*), verses (*ci*) and books (*shu*); they likewise "spread rumors" (*chuanbo yaoyan*) of an approaching cataclysm. As in the Jiangxi-Fujian network, in Huizhou Triad teachers and disciples also kept in touch with each other through letters as well as visitations, even over long distances.[48]

It was common practice in Triad, Buddhist, and Daoist traditions for followers to wear white or red clothing and turbans, as well as to display banners, talismans, and certificates written on white or red cloth. In some Triad initiation ceremonies neophytes wore white cloth bands around their head or waist, and in some cases wore white clothing. Because white customarily symbolized mourning in Chinese culture, initiations were meant to be rites of passage in which new members symbolically died and were subsequently reborn into the new society or sect; they became members of the Hong (Triad) family.[49] Hubert Seiwert also suggests that the use of the color white was a distinctive characteristic of Maitreya sects, and furthermore that "there was a connection between the symbol of white clothes and the expectation of a divine emperor or savior."[50] In other cases, at some Triad initiations new members wore red cloth bands around their heads or waist; this was also a common practice among Daoist priests, shamans, and spirit mediums, when performing exorcist rituals. Members of bandit and rebel groups also bound their heads with red cloth before the start of a battle. In Boluo before going on raids or into battle Triad leaders gave their followers red turbans on which were stamped protective charms, and they were also instructed to paste on the outer and inner doors of their homes red pieces of cloth with the characters *hong* and *ying* as amulets (see figure 13).[51]

Based on the above information, it is clear that the Triad groups involved in the Huizhou uprising belonged to a much larger, but somewhat loose, network of secret society and lay Buddhist organizations that stretched across Jiangxi, Fujian, and Guangdong. Significantly too, much of this area was mountainous and settled by marginalized Hakkas, who often took matters into their own hands by forming self-contained groups for mutual-aid and self-protection. As noted above, many of these groups also practiced vegetarianism, recited sutras, and produced amulets in order to protect their health and improve their livelihoods. Others, particularly the followers of Li Lingkui, Du Shiming, and Xu Qianjin, believed in an approaching apocalypse in which only believers, namely those followers who possessed their charms, flags, and certificates, would survive. As David Ownby explains, one the chief attractions for marginalized men to join the Tiandihui "appears to have been the promise of access to supernatural power through the manipulation of spiritual forces."[52]

Intersections of Triad and Sectarian Teachings

As the Great Vehicle Teaching spread among the Hakka communities across Jiangxi, Fujian, and Guangdong during the late eighteenth century, it absorbed other folk teachings, including those of the Triads. To appeal to common people teachers needed to use symbols that were familiar to them; hence they routinely drew from a repertoire of common beliefs and practices, such as those about demons, apocalypses, and supernatural saviors. Over time as these groups developed, they repeatedly split up and adopted new names. Hence, after Wu Zixiang's death in 1784, the Dachengjiao continued to evolve and its name also constantly changed; similarly, the Tiandihui also evolved and took many new names. Not only did names change but so did their teachings. Although the beliefs and rituals of the lay sects and Triads were not identical, nonetheless there were important intersections. The secret society and sectarian milieu was not closed. It was part of a subculture within the larger popular culture that included many other subcultures. Symbols, beliefs, and practices were constantly exchanged between various diverse groups.[53]

The Dachengjiao was an offshoot of the Luo Teaching, which first appeared in the late sixteenth century and thereafter spread across China. By the eighteenth century, the Luojiao had split into numerous discrete sects

CHAPTER 5

with similar but different teachings.[54] Nonetheless, they all traced their origins back to Patriarch Luo, whom many later followers treated as a superhuman savior. As the teaching evolved several affiliate groups, including the Dachengjiao, adopted millenarian beliefs based on the anticipation of a new era or *kalpa* (*jie*) to be ruled by Maitreya, the Buddha of the Future. As for the Dachengjiao, it too had divided into many groups that shared the same name but were often unrelated to one another. Suffice it to say that the vegetarian halls that Wu Zixiang started in Jiangxi under the name Five Vessels Teaching (Wupanjiao) in the late eighteenth century later evolved into the Way of Former Heaven (Xiantiandao) and the Way of Pervading Unity (Yiguandao). Both of these sects recognized Wu Zixiang as the tenth patriarch.[55]

Huang Dehui, the ninth patriarch of the Xiantiandao/Yiguandao tradition, was Wu Zixiang's teacher. Huang's teachings were based on a mixture of the Luo Teaching and other popular religious traditions circulating in south China during the eighteenth century. As was common for leaders of sects banned by the government, Huang was known by many different names, one of which was Huang Tingchen. In 1734, Huang Tingchen came to the attention of the authorities investigating "heretic sects" in the border area of Jiangxi and Zhejiang. Two years earlier Huang and his son established a vegetarian hall in Nanchang, Jiangxi's capital. His sect was known by several names, such as the Patriarch of the Three Emperors Teaching (Sanhuang shengzujiao), Complete Earnest Great Vehicle Teaching (Yuandun dachengjiao), Nine Lotus Hall (Jiuliantang), and White Sun Society (Baiyanghui), among others. Devotees refrained from eating meat, recited sutras, and practiced Daoist-style meditation. Like other sects Huang recorded the names of members in registers (*tangbu*), and he also produced and distributed scriptures (*jingshu*), covenants (*mengbu*), certificates (*zha*), banners (*qi*), and dragon seals (*longyin*) on which were written titles of kings and marshals. According to the depositions of arrested members, they said their master (*zhu*) was someone surnamed Zhu (a reference to the Ming dynasty), who had amassed an army of some fifty thousand (spirit) soldiers at a place called Jade Mountain. Only those followers who posted the teaching's certificates (or charms) on their houses would be spared the army's wrath. Huang Tingchen proclaimed himself the Heavenly Father (*Tian laoye*) and his son claimed to be the incarnation of Maitreya. Fearing disturbances officials quickly rounded up suspected sect members before they had a chance to act.[56]

Among the scriptures that Huang Dehui/Huang Tingchen disseminated among followers were one or more versions of the *Nine Lotus Scripture*

(*Jiulian jing*), which included vivid mythological and eschatological narratives. Buddhas and deities, it explained, will descend to earth to rescue mankind from an apocalypse. Those who follow the doctrine will be saved from the destruction that attends the end of each cosmic era or *kalpa*. Everyone else will perish. The last change will be marked by the appearance of Maitreya, and the community of the elect will then join the myriads of buddhas in Cloud City. Wu Zixiang also distributed to his disciples some version of the *Jiulian jing*, as well as two works that he authored, the *Dacheng dajie jing* and *Enben jing*. In fact, the latter two scriptures derived from the *Jiulian jing*, a work that became the basic text for many subsequent sects, including the Way of Former Heaven and the Way of Pervading Unity. The *Jiulian jing* and these other scriptures were widely accepted because they represented literary condensations of ideas and beliefs common in popular lore.[57]

As noted earlier, as Wu Zixiang's sectarian network evolved and changed over the late eighteenth and early nineteenth centuries, several subsequent leaders became actively involved in Tiandihui cells. The result was an interesting (and somewhat confusing) mix of sectarian, Triad, and popular messianic symbols and beliefs. Li Lingkui, who transmitted the teachings espoused in the *Enben jing*, claimed to be a reincarnated emperor of the Tang dynasty and foretold an impending catastrophe. His disciple Liao Ganzhou not only learned about the apocalypse from his master but also from another teacher named Wang Tianzu, who claimed to be a manifestation of Maitreya. Wang Tianzu was a disciple of He Rui who had studied with Wu Zixiang. Both Li Lingkui and Liao Ganzhou also were Triad members.[58]

The best documented case in this network is that of Du Shiming, who was a disciple of both Wu Zixiang and Li Lingkui (see figure 14). In fact, Du Shiming and his followers venerated the two patriarchs Huang Tingchen and Wu Zixiang, whom followers treated as superhuman saviors, as well as Elder Brother Wan (that is, Wan Tixi), a key founder of the Tiandihui, and other protective deities (see figure 15). Du disseminated the *Enben jing* among his followers and wrote contracts (*hetong*) on white silk. He also produced certificates/amulets, such as the one depicted in figure 15, and distributed them among his followers for both identification and protection. Members were taught Triad lore, slogans, secret code words, and hand signals, as well as about the saviors Li Kaihua, Zhu Qigui, and Zhu Hongzhu. Du claimed that Zhu Hongzhu awaited in the secluded "Sealed-Tight Mountain" (Fengjinshan) in a mystical "lumber mill" (*muchang*), which served as a safe haven likely representing the City of Willows. He was supported, according to

CHAPTER 5

Du Shiming, by Triads in Jiangxi, Fujian, Guangdong, and Shandong, who were preparing for the great enterprise that would begin on the nineteenth day of the second lunar month in the following year (likely 1806). He also gave each member the new family name Hong (symbolizing Triad membership) and the shared generational name or "Buddha name" (*foming*), Jin (gold), followed by the last character in the original name; thus Du Shiming became Hong Jinming. Like his teacher Li Lingkui, Du Shiming divided his followers into vegetarians and meat-eaters, and espoused millenarian ideas of an approaching apocalypse in which only his followers would be saved. Clearly Du's group embraced a mix of sectarian and Triad teachings, lore, and practices.[59]

Although the Huizhou Triads were not directly connected to the Li Lingkui–Du Shiming network, nonetheless, because they had roots that can be traced back to Wu Zixiang both groups shared many similar beliefs and rituals. Unfortunately, the information on Xu Qianjin and his disciple Zhu Yajin, and on what they proselytized in Boluo, is fragmentary and limited. What we do know is that between them they had more than a hundred followers who belonged to Chen Lanjisi's Tiandihui. There is evidence too that their sect spread to other Triad camps in Yongan, Longmen, Zengcheng, and Dongguan. According to the confession of one of their followers named Huang Dawan, their teachings were circulated among the Triads in Goat Dung Mountain by several lay preachers and Buddhist monks who practiced vegetarianism, chanted sutras, and predicted the world's end. They made wood seals and distributed unnamed scriptures, as well as written covenants, certificates, and prognostications. Leaders took such titles as kings and marshals. During the battles with imperial troops and local militia, however, devotees systematically burned their scriptures and other sect documents.[60] Only the following ominous incantation (*gezhou*) remains extant (figure 16):

> In the *gengshen* year [1800] [demon] soldiers will arrive and all under Heaven, both men and women, will be in chaos.
>
> In the *xinyou* [year 1801] a thousand buddhas from the five directions will arise, awaiting the eighteen [arhats] to create Heaven on earth.
>
> In the *renxu* [year 1802] husbands and wives will have difficulties east and west, and the wicked multitudes [non-believers] will meet with the ten calamities.

In the *guihai* year [1803] peace and tranquility will return, and [followers] will be rewarded with titles as gods and buddhas.

In the *yichou* [year 1805] those who follow the [sect's] teachings and five Buddhist precepts will be reunited and become complete.[61]

This incantation, written and distributed by Xu Qianjin in 1799, presented a millenarian message of a looming catastrophe in the following year; it also gave hope to his followers that they would survive the disaster and afterward live among the multitude of gods and buddhas in paradise. Xu taught his adherents to prepare for the apocalypse by chanting this incantation each day while facing the heavens. The incantation, which presaged the Triad uprising that began in earnest in 1802, anticipated cosmic calamities before peace and tranquility would be restored in 1803. The eighteen arhats, who in the popular mindset were likened to miracle workers, were the guardians of the Buddhist faith who awaited on earth for the appearance of Maitreya, who would save the faithful elect. Although this incantation is somewhat obscure and open to several layers of meaning, nevertheless it fits within the sectarian tradition espoused by Huang Dehui, Wu Zixiang, and subsequent teachers, as well as with the eschatological teachings in the *Nine Lotus Scripture*.

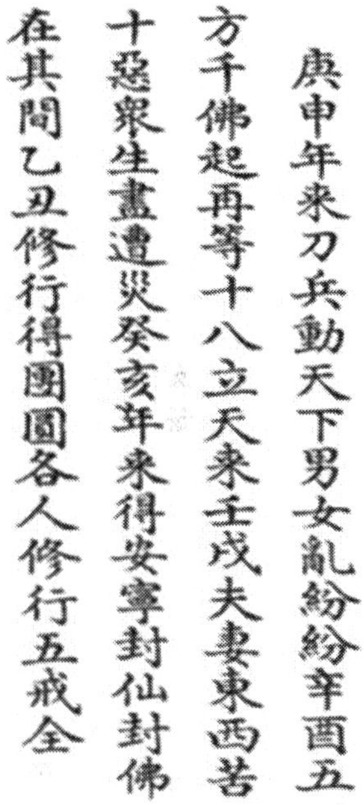
庚申年来刀兵動天下男女亂紛紛辛酉五
方千佛起再等十八立天来壬戌夫妻東西苦
十惡衆生盡遭災癸亥年来得安寧封仙封佛
在其間乙丑修行得團圓各人修行五戒全

Figure 16. Xu Qianjin's Incantation, 1799 (Source: First Historical Archives, Beijing)

There were, of course, other possible influences on Xu Qianjin, such as the teachings of two popular scriptures, the *Dragon Flower Scripture* (*Longhua jing*) and the *Scripture of the Five Lords* (*Wugong jing*). The former scripture, which derived from the *Jiulian jing*, depicted cataclysmic floods, famines, and plagues lasting many years, in which only upright believers would survive without harm. Central to its teaching was the idea that salvation could only be obtained through the divine intervention of a savior. Followers of this teaching, under the name Dachengjiao, led an uprising in 1622, and although quickly crushed, the revolt marked the start of increasingly clandestine activities for the Dachengjiao and its

CHAPTER 5

affiliates. The latter text also predicted terrible catastrophes and destruction of the known world, in which only individuals possessing the scripture and amulets of the Five Lords would be saved. The *Wugong jing* is also particularly relevant because it specifically mentions "ten calamities" attending the apocalypse and the arrival of saviors leading divine armies to save believers. Maitreya also plays a key role as a savior. The elect would then enter a state of "great peace" (*taiping*) in an ideal earthly paradise. The scripture was associated with a number of millenarian movements and revolts in the Ming and Qing periods. According to Barend ter Haar, this scripture had a tremendous impact on the development of the demonological messianic tradition among the Triads, and Li Lingkui's group in particular. Both the *Longhua jing* and *Wugong jing* were widespread popular texts that did not belong to any one particular teaching.[62]

Although we cannot draw a direct connection with Xu Qianjin's prognostication, Chen Lanjisi's group also believed in a looming disaster of cosmic proportions. In Xu's case the saviors were buddhas and arhats (as well as the unnamed Maitreya), whereas in Chen's case they were Li Taohong, Zhu Hongying, and other demonological saviors (discussed in the previous chapter). For example, on the Triad banner (figure 13) was the following seven-character couplet:

Unite the ten thousand [Triads] in contract; Li Taohong follows [the way of] Heaven.
Floods will overflow their natural channels and inundate all under Heaven.[63]

The second line in this couplet comes directly from the ancient *Book of Mencius* in which the author described a cataclysmic flood that covered the whole earth during the time of the legendary Emperor Yao. Li Taohong, in the first line, was a mythical founder of the Tiandihui and a savior, who righteously follows the way of Heaven to save the Triads (who have united with him by contract) from the deluge, a great flood that will destroy mankind.[64] According to Kristofer Schipper, in vernacular Daoism seven-character verses were "poetic spells," used to summon the gods who must obey the master who has a covenant or contract with those gods.[65] While there is no explicit reference to the destruction of the Qing dynasty, it is implied that the imperfect world under Manchu rule will be replaced by a perfect new world.

The inspiration for the Huizhou Triads derived not only from Tiandihui lore and Dachengjiao teachings, but more importantly from south China's shared oral culture in general. Popular beliefs in calamities and otherworldly saviors were part of popular lore and therefore something easily understood by most individuals who joined the Triads and lay Buddhist sects. Because such ideas and symbols were widely diffused throughout Chinese culture there was no need for people to be highly educated to understand them. The mention of saviors like Li Kaihua and Zhu Hongzhu were not necessarily derived from either the Triad or sectarian traditions, but rather from pervasive customary beliefs emanating from the demonological messianic tradition. Beliefs in Maitreya as a demon-slaying savior also were widespread not only among lay Buddhists groups but also generally among the wider population. In fact, in the Qing period Maitreya frequently appeared together with other saviors, such as Li Kaihua, a clear indication that the original Buddhist ideas had become interwoven with popular religious motifs.

Such beliefs belonged to the wider popular religious milieu, not necessarily to any particular teaching or tradition. While the symbols remained the same, individuals could interpret them in different ways. Apocalyptic fears about disasters, famines, floods, and wars, which closely corresponded to the actual experiences of common people, were etched in their collective memory. Real calamities often had apocalyptic dimensions (as we noted in chapter 2 about the disasters during the Ming–Qing transition). Anxieties about impending catastrophes were not farfetched prophecies, but had a basis in the actual conditions of people's lives. For many people, therefore, teachings about apocalyptic disasters were not absurd. Such beliefs were part of the oral culture that had been handed down generation by generation since antiquity.[66]

Conclusion

The Triad and Dachengjiao traditions in the tri-province area of Guangdong, Jiangxi, and Fujian merged and closely interconnected with each other, not only through a common membership of leaders and followers but also through shared customs, rituals, and beliefs. This mountainous borderland was linked together by cultural, social, and economic ties that traversed provincial boundaries and Skinnerian macroregions.[67] A highly mobile population of itinerant laborers, peddlers, coolies, actors, healers, barbers, monks, geomancers, and martial artists—the mainstay of sect and secret society teachers and members discussed in this chapter—routinely circulated across this vast area via rivers and mountain paths. This was a marginal and ethnically mixed contact zone of endemic feuding and weak state control, an area

CHAPTER 5

where Hakkas were a major component of the population. On the one hand, Triad and lay Buddhist groups formed along the nodes of communication and trade routes, in market towns where rivers and roads intersected. One such place was Wan'an on the Gan River, a necessary stopover for travelers between Jiangxi and Guangdong; in the early nineteenth century the Tiandihui and lay Buddhist groups were active there.[68] On the other hand, as the late Ming scholar Xiong Renlin explained, "Various mountain ranges of northern Guangdong, southeastern Hunan, southwest Fujian, Jiangxi, and south Zhejiang were connected, providing tracks for the dye-growing [indigo] migrants of Tingzhou. Such paths . . . were hidden from the eyes of the state."[69] These were the mountain paths used by smugglers, bandits, and dissidents, particularly those individuals and groups that wanted to remain hidden from officials. They were in large part Hakkas.

A large number of the individuals mentioned in this chapter, in fact, regularly trekked back and forth between Jiangxi, Fujian, and Guangdong. We have noted how Li Lingkui, Liao Ganzhou, and Du Shiming, as well as their followers, frequently traveled between Fujian and Jiangxi where they disseminated Triad and lay Buddhist teachings and preached about sword-bearing demons and impending cosmic catastrophes. In 1801 and 1802 officials reported to the throne that Fujianese sojourners, such as Wu Tao and Cai Buyun, had helped to disseminate Triad teachings from their home province of Fujian to neighboring Jiangxi and Guangdong.[70] Chen Lanjisi's family had originated in Taihe county in Jiangxi, moved to Xingning county in the fourteenth century, and then resettled in several places in Huizhou prefecture in Guangdong in the late Ming and early Qing; until today they still maintain contacts with relatives in Jiangxi and elsewhere.[71] Sect and secret society members regularly communicated with one another through visitations and letters, often over long distances across the three provinces. There was in fact a discernable pattern here, involving the never-ending flow of sojourners who earned their livings in various places and through multiple occupations. For itinerant peddlers, monks, barbers, and actors—many of whom were Hakkas—the distribution and selling of scriptures, charms, secret society handbooks, hand signals, and secret codes was an important supplement to their other incomes and in some cases their main source of livelihood.

It is clear too that the Triad and Dachengjiao traditions derived from common cultural and religious traditions found in local society. The repeated and widespread appearance of particular rituals and folk beliefs over a long period of time and over an extended area of south China was not the result of coincidence but rather of a shared well-known heritage. For example, charismatic teachers such as Wang Liangchen, Wang Tianzu, Li Lingkui, Du Shiming, Xu Qianjin, and Chen Lanjisi, circulated similar apocalyptic stories to audiences that readily accepted such forebodings. Marginalization and hardships of everyday life conditioned people's perceptions and beliefs about a cosmos in which the natural and supernatural realms were thoroughly entwined. Because folk beliefs that natural and man-made calamities could be averted by the aid of imperial descendants, saviors were often said to be royal figures, and therefore the surnames Li of the Tang dynasty and Zhu of the Ming dynasty were popular. Besides the frequent usage of names like Li Kaihua and Zhu Hongzhu in numerous messianic movements, we also find on the talisman of Wu Wenchun (figure 15) and banner of Chen Lanjisi (figure 13) the three surnames Li, Zhu, and Hong, whose names were invoked as talismanic protection, as well as to foster fraternity and common identity among Triad followers.[72]

For the Hakkas in Huizhou the Triads and their affiliations with sectarianism helped construct and define Hakka ethnic identity. According to Sow-Theng Leong, Hakka ethnicity developed as "a particularistic ethos" that first appeared in the early nineteenth century when Hakkas began to think of themselves as a distinct ethnic group. I would argue further that Hakka ethnic identity (at least in the Huizhou area) was a sociocultural process that began during and was, at least in part, an outcome of confrontations with rival Punti groups during the Tiandihui uprising in 1802. As a socially marginalized group Hakkas formed Triad and lay Buddhist associations as ways to create a new identity to offset the negative identity that they had been ascribed by dominant society.[73] These organizations helped build solidarity by providing an organizational framework that went beyond kinship and lineage, and by constructing networks of mutual obligations among the Hakka communities. Triad identities, in fact, overlapped with Hakka identities, and furthermore acted as visible markers that distinguished them from the Punti. For Hakkas the Tiandihui became a means of agency and empowerment, as well as an important vehicle for articulating Hakka identity and ethnicity.[74]

Finally, what should we make of the Triad uprising in Huizhou in 1802? On the most basic level it represented the culmination of long-standing antagonisms and rivalries between the Hakka and Punti. In this sense it was an ethnic conflict in which animosity and vengeance were primary motives. On another level, the Qing state viewed the uprising as a politically motivated attempt to topple the dynasty. In the eyes of the government, organizations such as the Triad and Dachengjiao were seditious in nature as evidenced by their production of slogans, charms, scriptures, and books, which to officials appeared unorthodox and dangerous. To simply belong to such organizations was a serious criminal offense. The Qing state treated the confrontation with secret societies and sects as a conflict of belief systems and as a contest for power.[75]

But I believe there is more to the story. On a higher level, the eschatological message preached by sect members, and perpetuated by the Tiandihui as well, went beyond the overturning of the dynasty. They called for a profound cosmic change. The aim was to usher in a new age of great peace, a new form of existence in which Hakkas would play a dominant role. As Hubert Seiwert has explained, the new ideal world was not necessarily a political utopia but a religious eschatology. It represented the end of the current world as we know it and the formation of a new transcendental world.[76] In the words of the Boluo sectarian teacher Xu Qianjin, Heaven would appear on earth and buddhas would descend to save the true believers who would thereafter live in complete tranquility and peace. This would be nothing less than a Hakka paradise.

Interlude 2

What Ever Happened to Broken Shoes Chen the Fourth?

Qing soldiers captured Chen Lanjisi or Broken Shoes Chen the Fourth on Friday, October 15, 1802, in the northern foothills of Luofushan, just a few months after the start of the Hakka uprising in Huizhou. The next day, after giving his confession, he and eight family members were summarily executed without a formal trial in front of the gathered officials and soldiers. As leader of the rebellion in Boluo county, Broken Shoes suffered the harshest form of capital punishment under Qing law—death-by-slicing (*lingchi*). In the face of certain death, he remained calm and defiant, and as one official noted, he "stood erect and bold, and betrayed not a bit of fear."[1] His confession, obtained under torture, read in part:

> *I am a Boluo native and this year am twenty-six years old. My stepgrandmother is surnamed Zhong, my father is Chen Shizhuang, and my mother is surnamed Liao. My elder brother is Chen Zhixi and my younger brother is Chen Yaqi. My wife is surnamed Peng and I have one son and one daughter. In the seventh lunar month of the sixth year of the Jiaqing reign [1801], I decided to gather people to form a sworn brotherhood and within two years [?] had more than 10,000 recruits. Because I had such a massive following, this year [1802] in the seventh lunar month I decided to rebel. I made several tens of large and small five-colored banners on which I wrote the characters "follow Heaven to carry out the way," prepared knives and other weapons, and gave followers red turbans to wear around their heads. Because I believed it would be difficult for soldiers*

Interlude 2

to attack, I made my headquarters at Luoxiying, which is surrounded on four sides by mountains and accessible only through a narrow pass. A month later I made a sacrifice to our banners. My father donned a yellow robe and took the title Venerable Great King and I sat beside him taking the title Great King. . . . Afterward I led my followers down the mountain to loot and burn several tens of [Punti] towns and villages. . . . On the fifth day of the ninth lunar month [October 1] soldiers attacked Luoxiying. When our defenses faltered we fled. Hu Ermei and I got away on horses . . . to Luofushan. By then several of my family members had been captured. On the nineteenth [October 15] I was captured at Zhoushan, on the border of Boluo and Zengcheng counties.[2]

Under Qing law his family members, even if they had not actively participated in the uprising, were held culpable. The family members who were executed with Broken Shoes included his father, mother, step-grandmother, elder brother, wife, and three paternal cousins—Chen Zhiyuan, Chen Yagui,

Map 6. Geographic Scope of Cheng Lanjisi's Adventures (Source: Created by author)

and Chen Yawu. Soldiers had killed the younger brother, Chen Yaqi, during the exodus from Luoxiying. A few weeks later soldiers captured Lanjisi's son and daughter who also were promptly executed on the spot.[3] Over the next few weeks imperial forces and local militias quickly crushed the Hakka-Triad rebellion in Boluo.

But the situation was not so simple. These and other official reports are problematic. They not only suffer from internal inconsistencies, but also are contradicted by Chen family records and information I collected from interviews with family members who stated that Broken Shoes had not been captured and executed in 1802. Rather, he had escaped and ended up several years later in the mountains of Lianzhou, a remote area in northwestern Guangdong bordering Hunan and Guangxi, where he changed his name, established a new Chen lineage, continued to organize Triad cells, and then went on in his seventies to help lead the Red Turban Rebellion in the 1850s–1860s.

Broken Shoes is a relatively unknown historical figure and most of what we are told about him cannot be verified. Who was he? Where did he live? When was he born and when and how did he die? This interlude looks at the various official and family claims about Broken Shoes and attempts to unravel his hidden history. Map 6 depicts the geographic scope of Chen Lanjisi's real and purported activities and adventures across Guangdong, Guangxi, and Hunan.

From Riches to Rags—The Chens of Boluo

We must begin our discussion with Chen Lanjisi's unusual name. Why was he called "Broken Shoes Chen the Fourth"? Does his name give us any insights into his personality and social status? In the Chen family's 1833 genealogy his given name is Xisi, which is also a curious name with a literal meaning of "Straw Mat the Fourth." He was the fourth son of Chen Shizhuang, and his mother was not Liao, as given in his confession, but rather his father's second wife or concubine, whose surname was Zhan. He had three older brothers, all born of Madam Liao, and a younger brother, who like himself, was born of Madam Zhan. In the genealogy, his younger brother's name was Xiwu, "Straw Mat the Fifth," not Chen Yaqi, as stated in the confession, a name implying that he was the seventh son (but Chen Shizhuang only had five sons). It is more likely that Yaqi was a cousin. "Broken Shoes" was a nickname, one shared with his younger brother—they were known as Broken Shoes the Fourth (Lanjisi) and Broken Shoes the Fifth (Lanjiwu) by everyone in their community. The character that I translate as "shoes" is *ji*, which in fact was in the past a common peasant footwear made of wood or at least wooden soles with cloth or straw coverings (similar to the Japanese *geta*). Why "broken shoes"? In interviews with descendants in Boluo in 2002 and in Lianzhou in 2015, family members told me that he simply liked to wear a pair of torn and broken shoes. Several family elders explained further that he was a thrifty person who empathized closely with poor peasants like himself, and also that his family's past affluence was in a state of decline, so he could not afford new shoes.[4]

This last point needs further explanation. Was Broken Shoes and his family in a state of decline in 1802, at the start of the uprising? According to Chen Shizhuang's confession he had a purchased title as Commissary of the Seal in the Provincial Judge's Office (*anchasi zhaomo*) and his first son, Chen Zhixi, had a Collegian of the Imperial Academy (*jiansheng*) degree, which too would have been purchased.[5] The father also had two wives (or a wife and a concubine).[6] "Clearly Broken Shoes' family was well-off," Governor-General Jueluo Jiqing remarked, adding that "he didn't foment rebellion because the family was indigent and hungry."[7] In fact, the Chens steadily grew in numbers and prospered after moving to Boluo in 1573. By the early Qing some family members owned mountain lands, had purchased concubines and scholarly degrees, and even held minor positions in the local government. For example, Broken Shoes' great-grandfather, Chen Zhongru, who was born in 1671, became a prefectural secretary (*bapin jingli*), owned hundreds of hectares of farmland, and had a wife and concubine. He was said to be honest, upright, and loyal, a man who was filial toward his parents and respectful of his siblings. As the genealogy put it, by 1784, the year that Chen Jiaxun had revised the genealogy, the lineage was large and prosperous (*zuren fanyan fugui*).[8]

After Chen Jiaxun died in 1788 at age sixty-four, however, the lineage plummeted. This decline was as much moral as it was economic. As the 1833 genealogy explained:

> *Family members became licentious and dissolute. Elder brothers disregarded younger brothers, and younger brothers disrespected older brothers. Younger members violated the [lineage] rules and overstepped their bounds. During the day they went into the mountains to fornicate, and at night they gathered in gangs to gamble. There were those who became*

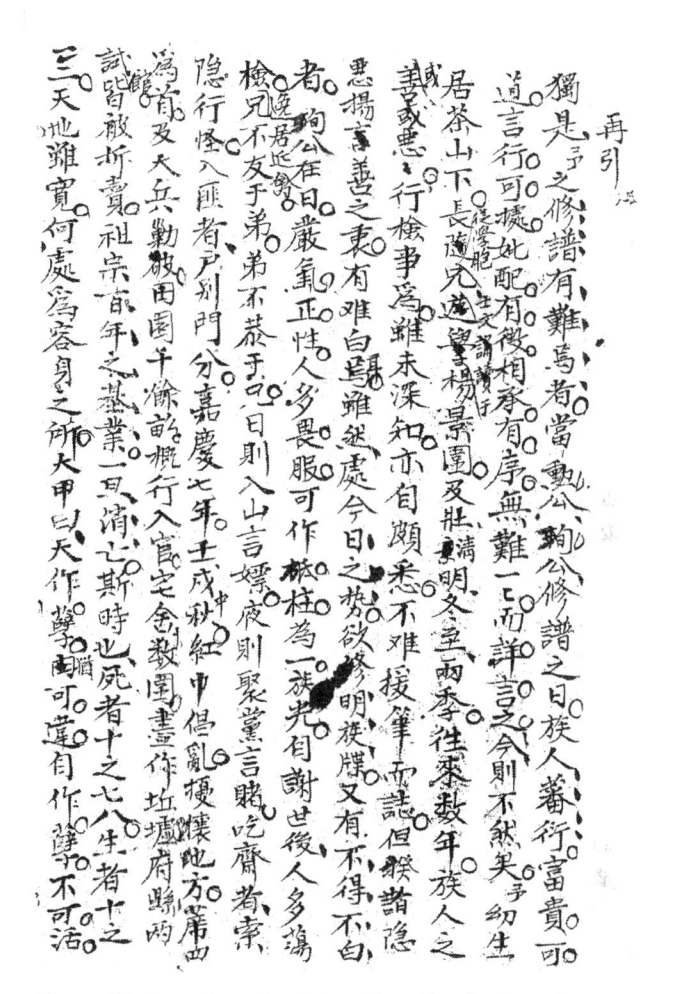

Figure 17. Page from the Boluo Chen Family Genealogy, 1833 (Source: Author's copy)

vegetarians and practiced sorcery. Others became bandits and were divided into many cliques.[9]

Broken Shoes grew up during a time of increased tensions not only within his lineage but also with neighboring Punti villages. Being the son of the second wife or, more likely, a concubine, his position and status within the family would have been low and insecure. One of the family elders in Yangjingkeng mentioned to me an adage that he said related to Broken Shoes' situation: "The straw mat is rich and the wooden shoes are thick" (*xifeng jihou*), said of someone who will have a rich inheritance. But since his shoes were broken, the elder explained, Lanjisi could not inherit his father's property or become rich.[10]

No matter if Broken Shoes was rich or poor, one thing that is certain is that his rebellion brought ruin to the family and lineage. According to the 1833 genealogy (figure 17), "A hundred years of hard work by our ancestors was all destroyed in a single day." Nearly 80 percent of the family had been killed during the fighting, and with defeat the government also had confiscated most of their lands and property. Soldiers and Punti militiamen also desecrated the Chen family's ancestral graves in Yangjingkeng, as a gesture of contempt that aimed to wreck the family's posterity. Lanjisi's family never fully recovered from the catastrophe and the surviving family elders at the time put the blame squarely on Broken Shoes.[11]

From Broken Shoes to Southern Efflorescent King— The Chens of Lianzhou

What about the official reports that Broken Shoes was captured and executed? As mentioned above, family members in both Boluo and Lianzhou insist that he was not captured and executed, but that he had escaped and eventually ended up living in the foothills of the Yao mountains in faraway Lianzhou. What they told me was that actually his younger brother, Chen Lanjiwu (or Chen Xiwu), was executed in his place. This hypothesis, however, is challenged by a government report stating that Chen Lanjiwu was arrested and executed in Boluo on February 4, 1803.[12] Of course, the official reports could be completely wrong. Someone claiming to be Lanjisi and later Lanjiwu could have been the persons executed. But then why would anyone want to claim to be a wanted felon and face certain death?

In south China there was a common tradition of "substitution" called *dingxiong*, whereby an individual volunteered to take the blame and suffer punishment for another person's crime. Although the practice was illegal, it was not unusual. According to longtime China-hand William Hunter, "It is a well-known and remarkable fact, that substitutes may often be found for a very small sum to undergo the last penalty [death]. Men appear at the prison and offer themselves, instigated by some such motive as extreme poverty of aged parents, to whom the money agreed upon shall be paid after the execution."[13] During armed feuds between rival lineages or ethnic groups, such as Hakka and Punti, adolescent boys would be purchased as "adopted sons" and then ordered to fight or become substitutes for family members who were wanted for capital crimes.[14] Another eyewitness, John Scarth, wrote that during the Red Turban Revolt (see below), "a man gave himself up as a [rebel] chief when he was perfectly innocent, choosing to represent that character, as the reward was considerable."[15] The practice was so common in Guangdong that a literatus named Chen Weiyan wrote this ditty concerning people in neighboring Chaozhou, an area sharing similar customs as Boluo:

> Chaozhou people are obstinate;
> They'd rather treat their lives as broken shoes [worthless],
> And willingly throw their lives away for others,
> Because the money they get will gratify their families.

Elaborating on why people willingly became substitutes to undergo capital punishment, Chen Weiyan said it was not only for the money but also because their families and villages would respect and venerate them as martyrs and heroes.[16] Therefore, it would not be unreasonable to accept Broken Shoes' family's claim that a substitute, perhaps his younger brother, was executed in his stead.

Assuming this story true, Broken Shoes spent the next ten years on the run. He apparently changed his name several times as he moved from one place to the next, following well-traveled routes along the East and West Rivers into eastern Guangxi and less-traveled mountain paths across northern Guangxi and Guangdong. He would have depended on known Hakka networks in his travels, staying with distant cousins and other acquaintances. Finally, in 1812 (some sources say 1815) he settled down with another Boluo Hakka and his sworn brother, Qiu Yajiang, in Lianzhou in Tiandeng village. Various members of the Qiu family had previously moved into this area from Huizhou in the late Qianlong and early Jiaqing reigns, about the same time that the Hakka-Punti disturbances were intensifying in Boluo.[17] By then Broken Shoes had taken the name Chen Jinjiang; he also had a new wife whose surname was Ye, and together they had four sons. For the next forty or so years the Chens lived quietly as farmers in the secluded foothills of the Yao mountains. During that time, nearby on the Lian River in Longtan market, Chen Jinjiang and Qiu Yajiang opened a general store and operated a press that made lamp and cooking oils from the teas, peanuts, and hemp grown by Hakka farmers.[18]

Interlude 2

During those quiet years in Tiandeng village, his descendants told me that Chen Jinjiang continued to organize Triad cells among the Hakkas. His store became the headquarters for clandestine secret society gatherings. By the early nineteenth century Hakkas were the dominant group in this area, having pushed the original Yao inhabitants further into the surrounding mountains, resulting in great animosity and resentment between the two groups lasting even to today. Although members of the Chen and Qiu families did not specifically mention any involvement in the great Yao uprising in Lianzhou in 1832 (discussed in the next chapter), they told me about frequent incidents of crop and cattle thefts and armed clashes around their homesteads. In response the Hakka families built stone stockades behind their villages for self-defense against Yao attacks. The Chens and Qius may have also met Taiping leaders Hong Xiuquan and Feng Yunshan in 1844, when they were proselytizing among fellow Hakkas in Yingde, Yangshan, and Lianzhou. After 1850 both Triad cells and Taiping sympathizers were active in the mountains bordering Guangxi, Guangdong, and Hunan.[19]

When the Red Turban Rebellion erupted in 1854 much of Guangdong was already in a state of turmoil. Banditry, piracy, secret societies, and armed feuds had engulfed most of the province. If we are to believe family records, Chen Jinjiang, who would have been in his seventies, led a ragtag army of Triads to join the uprisings in western Guangdong with the avowed purpose of overthrowing the Qing dynasty.[20] Sometimes using the name Chen Jingang and at other times Chen Jinjiang, he led attacks on Sanshui and Qingyuan counties that summer, and in 1855, after being defeated by Qing armies and local militias, he took his forces up the North River to Chenzhou in Hunan, and for the next two years they continued to campaign across Yangshan and Lianzhou in Guangdong. By that time Chen reportedly had an army exceeding 10,000 men. In 1857 his army occupied large portions of Yingde, Yangshan, and Huaiji, where he established the Great Hong [Triad] Kingdom (Taihongguo) and took the title Southern Efflorescent King (Nanxing wang). Four years later he moved his headquarters to Xinyi county and for the next two years his army held roughly forty towns and several counties along the Guangdong-Guangxi border (see map 6). In 1863, with defeat imminent, some sources say he was assassinated in Xinyi by his lieutenant Zheng Jin, while his descendants assert that he secretly escaped back home to Tiandeng, where he again took a new name, Chen Xingcai. Next year he died at age eighty-three and was buried by the Lian River near his old

Figure 18. Grave of the Southern Efflorescent King with his Descendant and the Author, 2015 (Source: Photo by Lanshin Chang)

store in Longtan. Today his simple grave is marked with the name Southern Efflorescent King (figure 18).[21]

Both the names Chen Jinjiang and Chen Jingang appear in historical sources, but were they the same person? In Sanshui a different story is told. Chen Jingang was born in 1820 in Fanhu, a small market town in that county, where at a young age he became a cooper by trade. In 1854 he joined the Red Turban movement and led a Triad uprising among fellow artisans and peasants in Sanshui under the slogan "destroy the Qing and restore the Ming." They overran Sanshui and Qingyuan, and later occupied Huaiji and Xinyi, where he established his kingdom. He was assassinated in 1863.[22] In this version, Chen Jinjiang and Chen Jingang are two completely different people.

What is missing from both versions of events, however, is any mention of the great Hakka-Punti War that was blazing across western Guangdong during these same years of turmoil. Amid the Taiping and Red Turban Rebellions, ethnic tensions were flaring out of control. Several scholars have pointed out that ethnic strife between Hakka and Punti was a major cause of the

Red Turban disturbances that began in the western Canton delta (Heshan, Xinhui, Kaiping, Enping, Gaoyao, Xinxing, and Xinning) and then spread like wildfires across most of northwestern Guangdong (Qingyuan, Yingde, Yangshan, Lianzhou, and Huaiji) and eastern Guangxi (Rongxian, Cenxi, Tengxian, Pingnan, Zhaoping, Pingle, and Hexian) between 1854 and 1867 (see map 6). Each side took advantage of the disorder to seek revenge against their long-standing rivals and to enhance their own positions. The Hakkas built blockhouses in their villages and stockades in the mountains and raised armies divided into red and white banner forces (as in Huizhou) that numbered in the thousands. In fact, as much actual fighting occurred between Hakka and Punti paramilitary forces as between rebels and Qing soldiers. Once the Red Turban movement disintegrated in 1856, ethnic violence actually accelerated. Punti militias, often with the support of local authorities, attacked and burned down thousands of Hakka villages and killed several tens of thousands of people. Countless numbers of Hakkas fled their homes to become "wandering bandits" who set up "little republics" in the mountains, while thousands who had been taken prisoner were sold and shipped off to Southeast Asia, the West Indies, and South America as coolies. The so-called Hakka-Punti War became the largest ethnic feud in Chinese history.[23] This was the reality of life for men like Chen Jinjiang and Chen Jingang.

FROM THE FAMILY'S ARCH-CRIMINAL TO THE PEOPLE'S HERO

History is never static. In 1833, some thirty years after the failed rebellion in Huizhou, Chen Shidun, the compiler of the updated genealogy, condemned Broken Shoes as an arch-criminal, the one person most responsible for the downfall of his family. Some 160 years later another compiler of the genealogy, Chen Fangqi in Lianzhou, lauded Broken Shoes or Chen Xingcai, as he was later known, as a people's hero. In Tiandeng village his purported former home has been turned into a small memorial hall and museum, dedicated in 2010. Among the memorabilia are newspaper clippings, photos of his descendants, and an imposing portrait of a young Southern Efflorescent King brandishing a sword astride a galloping white horse (figure 19).

Beginning in the 1990s, Chen Fangqi and a few other family members began a quest to find their lost roots, and in the process they historicized the family's past by making Broken Shoes into a model hero consistent with PRC historiography. He became a courageous, incorruptible peasant leader who consistently fought on the side of the people against tyrannical officials and rapacious landlords. He was a heroic freedom fighter who espoused "self-sacrifice for the collective good" and led a "righteous rebellion" against the oppressive alien Qing dynasty. I was told by more than one descendant that in 1802 Broken Shoes' "righteous army" (*yijun*) fought under the slogan "rob the rich to help the poor." Later in the 1850s Chen allied with the Taiping armies in campaigns in southern Hunan and northern Guangdong, and after establishing the Great Hong Kingdom in 1857, he levied taxes on rich landowners (what he called "Triad rents" [*hongzu*]), lowered taxes on peasants, promoted trade, and opened the granaries to feed the poor, thereby receiving strong support from the masses.[24] Although these family claims are not substantiated in any historical sources, they have occasionally appeared in local newspapers and online as historical truths.[25]

Figure 19. A Modern Representation of the Southern Efflorescent King (Source: Photo by author)

Broken Shoes has remained little more than a local hero, virtually unknown outside family members and their Hakka neighbors in Boluo and Lianzhou. Most people, in fact, have never heard of him. Those people in Lianzhou who do know anything about him know him as the Southern Efflorescent King and not as Broken Shoes. Yet the Chen family's portrayal of him as a hero resonates larger ideological themes in post-Liberation Chinese historiography, which underscore the roles of peasant rebellions and class struggle as the prime movers of history. Since 1949 the subject of "righteous peasant uprisings" (*nongmin qiyi*) have been glorified in thousands of scholarly books and articles and popular histories, novels, movies, and television dramas. According to James Harrison, one of the greatest successes of the PRC has been the "popularization of history" according to communist principles. In Communist China heroes are produced from the deeds of history as well as from the needs of the people. Popular movements and peasant rebellions have had to be rewritten from the perspective of the masses.[26] The Chens of Lianzhou have been the prime movers in eulogizing Chen Lanjisi/Chen Xingcai as a "revolutionary hero" whose self-sacrifice for the benefit of the people serves as an exemplary model and inspiration for proper family behavior and good citizenship.[27] As a local hero his image symbolizes values relevant to China today. His history has become mythologized.

It is unlikely that we will ever know who Broken Shoes really was or who is buried in the grave of the Southern Efflorescent King. The details of his history will remain hidden. Family members passionately believe that the Southern Efflorescent King is Broken Shoes and that he is interred in the grave. This assumes that Chen Lanjisi, Chen Jinjiang, Chen Jingang, and Chen Xingcai are all the same person. All these men were real people, and although possible, it seems unlikely that they were the same person. Their true historical lives have been mostly lost. The lack of reliable historical sources has allowed the gaps to be filled in with myths and legends about Broken Shoes and the Southern Efflorescent King, as well as for the creation of his hero's image. What became most apparent to me from interviews with his descendants was that in retelling Broken Shoes' story, historical myth became more important than historical reality. Today it is impossible to separate the man from the mythologized historical image. For the Chen family the enduring image is of a heroic young Southern Efflorescent King charging into battle astride his white horse.

CHAPTER 6

Identity, Messianism, and Rebellion on the Yao Frontier

At the end of December 1831, a Yao tribesman came down from his mountain farmstead to sell his crops in the local Chinese market in Jianghua county, Hunan, in exchange for silver. Later he discovered that the silver had been mixed with tin, but when he sued the merchant in the county court, the magistrate adjudicated in favor of the merchant, and in fact the Yao farmer was then accused of theft and thrown into jail.[1] Not long afterward, to the south in the Yao mountains of Lianshan, Guangdong, Chinese "scoundrels" pillaged the tiny Yao hamlet of Huangguachong, where they stole oxen and grain. While in this instance, the county magistrate decided in favor of the Yao victims and adjudged that the culprits pay the equivalent of 1,200 pieces of gold to the victims, they ignored the judgment.[2] In both cases, the Yao retaliated by gathering bands of several hundred tribesmen and raiding nearby Chinese villages and markets. Although these two incidents, which were spontaneous and unconnected, were not the cause of the Yao uprising, which began in earnest in January 1832, they exemplified the mounting tensions and conflicts on the Yao frontier that had been simmering over the previous decades.

The Yao Rebellion of 1832 was the largest Yao uprising in the nineteenth century. It erupted in the mountainous borderland between Guangdong, Guangxi, and Hunan, a remote area with the largest concentration of Yao people and an area that many of them considered as their sacred homeland. It took the state and local power brokers more than a year to subdue the revolt, which came to involve tens of thousands of Yao insurgents, Chinese bandits

CHAPTER 6

and Triads, soldiers, mercenaries, and militiamen. This area had a long history of poverty, ethnic conflict, banditry, and secret society activism. The earliest recorded Yao uprisings were in the tenth century, and in the Ming dynasty there was a century of intermittent fighting that scholars have called the Great Yao Wars between the 1440s and 1540s. In the early Qing strife continued with a Yao uprising in 1701 and several other smaller disturbances throughout the eighteenth century.[3] When the next large-scale uprising flared up in the winter of 1832, the Yao foothills already had become crowded with Chinese settlers who had grabbed up the most productive lands, plunging the indigenes into unrelenting cycles of debt and poverty. An expanding Qing state and corrupt yamen underlings, soldiers, and officials only further incited Yao resistance.

This chapter begins with a discussion about Yao identity, which was imposed by successive imperial regimes on certain highland aborigines in south China who in time also came to view themselves in similar ways. The Yao identified themselves as descendants of a fabled dragon-dog named

Map 7. The Hunan-Guangdong-Guangxi Borderland during the Yao Rebellion, 1832 (Source: Created by author)

Identity, Messianism, and Rebellion on the Yao Frontier

Panhu whose stories were first recorded in official accounts during the ancient Han dynasty. In the Yao adaptation Panhu became a messiah who vowed to return to lead his people to a promised land that many indigenes believed to be located in the internal mountainous frontier on the Hunan-Guangdong-Guangxi border (map 7). The Yao frontier and messianism are discussed in the second and third sections of this chapter. The final section considers how a charismatic Daoist ritual master named Zhao Jinlong (Golden Dragon Zhao) ignited the rebellion in 1832 by mobilizing thousands of followers with claims of being a Yao King and the reincarnation of Panhu who had returned to earth to lead his people to an earthly paradise. The Panhu myth, I argue, is the key to our understanding of Yao identity, the Yao frontier, and the Yao Rebellion of 1832.

Who Are the Yao?

To delineate the Yao is no easy task, as there was no distinct, unified group of people in the past that we can call Yao. Rather, the Yao as an ethnic group in China was constructed over a long period of time by successive imperial dynasties and culminating with the Communist state's classification in the 1950s.[4] Yao ethnic identity was imposed by outsiders, and in fact the Yao themselves had little to say in the matter. It was a term of political expediency and practicality. The Yao were (and still are) made up of discrete groups of people speaking a variety of mutually unintelligible languages, who came to be lumped together mainly because of shared ritual practices and cultural traits, especially a common founding mythohistory relating to a dragon-dog named Panhu. As Ralph Litzinger explains, the Yao were "the creation of the imperial imagination," existing "only as a noncultured other, situated on the borders of empire and civilization."[5] Nonetheless, once those people labeled as Yao accepted that label they interpreted and manipulated their imposed ethnic identity to redefine themselves in ways that the state had never imagined or could control.

The Panhu myth is one of the best-known features of Yao culture and has played a key role in creating Yao identity. While the origins of the myth are obscure, it likely circulated orally among local tribes in southern China before it was recorded in Han dynasty accounts. Over the centuries the Yao elaborated on this story to elucidate their origins in terms of their relationship with the Chinese imperium and the two very different sociopolitical orders. As recorded in the so-called Yao charters (*die*), in brief the story explains:

Chapter 6

*In ancient times barbarians known as the dog tribe (*quanrong*) repeatedly invaded China during the reign of an emperor named Ping. Unable to militarily defeat this enemy, the emperor proclaimed that whoever could obtain the head of King Gao, the enemy chieftain, would be rewarded with a fiefdom, gold, and the hand of his daughter in marriage.[6] None of Emperor Ping's officers, soldiers, or subjects were able to complete the task, save one, his faithful dog named Panhu, who not long after the proclamation was read, appeared at the palace with the head of King Gao. The emperor was delighted but reckoned that a dog could never marry his daughter or be elevated to noble status. Upon hearing this, however, the princess insisted that the emperor fulfill his public pledge, and so she married Panhu and together they left to live in a cave in the wild, inaccessible southern mountains. His wife gave birth to twelve children, six of each sex, who married one another and had many offspring. They lived together in the mountains, feeding upon roots and wild beasts. At some point the emperor rewarded Panhu with the title King Pan (Pan Wang). After he died the princess returned to the palace and related her story to the emperor, who summoned the children to court. Unaccustomed to living in a palace and on the open plains, Ping allowed them to return to their mountain home, promising them perpetual freedom and exemption from taxation. They established a utopian kingdom called the Thousand Family Grotto (*Qianjiadong*) deep in the mountains of southern China, but sometime later, after being driven out by a Chinese army, they became highland nomads.[7] From these ancestors it is said the people called the Yao have sprung.[8]*

Although in the past many Yao and Chinese have taken the Panhu story at face value as historical fact, both sides attributed different meanings to it. On the one hand, the Yao emphasized the mystical origins of Panhu and the Yao people, as well as the special privileges and honors that the Chinese emperor had granted them; on the other hand, the Chinese emphasized the dog and thus the lowly, bestial origins of the Yao. The sexual union between the dog (Panhu) and the human (princess) simply confirmed Chinese preconceived views that the Yao were at the least barbarians, or even worse, a subhuman race of freaks. In the past, many Cantonese actually believed that Yao children were born with tails that fell off when they reached twenty.[9] For the Yao, however, identity became largely based on claims of descent from Panhu and a core of common ritual practices associated with the Panhu cult, which legitimized their clan system and linked them into a vast chain of deceased and living Yao.[10]

Yao identity actually owes much to meanings derived from China's imperial officials and scholars. What emerged was not an ethnic but rather a sociopolitical marker of demarcation and categorization. According to historian Leo Shin, ethnic labels, such as Yao or Miao, were not "self-evident truths," but rather "historically constructed categories whose precise contents shifted with time and space."[11] The term "Yao" was an administrative label imposed on highland peoples of the Hunan-Guangdong-Guangxi borderland who were not *min*, that is, registered tax-paying subjects of the imperial state. In fact, some of the earliest Chinese records, dating to at least the Tang dynasty, specifically used the term *moyao* to identify certain barefoot mountain aborigines as a distinct group of people who did not pay or were exempt from paying taxes.[12] Later on one of the most important assumptions of being Yao was exemption from taxation, which can also be traced back to the Panhu story.[13]

From the Ming dynasty onward, officials used the term "Yao" to designate indigenous peoples living in the southern mountains and practicing swidden agriculture. They were removed both physically and culturally from Chinese civilization, and according to Qu Dajun, they exhibited exotic, wild, and savage customs.[14] They epitomized the antithesis of order and stability. "To stand outside the realms of regulation and taxation," Hjorleifur Jonsson has explained, "is to be defective or illicit."[15] This attitude is perhaps best illustrated by the Ming statesman, Zhang Juzheng, who believed that the Yao should be treated as dogs:

> *The important principle is for the officials in charge [of overseeing the Yao] to deal with them in a flexible manner: Just like dogs, if they wag their tails, bones will be thrown to them; if they bark wildly, they will be beaten with sticks; after the beating, if they submit again, bones will be thrown to them again; after the bones, if they bark again, then more beatings. How can one argue with them about being crooked or straight or about the observation of law?*[16]

At the same time, over the course of the Ming dynasty, those people that the state were labelling as Yao also began to elaborate on their own traditions, especially in the form of stories, the most important of which was that of the dog-king Panhu. It may be no accident therefore that by the Qing period the term "Yao" was routinely written with the dog radical, a pointedly

CHAPTER 6

dehumanizing characterization based on Chinese misunderstandings of the Yao myth of their primordial ancestor Panhu.[17] Since the Yao considered themselves the progeny of a dog, however, they viewed this characterization more positively. For them the dragon-dog was a powerful totem that not only symbolized the Yao as an ethnic group, but also as their primal ancestor, provided them divine or magical protection.

China's imperial states also demarcated the Yao in other ways. The most common label was the paring of the Yao, and other minority groups, into "cooked" (*shu*) and "raw" (*sheng*) categories. The most important consideration in this schema was whether a group was considered to be subordinate to the local Chinese administration (cooked) or outside it (raw). According to Magnus Fiskesjö, the terms "cooked" and "raw," as used in official discourse, denoted the civilizing process (from raw to cooked to civilized) and had nothing to do with ethnic identification.[18] On the one hand, cooked Yao lived near Chinese villages, wore Chinese-style clothing, practiced stepped-riziculture, and engaged in trade. They were, at least in theory, in the process of becoming civilized (becoming *min*). On the other hand, raw Yao lived in remote mountains and had little or no contact with Chinese; they were considered wild, uncivilized, and dangerous. The cooked Yao acted as a buffer between raw Yao and Chinese. There also were the "lowland" (*pingdi*) and "highland" (*gaoshan*) Yao, as well as "settled" (*zhu*) and "wandering" (*liu*) Yao. Lowland and settled Yao were normally associated with cooked Yao, and highland and wandering Yao were normally associated with raw Yao. During times of disturbances, officials often branded Yao people simply as "good" (*liang* or *shan*), "rebellious" (*ni*), "bandit" (*fei*), or "violent" (*xiong*), according to circumstances. These categories, however, were not mutually exclusive, but were constantly changing, and these characterizations likewise were interdependent and interchangeable.[19]

By the nineteenth century, perhaps earlier, the Yao and Chinese had come to define themselves in terms of the "other," ideas often based on preconceived notions and past experiences. For the Yao, their own understanding of themselves derived from their confrontations and collaborations with Chinese over several centuries. The label "Yao," as it came to be accepted by both sides, was in fact the result of mutual "intercultural misunderstandings" that had very little to do with how those people labeled Yao had originally perceived of themselves.[20] Misunderstandings and miscommunications often led to interethnic violence, which in itself was an important factor fixing ethnic identities. According to R. Brian Ferguson and Neil Whitehead,

"Violence may be an expression of fundamental cultural practice and a sanctioned means of collective communication and exchange, such that the 'enemy' becomes integral to cultural identity."[21] Yao uprisings against a common enemy, the Chinese, likely helped to sharpen the focus of ethnic identity and increased the importance of maintaining it.[22]

The Yao Frontier

As disparate groups, without a unified culture or language, there was no single Yao frontier (*Yao jiang*), but rather many frontiers. The various groups lumped together as Yao, in fact, were spread across a wide area of southern China, from Guangdong to Yunnan, as well as across much of Southeast Asia. Here I take a close look at only one particular Yao frontier, namely that of the internal borderland of Hunan, Guangdong, and Guangxi provinces, where the Guoshan Yao and Pai Yao lived in scattered communities throughout the rugged Wuling mountain range. The Guoshan Yao (Crossing the Mountains Yao) practiced slash-and-burn agriculture and therefore continuously moved (roughly every two or three years) to exploit new lands. As late as the 1930s, most of them had no fixed settlements, lived in makeshift bamboo sheds, ate maize and wild vegetables, and were largely illiterate and poor.[23] The Pai Yao (Row Yao) were scattered across the mountains where they lived more or less in permanent settlements that were organized into loose confederations. Their larger settlements, such as Youling (figure 20), were stockades (*zhai*) protected with bamboo palisades and the passes leading to them had fortified stone gates. They practiced both swidden and paddy agriculture depending on the terrain. By the late eighteenth century some of the Guoshan Yao and Pai Yao had moved down from the mountains into the hills and valleys, where they established communities in relatively close proximity to Chinese settlements. The largest number of Yao, nonetheless, remained in the mountains where hunting and gathering was as important to their livelihoods as was farming.[24]

The Yao laid claim to their mountainous frontier based, in large part, on the Panhu story and the Yao charters. Beginning in the Ming dynasty the Yao created several imperial charters which retold and expanded the Panhu story. Although several Chinese and Yao scholars have regarded them as true historical sources on the early history of the Yao,[25] there is no conclusive evidence that such charters ever existed. Barend ter Haar and others have shown that they were actually "composed by the Yao themselves on the basis of orally transmitted mythology in order to create a positive identity vis-á-vis

Figure 20. Youling Stockade, c. 1837 (Source: *Lianshan suiyao tingzhi*, 1837)

the Chinese."[26] They were also an important instrument that the Yao often used to defend their rights to occupy frontier lands. The most important of these documents, the oldest of which the Yao claimed dated back to the Tang dynasty, are called *Pinghuang quandie* (*Charter from Emperor Ping*) and *Guoshan bang* (*Proclamation of [the right to] cross the mountains*). Written as scrolls in an awkward, unconventional classical Chinese style, the charters not only recounted Panhu's story, but also delineated a number of rights accorded to the Yao by Chinese emperors in perpetuity, especially grants of land, the right to live and freely roam in certain mountains, and exemptions from taxation or corvée labor. Charters were statements of Yao identity and rights; they also claimed Yao independence and separation from the imperial Chinese polity. Some charters, ostensibly written in the thirteenth century, recounted the settlement history of specific Yao surname groups. Other charters named specific idyllic locations as their vested homeland, the most important of which was the Thousand Family Grotto. The Yao insisted that they had been rewarded these lands for the meritorious deeds they had performed for the country, particularly Panhu's defeat of China's foreign enemies for which he and his descendants were granted an autonomous kingdom in the southern mountains. Whenever the Yao negotiated with the Ming and Qing imperial governments, they always produced charters to bolster their claims to land and to their rights to live and wander in certain frontier areas.[27]

The Yao frontier was characterized by rugged mountain ranges, poor soil, and weak infrastructure. Roughly 70 percent of the area consisted of mountains exceeding a thousand feet, with some peaks reaching over 5,000 feet. One eighteenth-century Qing official described the Yao frontier as "ten thousand mountains stretching for a thousand *li*."[28] Despite the division of the Yao frontier between the three provinces of Hunan, Guangdong, and Guangxi, it is best to think of this internal frontier as an organic whole stitched together by an intricate web of mountain paths and rivers (see figure 20). For the Yao there were no boundaries or political borders. The mountains were open spaces defined not by artificial boundaries but by the natural environment.[29] Mountains were no hindrance to people accustomed to living in such a rugged environment. "Daily they [Yao] cross back and forth; to them there are no borders."[30] Yao self-identity also derived from their intimate, innate relationship with their mountain homeland, often described to me as a place imbued with numinous power (*diling*), which they believed had been wittingly set aside for them by their gods and ancestors.[31]

Among rugged mountain ranges, life on the Yao frontier was never easy, particularly for Chinese frontiersmen. The area was a contact zone where diverse groups of peoples—indigenes, pioneers, soldiers, and officials—met, mixed, mediated, and fought with each other to create something new. In the mid-Qing no one side was strong enough to forcefully impose its will over the other. Essential for survival, in a desolate space with limited resources,

CHAPTER 6

the inhabitants, both Yao and Chinese, had to accommodate one another. The frontier became a "middle ground" in which a network of relationships was facilitated through perceived local practices and shared meanings. In the absence of overriding state authority, as Richard White has explained for North America's colonial frontier, something new emerges through adaptation, hybridization, and recombination. Either through cooperation or conflict all sides constantly adjusted to new evolving patterns of life on the Yao frontier. In coming together they negotiated commercial, political, social, and cultural relationships out of which they forged new patterns of interaction through both innovation and misunderstanding. What this meant was that all sides were dynamic agents of change.[32]

From the gaze of the imperium, however, the Yao mountains were wild and the people living there uncivilized. The frontier was what James Scott described as a non-state space.[33] In fact, the expansion of the state into the Yao frontier in the early and mid-Qing periods did not aim primarily at assimilation but rather at demarcation and quarantine (see figure 21). This arrangement left the Yao nearly independent and self-governing. A large variety of hereditary chieftains, headmen, and Daoist ritual specialists ruled

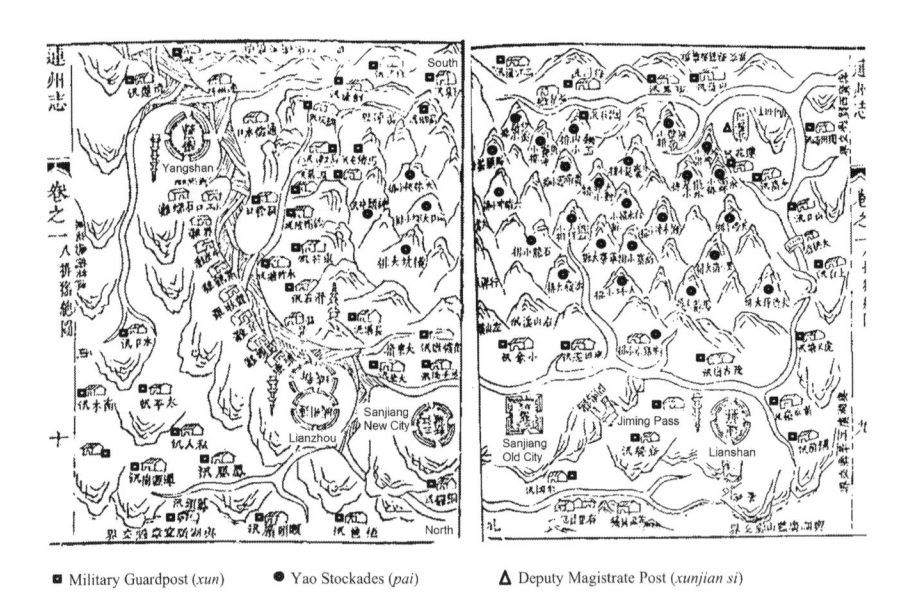

■ Military Guardpost (*xun*)   ● Yao Stockades (*pai*)   ▲ Deputy Magistrate Post (*xunjian si*)

Figure 21. Yao Stockades and Qing Military Posts in the Lianyang Region, c. 1771 (Source: *Lianzhou zhi*, 1771)

over the various indigenous mountain people, usually with tacit recognition from the Ming and Qing states. Among the Pai Yao, in what is today Liannan Yao Autonomous County, "Celestial Masters" (*tianzhanggong*) oversaw virtual fiefdoms from fortified stockades, much like the county magistrates in lowland walled cities. They exacted a variety of tribute from subordinate hamlets (*chong*) and their authority was derived from religious custom as well as from titles given to them by the state. Although in the Kangxi period the government attempted to weaken the chieftain system and pull the Yao closer into the Qing political orbit, such attempts met with little success.[34] The Yao frontier was actually a gray area that the imperial state mostly ignored; only in times of disorder did the state take direct action.

The Qing court had no overarching ten-year plan for the Yao, but rather policies tended to be piecemeal and were in constant flux. In most cases policies developed as reactions to Yao disturbances. A few examples will suffice. After a Yao uprising in the Shunzhi period (in 1652), the government established a Lianyang Battalion (Lianyang ying), but afterward, following a long period of relative tranquility, did not enact other substantial policies for half a century. Then, after a Yao uprising in 1701, the Kangxi emperor in the next year began to set up a series of new civil and military posts surrounding the frontier, in an attempt to delimit the Yao inside the mountain areas. First the government established a Sanjiang Battalion (Sanjiang xieying) with some 2,000 soldiers deployed across thirty-six guard posts (*xun*) encircling the Yao mountains (see figure 21). All the guard posts were located at mountain passes to better regulate the flow of traffic both in and out of the mountains. According to a stone inscription dated 1714, for example, two of these guard posts were strategically placed near the village of Shanxi on the narrow mountain road connecting Guangdong and Hunan.[35] The court next assigned a Subprefect for Pacifying the Yao (Li Yao tongzhi) in 1705 to the new walled city of Sanjiang, and the nearby battalion was renamed Battalion for Pacifying the Yao (Sui Yao ying). Several deputy magistrate posts (*xunjiansi*) were likewise established in Chinese villages near the Yao mountains, where these officials had specific responsibilities to help the subprefects oversee and regulate the activities and movements of the Yao and Chinese, and in particular to mediate disputes between the two parties. New roads were built connecting the lowland walled cities with these frontier outposts. In 1729 Lianzhou became an independent department (*zhilizhou*), but not until 1816 was Lianshan upgraded to an independent subprefecture (*zhiliting*); in both cases officials and soldiers stationed in these areas had specific duties to

CHAPTER 6

control and pacify the Yao.[36] During the early nineteenth century these posts were occasionally changed or upgraded to address disturbances or various new contingencies.[37] Inside the vast Yao mountains, however, the indigenes remained separate and largely on their own.

The Yao frontier evolved in stages marked by the influx of Chinese settlers, which culminated in the great migrations of mostly Hakka pioneers in the eighteenth and early nineteenth centuries. Up until that time, the Chinese population remained much smaller than that of the Yao, probably no more than a third of the Yao population. At first the Qing government's promotion of land reclamation in the wake of the devastating Ming-Qing dynastic wars and later population pressure in China's central plains prompted an extraordinary movement of migrants into the empire's peripheral and internal borderlands. Large numbers of Hakkas relocated from their homes in Jiangxi, as well as from elsewhere in Hunan and Guangdong into the Yao mountains.[38] Although after the 1760s officials no longer encouraged migrations, nonetheless Hakkas continued to move into this area into the early nineteenth century, and in particular following the suppression of the Hakka-Triad uprising in Huizhou prefecture in 1802.[39] Indicative of the Hakka impact on the Yao frontier, the lingua franca, in fact, became the Hakka dialect, not only for communications between Chinese and Yao, but also for the Pai Yao and Guoshan Yao, whose languages were incompatible. Hakka remains the major language of communication today.[40]

While we do not know for sure how many new settlers arrived in the area as a whole, the Lianshan gazetteer claimed that by the 1680s the registered Chinese population (*min*) was already slightly larger than that of the Yao in the mountainous area.[41] Likewise, reports from Jianghua county in Hunan estimated that by 1729 half of the population was Chinese, mostly new settlers who came to open up lands for agriculture.[42] While the Han population continued to increase mainly through spontaneous and uncontrolled in-migration, that of the Yao increased slowly and naturally through procreation. One official, Qian Yikai, estimated that in the eighteenth century there were no more than 10,000 Bapai Yao in what is today the Liannan autonomous county; another official reported that the Yao population, as a whole, at the start of the rebellion in 1832 was between 50,000 and 60,000 people.[43] Although the numbers are not statistically exact or reliable, nonetheless, they do indicate that by the time of the uprising in 1832 there already was a sizable Chinese, largely Hakka, population advancing into the Yao frontier.

As the more fertile lowlands were already occupied by Chinese from earlier migrations, the newcomers moved into the more mountainous areas and lived in close proximity to and among the Yao. Once in this inhospitable mountain environment frontiersmen needed to adopt traditional Yao slash-and-burn farming techniques as well as hunting and gathering to eke out a subsistence livelihood. As more and more settlers, particularly Hakkas, moved into the Yao frontier during the eighteenth and early nineteenth centuries, they established new homesteads deeper and deeper into Yao lands, with some frontiersmen adapting to Yao culture and lifestyles. Much to the disdain of Qing officials, a number of Chinese pioneers went native. Because of their distance from the seats of power, most of these new Hakka homesteads remained beyond the control of Qing officials in lowland walled cities.[44]

Backcountry Hakka pioneers were a heterogeneous throng, in some ways like the Yao whom they settled among. They were, in many cases, an unruly rough-and-tumble multitude of mostly single men who could never be fully restrained. The Qing government always feared the presence of such uninhibited Chinese in Yao territory. Much of the Qing policy with regards to aborigines, such as the Yao and Miao, in fact, was designed to regulate and minimize contacts between the two groups.[45] In the eighteenth century, the central government and local officials initiated a series of regulations and policies aimed to limit the number of settlers entering Yao territories, and at the same time also required Yao to follow certain paths down mountains and to trade in specified lowland markets. The state imposed regulations on border markets and assigned deputy magistrates to enforce them. In 1708, for instance, following minor Yao disturbances in the Lianshan mountains, the authorities blockaded the Yao by closing the roads coming out of the mountains and thereby preventing them from conducting trade in the lowland markets. The disturbances escalated and only ceased after officials rescinded the policy.[46] Of course, as the above case demonstrates, separation and strict regulations were impossible to enforce and often backfired. Chinese traders and settlers flaunted the rules; they traveled and traded wherever they chose. Many Chinese moved into areas where they were not supposed to settle. Whenever possible, local officials ignored the highly rigid regulations in order to avoid unnecessary trouble.

Tensions and Messianism on the Yao Frontier

The Yao Rebellion arose out of the contradictions and tensions inherent in the mountainous Yao frontier. Indigenous groups, such as the Yao or Miao,

CHAPTER 6

responded to contact with invasive and often violent outsiders in various and sometimes conflicting ways—accommodation, resistance, flight, increased inter-tribal banditry and feuds, and messianic uprisings. The Yao, at one time or another, adopted all these methods in dealing with Chinese intruders who increasingly stole their lands, resources, and women. The Yao Rebellion of 1832 was the most violent response, one that expressed pent-up frustrations and anger that had been festering for years. With this uprising the Yao sought revenge against those Chinese settlers who most threatened and harmed them and their way of life. Messianism, in particular, played an important role in mobilizing the Yao at the start of the rebellion.

The Yao frontier began to show stress in the several decades before the start of disturbances in late December 1831. As mentioned above, over the course of the eighteenth century the population, both Chinese and Yao, increased rapidly in the mountainous borderland. By the early nineteenth century the Yao frontier experienced a demographic crisis with usable land and hunting grounds in increasingly short supply. The newcomers, who were mostly Hakkas, were a disparate mix of farmers, petty traders, wanderers, and con men. They brought with them their own forms of social organization, which included Triad secret societies. Living in close proximity to one another produced tensions and conflicts, and sometimes horrific violence between indigenes and settlers.[47] Assaults and murders became increasingly common and routine facts of life in the Yao mountains; so did theft and robbery, especially of scarce resources, such as grain and cattle. The assaults, murders, thefts, and robberies were not one-sided, as both Yao and Chinese were culprits. Violence was not only inter-ethnic (between Chinese and Yao), but also intra-ethnic (Chinese against Chinese and Yao against Yao). The Yao frontier was a breeding ground for both accommodation and predation.

As the Yao mountains became crowded and good land became increasingly scarce, inevitably there were more conflicts. The chronicler of the Yongming gazetteer reported, on the eve of the rebellion, that Yao and Hakka fought one another for the uncultivated highlands in Tangxia and Leidong in Hunan. Local officials, unable to mediate a compromise, ended up calling in troops to drive both parties out of the area.[48] The theft of land, however, was decidedly one-sided. Typically Chinese moneylenders grabbed up lands from poor, indebted Yao who could not repay loans made at usurious rates. Many Yao, as a result, became tenant farmers to Chinese landlords. Sometimes Yao men also had to hand over wives and daughters to repay debts.[49] Chinese rascals also acquired Yao lands using forged deeds. In one case, a Chinese named

Yu Youxing from Lianshan produced a bogus deed claiming that Yao forest lands in Dazhangling belonged to him. He then placed a wooden placard on the site announcing that the Yao had illegally cut down firs worth more than a thousand taels of silver that they needed to pay back to him.[50] Chinese also stole Yao crops and livestock claiming that they took such actions because the Yao had refused to repay their debts.[51]

Chinese who owned and controlled the markets also swindled the Yao, and unscrupulous runners, soldiers, and officials took advantage of Yao weaknesses to protect and collude with settlers and to extort the Yao for money, resources, and sex. In the scholar-official Wei Yuan's opinion, because the Yao were simple-minded and illiterate, Chinese took advantage of their naivete to insult and cheat them, while officials turned a blind eye.[52] Over the course of the eighteenth century the Yao came to increasingly rely on markets to sell their mountain products and to buy daily necessities, such as salt, lamp oil, ironware, dry goods, and even rice. What they were unable to exchange through barter they had to purchase with hard cash, which meant that they were at the mercy of Chinese merchants who bought low and sold high. For many Yao there was an inescapable, endless cycle of debt and poverty. As local officials in Guangdong reported at the end of the rebellion, conflicts always occurred in the market areas where Chinese and Yao settlements were in close proximity to one another.[53] The failure of both sides to agree on appropriate mechanisms of exchange frequently resulted in violence. To the Yao backcountry Chinese increasingly became seen as enemies and bandits, and for the Yao an appropriate, justifiable response was to rob them. When the Chinese responded in kind, violence and bloodshed often escalated out of control.

With tensions rising, in the months leading up to the rebellion, a number of Yao prophets emerged, claiming that they had received visions from their great ancestor, Panhu the dog-king, to discard foreign ways and return to their own traditions. The intrusion of Chinese outsiders during the eighteenth and early nineteenth centuries had a destabilizing impact on Yao culture and prompted serious questioning of their beliefs and customs. In times of crisis, seers or prophets appeared among the Yao who promoted various religious interpretations of catastrophic events and violence that they believed threatened their existence. Some seers combined religious creativity with political resistance, drawing from both Daoist and native traditions.[54]

Several prophets appeared among the Yao in 1831. Li Deming and Zhao Fucai, both Daoist ritual masters (*shigong*), predicted the imminent appearance of the Sky Spirit (*tianxian*) among the Yao people. In some stories, the Sky Spirit assisted Panhu in his quest to kill the Chinese emperor's nemesis, and thus became the dog-king's emissary and harbinger of impending disturbances.[55] On the eve of the rebellion both prophets foretold cosmic cataclysms, Yao armies clearing away the outsiders and advancing to Beijing to kill the Daoguang emperor, and a Yao messiah leading his chosen people to an earthly promised land.[56] The Yao promised land was the previously mentioned Thousand Family Grotto, which was the legendary primordial homeland of the Yao people that many believed to be in Hunan.[57] This traditional vision of an earthly paradise, however, was illusory, but spoken of in many stories, and would have been quite familiar to most Yao.[58] It was a promised land that the Yao reached out for, but was always just beyond their grasp. Now the prophets assured their people that it was attainable.

Zhao Jinlong was the most important Yao prophet. He was a Guoshan Yao, a ritual master, and village headman (*touren*). Zhao Jinlong, whose clan name (*zuming*) was Wanyuan, originally came from Dalongchong in Jianghua county, Hunan. Later he moved with his family to Changtangping, where he farmed mountain land. Although he apparently mingled freely among the Chinese communities and spoke their language, he had not shaved his head in recognition of Qing rule and he continued to dress in traditional Yao fashion. Following Yao custom, he became an apprentice to two ritual masters, Li Deming and Zhao Zaiqing, learning from them the more complex Daoist exorcist rituals and scriptures that were necessary for his own advancement. Sometime before the uprising began, the deputy magistrate of Jintian sanctioned Zhao Jinlong as a native headman in charge of 200–300 households in recognition of his leadership abilities.[59] By then he had a growing reputation among the Yao as a magician, healer, and martial artist.[60]

At the start of the uprising Zhao Jinlong took the appellation of Yao King (Yao Wang), a title not recognized by the Qing state, but rather a Yao designation said to date back to the fourteenth century, and therefore several centuries before Qing rule. The tradition of Yao Kings undoubtedly derived from the Panhu mythohistory whereby the dragon-dog had been rewarded the rank of king by the Chinese ruler. In fact, the Yao tribes that Hans Stübel studied in Guangdong in the 1930s venerated a deity called the Yao King, which he identified with Panhu.[61] Yao Kings, who were also Celestial Masters, were the highest ranking politico-religious leaders in the so-called Yao Lao system of local governance among the Bapai Yao in Lianzhou. Panhu was the source of their ritual power and magical arts.[62] The appearance of the Yao King in December 1831 acted as a tool for recruitment and a catalyst for revolt; he became an important symbol for mobilizing the Yao, who were scattered across hundreds of miles of rugged mountains and who had no established leaders beyond their own village headmen. As Donald Sutton has explained for the Miao uprising in 1795, indigenous kings provided an important transcendent meaning and legitimacy to the revolt as well as a means to articulate its motives and goals.[63] Zhao Jinlong served a similar purpose.

Zhao Jinlong could also find support and rationale for his claims as the Yao King from a rich tradition of oral folklore that had been handed down from generation to generation for hundreds of years. The story of Doufu Bagui, in particular, depicted a superhuman hero of incredible strength (he could uproot a large tree with his bare hands), who resisted the encroachments of the Ming dynasty. The Yao greatly respected and honored him as a Yao King and savior. Armed with a magical sword bestowed on him by Heaven, he led his forces to fight the Ming all the way to Beijing, completely defeating the imperial armies sent to stop him. Henceforth, the Ming emperor dared not attack the Yao people. Other folktales depicted ritual specialists who possessed magical powers that they could muster to overcome Yao enemies, even the Chinese emperor himself. One such tale was called "Zhao Jie the Second Kills the Emperor." According to folklorist Xu Wenqing, all of these folktales expressed the Yao people's idealized desire for ethnic autonomy and peace after a long period of suppression and humiliation by Chinese imperial states, as well as their love of freedom and willingness to use violence to attain it.[64] Such tales undoubtedly provided models for resistance and rebellion.

Zhao Jinlong not only took the title of Yao King, but also more importantly he declared himself the reincarnation of Pan Wang (King Panhu), who was not only the primordial ancestor but also treated as the Yao savior, who promised to send forth from Heaven his "Five Banner Calvary" to rescue the Yao people in time of trouble.[65] Other ritual specialists supported Zhao Jinlong and his claims: he was the prophesied messiah. In late December 1831, he declared himself the "Golden Dragon King" (*jinlong wang*), donned a yellow robe, made sacrifices to Heaven and Earth, and announced the start of the great Yao revolt. He distributed yellow and red banners, red turbans, and amulets among three hundred followers, and posted placards everywhere with the words "First Year of Jinlong."[66] The name "golden dragon" (*jinlong*) is significant because this was an alternate name for the dragon-dog Panhu.[67]

At the start of the revolt, Zhao Jinlong also proclaimed that he was "redeeming the vow of King Pan," that is Panhu's promise to send his Five Banner Calvary to save the Yao in time of crisis. As a ritual master, Zhao Jinlong possessed Daoist sacred texts, incantations, and talismans that he could use to call forth spirit soldiers.[68] In fact, his authority (and that of other ritual specialists) was based on his ability to manipulate the spirit world to call down divine warriors to his aid. According to Jonsson, Yao leaders, such as Zhao Jinlong, were men known for their military prowess, which in large measure depended on their possession of Daoist ritual objects (sacred texts, incantations, talismans, swords, etc.) that could be used to make contact with powerful spirits who would come to their aid whenever needed.[69] Based on the confessions of captured Yao rebels, Zhao Jinlong possessed strong magical powers to cure illnesses as well as to transform water into fire and change grass into oxen.[70] If we read between the lines in official documents, it was likely that he promised his followers that he would lead them to the Thousand Family Grotto where the Yao would "live in peace and prosperity," be "independent," "represent themselves," and "pay no taxes."[71] Actually in the Daoguang period there were rumors among the Yao that the promised land was at hand, and that the Thousand Family Grotto was nearby in the Hunan mountains.[72] Although Zhao Jinlong would not live to see the promised land, his name lives on in legends among the Yao in Hunan and Guangdong.[73]

THE YAO REBELLION OF 1832

The Yao Rebellion was a series of separate and loosely linked uprisings. In several areas in Guangxi and Guangdong, Yao disturbances erupted spontaneously and were not, for the most part, connected with the larger rebellion initiated by Zhao Jinlong and others in Hunan. Indeed, attempts to forge a lasting unified front to fight the Chinese failed to materialize. There never was a pan-Yao alliance across the three provinces, nor did all the Yao support the rebellion. There were always groups of "good" Yao who not only abstained from fighting but also helped the Qing government combat the rebels.[74]

Officials tended to blame the outbreak of disturbances in late 1831 on Chinese scoundrels who had organized Triad gangs that wantonly robbed and murdered Yao people, and on local officials, yamen underlings, and soldiers who refused or were unable to restrain them.[75] In his account of the rebellion, Wei Yuan said the troubles caused by the Triads were much worse than those caused by the Yao.[76] Later on, according to the confession of Zhao Fujin, son of Zhao Jinlong, a Triad band, led by a Hakka ruffian (*feigun*) named Deng Chaoxiang, ignited the rebellion after pillaging Yao stockades in Jianghua county, Hunan, stealing their cattle and grain and murdering innocent people.[77] In retaliation in January some six hundred Yao tribesmen attacked Hakka-Triad walled settlements at Lianghekou, Hongjiangzhai, and Huangzhuzhai in Hunan near the Guangdong-Guangxi border. They killed about sixty men and women, as well as one soldier.[78] What had started as a raiding party to redress local grievances soon escalated into a full-fledged insurrection, which would take the Qing government more than a year to suppress.

Three charismatic leaders—Zhao Jinlong, Zhao Fucai, and Zhao Wenfeng—emerged and over the next several months gathered a ragtag army exceeding a thousand men and women. In February local officials and villagers in Jianghua quickly put together a small force of several hundred soldiers and local stalwarts to attack Yao strongholds in the snow-covered mountains. Although about three hundred Yao rebels were killed, the main body escaped into the Lanshan mountain range on the border with Guangdong. After several indecisive skirmishes, the emperor ordered a full-scale attack to wipe out the Yao rebels once and for all. In March Hailing'a, commander-in-chief in Hunan, led nearly five hundred soldiers and local militiamen deep into the Yao mountains, where at Chitang Market—"where the mountains steepen and the road narrows"—Yao rebels, who had lain in ambush, rushed down the mountain and slaughtered all of the troops, including Hailing'a.[79]

As word spread after the victory over Hailing'a, other Yao groups rose in response. The uprising spread further into Guangdong and Guangxi. At the same time, several Yao leaders were able to galvanize their forces into better fighting units. They organized themselves into three routes (*lu*) or detachments. Zhao Jinlong led one detachment made up of Yao from the Bapai area of Lianzhou and Lianshan in Guangdong and from Jianghua and Jintian in Hunan; Zhao Fucai led another detachment of Yao from Changning and Guiyang in Hunan; and Zhao Wenfeng led the third detachment of Yao from the Xintian, Ningyuan, and Lanshan areas. Probably a total of 6,000 to 9,000 Yao, including both Guoshan Yao and Pai Yao, and both cooked and raw Yao, joined the rebellion. Each of the three leaders assigned loyal subordinates as "generals" (*jiangjun*). For example, Zhao Jinlong's younger sister held the rank of general, as did several of his brothers and cousins. Below the generals were "captains" or "headmen" (*touren* or *toumu*), who commanded banner units consisting of roughly a hundred troops. Many commanders were, in fact, ritual masters, who in ceremonial dress and bearing

Daoist paraphernalia, led troops into battles.[80] Based on Yao clan customs, subordinates in most cases were kinsmen, either through blood or marriage. Blood oaths among leaders and followers further extended and reinforced the organizational networks beyond kin groups. Yet despite the apparent organizational structure there was never any coordinated military campaigns between the various detachments.

During the bitterly cold winter months Yao insurgents descended from their mountain stockades to plunder lowland Chinese villages, markets, and government outposts. Because over the previous two years much of Guangdong and parts of Guangxi and Hunan provinces had experienced severe droughts and famines, the Yao bands conducted raids to obtain desperately needed food and supplies, including weapons. Revenge was also another important motive driving Yao attacks. After each raid they returned to their mountain retreats, to areas out of the reach of soldiers sent to suppress them.[81] Later that spring the Qing armies, now supported with village militia units and loyal Yao irregulars, counterattacked, and during fierce fighting Zhao Fucai and more than a thousand rebels were slain. When Zhao Wenfeng's troops heard about the defeat roughly half of them deserted. In separate actions, in April Zhao Zaiqing led 2,000 Guoshan Yao to pillage villages in Lianzhou; but he was soon afterward captured and executed. Also in April imperial soldiers cornered and killed Zhao Jinlong and several thousand rebels at Yangquan, a small market town on the Hunan-Jiangxi border. On his person were found a double-edge sword, a wood seal, and a small wooden statue of the ancestral deity Panhu—all essential Yao or Daoist paraphernalia used in performing exorcist rituals, conjuring magic, and curing ailments. During these campaigns officials also ordered soldiers to find and desecrate the ancestral graves of Yao leaders, so as to destroy the *fengshui* that protected their families and to spoil their chances of success.[82]

The situation in the Yao rebellion, however, was much more complicated than it first appears. Not only was there no single unified or coordinated rebel movement, but also the entire area was infested with Chinese bandits and Triads, who either attacked the Yao or collaborated with them. Some resourceful Chinese, whom officials labeled traitors and bandits, sold gunpowder and weapons, including cannons, to Yao rebels, while others gave them shelter and protection.[83] Many backcountry Chinese took advantage of the chaos to conduct raids on both Yao and Chinese communities. Triads, who had entered the area with the Hakkas in the early nineteenth century, were a constant menace noted by Qing officials; they too plundered both Yao and Chinese villages and markets. Also, in many cases those Yao that officials labeled as "bandits" were simply that: they were not rebels, but also had taken advantage of the chaos to rob both Chinese and Yao. In some cases, Chinese and Yao bandits joined forces to rob and kidnap just about anyone they came across.[84]

With the death of Zhao Jinlong in April 1832 no other messianic leader appeared and there were no new Yao kings able to replace him. Nonetheless, scattered bands of Yao insurgents continued to spontaneously rise up during the summer and early autumn. Although the fighting had slowed down by midsummer on the Hunan side of the mountains, still Yao disturbances continued to spread across several borderland areas: Yangshan, Deqing, Fengchuan, Lechang, and Ruyuan counties in Guangdong, and Hexian, Huaiji, Fuchuan, and Guanyang counties in Guangxi. New leaders also appeared. For example, in Guangxi, Pan Junhua led nearly 2,000 Yao rebels to attack Chinese villages and markets in Hexian; and in Guangdong Liu Wencai led a thousand Yao rebels to plunder several tens of Hakka villages in Yangshan.[85] In most cases continued disturbances were piecemeal and aimed at specific local grievances. Despite several Yao successes in the battlefield by August the fighting had bogged down to a standstill with neither side capable of overpowering the other. Even so, Yao raids on lowland settlements continued in Guangxi and Guangdong, as did skirmishes with Chinese soldiers and local militia, to the end of the year.[86]

At the start of the rebellion the government had only dispatched a few hundred soldiers who were handily defeated during those early stages by Yao insurgents. Gradually over the winter and spring of 1832, the number of government troops increased to about 4,000 in Hunan, roughly 4,000 in Guangdong, and another 1,200 in Guangxi. Local militia, mercenaries, and loyal Yao irregulars, which came to number more than 3,000 fighters, supplemented the regular army. By the time the major fighting ended in late September the government had between 13,000 and 15,000 soldiers, militiamen, and irregulars in the field.[87] As for the Yao rebels, it is likely that they never exceeded a total of 10,000 fighters, including men and women, who were scattered across the Yao mountains in numerous discrete forces.

Despite the fact that the Yao were not a well-organized or unified fighting force, the rebellion was able to last as long as it did, for more than a year, because the terrain where most of the fighting took place was in extremely remote and rugged mountains, areas where the Qing suppression forces were unfamiliar and unaccustomed to fighting. Furthermore, large numbers of

CHAPTER 6

soldiers in Guangdong were opium addicts, which greatly inhibited their fighting ability.[88] Only by September did the government make some headway in its campaigns against the Yao rebels and bandits. First, Qing forces were able to defeat Yao insurgents by drawing them out of the mountains to do battle on the lowlands. This was accomplished after initiating a blockade in the spring and summer that aimed to starve out the Yao living in the mountains. Second, officials encouraged local communities to hire mercenary "braves" and to form militia, and officials also employed "loyal" Yao irregulars to combat the rebels hiding in the mountains. Local militia and Yao irregulars proved quite effective because they were more familiar with the mountains and rebel hideouts, and besides they were fighting to defend their homes. Finally, military campaigns were accompanied by an "appeasement" (*zhaofu*) policy, which offered pardons and monetary rewards to rebels who surrendered. Appeasement was a policy of compromise and accommodation, one that acknowledged the reality of the Yao frontier where the state was not powerful enough to overcome the rebels. Instead, it recognized a rough balance of power. The Yao Rebellion collapsed in the late fall of 1832, at a time of crop failures and increasing pestilence. Faced with starvation many Yao came down from the mountains to surrender; others remained in the mountains and continued their resistance. Qing mopping-up operations against "fugitive" rebels and bandits continued into 1834.[89] In the aftermath of victory, the Qing government increasingly attempted to impose its will over the Yao frontier. However, in the long run assimilation policies never fully succeeded or replaced accommodation.

Conclusion

At the core of this chapter is the Panhu myth and the role and power it has played in Yao history. As I have argued, this mythohistory is the key to understanding Yao identity, the Yao frontier, and the Yao Rebellion of 1832. As noted in the prelude, myths, when taken as popular truths, have a persuasive influence on the minds and actions of individuals and groups. According to folklorist Douglas Cowan, the purpose of origin myths depends less on historical truths than on their ability to "establish frameworks of meaning" that legitimate sociocultural practices and "structure credibility."[90] The Panhu myth provided the Yao with a proud cultural heritage that stood in stark contrast to the negative histories propagated by the Ming and Qing imperium and China's cultural elite. By refashioning the Panhu myth within the context of their own culture, the Yao both rejected and challenged the

Identity, Messianism, and Rebellion on the Yao Frontier

hegemonic narratives of the Han Chinese majority. For subjugated peoples, such as the Yao, mythology allowed them to envision a world where oppression was not seen as a preordained fact. The Yao rewrote history according to their own understandings of the past.

Yao identity as a distinct ethnic group was largely based on beliefs of descent from the mythical dragon-dog Panhu, beliefs which helped them create social and cultural cohesion that transcended individuals and families. The myth became the basis for a return to Yao roots and to an identity predating Han Chinese domination and subjugation. One of the most important assumptions of being Yao was their autonomous rights to occupy frontier lands in the mountains of southern China, where they would be exempt from paying taxes and free from interference from the Chinese state. Yao charters, which reiterated the Panhu story, were important instruments that the Yao often used to defend and legitimize their claims to their sacred homeland. The Yao repeatedly insisted that they had been rewarded inalienable rights to these lands for the meritorious deeds that Panhu had performed for China in the ancient past and for which the emperor had granted him an independent kingdom in perpetuity. According to this mythohistory the Yao consequently enjoyed an idyllic existence in the Thousand Family Grotto located in the mountains along the Hunan, Guangdong, and Guangxi border. The Panhu myth provided the Yao with a utopian nostalgia set in a romantic mythical past.

But that ancient utopian kingdom was ephemeral. After a vindictive Chinese ruler expelled the Yao from their homeland, Panhu promised to return one day to destroy his enemies and reclaim the Yao earthly paradise. He would descend from Heaven to lead an army of spirit soldiers (his Five Banner Calvary) that could be called to arms by Yao ritual specialists. For many Yao the time of reckoning came in 1832, when an enigmatic ritual master named Zhao Jinlong proclaimed to be the Yao King and the reincarnated Panhu. Apparently fulfilling Panhu's vow, Zhao became an important symbol that helped mobilize the Yao people for rebellion.

However, the viability of recovering their promised land once again proved illusory and short-lived; sustained resistance lasted only as long as the savior Zhao Jinlong remained alive. Once he died, only months after starting the uprising, there was no one strong or charismatic enough to replace him and the rebellion soon afterward disintegrated. The Panhu myth, nonetheless, served as a counter-hegemonic narrative and rallying cry that for a short time during the rebellion empowered the Yao in their struggles for recognition

CHAPTER 6

and a semblance of independence. Like the Ming dynasty Yao hero Doufu Bagui, today Zhao Jinlong is eulogized in folklore as a heroic Yao King and savior who opposed the Qing and fought for ethnic autonomy.

CHAPTER 7

Water Chicks, Amazons, and Goddesses

LIKE THE SEAS, WOMEN HAVE BEEN REGARDED VARIOUSLY AS MYSTERIOUS, precarious, dangerous, nurturing, and life-giving. Although in the West during the age of sail women were not allowed to go to sea (though many did disguised as men), in south China there were fewer restrictions on women working and living aboard ships. Women went to sea as mothers, wives, daughters, and sisters, and worked aboard ships as sailors, pirates, and prostitutes. Many of the most important Chinese sea deities were female: the Empress of Heaven (Tianhou), the Mother of Typhoons (Jumu), and the Third Old Lady (Sanpo, discussed in the following chapter), among many others. Even several female pirates—the spouse of Yang Yandi and the sisters of Wu Ping, Lin Daoqian, and Zheng Chenggong—were venerated locally along the southern coast as sprites and goddesses (discussed in the first interlude). Based largely on Qing dynasty archival sources and modern anthropological studies, as well as field research carried out by the author on the Fujian and Guangdong coasts, this chapter argues that in the early modern and modern periods the waters along the southern coast of China were a highly feminized space.[1]

This feminization of south China's water world provides an important alternative approach to understanding China, one that emphasizes the agency of women in shaping their own destinies and history. Boat women and female pirates represented the most radical departure from the traditional norms of dominant patriarchal society and culture on land. They represented a threatening "other" that defied the accepted notions of womanhood, breaking with the established codes of female propriety, virtue, and passivity.[2] Female sea deities reinforced notions of "otherness" and provided boat

CHAPTER 7

women with positive models of womanhood, strength, and defiance in an otherwise male-dominated and terra-centered society.

This chapter focuses on the water world of Dan boat women in Fujian and Guangdong provinces between the Ming dynasty and late Republican period. Taken together these two provinces accounted for more than a third of China's littoral. Besides the shoreline with its innumerable bays and harbors, there were thousands of small offshore islands seasonally inhabited by fisherfolk, traders, smugglers, and pirates. Countless rivers and creeks also connected the coast with the hinterland.[3] In the early nineteenth century, the boating population of fishers and sailors numbered in the hundreds of thousands. Besides them there were even more men and women in auxiliary occupations—merchants, ship chandlers, stevedores, coolies, artisans, farmers, innkeepers, healers, seamstresses, entertainers, and prostitutes—who depended on the seas and rivers for their livelihoods. Together they constituted south China's vibrant maritime society, one that both complemented and clashed with dominant society on land.

Chinese boat people were usually lumped together by officials and landed society under the rubric Tanka (Danjia), a highly offensive and pejorative term literally meaning "egg families." The term was explicitly dehumanizing—for many Chinese, Dan boat people were a subhuman species hatched from eggs like amphibians or reptiles. No one is quite sure how or when this term developed. In Guangdong the name first appeared in written form in the Song dynasty in reference to pearl-fishers, and by the Yuan dynasty there was mention of Dan pearl-fishers in Fujian. In the Ming dynasty and thereafter the name Dan came to signify various boat people who engaged in fishing and resided aboard junks and sampans and in makeshift shacks on the reclaimed lands—the so-called sand fields—of the Canton delta.[4] In Fujian one of the names for the Dan boat households of Fuzhou was *quti*, another derogatory term meaning "twisted hoofs," because it was commonly believed that all Dan had twisted feet or legs as a result of spending generations squatting on boats.[5] The dominant society on land scorned them as thieves, savages, slaves, floating twigs, vagabonds, and the like. While the men were often deemed pirates and the women shameless whores, such simple characterizations are misleading. The boat women, in particular, actually played key roles in south China's water world, giving it a perceptible feminine essence.

What made this water world feminine? We can start with a description by Qu Dajun, the famous seventeenth-century Cantonese scholar who wrote *New Discourses on Guangdong*. His book included an interesting section titled

"Sea Water" (*haishui*), where among other things, the author discussed the differences between fresh or river water and salt or sea water. He does this by juxtaposing the ancient Chinese philosophical concepts of *yin* and *yang*—the ideas of complementary opposites so fundamental to the ways of thinking not only in China but across East Asia. We are all familiar with these paired opposites; they hardly need elaboration:

Yang	Yin
bright	dark
hot	cold
sun	moon
positive	negative
order	disorder
man	woman

In one passage, Qu Dajun described sea water as being *yin*.[6] If sea water is *yin*, then it stands to reason that the seas must also be dark and feminine. Other writers also associated rivers, lakes, and other bodies of water with the feminine (thus *yin*). In fact, water is the symbol par excellence of *yin*. As Edward Schafer explains, "Women represented metaphysical water in human form."[7] On traditional Chinese maps the seas offshore were often labelled "black waters" (*heishui*) or some similar term, and the further one moved away from land, we can presume, the darker and more feminine the waters became. Bodies of water, such as rivers, lakes, and seas, were likened to a woman's womb pregnant with life. In traditional Chinese medicine the womb is described as a "sea of blood" (*xuehai*), the location in the body that stores life's essence. Ancient myths described China's rivers and oceans as being inhabited my myriad creatures, both mythical and real, including water spirits, sprites, nymphs, deities, monsters, and demons, many of which were female in nature. "In many ways," Lee Irwin writes, "the feminine principle [which] is regarded in Chinese mythology as fluid, spontaneous, flowing power [is] also aptly symbolized by its associations with water."[8] For Qu Dajun and other writers the essence of woman was the essence of water.

I take this as a starting point for my discussion about what made the waters along the south China littoral feminine. The story unfolds in three parts: first, the place of Dan boat women at sea, particularly on the coastal waters and estuaries along the south China coast; second, women at sea who were forceful and dangerous, namely female pirates; and third, female sea deities and water sprites, who could be both treacherous and protective. My emphasis is on the important role that Dan females played in shaping south China's maritime society and culture.

Women on the Waters

Unlike many other areas of the world, in the seas around southern China there were few taboos on Dan women working and living aboard ships. They were, as one boat woman told me, "women on the waters" (*shuishang nüren*). In fact, it is estimated that one-third to as much as one-half of the seaborne population was female. Because in maritime south China whole families went to sea, it was not unusual to find women and children aboard most boats. Entire families, as well as hired hands, all lived, ate, worked, and slept together in generally very cramped quarters. Often too on the rivers and estuaries women and even young girls operated their own boats or sampans, ferrying passengers, transporting cargoes, and hawking their goods and services, including sex.

Here is what the English traveler John Barrow had to say about the boat women he encountered near Canton in 1792:

> *The boats before this city were mostly managed by young girls, whose dress confided of a neat white jacket and petticoat and a gipsey [sic] straw hat. Having for so great a length of time scarcely ever set our eyes upon a female, . . . though in reality very plain and coarse-featured, [they] were considered, as the most beautiful objects that had occurred in the whole journey. To the occupation of ferrying passengers over the river it seemed they added another, not quite so honourable, for which, however, they had not only the consent and approbation of their parents, but also the sanction of the government, or perhaps, to speak more correctly, of the governing magistrates, given in consideration of their receiving a portion of the wages of prostitution.*[9]

Nearly a century and half later the scene was much the same. When C. S. See, a Malaysian Chinese, visited Canton in 1936, he described the waterfront's "saltwater girls" (*xianshuimei*) this way: "They live a peculiar and hard existence. During the day they row far out to sea to catch fish. In the evening on their return to the shore they first sell their fish and then put on their gayest clothes. Many of them parade the water-front for immoral purposes."[10] In pursuing a livelihood on the margins, often Dan women found it necessary to move back and forth between fishing, ferrying, and prostitution, normally using the same boat for these multiple purposes. Not all boat women, however, engaged in sex work.

The apparent freedom and laxity of seafaring women that Barrow and others came across were quite different from the roles that women were supposed to play in China's male-dominated patriarchal society. On land, women were expected, often even required, to remain at home in the so-called inner quarters. They were supposed to be docile, meek, obedient, subservient, and chaste. In general, in traditional China, the public mixing together of men and women was taboo. Major exceptions to the rule were that of Hakka and indigenous minority women, such as the Yao and Miao, who also worked alongside their menfolk in the fields. They too were frowned upon by polite society as being indecent.

On water, Dan women were another exception. To most people on land boat women represented an exotic "other." They seemed to snub their noses at polite society. They were unconventional in their habits and dress. Their language was described as rough and foul. Unlike most other women who followed the fashion of the day and bound their feet, boat women (as well as Hakka, Yao, Miao, and Manchu women) had natural feet. In the old days they did not wear girdles and brassieres, and they went about barefoot the same as men.[11] In the eighteenth century, the poet Xu Kun gave this vivid description of Dan boat girls in Fuzhou harbor: "Those who paddle the boats are all women.... Captivating, young and lovely, they wear simple tunics and have bare, unbound feet."[12] From early age girls were expected to contribute their fair share of the chores aboard their family's boat. They were not only trained to cook, wash, and mend clothes, but also to row and sail boats, to fish or dive for pearls, and to mend sails and nets. They were required to earn their keep, and according to the anthropologist Hiroaki Kani, who did fieldwork in Hong Kong in the early 1960s, boat girls were generally strong and could do most of the same work as men.[13] Figure 22 depicts early twentieth-century Dan boat people living aboard small sampans in families on the Min River near Fuzhou.

Because they lived and worked side by side with their husbands, fathers, brothers, and sons, as well as other non-family males, most people on shore considered Dan boat women to be not merely exotic but also promiscuous. From the traditional dominant male perspective, boat women upset the

Chapter 7

Figure 22. Dan Boat Families on the Min River, c. 1910 (Source: Wikimedia Commons)

natural boundaries between men and women. They were unnatural and dangerous because they overturned accepted orthodox values and were intractable.[14] For those people on land, and when viewed against the Confucian standards of the day, boat women were bawdy and licentious. In fact, the sexual mores and standards of boat people, in general, were quite different from those on shore. In many ways, it can be argued, Dan women self-consciously defied the sexual customs and family values of patriarchal society. Unlike marriages on land that were arranged, among boat people couples largely made their own choices of partners, only afterward receiving their parent's approval. Divorce simply needed to be agreed upon by husband and wife, and divorced or widowed women remarried without stigma or shame. Virginity was not a prerequisite for marriage. What dominant landed society considered to be illicit sex for females, namely sexual relations outside the bonds of marriage or concubinage, actually was an acceptable custom among boat women. According to anthropologist Eugene Anderson, who did research on Dan fishing communities in Hong Kong's New Territories in the 1960s, among the Cantonese boat people, premarital sexual experimentation among teenage boys and girls was taken for granted and in some cases even encouraged. Also what today we would call infidelity or adultery among married couples was not unusual.[15] Cantonese boat women, in fact, were famous for their lusty, erotic "saltwater songs" (*xianshuige*), which were sung by courting couples and prostitutes alike. The themes of these songs were mostly sexual, and in fact extremely explicit and regarded by polite society as obscene.[16]

Prostitution among boat women and teenage girls was also commonplace, but not universal. While in some cases young girls had been abducted and forced into prostitution or had been pimped by their fathers, brothers, or husbands, in other cases they freely sold their services as a means of making a living or to earn extra money. Perhaps the more permissive attitude that boat people had toward sex made it easier for Dan girls to become sex workers. Based on research done in the 1930s on boat people in Sanshui county, sociologist Wu Ruilin declared that the Dan prostitutes he interviewed had freely chosen their profession and, in his opinion, apparently enjoyed their work. One of the prostitutes, in fact, had been married to a fisherman, but because he earned too little money, she left him to work as a prostitute. In another case, two sisters, one nineteen and the other twenty-four years old, who had been prostitutes since their early teens, followed their mother's example to engage in sex work.[17] A Chinese poet in the 1920s noted that young prostitutes, who sat aboard their boats dressed in beautiful clothing, called out to passersby on shore "without any feeling of shame."[18] It is doubtful, however, that all prostitutes enjoyed their work or felt no shame. It is more likely that in most cases women engaged in sex work because of economic necessity and the need to support family members.[19] In her study of early twentieth-century Shanghai prostitution, Gail Hershatter explains: "Women took work where they could find it, and the particular nature of sex work did not automatically make it the least desirable job available."[20] The same was probably true in south China.

These were the common prostitutes, called "water chicks" (*shuiji*), who mostly serviced workers and sailors, including those on Western ships that anchored at Whampoa in the Canton delta. Throughout the Pearl River estuary girls in their teens plied their trade singly or in pairs from small sampans, which they also used to transport passengers and cargo.[21] Some Dan prostitutes also operated out of shanties along the banks of rivers and creeks among the sand fields in the Canton delta. Figure 23 shows the former archway to the "water chicks" anchorage in Macau, which remained active until the 1970s. After visiting the anchorage in Macau, one displaced Portuguese customer described the girls as "lowly and with no touch of finery, reeking of wretchedness and poverty."[22] But for most Western sailors, after a long voyage, they found pleasure at Lob Lob Creek, between Whampoa and Canton, where floating brothels were "well stocked with a number of beautiful young women, of different ages, to whom everybody, Chinese or European, may have access at any time."[23] Foreigners referred to such common prostitutes as "saltwater girls." On the Han River in Chaozhou and Jiaying, where the boat people made their livings by transporting goods and making bamboo matting, it was said that half of the sex workers in the late nineteenth century were Dan females.[24] In Fuzhou harbor people on shore disapprovingly referred to Dan ferry boat operators who doubled as prostitutes as "twisted-hoofs hags" (*quti po*), denoting their debauched unnatural appearance and behavior.[25] Besides sex these young women also sold food, liquor, and opium, as well as washed and mended clothes. If customers did not go to visit them, prostitutes would sail out in their sampans to service sailors aboard their ships. Boatloads of prostitutes even visited pirate ships along the coast and Western ships at Whampoa.[26]

Another class of prostitutes was the well-known "flower boat" girls of Macau and Canton, usually referred to in the foreign literature as "sing-song-girls." In both cities floating brothels anchored in groups of anywhere from ten to thirty boats, forming discrete floating neighborhoods firmly managed by a procuress or madam. The larger boats had lavishly decorated private rooms and could accommodate dozens of guests. The young women aboard these boats were the high-class sex workers whose customers were mostly Chinese men of wealth and affluence—officials, scholars, and well-to-do merchants. These high-class prostitutes, however, were generally off-limits to Westerners. In most cases flower boat girls began their careers at a noticeably young age after being kidnapped or sold to boat operators or madams. Their feet were bound and only after several years of training in the polite arts of music, literature, and art did they begin to earn their keep as prostitutes once they reached puberty. They wore expensive, fashionable clothing, often made of silk, and offered their patrons an elegant and sophisticated female companionship in addition to sex. Besides the Canton delta, the girls came from many areas all over China—Chaozhou, Jiangxi, Yangzhou, Hunan, Hubei, Henan, and so forth—and therefore were not regarded as Dan. In any case, the life experiences and behaviors of flower boat girls were quite different from those of ordinary Dan women and common prostitutes.[27]

According to Anders Hansson, there was a marked increase in the middle of the eighteenth century of Dan prostitution, perhaps as a result of the so-called Yongzheng emancipation edict in 1729, which removed their

Figure 23. Gateway to the Former "Water Chicks" Anchorage in Macau's Inner Harbor, 2008 (Source: Photo by author)

pariah status and made mobility easier. In 1770, one local Chinese official estimated that there were as many as 8,000 Dan boats in the Pearl River estuary that were used for prostitution.[28] Before Liberation in 1949, I was told,

Chapter 7

at the small Fujian port of Yunxiao, there were usually about twenty to thirty Dan boats, which during daylight engaged in fishing and transporting goods, and after dark prostitution.[29] Today Dan floating brothels have virtually disappeared in the larger cities of Canton, Fuzhou, Macau, and Hong Kong, but they still persist clandestinely in many of the smaller fishing ports along the coast and inland rivers.[30]

But should we only view or judge boat women based solely on the values and criteria of landed society or by Confucian patriarchal standards? I think not. We should also view and judge people by their own standards and values, based on their lifestyles, actions, and beliefs. For south China's boat people, both men and women, it goes without saying that life on water was quite different from life on land. Seaborne life was indeed a lot tougher and boat people were generally a lot poorer and certainly greatly discriminated against. What was taken for lax moral standards were in fact often well thought out economic strategies and routines necessary for subsistence. The material conditions of boat people required different lifestyles and standards of behavior that were contrary to those of their more affluent counterparts living on shore. They had to devise their own strategies, often at odds with dominant society, for survival in an extremely competitive and often hostile environment.

To survive at sea required cooperation and hard work. The ship was a small community. Men, women, and children all lived and worked together in their wooden world. Shipboard life included family members and hired workers who were not necessarily kinfolk. In this rather closed world, the mixing of the sexes was a necessary and unavoidable aspect of seafaring life. Boat people were much more independent and nonconformist, or as Anderson has explained, they adopted "a form of Chinese traditional culture that fit their own needs."[31] In doing so they created a flexible alternative lifestyle that enabled them to survive and thrive. Many Dan, in fact, were proud of their unique lifestyles and accomplishments. As one late nineteenth-century Japanese writer, Sakura Magozō (using the Chinese pen name Dashan), observed, for the boat people around Fuzhou "life upon the waters is not as dirty, rude and narrow as that of the land people."[32] Their self-consciously planned society and culture allowed them their own space at the margins of dominant society and helped them to fashion their own identity as a separate ethnic group.[33]

Dan women were known to be strong and independent. Although male-female relations were complex, nonetheless, boat women had more egalitarian relationships with male shipmates than their counterparts on land. In the Pearl River estuary, aboard ship adult women, particularly wives and mothers, shared in decision making and fund allocation. Because they shared in all shipboard chores and were familiar with the ways of the ship, men took their opinions and suggestions seriously.[34] The situation in Fuzhou harbor likewise emphasized the importance of Dan women. According to a report by the sociologist Wu Gaozi, made in 1930,

> *in Dan families, primary authority belongs to the man ... [but] the work of really attending to day-to-day matters relies primarily upon the women. The women, not the men, do most of the work in directly creating family income. Paddling the boat and ferrying people about is largely the responsibility of women. The Dan women of Fuzhou are generally quite strong, having muscular strength surpassing most people. They use their strength and sweat to earn money.*[35]

Their self-declared strength and independence aboard ships is perhaps best exemplified in a 1946 song that boat women in Hong Kong sang every year at dawn on the first day of the third lunar month at the start of the fishing season. Just as they set sail they would gather and sing together in chorus:

> Strong are we, the Women.
> Elder sister, younger sister, mother, grandmother,
> Strong are we, the Women,
> Working together in a concerted effort,
> In our hands here lies,
> Our whole strength and power.

As the song clearly shows, women were self-consciously aware of their important functions, responsibilities, and strengths in keeping their boats afloat and making sure their voyages were successful. For boat women, their "whole strength and power" derived from their own hands.[36]

Female Pirates

If boat women, in general, were considered threatening because they overturned the Confucian standards of the day, even more so did women who became pirates. Because in south China many women (particularly among Dan boat people) made their homes aboard ship and worked alongside the men, it should not be surprising to find females also among the pirates. As witnessed by Fanny Loviot, who had been abducted near Macau in 1854, "pirates of the Chinese seas make their junks their homes, and carry their wives and children with them on every expedition. The women assist in working the ships, and are chiefly employed in lading and unlading the merchandise."[37] Some pirate captains reportedly had five or six wives, as well as other family members all living with them aboard their vessels. For them, piracy was literally a family business. One early nineteenth-century pirate captain named Huang Shengzhang, for example, kept his entire family with him at sea—his mother, wife, two sons, four other female relatives, and a servant girl.[38] The Fujian pirate chief, Zhu Fen, who called himself "King of the Southern Seas" (*hainanwang*), likewise surrounded himself with his wife and children, several adopted sons and daughters, as well as his uncles and brothers and their families. When his younger brother, Zhu Wo, surrendered to the authorities in Fujian in 1809, he took with him some 3,300 followers, including not only men but also a large number of women and children.[39] Evidently women and children composed a sizable percentage of the pirate population.

Substantial evidence from official documents show that several female pirates had married, either voluntarily or by coercion, into the pirate profession, and in either case willingly lived the lives of outlaws, no different than male pirates. In several instances women who had originally been abducted by pirates and forced into marriage gradually adapted to their new lives and raised families with pirate spouses: the wife of Huang Zhenggui, whose surname was Su, had two sons; the wife of Luo Xingda, whose surname was Zhong, had one son; and the wife of Wu Xinzhi, whose surname was Yang, had a son and a daughter.[40] Most pirate wives spent much of their time cooking, mending sails, and handling the loading and unloading of stolen goods. Others fought alongside their husbands; some died fighting in battle. In one case, the wife of a pirate named Chen Acheng, who had the surname Li, participated actively in more than ten piracies; she was Vietnamese and both she and her husband were members of Fan Guangxi's gang. After her arrest and trial she was sentenced to exile as a military slave in Xinjiang.[41] In another case, in 1809, during a battle with the Qing navy in the Pearl River near Macau, one female pirate, the wife of a pirate captain, fought to her death with swords in both hands.[42] One of Zhu Fen's sisters-in-law also fought to her death in a desperate naval battle in 1809.[43]

Dan boat women, who lived their entire lives on water, also played important auxiliary roles supplying pirates with food, weapons, and intelligence, as well as fencing stolen goods. One female, only known to us as Madam Big Foot (Da Jiao Sao), was the widow of a pirate named He Sanfa, who operated in the waters around Hong Kong in the mid-nineteenth century. After her husband died she collaborated with his associates by helping to distribute safe-conduct passes and recruit gang members. Although arrested by Qing soldiers for aiding pirates, she was later released due to insufficient evidence. One of her contemporaries, Ng Akew (Wu Ajiao), who had been "purchased" in 1849 by an American captain and opium trader named James Endicott, actively engaged in the illegal opium trade and colluded with pirates, including the notorious Shap-ng-tsai (Shiwuzai), by selling their loot. She acted as an important go-between for pirates and unscrupulous Western traders, like Endicott. One Hong Kong newspaper in 1849 described her as "a clever woman, of extraordinary activity as well as enterprising." With her connections to foreigners in Hong Kong and the Chinese underworld within a few years she had accumulated a small fortune through dealings in the opium and coolie trade, land speculation in Hong Kong, moneylending, and prostitution. Through their association with pirates, both Madam Big Foot and Akew derived economic benefits that allowed them a large degree of personal independence unheard of among other women of their time.[44]

Several female pirates became chieftains themselves. The most famous examples are Zheng Yi Sao and Cai Qian Ma in the early nineteenth century, and Lai Choi San in the early twentieth century. Zheng Yi Sao was originally a prostitute on one of Canton's floating brothels. She was a Dan boat woman, probably born around 1775 in Xinhui county, and was well known for her charm and beauty. Her family name was Shi (Stone) and we are told that she was called Fragrant Lass (Xianggu), a nickname or perhaps the name she used as a prostitute. Today she is best known as the Wife of Zheng Yi (Zheng Yi Sao). Her husband, Zheng Yi, in fact, was one of Guangdong's most powerful and notorious pirates at the end of the eighteenth century and start of the nineteenth century. Like other boat women, Shi Xianggu worked her entire life aboard ships, first with her natal family, then as a prostitute, and later as the wife of a pirate. In her latter role, she developed a reputation as a fearless warrior and capable leader. According to Dian Murray, she was instrumental in helping her husband consolidate his authority over the unruly and disparate gangs of pirates.[45]

When Zheng Yi suddenly died in 1807, Shi Xianggu did not quietly step aside, but instead she successfully maneuvered to take command of her husband's gang, the largest and most powerful Red Banner Fleet. Suddenly she came to command between 15,000 and 20,000 pirates, mostly men but also a considerable number of women. In taking power she was assisted by the charismatic twenty-one-year-old Zhang Baozai, her husband's adopted son and her lover. For the next several years, between 1807 and 1810, Zheng Yi Sao and Zhang Baozai had virtual control over the waters in the central coastal region of Guangdong, which included the rich Canton delta. Together with five or six other powerful Cantonese pirates, they formed a massive confederation of as many as 70,000 pirates, who effectively challenged the power and authority of the Qing state along the southern coast of China for nearly a decade. In 1809, at the height of her power and at a time of a severe famine in the Canton delta, Zheng Yi Sao launched naval expeditions deep into the inland river system, even threatening the provincial capital at Canton at one point.[46]

But by that time, after so many years of fighting, the pirates were exhausted. There were also squabbles and dissent among the pirate bosses, which added to a growing weakness that led to schism by the start of 1810. At the heart of the dissention was Zheng Yi Sao, who became the object of rivalry between Zhang Baozai and another chief named Guo Podai, leader of the formidable Black Banner Fleet. In fact, in January the two male pirate leaders clashed in a brief skirmish off the Guangdong coast. Although the battle was indecisive, soon afterward Guo Podai surrendered to the government, and not too long after that, with the confederation disintegrating, Zheng Yi Sao negotiated with the provincial authorities for the surrender of her fleet. After much haggling, the surrender was accomplished in April; she and Zhang Baozai surrendered with 17,318 followers, including roughly 5,000 women and children.[47]

After retiring from the pirate trade, Zheng Yi Sao moved on shore in Macau, where she reportedly operated a gambling parlor and opium den in the Chinese Bazaar in the Inner Harbor. Later she moved to Canton where she continued to run gambling and opium establishments until her death in 1844. Yet even after her death, she has lived on in legends. According to C. Nathan Kwan, "By the mid-nineteenth century . . . Zheng Yi Sao had entered the popular imagination, and Chinese women pirates were referred to as her descendants."[48] Her colorful life, adventurous exploits, and alleged love affairs have been told and retold many times in oral lore, novels, and movies. In 1993 a Hong Kong movie called *Angry Sea and Good Pirates* (*Nuhai xiadao*) featured Zheng Yi Sao battling against British imperialism, and a somewhat misplaced Zheng Yi Sao even appeared in Disney's 2007 blockbuster *Pirates of the Caribbean: At World's End*, as the haunting pirate Mistress Ching.

Another famous female pirate and a contemporary of Zheng Yi Sao, we know only by the name Matron Cai Qian (Cai Qian Ma).[49] Her name is derived from her husband, the pirate boss Cai Qian, who commanded a formidable fleet of several thousand pirates in Fujian province in the early nineteenth century. We know little about her life, but we do know that she was born in Pingyang county in Zhejiang province probably sometime in the 1770s or 1780s. Like Zheng Yi Sao, Cai Qian Ma was a Dan boat woman and a famous beauty, but had a reputation as a loose woman. Her first husband, we are told, sold her to a waterfront barber in one of the ports in southern Zhejiang, where one day Cai Qian was having his hair cut when he took notice of the barber's young wife. He at once made an offer the barber could not refuse, and for a third time she was sold in marriage. Yet even after her marriage to Cai Qian, she reportedly continued her promiscuous affairs.[50] According to legends, she kept a harem of young men from among the male captives. Like her husband, she too was addicted to opium and strong drink. Nevertheless, Cai Qian Ma played an important role in her husband's rise to power among the Fujian pirates. Aboard ship she proved to be a skillful and resourceful leader and a cunning and fierce fighter. At least one source claimed that she was second-in-command of her husband's fleet and even led her own flotilla of several ships with crews of "amazon warriors" (*niangzi jun*).[51] In some accounts, she died in a naval battle in 1804; in other accounts she fought to her death with her husband in 1809. Today she is something of a heroine in Fujian, with her stories appearing occasionally in cartoons and in newspapers.[52]

The third female pirate boss was Lai Choi San, who lived in Macau in the early twentieth century. Much of what we know about her comes from the journalist Aleko Lilius, who wrote a best-selling account of her life in *I Sailed with Chinese Pirates*, first published in 1931. According to Lilius her name means "Mountain of Wealth," though this was doubtful her real name. She too was a Dan boat woman. Unlike Zheng Yi Sao and Cai Qian Ma, who had married into the pirate profession, Lai Choi San had been born into it. Her father and brothers were all pirates and smugglers in Hong Kong and Macau. At the time of his death in the early 1920s, her father owned seven heavily armed junks. The family reportedly controlled Macau's lucrative fishing industry through a systematic and extensive protection racket that was shielded by close connections with local officials and businessmen. After her father was killed in a fight with a rival gang, Lai Choi San (not her brothers) inherited the family trade. Afterward she added five more junks to the fleet,

CHAPTER 7

and by ruthlessly eliminating her rivals she retained firm control over the local fishing trade. She became so powerful that Lilius called her the "Queen of Macau pirates."[53]

Lai Choi San received formal recognition after an official in Macau gave her the title of "Inspector," which gave her operations the appearance of legitimacy. In a sense, therefore, her activities became sanctioned by Macau officials, who were certainly receiving kickbacks from her in return for immunity from prosecution. This meant she could lead her fleet in the waters around Macau collecting tribute from local fishermen without interference from police. Those who paid her were protected from rival gangs in the area, but those who refused were either murdered or kidnapped for ransom. Extortion rackets, in fact, had been common practice among pirate groups in this area for centuries and provided a major source of their income and power. To avoid being attacked, cargo junks and fishing craft paid large sums of money to the pirates, who then issued passports guaranteeing safe passage. For a decade the pirate queen maintained her power over Macau's fishing industry and rival gangs through murder, kidnapping, blackmail, and extortion.[54]

According to Lilius, she was cunning, cold-blooded, and cruel, a sort of female Fu Manchu. She also had "barrels of money, and her will is law." The pirate queen is said to have loved the sea and the life of a pirate and never had any ambition to settle down to a peaceful life on shore.[55] In 1935, she was immortalized as the archetypal "Dragon Lady" in the American comic strip *Terry and the Pirates*, and more recently she was featured as the sinister but super-sexual villain in a novel authored by the actor Marlon Brando.[56] Nowadays she is still remembered by old-timers in Macau and Hong Kong as a feminine Robin Hood who robbed the rich and helped the poor.[57]

Besides these three famous female pirates, of course, there were many other women among the male pirates along the southern coast of China. Unfortunately, we know very little about them. What we can surmise is that they were able to survive in a male-dominated society because they proved themselves to be as capable as men in battle and in their duties aboard ship. In many cases, they even surpassed their male crewmates. Women were not merely tolerated by male shipmates, but, as we have noted above, took active leading roles aboard pirate ships. Although Zheng Yi Sao and Cai Qian Ma took advantage of their marriages to pirate leaders to gain access to power, they were able to maintain their power through their own abilities. Lai Choi San did not have to marry into the pirate profession; she had inherited her leadership position from her father because she had proven herself a skilled, forceful leader. Their examples offered an important alternative image of womanhood in Chinese history, one that challenged and contradicted the ideals of dominant patriarchal society. Female pirates represented a dangerous "other" and the most radical departure from dominant society on land.

Female Sea Deities

Like the sea itself, goddesses could be nurturing at times but destructive at other times. Boat people tried to understand their watery world through natural observations and to master it through omens, magic, and religious rituals. For them, like most people on shore, religious activities were basically pragmatic and reflected this-worldly hopes, needs, and anxieties of individuals and family members. In general, concerns for the afterlife and salvation were secondary to concerns about survival in the here-and-now.

The view of boat people of the supernatural was shaped by their daily confrontation with the sea and nature, as the following story from late nineteenth-century Fujian reveals. Sailors and fishermen in the area around Amoy had a peculiar yarn about how sudden storms arose at sea. They believed in a fierce and vulgar female spirit that they called the "Pissing Woman" (*ts'oa jio po*). This female sprite, according to legend, was once a real woman married to a cruel, brutal sailor, who cursed and abused her whenever he could. Preferring death to such a life, she committed suicide by throwing herself into the sea and thereby becoming a vengeful wandering ghost. "Since then she rages at sea, a wrathful demon, against every junk she sees, in the hope that her husband may be amongst the crew and be sunk into her own watery grave." She appears on the open sea as a sudden storm in a black cloudy mass that will toss and capsize any boat. "She is so unmannerly as to pass on high a flood of urine, which will fill the ship in a moment up to the deck." To counteract the wrath of the Pissing Woman, as soon as her dark specter appears the sailors must close all hatches, and immediately begin an exorcism. At once the crew burns paper money on deck to appease her anger; they also set off firecrackers and blunderbusses to try to scare her away. Then one of the sailors, stripped naked, climbs up the mast, his hair disheveled, and brandishing a sword, axe, club, or spear. He then sets about abusing and cursing the demon in every way imaginable. Meanwhile on deck another sailor, especially appointed for the task, dressed in a black gown with long spacious sleeves, begins a ritual exorcistic dance to the sound of gongs beaten by a mate. In his hand he brandishes a stick upon which a red cloth is attached to the end. The combined efforts of the naked sailor atop the mast and the exorcist dancing below on deck finally scare away the demon and the sea becomes calm.[58] This story about the Pissing Woman is interesting for what it reveals about common folk beliefs of seafarers and the exorcistic methods they used to counteract angry spirits.

Although there were many sea deities who were male, there were equally as many, possibly more, who were female. One Chinese scholar, Niu Junkai, for example, discovered more than thirty female deities devoted to protecting seafarers just along the coast of the Gulf of Tonkin.[59] Based on my own fieldwork between 2009 and 2013, along the Guangdong coast between the Leizhou peninsula and the port city of Jiazi there were hundreds of temples with both primary and secondary female deities, who (like Zuxi) are mostly unknown outside their local communities. In fact, the majority of temples I visited along the coast were dedicated to goddesses. Throughout south China's maritime world, as Hugh Clark has explained, "it was common to identify the protection of mariners with female deities."[60]

Undoubtedly the most important and famous sea deity, male or female, is the Empress of Heaven (Tianhou). What began as a minor local cult among fisherfolk in Putian county in Fujian in the tenth century had by the fifteenth century developed into a major cult all along south China's coast, and by the eighteenth century her cult had spread to Japan and Southeast Asia. Born into what was likely a poor Dan fishing family on Meizhou island, she refused to marry and remained childless—thus ensuring her purity—and at an early age developed a reputation in her village as a miracle worker or spirit medium (*wupo*). Stories abound about how she used her magical charms and incantations to save seafarers in storms at sea. Soon after she died, some say at age sixteen and others at twenty, local seafaring communities in Putian began worshipping Lin Moniang as the Divine Woman of Meizhou (Meizhou shennü), and gradually as her reputation spread along the southern coast she became known more familiarly as the Maternal Ancestor (Mazu). She continued her miraculous intercessions to save imperiled seafarers. Some versions of her legend credit her with subduing demons to protect sailors by quelling storms far out at sea or destroying pirates who threatened their ships.

Because of her popularity along the southeastern coast of China, beginning in 1156 with the title Lady of Numinous Grace (Linghui furen), she started receiving a series of honorific titles, whereby she became incorporated into the state's official pantheon. In 1278, Kublai Khan honored her with the title Celestial Concubine (Tianfei), and in 1683 the Kangxi emperor bestowed on her the title Empress of Heaven in recognition and appreciation for help in securing Taiwan for the new Manchu rulers.[61] Undoubtedly official recognition was important in the spread of the Mazu cult.

While Mazu is best known for helping to protect and rescue sailors at sea, nonetheless, at times she could be violent and unpredictable. The fierce storms that erupted each year in the third lunar month were associated with Mazu; sea people of Fujian called these storms the "Mazu gales" (Mazu *ju*).[62] Sailors reported that sometimes during storms the goddess appeared as a ball of fire either going up or down the mast. If it was seen going up, this was a bad omen for it meant that she had abandoned the ship and there would be certain disaster; if it was seen going down, then this was a good omen and the sailors felt assured that they would survive the storm.[63] In some instances Mazu, as well as a number of other goddesses, was depicted in temples and popular iconography as an Amazon-like warrior, wielding a sword or command flag ready to do battle against unseen demons or real pirates. In a story told to anthropologist James Watson, in one temple in Hong Kong's New Territories, the statue of Mazu sits atop the remnants of a stone image of an earlier rival male deity that she had not only defeated in battle but also devoured.[64] More to the point, the early thirteenth-century scholar Ding Bogui warned devotees that unless they properly placated the Divine Woman, whom he depicted as a terrifying Dragon Lady (*long nü*), she was dangerous and would harm people.[65]

On the Leizhou peninsula and Hainan island, one local deity is called Mother of Typhoons (Jumu), because she was believed to be the progenitor of storms and typhoons at sea. Qu Dajun, who classified typhoons as a *yin* element and therefore feminine, recounted how people prayed to Jumu in hopes of preventing storms. A somewhat precarious deity, however, she would either create or prevent storms depending on her mood. It was therefore the custom in this area for boat people before setting out on a voyage to visit her temple to beseech her blessings and protection while at sea. Another similar deity worshipped in coastal south China was called the Mother of Winds (Fengmu).[66]

In Fuzhou, besides Mazu, the boat people venerate the Lady of the Seventh Star (Qixing Niangniang) as a patron deity. She was associated with the popular story of the Weaving Maid, but also was something of an Amazon-like warrior who miraculously saved the women and children of the city during the Mongol invasion. In 1368, the Hongwu Emperor canonized her with the title Lady Who Protects Children and Registers Births (Baochan zhusheng yuanjun), and sometime later she also received the title Sage Mother

(Shengmu). Because she was considered the protector of young girls, parents have traditionally placed their daughters under her ritual protection, making the Lady of the Seventh Star their adoptive mother. On her festival, celebrated on the seventh day of the seventh lunar month, women still go to her temples to make offerings of embroidered shoes, cosmetics, combs, handkerchiefs, and fans, and girls of sixteen *sui* perform nubility rites, which mark their availability for marriage.[67]

There were, of course, other female spirits and goddesses who were protective and beneficent. On both the Guangdong and Fujian coasts, among the Dan boat people, there were the so-called Little Old Ladies (Pozai), also commonly referred to as the Milk Ladies (Nainiang), whom women prayed to for protection and good health for both themselves and their children. They belonged to a large group of minor female deities who assisted women in childbirth. Their shrines could be found aboard ships and in makeshift shanties on shore.[68] On Hainan island one local goddess, Holy Mother of Shuiwei (Shuiwei shengmu), was especially worshipped by women seeking good health for their children and the retention of their own youthful beauty. On her birthday, either the fourth or twenty-fifth day of the second lunar month depending on location, female worshippers took to her temple offerings of perfume, face powder, and handkerchiefs, which they brought home after being blessed.[69] In Macau's Kanggong Temple in the Inner Harbor at a side altar near the entrance is a shrine dedicated to a goddess known as the Powdered Lady (Huafen furen), who was the patron deity of local prostitutes on the floating brothels whose main anchorage was nearby (figure 24). Prostitutes made offerings of perfume, face powder, and bead trinkets, and prayed for good health (particularly avoidance of venereal infections). While several of the deities mentioned above were not specifically sea goddesses, nonetheless boat women were among their most fervent devotees.

Besides the officially recognized cults and temples, such as those dedicated to Tianhou, innumerable unregistered, illicit temples and cults dotted the south China coastline. In fact, Lee Irwin has posited that the majority of female divinities "were generally unconnected with orthodox rites and were unsanctioned by religious and secular authorities." What is more, they were "regarded as a threat to the masculine, hierarchic authorities."[70] These were what the Ming and Qing governments labeled heretic cults and licentious shrines. Sometimes they began as modest matsheds located in small fishing villages and port towns that engaged in clandestine trade and were not sanctioned by the government. Frequently too the cults that developed around

Figure 24. Side Altar of the Powdered Lady in the Kanggong Temple in Macau, 2019 (Source: Photo by author)

these temples and shrines included not only fishers and sailors but also pirates and smugglers. Devotees often practiced exorcistic rituals and spirit possession, activities that the state considered unorthodox (*xie*) and licentious (*yin*), though certainly devotees never depicted them as such.[71] An example of such a cult was that of the Third Old Lady, discussed in chapter 8.

The idea of ambivalent identity is deeply embedded in the narratives about Chinese female sea deities. They reflected the incongruity of the seas themselves, which at times were calm and benevolent yet at other times wild and destructive. On the one hand, like Dan boat women the sea goddesses were strong and independent, and on the other hand, like female pirates the goddesses were forceful and violent. Furthermore, it is important to point out that there was not only a distinction to be drawn between deities and demons, but also between deities whose actions were at times good and at other times vile. Even goddesses could at times act like demons. Nonetheless, however they are characterized, goddesses and sprites have remained an omnipresent feature of south China's water world.

Conclusion

We are told that in the West, at least in the past, women who went to sea were frowned upon by most people. In fact, we know from sailors' lore and pirate codes that women were expressly forbidden aboard ships. Their presence was considered too distracting and disturbing, and many sailors also believed women brought bad luck. Nevertheless, we do know that in the West women did venture out to sea as sailors and pirates, but when they did so they typically disguised themselves as young men.

In southern China, Dan women did not have to go out to sea; they were born, raised, and lived their entire lives on the sea. Unlike Western seafaring women, their Chinese counterparts did not have to disguise as men, but rather they dressed and acted as women. Unlike most of their counterparts on land, Dan boat women did not bind their feet. On Chinese ships women worked alongside the male sailors and they worked just as hard and often even harder. Yet they too were frowned upon and marginalized by landed society. The marginal status of boat women, I would argue, was liberating, at least in the sense of releasing them from the norms of dominant society on land that restricted women to the "inner chambers" and to only certain types of work men deemed suitable for respectable women. Unlike other non-elite women, ideally expected to remain at home cooking and weaving, south China's boat women were able to spend their lives outside the confines of the home, working openly on rivers and seas as ferry boat operators, fisher women, prostitutes, and pirates.

As I have argued, boat women represented a threatening "other" that people on land (especially men) criticized as immoral and shameful. Dan women self-consciously defied the accepted notions of womanhood, breaking with established codes of female propriety, virtue, and passivity. Female seafarers were subversive and dangerous. Although some women in elite families and a few women of commoner status were able to gain a degree of independence, they normally did so without rejecting the accepted values of the patriarchal system. Boat women, however, enjoyed freedoms unheard of for most women on land, and in effect turned Confucianism on its head. From the perspective of dominant society on land, women who acted like men perverted the accepted social order and normal gender relations. In short, they challenged the patriarchal hierarchy upon which both state and society rested. Female pirates and female sea deities reinforced these notions of "other" and provided boat women with positive alternative models of womanhood, strength, and defiance in an otherwise male and land-centered Chinese cosmos.

Let me end with a few thoughts about where I started this chapter—the feminization of south China's maritime world. According to tradition the sea symbolized the *yin* forces in nature, which is female. Water belonged to the dark and cold. Water is soft and weak in the same way that China's traditional society depicted women. Yet as the ancient philosopher Laozi has pointed out, although the weakest of things, water can overcome the strongest, just as women can overcome men and male-dominated society. The sea is a life-giving source but one that is also dangerous and life-threatening. The seas are pregnant with aquatic life, yet also cold and dark. Like *yin*, the seas are deep and mysterious, and full of dangers. In the natural order of things, according to orthodox Confucian teachings, men take precedence over women, just as *yang* takes precedence over *yin*. This was the proper and natural order of things, the way it was supposed to be. But the world of Chinese seafarers was inverted and Confucianism was turned upside down. Instead, southern China's watery world was one in which women played active, not passive roles and at times even leading roles. They became active agents in their own lives and in the shaping of history.

CHAPTER 8

Weizhou Island, Dan Fishers, and the Mysterious Third Old Lady

THE WORSHIP OF A LITTLE-KNOWN DEITY NAMED THE THIRD OLD LADY (Sanpo) began as an obscure local cult in the Gulf of Tonkin, but her precise origins are unclear. What does seem certain is that her cult was deeply intertwined with the history of Weizhou island and its connections with fisherfolks and pirates. Before her transformation into Sanpo she may have been a water sprite who watched over a natural spring on the island. By the eighteenth century Sanpo had a growing following among the Dan fishers, seafarers, pirates, and smugglers who frequented Weizhou, and who in 1738 or 1739 erected a temple in her honor at South Bay (Nanwan). By the end of the century her temples peppered the Lienzhou coast and Leizhou peninsula, and by the start of the following century there were Sanpo temples in the Canton delta. Map 8 presents the distribution of Sanpo Temples on the coast of Guangdong in the second half of the nineteenth century. In this chapter I look at how fishers and pirates played key roles in the spread of the cult from west to east along the Guangdong coast, as well as how this originally local cult was co-opted into the state-recognized cult of the Empress of Heaven (Tianhou), also known colloquially as the Maternal Ancestor (Mazu). In reality, as we will see, the story of the Third Old Lady is complicated and nuanced.

Although less than ten square miles in size, Weizhou is the largest island in the Gulf of Tonkin after Hainan. Weizhou is situated west of the Leizhou peninsula and south of Hepu (roughly thirty-five nautical miles south of present-day Beihai City). Fishing, pearl cultivation, and subsistence

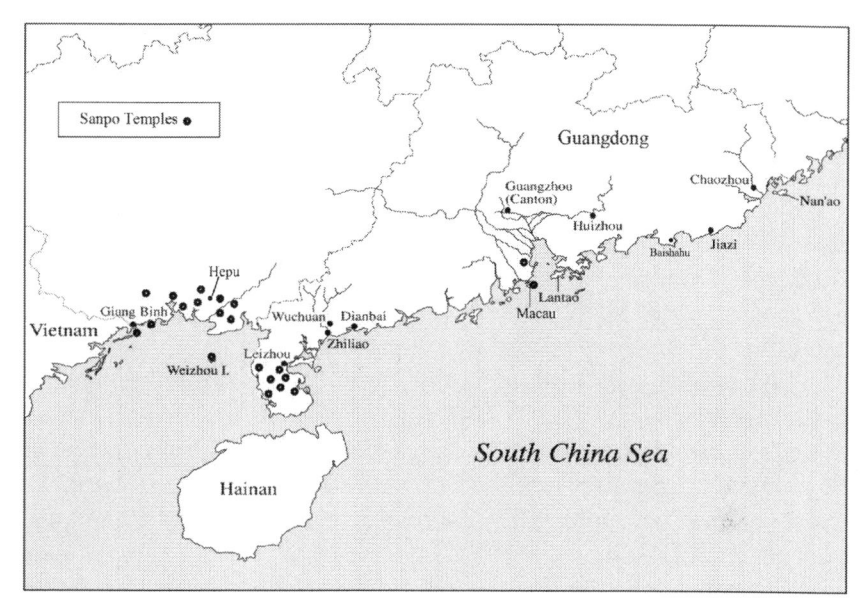

Map 8. Distribution of Sanpo Temples on the Guangdong Coast, c. 1850–1900 (Source: Created by author)

agriculture have continued as the main economic activities of the islanders. South Bay, which was formed out of a crater from an extinct volcano, was, and still is, the main harbor. Local legends relate how seafarers from as far back as the Han dynasty continually frequented the bay to careen their ships and replenish their supplies of fresh water from a well-known spring. Writing at the end of the sixteenth century, Guo Fei explained that because the waters around the island provided a safe harbor for as many as fifty vessels during the southerly monsoons, it became a frequent resort of fisherfolk, pearl thieves, smugglers, and pirates. Although officials repeatedly attempted to make the island off limits, they were never successful. Before the eighteenth century, in fact, the island had a regular, persistent transient population, whose makeshift communities came and went with the changing seasons. During the turbulent Ming-Qing transition, Yang Yandi and other pirates used the island as a staging area for forays in and beyond the gulf. In the late eighteenth and early nineteenth centuries, several pirate chieftains, such as Zheng Yi and Wushi Er, established permanent camps on the island. When a Qing military expedition attacked Weizhou in 1808, for instance, soldiers found roughly five hundred men, women, and children: 223 pirates and their families, 56 kidnapped victims being held for ransom, 150 illegal squatters, 72 laborers and beggars, and 3 men who fenced booty or handled ransom payments for the pirates.[1] Despite repeated naval campaigns and government prohibitions, Weizhou continued as a pirate and smuggler haven well into the twentieth century.[2]

Before the Yuan dynasty there is no record of any government outpost on the island. In 1294 the Mongol rulers established a Patrolling Inspector (*xunjian*) post on the island, which was responsible for guarding nearby waters and keeping the island free of miscreants and dissidents. Nonetheless, because of the remoteness of the island, the post apparently did not remain for long.[3] When the Mongol soldiers first arrived at the island they found it desolate and sparsely populated with only a few fisherfolks and pearl gathers living in impermanent hovels. According to local lore, they also discovered at South Bay a mysterious natural spring enclosed in a straw hut. After restocking their ships with spring water and not having found anyone around, the soldiers torched the hut, afraid that it would be used by illegal sojourners who frequented the island. Back aboard their ship, however, they were unable to weigh anchor and set sail, being prevented by a strange female apparition, whom they quickly realized was the "spirit of the spring." Only after beseeching forgiveness for destroying her "home" and promising to build a shrine in her honor did she allow them to leave. We do not know if they actually built a shrine, but what we do know is that directly behind the spring there is a grotto in the side of a precipice with an ancient shrine inside. At some point (islanders simply told me "a long time ago") fisherfolk attached a small matshed to the grotto where they worshipped Sanpo. In 1738 or 1739, because of her increasing popularity, local fishers and regular sojourners built a Sanpo Temple in South Bay (this temple still stands today behind a new temple built in the 1980s). Some devotees believe that Sanpo is the metamorphosis of the water sprite who protected this "sacred spring."[4]

Between the Yuan and Qing dynasties, Weizhou island had no permanent villages. While no one was permitted to settle on the island, many people tried to do so, and whenever they did the government issued new prohibitions and sent soldiers to clear away their homesteads. Today, in fact, in front of the Sanpo Temple there is a stone stele dated 1811 in which Governor-General Bailing permanently prohibited anyone from settling on the island; nonetheless, such sweeping prohibitions were unenforceable.[5]

The Dan were the most persistent group returning year after year to the island. For the most part, they engaged in fishing and pearl gathering for their livelihoods, but because of prejudice and poverty, many of them supplemented their legitimate occupations with predatory activities. In the Gulf of Tonkin the label Dan was a catch-all term used by officials to describe the sundry groups of Chinese and Vietnamese fishers, pearl gathers, and boat people living and operating in the area. In the Ming and early Qing periods the imperial government monopolized the pearl industry and strictly regulated the collection and distribution of pearls, much to the disadvantage of the pearl divers who found it increasingly hard to earn a living. Since the state always found it difficult to distinguish honest fishers from pirates, officials tended to practice ethnic profiling, lumping together all Dan as criminals. For roughly two centuries, between 1450 and 1650, loosely organized bands of so-called pearl thieves operated from bases on Weizhou island. They were mostly poor Dan boat people who clandestinely gathered and sold pearls to merchants in Qinzhou, Hepu, and Vietnam.[6]

One of the largest episodes involving pearl thieves occurred in the late 1570s when two Dan boatmen, Su Guansheng and Zhou Caixiong, gathered a force of roughly a thousand pearl gatherers and fishers to rob pearl beds, ships, villages, and government installations throughout the gulf region. Although soldiers captured and executed Su and more than four hundred followers in 1581, Zhou apparently escaped and was never heard from again. A few years later in 1589 officials again reported to the throne that soldiers had apprehended nearly a thousand pearl thieves who had been operating in hundreds of large junks in the waters around Weizhou. When times were tough, as they so often were, the pearl thieves became outright pirates plundering ships and villages throughout the Gulf of Tonkin.[7]

In the Tianhou Temple in Xiajiang in the suburbs of Leizhou City there is a large Ming dynasty stone inscription dated 1587 commemorating a major renovation of the temple. Originally this temple was built several hundred years earlier in the Song dynasty along the river leading into the city's commercial port. The inscription described how in the 1580s, because pearl thieves had gotten out of hand, the government forcefully relocated the Weizhou islanders back to the mainland, with many of them being resettled in the Leizhou peninsula. They brought with them their local deity, Qinghui, who was introduced into the Tianhou Temple (at that time still called Tianfei Temple). Qinghui was none other than Sanpo. According to an old handwritten liturgical text called the "Classic Book of Qinghui" (*Qinghui jingjuan*) that I found in Shanwei village on the Leizhou peninsula, she was born in Putian county in Fujian on the first day of the seventh lunar month into the Lin family around some mysterious circumstances. This of course refers to the same Lin family that Tianhou or Mazu also belongs, and therefore it is clear that Qinghui was Mazu's sister and someone quite special in her own right.[8]

In an alternate story written much later, in 1995, however, Qinghui was said to be a Russian warrior princess, born on the twenty-first day of the seventh lunar month in 976, who came to the aid of the Song emperor in his war against invading Khitan armies. After performing many heroic deeds in fighting China's enemies, she became the "sworn sister" of Tianhou and Zhaobao. After Qinghui died she was enshrined next to her two sworn sisters in the Tianhou Temple. The local people today refer to them as the "Three Sisters" (Sanjiemei)—Tianhou the elder sister, Zhaobao the second sister, and Qinghui the third sister. Therefore, Qinghui is colloquially known as Sanpo (Third Sister).[9] Although the stories are completely different, nonetheless, in both accounts Qinghui or Sanpo is considered to be the third sister of Tianhou. Like Tianhou, Sanpo too refused to marry and was a fearsome warrior sea goddess. At this point in the story Sanpo already had a close association with Tianhou.

Starting about the same time that Sanpo was being introduced into the Leizhou peninsula by Dan fishers and pirates from Weizhou island, and continuing over the next century, her cult spread to other communities across the Gulf of Tonkin. One obscure nineteenth-century document, which was later recorded in the *Xu Xiu Siku Quanshu*, cited an 1812 stone inscription stating that Sanpo was Tianhou's third elder sister whose birthday was on the twenty-second day of the third lunar month, that is, one day before Tianhou's birthday, and furthermore that the Sanpo cult was especially popular along the Lienzhou coast.[10] During my fieldwork in 2010 and 2011, in this area I found Sanpo temples in Hepu, Qinzhou, Fangcheng, Jiangping, and Zhushan on the border with Vietnam, as well as throughout the Leizhou peninsula. In most cases the temples were dedicated specifically to Sanpo or Qinghui; but in some cases, Sanpo was a secondary deity in a temple dedicated to another god. That was the case, for example, at the Kangwang Temple outside Qinzhou, which had a side altar venerating Sanpopo (an alternate designation of Sanpo). I also discovered many household shrines that included Sanpo as part of family worship. Appendix 3 lists the mostly extant Sanpo temples in coastal Guangdong and Guangxi. The list, however, is not exhaustive. There certainly are more temples and side altars dedicated to Sanpo than the ones listed in this appendix; nonetheless, I believe the list is a fair representation of the distribution of Sanpo temples in Guangdong and Guangxi.

Although there is a large concentration of Sanpo temples on the Lienzhou coast, it is unclear whether they all honor the same deity. It appears that the name Sanpo was in common use and referred, in a generic sense, to any one of several female deities or combinations of deities. Also, it is likely the names of deities evolved and changed over time. For example, in Teng county, Guangxi, in the Dragon Mother (Longmu) Temple people refer to its three enshrined deities—the Dragon Mother, Mazu, and another local deity known as the Third Elder Sister Liu (Liu Sanjie)—collectively as Sanpo (Three Old Ladies). In another example, off the Qinzhou coast three natural stone monoliths are worshiped as the Three Ladies (Sanniang) or Sanpo. According to one local legend, the three stone pillars are the metamorphosed incarnations of three sisters who lived in a nearby fishing village and were miracle workers, much like Mazu, who protected and saved sailors whose ships were wrecked in storms. According to another legend, the three sisters, who died at sea in a storm in their fishing boat, were magically transformed into stone pillars by the Daoist immortal Jade Emperor because they were chaste and righteous virgins.[11] The Sanpo temples in and around Jiangping (Giang Bình in Vietnamese) need special mention. At the time that the Sanpo cult was developing on Weizhou island in the Ming period, groups of Vietnamese fisherfolks, known today in China as the Jing minority, were settling on several islands near Jiangping on the Sino-Vietnamese border. They too brought with them their own language, culture, and religious beliefs, which included the worship of Sanpo, which some villagers said referred to three deities: the Buddhist Goddess of Mercy (Guanyin laomu) and two other local (Vietnamese?) deities. Other villagers, however, told me that Sanpo was a single deity and none other than Guanyin.[12]

Probably at some point in the second half of the eighteenth century, fishers and pirates from Weizhou island brought the Sanpo cult to the Canton delta. We know for certain that Dan fishers from Xiangshan (present-day Zhongshan), Macau, and Hong Kong had been fishing in the Gulf of Tonkin for centuries, and that Weizhou was a frequent anchorage. Several years ago, at the University of Hong Kong Library, I came across an old faded map dated c. 1930 showing the sailing routes used by fishers between Hong Kong and Macau and the Gulf of Tonkin (map 9). These same sailing routes would have been used by fishers and pirates in the eighteenth and nineteenth centuries and surely even earlier. We also know for a fact that pirates—who in many cases were themselves Dan fishers—from the Canton delta often went on extended raiding expeditions into the Gulf of Tonkin and used Weizhou

CHAPTER 8

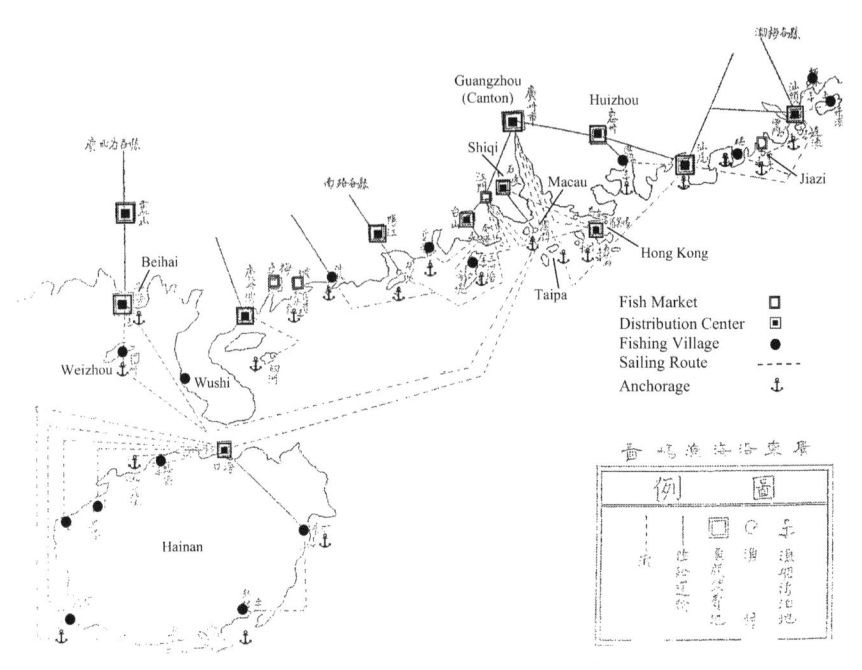

Map 9. Sailing Routes of Fishers between Hong Kong and the Gulf of Tonkin, c. 1930 (Source: Created by author; based on c. 1930 fishing route map)

as one of their main anchorages.[13] During the upsurge in Guangdong piracy between 1790 and 1810, Cantonese pirates Zheng Qi, Zheng Yi, and Guo Podai had bases on Weizhou, as did Wushi Er and Donghai Ba.[14] The great pirate chief Zhang Baozai, who began his outlaw career after being abducted at age fifteen by Zheng Yi, also would have spent much of his early years as a pirate on Weizhou. Significant too, Yuan Yonglun reported in his book, *A Record of Pacification of the Seas*, first published in 1830, that Zhang Baozai and other Cantonese pirates worshipped Sanpo at a temple in Huizhou prefecture as early as 1805.[15]

Huizhou, however, needs further consideration. Although I have not found any references to Sanpo in any extant gazetteers or other textual sources, during my field research in coastal Huizhou in December 2012, I came across a number of temples dedicated to sea goddesses, particularly Mazu, many of which had statues of three female deities on their altars. But none of the temple caretakers or worshipers were familiar with Sanpo or Qinghui. Take the example of the ancient port town of Jiazi in Lufeng county, where there is a Tianhou Temple that dates to the Song dynasty. Inside the temple on the main altar are three statues all said to be different Mazus—one of Lin Moniang, called Great Mother (Da Ma, birthday on the twenty-third day of the third lunar month), another called Second Mother (Er Ma, birthday on the twentieth day of the eighth lunar month), and the third called Third Mother (San Ma, birthday on the tenth day of the fourth lunar month). As explained in the first interlude, each deity is a separate, unique Mazu. According to the caretaker, Mr. Lin, who at the time was seventy-eight, he never heard the name Sanpo or Qinghui, and in fact he told me that it would be an insult to use the word *po* to refer to Tianhou or other female deities because the term was disrespectful; no one, he said, would call a deity "old lady" (*po*). Of course, it is possible that over the past centuries the identities of the female deities in these Huizhou temples have changed. This was not uncommon in China.[16]

It is also possible that Zhang Baozai, other pirates, and fishers worshipped Sanpo on Taipa, a small island and popular anchorage just south of Macau. On the island there is a small Sanpo Temple, which according to stone inscriptions was constructed in 1843 or 1845, and what is more, the cult on Taipa had close links with Weizhou and Leizhou (see the discussion below). Sanpo was described as the third elder sister of Tianhou with her festival celebrated on the twenty-second day of the third lunar month. On the temple's stone inscriptions, the Third Old Lady is referred to as Qinghui Sanpo, thus linking her directly to the cult in the Gulf of Tonkin. The actual shrine, where the statue of Sanpo was placed, is in a grotto at the rear of the temple. This is quite similar to the situation of the Sanpo Temple on Weizhou island—in both cases long before any temple was constructed a shrine was placed inside a grotto on a precipice. Later, as the deity became more popular, a matshed would have been attached to the grotto's entrance, and finally, after many years, a temple would have been built. So although the Sanpo Temple on Taipa was built in the 1840s, it is likely that several decades earlier fishers and pirates—such as Zhang Baozai (who died in 1822)—were worshipping Sanpo in this grotto. By the early nineteenth century there were also Sanpo temples in adjoining Xiangshan county and even on Lantao island in Hong Kong.[17]

Legitimizing the Sanpo Cult
Like the goddess Zuxi, the Third Old Lady was never formally recognized by any imperial government; she was never registered in the official pantheon of orthodox deities, as was Tianhou. Despite her growing popularity among

CHAPTER 8

Guangdong's boat people, Sanpo remained, in the eyes of officials, a licentious and unorthodox deity. The reasons for this rebuff are not difficult to understand. After all, from the state's perspective, the cult began among Dan fishers, who officials viewed as pearl thieves and pirates. To them the Dan were a despised underclass discriminated against in both law (before the late 1720s) and social custom, and pearl thieves and pirates, of course, were criminals. In her original form, the Third Old Lady protected these same despicable people, who honored her by installing her in shrines on their boats and in temples on shore. Officials were also disturbed by the exorcistic practices of her spirit mediums and worshippers, which they viewed as sorcery. In some stories Sanpo was a sword-wielding warrior goddess who came to the aid of anyone (including pirates) who worshipped and sacrificed to her.[18] According to the 1879 edition of the Xiangshan county gazetteer, Dan fishers in Niukoushan village had erected a small Sanpo temple in which devotees, both men and women, became possessed, spoke in tongues, and flagellated themselves. Then in 1854, the county magistrate, who viewed these practices as heretical, suppressed the Sanpo cult in Xiangshan and punished the "sorcerers" by flogging them in public, thereby putting an end to the cult in that county (though not in Taipa).[19]

Suppression, however, often drove cults underground, only for them to reemerge at some later time. Religious practices that were in the past considered unorthodox and illegal, in fact, have persisted to today in Leizhou and Weizhou (as elsewhere in China), despite condemnations as feudal superstitions (*fengjian mixin*) by the current Chinese party-state. In Shanwei village in Leizhou, a female spirit medium (*huapo*) surnamed Liu told me that when she first became possessed by Qinghui during the Cultural Revolution local cadre endlessly persecuted her, and only gradually in the late 1980s was she accepted and recognized for her "special powers" by her fellow villagers, who frequently consulted her mostly on matters of health and marriage.[20] Also in Leizhou during the lunar new year festivals and other religious holidays, including the birthday of Qinghui, spirit mediums in trance parade in the streets and villages with metal skewers piercing their cheeks or tongues (figure 25).[21] On Weizhou island at the Sanpo Temple, each year her festivals in the third and eighth lunar months include exorcist rituals, such as walking on fire (*guohuoshan*), climbing a ladder of knives (*padaoti*), and mediums in trances piercing their bodies with metal swords or spikes (*chuanling*). People regard such rituals as a form of war magic pitting Sanpo against demons who threaten the community. Like Mazu and Zuxi, Sanpo is a fearsome evil-expelling deity yet also one who is nurturing and protective. Today rituals labeled feudal superstitions, though technically illegal, are generally tolerated by local Communist cadre in Leizhou and Weizhou as expressions of traditional culture and forms of entertainment good for tourism. They are treated as cultural heritage.[22]

Figure 25. Spirit Medium in Trance with Long Metal Skewer Piercing His Cheeks, Shanwei Village, 2010 (Source: Photo by author)

CHAPTER 8

A turning point in the worship of Sanpo occurred between the 1840s and 1850s. On the one hand, in a deliberate attempt to disassociate Sanpo from pirates, stories began to appear about how she helped fishers, seafarers, and officials suppress piracy. This is most evident in the written versions about the Sanpo legend that always credit her with the suppression of pirates and other wrongdoers who threatened the peace and stability of the realm. On the other hand, in an effort to rid Sanpo of the stigmatism of heterodoxy devotees intentionally associated her with the state-sponsored cult of Tianhou; in some cases she was actually transformed into Tianhou.

Information on Taipa and the Sanpo Temple on that island are instructive. On one of the temple's extant stone inscriptions, dated 1859, it explained that the island was a busy anchorage for fishing junks and that fishers all depended on Sanpo for protection from storms and other dangers, namely pirates. According to the inscription, local Dan fishing fleets on several occasions joined forces with the imperial navy to fight pirates and rebels. We know for certain that on the heels of the Opium War tens of thousands of coolies, porters, and day laborers in the Canton delta were thrown out of work and many of them turned to piracy to survive. The turmoil, of course, continued unabated with the Taiping Rebellion and in Guangdong in particular with the Red Turban uprising and Hakka-Punti War that lasted until the late 1860s.[23] In 1843, a man named Zheng Shangpan from Iron City (Tiecheng, present-day Shiqi), the county seat of Xiangshan, organized a Dan flotilla to cooperate with Lai Enjue, the Guangdong provincial naval commander, on campaigns against pirates operating in the Gulf of Tonkin around Weizhou and Leizhou. By 1855, Red Turbans, Triads, and large bands of pirates were active in the waters around Macau and again the fishing fleets were called upon to quell the disturbances, and two years later provincial authorities once again summoned the fishers to sail up the West River to Wuzhou in Guangxi province to fight the Red Turbans who occupied the city. In each case fishers and officials thanked Sanpo for her protection and for helping them to victory over pirates and rebels.[24]

There are also similar stories from Weizhou about Sanpo protecting sailors and aiding the imperial navy defeat pirates in the Gulf of Tonkin. One interesting story relates to a Qing military officer named Huang Kaiguang, who in the 1840s had been stationed on Hainan island and was a renowned pirate fighter. In 1849 he cooperated with the British Royal Navy in a campaign against the Cantonese pirate Shap-ng Tsai (Shiwuzai) who was active in the area at that time.[25] After a successful campaign, Huang went to Weizhou to personally thank Sanpo for protecting his soldiers and helping in the defeat of the pirates, and according to some local stories it was Huang who built the Sanpo Temple. A native boatman named Lin Kuan told me another legend about Huang Kaiguang, which is similar to other stories that I heard about Sanpo. What he told me is worth retelling:

> *Once Huang Kaiguang led a naval force to Weizhou to suppress pirates, but when he arrived at the island, he found no trace of either pirates or villagers. All that he saw was a dilapidated temple in front of a grotto where fishers venerated the local deity Sanpo. Angry that he could not find any pirates, Huang burned the temple to the ground. Not long afterward, the sky turned black and the winds rose up and his warships could not leave the bay. Huang understood that he had enraged the goddess for burning down her shrine and so he immediately returned to shore and knelt before the cave where he lit incense and prayed for forgiveness. He promised that if Sanpo protected his fleet and gave him victory over the pirates he would return to build her a proper temple. Thereupon the skies cleared and as his fleet moved out of the bay, he sighted a large cave where the pirates hid. For seven days and seven nights a fierce battle raged and in the end Huang was victorious. As promised, he soon afterward returned to South Bay where he constructed a large temple.*[26]

It is likely that Huang Kaiguang was responsible for a major renovation of the temple in the early 1850s, but he was not responsible for the original construction of the temple, which most likely was in 1738 or 1739. Huang is important, however, in helping to legitimize Sanpo by associating her with a Qing official's recognition and support.[27]

It must have been about the same time, but we cannot be certain, that the Third Old Lady was transformed into the Empress of Heaven. In the process Sanpo lost her identity as a unique deity while becoming legitimized as Tianhou. This change is not difficult to understand. Since the Song dynasty, Tianhou has been depicted in written sources as the arch slayer of pirates and protector of seafarers, and by the mid 1850s she already had long been officially recognized by the state. Sanpo's transmutation involved a simple name or identity change. On Weizhou island, at some point in the past, the Sanpo Temple became the Tianhou Temple and Sanpo became Tianhou or Mazu. As the temple's caretaker, Mr. Li, explained to me, because Mazu was the third sister in her family she was called Sanpo (Third Sister). I heard the same story at other Tianhou/Sanpo temples along the Lienzhou coast. Similarly, on Lantao island off Hong Kong, in Dongyong village, at the Tianhou Temple, worshippers simply told me that Sanpo was the name that local fishers gave to Tianhou, without further explanation.[28] In all of these cases the Tianhou/Sanpo festival is celebrated on the twenty-third day of the third lunar month, which is Tianhou's birthday. The appropriation of Tianhou's identity was significant because it gave Sanpo legitimacy as a state approved deity, one who had shed her old vestiges of heterodoxy and had joined the official pantheon of deities. Nonetheless, although there was a name change the ritual practices apparently remained the same.[29]

The situation on the island of Taipa and the Leizhou peninsula developed differently. On Taipa, after the 1840s, "Hakka merchants" (*keshang*) flocked to the island and built their own Tianhou and Beidi temples. About the same time, as more and more Dan fishers settled on shore as farmers and shopkeepers, they gradually shed their identity (and stigma) as boat people and also began to abandon Sanpo in favor of the two state-sanctioned deities. The island's center of gravity, in the meantime, shifted to the southwest to the area near the Tianhou and Beidi temples, and by the end of the century the fishing boat anchorage and fish market also had moved nearby the Tianhou Temple. By the 1920s the Sanpo Temple had fallen into disuse, only to be resurrected in the 1990s once Macau became a UNESCO World Heritage Site. On Taipa Sanpo had not transformed into Tianhou, but instead she lost her popularity, and likely also her efficacy, and faded away.[30]

In Leizhou Sanpo was neither transformed into Tianhou nor did she disappear. Instead, today Sanpo or Qinghui, as she is better known in Leizhou, is one of the most popular deities, especially with a large following among child-bearing married women who view her as a maternal (or vernal) deity. She is usually dressed in green (*qing*), the color representing springtime, growth, and fertility. Her annual festival, which is celebrated on the twenty-first day of the seventh lunar month, focuses on fecundity and the protection and health of young children and no longer has anything to do with the sea per se. Throughout the peninsula she is worshipped in countless temple side altars and family shrines as well as in her own temples.[31]

Conclusion

The story of the Third Old Lady evolved slowly over several centuries, yet there are still many unresolvable missing pieces and inconsistencies. As an unsanctioned deity, she never developed a standardized set of shared values and symbols, and she has remained open to several, often contradictory, interpretations about her origins, birthday, and identity. She meant different things to different people. She likely appeared first in the thirteenth century, or perhaps earlier, as a nameless water sprite protecting a sacred spring frequented by fisherfolks and pirates on the remote Weizhou island. Over the next several centuries she gradually transformed from water sprite into the sea goddess Sanpo, who was first enshrined in a grotto behind a sacred spring and later in a temple built by boat people in the early eighteenth century. Dan fishers and pirates proved crucial in the spread of her cult throughout the Gulf of Tonkin and then to the Canton delta. By the time that the Qing naval officer, Huang Kaiguang, rebuilt or renovated the Sanpo Temple on Weizhou in the 1850s, Sanpo was being redefined as a defender of the state and arch-enemy of pirates. At some point she became identified as Tianhou. Simply put, on the island Sanpo is just another name for Tianhou. Today on Weizhou island Sanpo has a new temple, built in front of her old one, and a new name—Tianhou Temple.

It is still uncertain how the water sprite turned into a goddess and got the name "Sanpo," which I have translated as Third Old Lady. As noted the term *sanpo* also is used in a generic sense to mean "third sister" (as in the case of third sister of Mazu), "third wife" (as in the case of Yang Er's Third Wife, discussed in the first interlude), and "Three Old Ladies" (as in the case of the three goddesses enshrined in the Dragon Mother Temple in Teng county). On Weizhou island, where the Sanpo cult probably originated, the name likely derived from the earliest known legends that she was the third sister of Mazu. Sanpo's association with Mazu, in fact, was closely related to the latter's growing popularity among seafarers who began spreading the cult in the Song dynasty. By the late sixteenth century we know that Weizhou's Sanpo cult had reached the Leizhou peninsula and that she was enshrined in the Xiajiang Tianhou Temple as the Third Sister of Mazu, with the formal name Qinghui. That Qinghui was none other than Sanpo is confirmed by the 1859 stele in the Taipa Sanpo Temple, which names her Qinghui Sanpo, who came from the Weizhou-Leizhou area.

A watershed metamorphous came in the early nineteenth century when the Third Old Lady became the Empress of Heaven, thereby losing her own separate identity. I have argued that this transformation was a deliberate attempt on the part of her devotees to legitimize her cult and expunge the state's stigma of licentiousness and heterodoxy. This was done, at least on Weizhou island and around the Gulf of Tonkin, by remaking her into a pirate slayer and defender of law and order, as well as by transforming her into the Empress of Heaven, a legitimate state-recognized deity. As an unsanctioned deity her cult had been liable to official suppression, in the same way as pirates and rebels. In fact, Qing officials in the 1850s did suppress her cult in the Canton delta (in an area where she had not transformed into Tianhou), and as a result her temples were destroyed and her cult disappeared. On the island of Taipa Sanpo gradually lost her followers and her temple fell into disuse by the start of the twentieth century, only to be resurrected in the 1990s as a UNESCO World Heritage Site. On the Leizhou peninsula, Sanpo (or Qinghui) continues to today as a unique local cult whose devotees are mostly married females of childbearing age. Finally, Sanpo's metamorphosis was different from that of Zuxi, discussed in the first interlude; Sanpo simply became Mazu, whereas Zuxi became one of many unique goddesses on the Huizhou coast referred to as Mazu.

Postlude
China's Culture Wars

During the coronavirus pandemic in 2020 in China, battle lines in the culture wars were drawn over the unlikely issue of chopsticks, and more specifically over the time-honored custom of the communal sharing of food at the dinner table with chopsticks. For Chinese, of course, chopsticks have had a long history. They represented an ancient social and cultural tradition, one not easily changed, not even with the threat of the pandemic. Chopsticks have been described as an "indispensable utensil" in people's daily lives and even as a clear marker dividing civilized people from barbarians. Sharing food always has been a central feature of how Chinese convey affection and chopsticks have been an important metaphor for life itself. Therefore, almost instinctively, when the PRC government began recommending as a public health measure the disuse of chopsticks in favor of Western-style utensils, many Chinese reacted in angry opposition. They took offense in the state's interference in family matters and viewed it as an affront to Chinese culture and traditions. Other Chinese, however, recognized the need to shift eating habits, at least for the moment, as necessary to stem the tide of contagion, in the same way as wearing face masks and social distancing. The debate over chopsticks largely played out differently between urban and rural areas, educated and less educated people, women and men, young and old, and north and south.[1]

The conflict over chopsticks epitomized a deeper rift in China's society following the tragic failures of Maoism, which resulted in the loss of trust in the party-state among millions of citizens. Communism, as the fundamental sociopolitical ideology in China, faltered after the death of Chairman Mao in 1976, leaving the party scrambling to find substitutes. Under Deng Xiaoping and later leaders, socialism with Chinese characteristics transformed into capitalism with socialist characteristics. "To get rich is glorious" quickly replaced "serve the people" as China's new popularist mantra. Today

POSTLUDE

Chinese business people pursue wealth with new gods of money, even venerating foreign moguls such as Amazon founder Jeff Bezos, depicted in figure 26. The consumer culture that took off in the 1990s was accompanied by a revival of Confucianism. If Kang Youwei at the end of the nineteenth century could repackage Confucius as a reformer promoting constitutionalism, then why couldn't Hu Jintao and Xi Jinping repackage Confucius to bolster communism? Although during the Cultural Revolution the ancient sage was condemned as a proponent of feudal values, today those same Confucian

Figure 26. Chinese Trading Company Venerating Jeff Bezos as the God of Money on Black Friday, November 26, 2021 (Source: Wikimedia Commons)

values—respect for hierarchy, social harmony, frugality, and sexual restraint—are held up as the moral foundation for modern socialist China. At a time when many Chinese have lost faith in communism, party leaders have come to believe that Confucianism holds promises for building a new "socialist spiritual civilization," and at the same time helping to offset the unbridled capitalism and growing bourgeois individualism.[2] In the post-Mao era, cultural conflicts have increased as China has become more economically and socially diverse and less ideologically dogmatic.

China's culture wars, as Damien Ma has explained, have always been about defining the soul of the Chinese people.[3] In China and elsewhere culture wars tend to flare up during times of rapid economic change and when there are high degrees of social and cultural fragmentation, as well as widespread civil malaise and questioning of existing ethical values. According to sociologist James Hunter, who coined the term in American politics in 1991, culture wars are public conflicts based on differing worldviews regarding national identity and moral authority. They involve power struggles over who defines, shapes, and creates reality.[4] The culture wars in China, for the most part, have been fought out in a metaphorical middle ground in which no one side has been strong enough to vanquish the other. Hence, dominant orthodoxies, both past and present, have resulted from constant co-optations based on compromise and accommodation.[5] In this postlude we will examine China's culture wars over folk traditions, beliefs, and ritual practices, gender and sexuality, and multiculturalism and ethnic relations.

Ox-Demons and Snake-Spirits

In 1966 at the start of the Cultural Revolution, when Mao Zedong and his supporters adopted the slogan "ox-demons and snake-spirits" (*niugui sheshen*), they intentionally had chosen a term derived from traditional folk culture. As used by the Red Guards, the slogan became a common metaphor to denounce and dehumanize individuals deemed as opponents of the ascending cult of Chairman Mao. In popular culture the term conjured up images of an ominous cosmos populated by malevolent spirits who brought plagues, wars, and destruction to the human world. Depicting his enemies as monsters, freaks, and non-people, Mao deployed his Red Guards as divine armies to exorcise his demons. By purposefully invoking the traditional religious language of demonic invaders, Cultural Revolution propagandists fused and confused state and popular discussions about old and new class enemies, whether real or imagined. In fact, as Yiching Wu explains, "China's traditional folkloric demonological paradigms contributed considerably to the cultural idioms of political discourse in Mao's China."[6]

The spectacle of ox-demons and snake-spirits parading through cities and villages exemplified the deep cultural and spiritual divisions in late imperial and contemporary Chinese society. During the Maoist era, parading political enemies with dunce-caps and self-denigrating placards around their necks recalled similar traditional processions of criminals or deities through town and village streets to publicly purge and purify communities of perceived evils. In 1645, during bondservant revolts, former masters were bound, paraded, and abused by agitated crowds who forced them to declare their crimes against the people.[7] In south China during temple festivals it was common for zealots dressed as criminals with cuffs on their hands and chains around their necks to parade the streets to atone for their misdeeds.[8] Even today in many areas of rural China vestiges of the Cultural Revolution remain. In 2010, for instance, I witnessed a Thunder God procession in Shanwei village on the Leizhou peninsula, in which a spirit medium with cheeks pierced with an iron rod rode atop the god's palanquin (figure 25). He was followed by several poorly dressed men—beggars and village outcasts hired for the occasion—donning dunce-caps on which were written the words "ox-demons and snake-spirits" and other Maoist-era slogans (figure 27). The Thunder God procession, by juxtaposing political and sacerdotal symbols, was an annual public exorcism considered necessary to purge all bad elements, both human and ghostly, from the community.

Battles over ox-demons and snake-spirits signaled China's larger culture wars that have raged continuously for centuries over traditional folk beliefs and habits. On the one side, political elites in late imperial and contemporary China waged these wars to control popular culture by suppressing what they viewed as licentious (*yin*), heterodox (*xie*), and superstitious (*mixin*), including unregulated cults and sects, false gods, magic, fortune telling, geomancy, and so forth. On the other side, local communities fought back in various ways to defend their deities and religious customs against centralizing, hegemonic governments. The culture wars over folk religion were conflicts of competing belief systems and moralities that reflected enduring tensions and contradictions between state and society.

Much like Communist China, Ming and Qing authorities sought to create an orderly and puritanical society through legislation. As part of its civilizing mission, the late imperial state enacted laws to punish with death or exile individuals who wrote charms, recited spells, gave themselves exalted titles,

Figure 27. "Ox-Demons and Snake-Spirits" in the Thunder God Procession, Shanwei Village, 2010 (Source: Photo by author)

promoted religious processions and gatherings, and pretended to call down heretical gods. These laws were lumped together, usually under the rubrics of heresy and sedition, with those prohibiting secret societies and heterodox sects because they were viewed contrary to Confucian norms and posed threats to the stability of the realm. Officials often employed the derogatory language of the "rivers and lakes" to discredit spirit mediums, diviners, and geomancers as tricksters who deceived the people and caused trouble. What made them particularly dangerous was that they were ingrained in local communities and impossible to control or eradicate.[9]

At various times in the late imperial period, officials launched suppression campaigns against specific deities and cults. In the early Ming, hundreds of so-called licentious temples (*yinci*), including those of Buddhist, Daoist, and popular religions, were destroyed or converted into community schools (*shexue*), where wayward, misled subjects were to be reeducated in orthodox Confucian teachings.[10] In an attempt to "purify local customs," in 1724 the emperor inaugurated measures to "expel heresy and return to orthodoxy."[11] In Guangdong in the Ming and Qing periods, more specifically, officials launched suppression campaigns against the cult of the Lady of the Golden Flower (Jinhua furen), the cult of the Five Emperors (Wudi), and numerous unnamed village cults, where male spirit mediums dressed as women, danced wildly, and made sacrifices to demons.[12] We have also noted in chapter 5 how the government outlawed and suppressed popular lay Buddhist sects and secret societies, and in chapter 8 how in the 1850s the local magistrate in Xiangshan destroyed Sanpo temples, thereby greatly weakening the cult in that area.

Although PRC policies on religion have been contradictory and often arbitrary, they clearly followed precedents established in the late imperial period. During the Mao years extreme secularist policies sought to suppress all forms of religion as feudal superstition. In the 1980s, even as the government loosened restrictions on the economy, society, and religion, it continued to dictate what was proper and allowable. In seeking ideological and cultural control over the population, Deng Xiaoping, and later Hu Jintao and Xi Jinping, conducted periodic crackdowns on what they called "spiritual pollution" (*jingshen wuran*)—including pornography, homosexuality, and feudal superstition—which was counterpoised with "spiritual civilization" (*jingshen wenming*)—a purified vision for post-Mao Chineseness peppered with Confucianism.[13] In December 1983, a *Beijing Review* editorial reiterated the party's policy of "opposing cultural contamination" while protecting "lawful religious activities."[14] The government, however, only recognized the registered institutional religions of Buddhism, Daoism, Islam, and Christianity as lawful; all other religious groups were labeled illegitimate "superstitious organizations" (*mixin jiguan*) or "heterodox sects" (*xiejiao*) and therefore liable to criminal prosecution. New laws in the 1980s and 1990s singled out individuals who organized "superstitious sects and secret societies" as counterrevolutionaries to be sentenced to no less than five-years imprisonment, and "sorcerers and witches" who performed superstitious acts for the purpose of spreading rumors or swindling people to be sentenced between two and seven years imprisonment. These laws, in fact, closely resembled Ming and Qing laws in terminology and approach. The government aimed to sanitize Chinese religion within the accepted framework of Confucianism, Buddhism, and Daoism, while at the same time to make sure that religion conformed to the dogmas of the atheist Communist Party.[15]

Among the countless crackdowns on banned religious groups since 1949, I will briefly discuss two cases: Yiguandao and Falungong. Categorized in recent scholarship as redemptive societies—spiritual groups emanating from the salvationist and millenarian traditions of the late imperial period—in China they are labeled "reactionary sects and secret societies" (*fandong huidaomen*), a term used since the 1950s in campaigns to eradicate unorthodox religious groups.[16] The Yiguandao (Way of Pervading Unity), which first appeared in Shandong in the late nineteenth century, was an offshoot of the much earlier Xiantiandao (Way of Former Heaven), which itself was an offshoot of the Dachengjiao (Great Vehicle Teaching) discussed in chapter 5. In the late 1940s, as the Yiguandao was becoming the largest redemptive society in China, the Nationalist government outlawed the sect and after 1949 the new communist regime began a systematic country-wide campaign of suppression. Although severely undermined during the Mao era, in the 1980s the Yiguandao reemerged as an underground religious movement, which (according to government propaganda) fabricated "apocalyptic rumors" to incite rebellion and promoted "absurd superstitions" to cheat gullible peasants and seduce innocent women. Adopting similar measures as those used in the late imperial age, hundreds of leaders were arrested and executed or sent to prison, while untold numbers of ordinary members were forced to undergo political reeducation.[17] In Taiwan, however, after the government ended persecutions in 1987, the Yiguandao has flourished.

In 1999, the Chinese government denounced the Falungong (Practice of the Wheel of Law) and ordered its total eradication. Communist propaganda described it as an "evil cult," a label that had become "a mark of political demonization."[18] The Falungong had appeared in the 1980s as one of many "healing practices" during the *qigong* craze, but one that the authorities viewed as dangerous because of its millenarian teachings.[19] According to official statements, Li Hongzhi, the founder of the cult, had "fabricated many rumors to make himself mysterious and to cheat believers." Followers believed that he was the reincarnated Maitreya, the Buddha of the Future, who was often identified with messianic movements. In 2000 there were official media reports that the Falungong had denounced Jiang Zemin, who was president at the time, as an evil spirit appearing as a toad and that he was assisted by another evil spirit in the form of a "ferocious crocodile"—in folk culture both toads and crocodiles were considered venomous creatures having demonic powers. Some followers, it was further rumored, had apocalyptic visions of a sword-wielding rider on a white horse, assumed to be Li Hongzhi, who would smite China's communist leaders and usher in a new age of great peace. In this scenario, only true believers would be saved from the cataclysm. Obviously, such portents derived from preexisting popular messianic traditions, which officials perceived as a threat to the existing government and therefore needed to be eliminated. Severely suppressed in China, today the Falungong has become an international movement with a large number of expatriate Chinese adherents as well as a growing number of Western supporters.[20]

While the state remained busy with suppression campaigns, persecuted religious groups and individuals fought back by adopting various strategies to protect themselves, their beliefs, and their practices. Subterfuge was one of their most common responses. In order to hide their identity from the authorities, outlawed sects frequently changed names. For example, the Dachengjiao used a variety of names, including Wupanjiao, Yinpanjiao, and Laomujiao, but such ruses seldom stopped government attacks. A more successful strategy was to align themselves with state orthodoxy or to claim to be defenders of traditional Chinese culture, while maintaining their own beliefs and ritual practices. As noted in chapter 8, during recent Sanpo and other temple festivals, activities that had previously been labeled "feudal superstitions" were converted into acceptable elements of "cultural heritage." Similarly, geomancers and diviners, whom the present government disparage as con men, have in some cases associated themselves and their arts with orthodox teachings, such as the *Book of Changes* (*Yijing*) and National Learning (*Guoxue*), thereby enhancing their social status and acceptability as upholders of authentic Chineseness. Thus, to put it simply, dubious religious groups and individuals have attempted to cloak their activities by appropriating the symbolism of what the state deemed orthodox.[21]

Alleged false gods also have been disguised as orthodox gods sanctioned by the state. It has long been common practice for devotees, whenever necessary, to give their deities alternative identities to conceal their true nature from their persecutors. As P. Steven Sangren discovered during fieldwork in Taiwan in the 1980s, some sects labeled heretic by the government placed images of the Goddess of Mercy on their altars, explaining to followers that in fact she was a "stand-in" for the Eternal Mother (Wusheng laomu), an unorthodox deity associated with the so-called White Lotus millenarian tradition.[22] As for the Five Emperors' cult, despite repeated suppression campaigns in Guangdong and Fujian in the Ming and Qing periods, it remained popular. To avoid persecution worshippers in Fuzhou refashioned the banned Five Emperors into the imperially endorsed Five Manifestations (Wuxian), yet keeping the original iconography and ritual practices. In Canton devotees converted the Five Emperors' temple cults into underground cults operating from their homes, and therefore away from the gaze of officials.[23] In the 1520s, after officials destroyed the Lady of the Golden Flower Temple in Canton, her cult continued in secret and eventually in the late seventeenth century she reemerged in a different form, as a protector of women in childbirth, and therefore more acceptable to Qing and later rulers. In the end she was simply tolerated by officials and since 2009 her main temple in Canton has been a cultural heritage site.[24] In this book we also noted how worshippers transformed the illicit goddesses Zuxi and Sanpo into the officially sanctioned Empress of Heaven as a way to avoid suppression.

In opposing folk religious cults and their ritual practices it is important to reiterate that officials responded not only with repression, but also with co-optation, accommodation, and tolerance. Despite sporadic crackdowns the state actually had little power to consistently enforce its religious policies. In fact, oftentimes officials found it difficult to establish clear boundaries between acceptable and unacceptable cults. Unless they appeared overly dangerous, therefore, authorities found it more expedient to tolerate popular cults and to incorporate wayward gods into the official pantheon, such as the case with Mazu. Officials willingly compromised with local communities because they realized that people would resist suppression of established cults. Nonetheless, whether labeled orthodox or heterodox, the gods, their cults, and ritual practices meant different things to different people. Even official co-optation and tolerance allowed room for a wide variety of alternative interpretations of popular religion within communities. As Michael Szonyi explains, although people did not always do what they were supposed to do, they frequently claimed that they did what they were supposed to do. In this way the myth of China's cultural integration could be maintained in name if not in fact.[25]

Women, Pollution, Power

One of the unintended consequences of the post-Mao economic reforms and opening of the country has been the emergence in the late 1990s of a New Cultural Revolution, one not aimed at collectivization but at liberating the individual. It was not a revolution led by the Communist Party, peasants, or workers, but rather by the new urban middle class, and in particular young women demanding sexual equality and the right to consume. Exemplified in the writings of Wei Hui's *Shanghai Baby* (*Shanghai baobei*, 1999) and Mian Mian's *Candy* (*Tang*, 2000), among others, contemporary female writers have shifted emphasis away from the masculinized "Iron Girls" of the Maoist era to a blossoming of female self-awareness, autonomy, and virtuosity as they redefine Chinese feminism. They are representative of the growing number of apolitical, consumerist young Chinese women. As Megan Ferry suggests, these so-called bad girls of literature are modern knights-errant who have turned the straitlaced strictures of the Communist Party and traditional Confucian mores on their heads.[26] They have drawn their battle lines in China's culture wars over the issues of sexual freedom and gender equality.

The most striking feature of this new feminism has been a concomitant sexual revolution. Less than a century ago it was common for parents to arrange marriages and for young brides to not meet their husbands until the wedding. Sex outside marriage for females was taboo and it was scandalous for women to remain unwed. In recent years, however, an increasing number of young urban women have chosen to stay single and larger numbers of couples are living together outside marriage.[27] In Beijing research has shown that the percentage of people who approved of premarital sex rose from 50 percent in 1986 to 70 percent in 1990; in one Chengdu survey in 2003, roughly 80 percent of the women said that a marriage certificate was not necessary to enjoy sex; and in Shanghai in 2004 several studies reported that between 52 and 84 percent of women said that they had sex before marriage. Rural trends in premarital sex, though still lagging behind cities, also have gone up in recent years; in a rural area outside Shanghai, for example, more than 20 percent of the women said they had premarital sex.[28] According to well-known Chinese sexologist Li Yinhe, "Sex has gone from a luxury to a common demand for the Chinese people."[29] For many women, the traditional gender model of men as breadwinners and women as homemakers, child-producers, and sex objects has changed to a new model of sex for pleasure. For them gender roles have been turned upside down: the male body has become an object of female desire and pleasure. *Yin* has overtaken *yang*.[30]

Even before the sexual revolution in the 1990s, Chinese women were not as prudish and chaste as we once thought. In the late imperial period, as recent studies by Paola Paderni, Janet Theiss, and others have shown, it was not unheard of for women of all classes to engage in premarital and extramarital sex.[31] In fact, some groups of women, such as Dan boat women discussed in chapter 7, were well known for their sexual freedom. In the early twentieth century the uninhibited behavior of China's "modern girls," although condemned on moral or patriarchal grounds by traditionalists, was praised by progressives for their carefree expressions of desire. In the 1932 serialized novel, *The Girl of the Modern Age* (*Shidai guniang*), the protagonist, Qin Lili (Lily), represented a sexually liberated Shanghai girl who shifted from one lover to another with clear exhibitionist pleasure. She was the ultimate embodiment of the modern girl, one pursuing the latest fads in clothes and in sex. Lily and other modern girls of the 1930s set in motion important changes in traditional Chinese cultural values that would not be realized for another half-century.[32]

Going beyond their early twentieth-century predecessors, contemporary Chinese women are noted not for simply challenging conventional orthodox values but also for stretching the boundaries of womanhood beyond customary limits. In recent years China's "alternative culture" (*linglei wenhua*) is driven by a popular and pervasive refrain of sex, drugs, and rock-and-roll. The fiction of Wei Hui and Mian Mian, the internet blogs of Muzimei, Sister Furong, and Hooligan Yan, and the punk rock of Wang Yue and Luo Qi embody some of the more salient elements of China's New Cultural Revolution. Their writings and music openly explore forbidden themes of female sexual prowess, hedonism, prostitution, lesbianism, sadomasochism, and pornography. In Mian Mian's semi-autobiographical novel *Candy*, the teenage protagonist, Hong, quits school and runs away from home to pursue a liberated lifestyle in the unruly border town of Shenzhen, against the backdrop of heroin addiction, music of Jim Morrison and Cui Jian, and countless one-night stands. Inspired by the so-called lower-body literature of Mian Mian, Wei Hui, and others, female bloggers began posting explicit accounts of their personal erotic experiences. Although mainly an urban phenomenon among young educated women, notably Muzimei, there also has been a growing number of working-class, middle-aged, and rural-to-urban migrant women, notably Sister Furong and Hooligan Yan, who likewise have become online "bedroom activists" for the female libido. Several female rock stars, by flouting their carefree lifestyle, drug use, and sexual freedom with provocative lyrics,

Figure 28. Light Porn Advertisement for a Female Rock and Dance Performance in Wushi Harbor, Leizhou, 2010   (Source: Photo by author)

have become well-known advocates for women's rights. At the same time that these defiant women were altering cultural assumptions about gender relations, they also were commodifying their bodies. Today in cities, towns, and villages the sexually liberated female is being marketed on shopping mall billboards selling lingerie and on the sides of trucks promoting scantily clad female bands performing in dodgy dance halls (figure 28).[33]

While many Chinese have praised the new feminist stance on sexuality and gender equality, many more have criticized it as indecent, immoral, and lacking in human values. Official media has branded these new feminists as problem girls, hooligans, whores, perverts, and as acting like animals. Editorials and letters from readers in *China Youth Daily* and other journals frequently have complained that the writings of Wei Hui, Mian Mian, Muzimei, and others were outright degenerate and disgusting and that they corrupted the morality of youth. Although loosening up restrictions in recent years, nonetheless the government has remained vigilant and tough on overt sexual promiscuity and pornography. Both *Shanghai Baby* and *Candy* were officially banned for profanity in 2000, and three years later Muzimei and other female bloggers were shut off the internet.[34] Echoing Mao's 1942 Yan'an talk on art and literature, in 2014 Xi Jinping explained that literature, film, music, and art should promote core socialist values to assist the party's agenda; more specifically, they should "serve the people" (*wei renmin fuwu*) to "inspire minds, warm hearts, cultivate taste and clean up undesirable work styles."[35]

It is noteworthy that censors condemned Mian Mian as the "poster child for spiritual pollution." In traditional and modern China, women often have been associated with pollution and uncleanliness. The coupling of women with an inherent impurity may have been one method for the male-dominated patriarchal society to perpetuate female inferiority and nullify their power. According to anthropologist Mary Douglas, pollution is related to any fundamental disorder or anything out of place and inappropriate, and is therefore considered threatening and dangerous to society.[36] Many people in China, past and present, considered the uninhibited and uncontrolled female libido a polluting menace to the moral health of the country. In the Qing period the unchaste wife or widow was a cause of great anxiety for the state and patriarchal order. Women were objects to be controlled.[37] Prostitution and homosexuality were inappropriate acts considered dirty and impure, and therefore consequently condemned in laws and social customs.[38] Today many Chinese still maintain these same ideas about sexual pollution.

The greatest sources of female pollution, however, were inherent excretions of bodily fluids from menstruation and childbirth. As Charlotte Furth explains, "Imagined as a source of contagion, liable to make crops wither and to offend the gods, it [menstrual blood] has been associated with female threats to forms of cosmic and social order managed and defended by men."[39] Menstrual and puerperal impurities represented the antithesis of what Chinese considered a clean and pure body. Menstrual discharges also symbolized death. Even today in many rural areas it is believed that if a menstruating woman walked through a paddy field, she would cause the rice shoots to die, or if she entered the stalls to feed the animals or to lead them out to drink, they would become sick or die. Menstruating women, because they are impure, are barred from visiting temples and from participating in any form of worship. Since it is generally believed that evil spirits easily attached to impurities, menstruating and parturient women were segregated in order to keep them away from harmful influences and to prevent others from contamination. Males were always the most vulnerable to female pollution. Today although such deep-rooted beliefs are still common in rural areas and among the older generation of men and women, many younger women simply consider menstruation as a natural phenomenon and not necessarily polluting.[40]

Pollution was not only a source of danger but also of power for women. "The power of menstrual blood," writes Emily Ahern, "can be seen as a symbolic representation of the actual social power of young married women."[41] Women intentionally and unintentionally used their powers of pollution as weapons directed at others, usually men, to obtain particular goals. They could apply menstrual and fetal blood to magically defeat enemies in battle, attract lovers and seduce men, prolong life, and help maintain a youthful appearance.[42] During the Wang Lun Rebellion in 1774 and the Boxer Uprising in 1900, both sides in these conflicts engaged in supernatural warfare by employing menstruating women (sometimes prostitutes) to use their negative *yin* powers to defeat their enemies. Conversely, the Red Lanterns, who were often pre-pubescent virgins, possessed extremely potent magical powers because of their purity, which could be used to counteract black magic.[43] For centuries abused women in China have empowered themselves by committing suicide—a form of death pollution—to become malevolent ghosts to avenge the wrongs done to them in life (such as the Pissing Woman in chapter 7). As a recent study by Hyeon Jung Lee argues, suicidal behavior among rural women was an important form of female agency that asserted their moral aspiration for freedom and individual rights.[44] Sex was not only polluting but also the ultimate female weapon in the battle for gender equality. Women who took control of their bodies became empowered.

Although still surrounded by controversy, today elements of China's sexual revolution have entered mainstream culture and commercial economy, even receiving tacit approval from the party-state. As literary critic Xu Kun has pointed out, the market has usurped government control over gender. China's new consumerist, apolitical culture has commodified the female body and sexuality.[45] Bad girl writers Wei Hui and Mian Mian have in recent years toned down their irreverence with safer, non-threatening stories about women's material life and self-fulfillment and with less sexually explicit content. In Mian Mian's second novel, *Panda Sex* (*Xiongmao*, 2004), the protagonist lives without sex, alcohol, and drugs; according to the author, the panda in the title symbolizes abstinence because in real life pandas have inactive mating habits. Recently she has also appeared in films and actively organizes "dance parties" to capitalize on the new consumer culture.[46] Another bad girl writer, Chun Shu, who authored *Beijing Doll* (*Beijing wawa*, 2002), was praised in 2010 by the All-China Women's Federation, the party's official women's rights organization, as an important young female author.[47] Despite being cast off the internet, female bloggers Muzimei and Sister Furong have cashed in on their popularity and fame—the former was hired as marketing manager for Blogchina.com, and the latter has received lucrative product endorsements, book and film contracts, and an independent modeling career that has given her access to a trans-global lifestyle.[48] In 1997 the rock singer and drug addict Luo Qi was arrested and put into a rehabilitation hospital. After her release the authorities posed her as a model citizen and spokesperson for its anti-drug abuse campaigns.[49] In recent years these former bad girls are full-fledged celebrities and prime shapers of China's youth culture.

ETHNICITY, BARBARISM, CIVILIZATION

In 2011 during field research on piracy in the Gulf of Tonkin I heard this story about the origins of the Three Islands, home of the Jing (Kinh) ethnic minority in China:

> *A long time ago on White Dragon Tail (Bailongwei) peninsula there was a giant centipede spirit (*wugongjing*) living in a cave. Whenever a boat passed it demanded a human to eat, otherwise the centipede would beckon heavy waves to capsize the boat. One day a beggar carrying a large pumpkin approached the captain of a fishing boat and asked for free passage. The captain, well aware of the centipede's appetite for human sacrifice, readily agreed, secretly planning to feed the beggar to the evil spirit. As the boat approached the centipede's cave, the crew gathered around the beggar preparing to throw him overboard. The beggar, who had been boiling the pumpkin all along, asked them to wait, and picking up the scalding hot pumpkin, threw it straight into the creature's mouth. The beast exploded into bits, whereupon the tail, head, and heart became the Three Islands—Wanwei, Wutou, and Shanxin. Witnessing this miracle, the sailors realized that the beggar was none other than the immortal Great King Who Pacifies the Seas (Zhenhai dawang).*[50]

While this has become the most popular and politically correct version of the legend of the Three Islands, it is not the only one. Hong Kong anthropologist Cheung Siu-woo recounted another version in which the centipede transformed into four islands, one of which was located in Vietnam. According to his Jing informant on Wanwei island, this was in fact an earlier version, but he said it was better to exclude the fourth island, Trà Cổ, "in order to avoid confusing the official national boundary and the identity of the local Kinh people."[51] Actually the story of the centipede spirit is likely based on the well-known fifteenth-century Vietnamese "Legend of the Fish Spirit," which described a huge demonic centipede that lived in the Gulf of Tonkin, caused storms, and ate humans. In this version, the Dragon King killed the creature by throwing molten iron down its throat, upon which the centipede exploded into pieces. Its tail became the White Dragon Tail peninsula and its head became Dog Head island (Goutoushan), areas that remained a part of Vietnam until 1877.[52]

The above legends about the origins of the Jing community in China raise questions about its ethnic identity and how the Jing fit into the larger Chinese politico-cultural milieu. Originally the people who settled on the Three Islands and neighboring areas near Jiangping (Giang Bình) were migratory fisherfolk who had come from northern Vietnam in waves beginning in the early sixteenth century. They would have thought of themselves as Vietnamese, as the Kinh people, who are Vietnam's majority ethnic group. For hundreds of years, however, Chinese were uncertain about how to classify them; they were variously called Man (a generic term for southern barbarians), Yue (another generic term for barbarians living in the areas of today's Guangdong, Guangxi, and northern Vietnam), Tanka or Dan (a generic term for despised boat people), and Annanese (an ancient term for Vietnamese people).[53] They were not officially labeled Jing until 1957, when the new Chinese communist regime divided the country into fifty-six nationalities. The Han, whom most people think of as the "Chinese" people, occupied more than 90 percent of the total population, with the remaining fifty-five nationalities designated as ethnic minorities.[54]

Regarding the Jing minority, although the current Chinese authorities do not deny Jing connections with Vietnam, they are downplayed or ignored (as we noted in the above politically correct version of the legend of the Three Islands); emphasis instead is placed on the integral part that the Jing play in creating a unified Chinese nation. As I was told by a local Wutou villager, the Chinese character *jing* means "capital" and refers explicitly to the "northern capital" (Beijing) and thus shows the close connections that the Jing people have with China as a whole. Yet at the same time the Jing living on the Three Islands retain many of their own distinct customs and Vietnamese language, marking them off from other Chinese.[55] Contradictions between unity and diversity, not only for the Jing but also for other minorities, are at the root of China's ethnic culture wars.

Postlude

In many respects ethnic diversity has bred animosity, prejudice, and intolerance. Han Chinese have been quick to point out differences between "us" and "them," between civilized people and barbarians. The minorities in south and southwest China (areas that I focus on in this section) were not only geographically marginal but more importantly also socially and culturally marginal. In late imperial and modern China, ethnic groups were contrasted unfavorably with Han Chinese. It was said that the Miao, Yao, and Li, for instance, did not bury their dead in coffins or follow prescribed Han funeral rites; they did not have ancestral halls or keep ancestral tablets; and their sacrifices to ancestors involved blood offerings of animals and rituals led by sorcerers. By their very nature they were backward and wild; they lived in remote mountains where they maintained a primitive lifestyle by hunting and gathering and they squandered their land with slash-and-burn farming. Many Chinese believed that they knew neither how to cook their food nor how to use chopsticks, two fundamentals of civilization. Since the 1930s Han-produced films have perpetuated stereotyped images of non-Han peoples as frail, backward, ignorant, and impoverished. Today internet blogs have become popular vehicles for Chinese "netizens" to not only express ideas about sex but also ethnic policies and multiculturalism. While some people have criticized the government's handling of minorities, especially in Tibet and Xinjiang, many more have expressed Han-supremist views that belittle minorities as inferiors and openly advocate strong assimilation policies to restore "the natural ethnic order" in China.[56]

As mentioned at the start of this book, there always has been a tendency for the Han majority to demean minorities, both literally and figuratively, as being intrinsically feminine in nature. Minority groups were like women not only because they were dirty and polluting but also because they inverted the positions of male and female. For Han Chinese, traditionally a well-ordered society was supposed to be based on male-centered patriarchal households in which females were expected to be subordinate, meek, and chaste. Minority women, however, exemplified the opposite. They engaged in what Chinese considered essentially men's work, such as farming and trade. They mingled freely with the opposite sex and did not bind their feet. Among the Miao, Yao, and Dan, women enjoyed a relatively equal social status with men. Most Chinese believed that minority women were morally lax; they dressed immodestly and had improper sexual freedoms, including premarital sex and marriages arranged by young couples themselves. During the traditional Ha festival among the Jing, in the past, young female ritual performers entertained the gods with lustful songs and dances, which prudish Chinese viewed as akin to whoredom. Today Jing, Dai, Dan, and other minority females are still considered promiscuous if not as outright prostitutes.[57]

Chinese have long held that because ethnic minorities were inferior, backward, and barbaric savages, they needed to be civilized. The basic assumption was that Chinese culture was inherently superior to native cultures. Although there were always some Chinese who believed that certain ethnic groups could never be civilized, nevertheless, the general consensus has been that most could be transformed and made to become more Chinese.[58] Education was the cornerstone of China's civilizing programs. In the past "barbarians" became objects of transformation, typically expressed in stages from "raw" to "cooked" to "civilized." As noted in chapter 6, the leader of the 1832 Yao uprising, Zhao Jinlong, appears to have been a transitional figure between raw and cooked—he dressed in customary Yao fashion and did not wear the queue, but he mingled freely among Chinese in markets, spoke one or more Chinese dialects, and received official recognition as a native headman. In the Qing, wearing Chinese-style clothing, having a queue, and speaking Chinese were not only important symbolic markers distinguishing raw and cooked aborigines, but also indicated the measure of one's transformation to civilization.[59]

According to Stevan Harrell, the ethnic classification campaign in the 1950s was a constructed political crusade disguised as a civilizing project. Under the concept of "unity in diversity," a term coined by Chinese anthropologist Fei Xiaotong (1910–2005), minorities all shared the same roots as part of a single Chinese family, an idea that dates back to the early Ming dynasty. As in the past, it is the intention of the present Chinese government to integrate minorities socially and culturally with the rest of China through a process of "ethnic fusion" (*minzu ronghe*). At the forefront of the PRC's ethnic policies is the promotion of "patriotic education" in order to better integrate minorities into mainstream Chinese society. In 2019, Xi Jinping obliged party cadres to help build a "spiritual homeland" by transforming minority cultures and identities to bring them in line with the collective consciousness of the nation. The idea was that Han Chinese, as the most advanced ethnic group, must lead the way to guide the less-advanced minorities toward the shared goals of socialism, harmony, and unity. To fulfill his "Chinese Dream," Xi Jinping has called for a "great revival of the Chinese people," which requires a homogenous nation in which differences of religion, culture, and ethnicity are played down.[60]

Acculturation and assimilation policies in late imperial and modern China, however, met with only partial success. Ming and Qing frontiers became contact zones where different peoples and cultures mingled to create something new through compromise and accommodation. Although in some cases natives found Confucian education and Mandarin Chinese to be beneficial tools for promoting their own status and facilitating communication, nevertheless, the marketplace proved to be the better classroom. Essential for conducting business, settlers learned one or more native languages and natives learned to speak various local Chinese dialects, such as Hakka. Interethnic marriages, though frowned upon by Qing rulers, were a common feature of frontier life that helped to blur the lines separating indigenes and migrants. On the frontiers, legal cases were often settled according to customary law rather than by imperial codified law. Acculturation actually worked both ways: while many natives became more Chinese in appearances and habits, there also were many Chinese frontiersmen who went native.[61]

Although the PRC government officially promotes multiculturalism, its ethnic policies have been ambiguous and seldom applied universally. Because communist civilizing projects, like those in the past, have failed to create a single unified sociopolitical culture, the current regime also has had to adopt compromise in dealing with certain minority groups, particularly in south and southwest China. This is especially evident in the state's promotion of ethnic tourism, which has attempted to create a standardized "authentic" culture by weeding out those qualities that might detract from its vision of multicultural unity. Yet "the notion of authenticity," explains folklorist Juwen Zhang, "is but an imagined empowerment over the claim of those who possess the power of discourse."[62] Authenticity is a fluid and constantly negotiated concept.[63]

While some scholars have noted that tourism has destroyed native cultures, others have argued that this was not necessarily the case. Based on fieldwork among the Dong in Guizhou province, Timothy Oakes discovered that tourism actually was an important factor in the ongoing official and local construction of ethnic identity. Tourism, in other words, provided indigens a certain amount of agency to express who they were and how they lived, while at the same time allowing them to "embrace modernity without losing their traditions." As Harriet Evans explains in her study of the Naxi in Yunnan: "With the arrival of the market, they welcomed the prospect of deploying their ethnic identity in the service of commercial gain."[64] For the Jing minority, the Three Islands, which were once bases for pirate and smuggling operations, have been transformed into sandy beaches with upscale resorts. Jing leaders also have made compromises with officials by playing down their Vietnamese heritage and by modifying Ha festivals into grand spectacles of modern song and dance performances while keeping their original sacerdotal purpose in the background. Tensions between extralocal and local traditions in many instances, therefore, have been adjusted through cooperation and accommodation. In fact, traditions are continued, revitalized, or reinvented through a process of cultural hybridity, which inevitably results in something new.[65]

Conclusion

Although many scholars agree that over the course of the late imperial and modern periods China has become a more culturally homogeneous country, this was not universally true. On the one hand, Chinese culture and society share certain fundamental beliefs and values, yet on the other hand, there is still much diversity and heterogeneity. Large segments of the population, notably among ordinary people and youths, have lifestyles and habits that do not correspond with or are contrary to those desired by the hegemonic state and cultural elites. Many of today's women and youths, although paying lip-service to the party-state dogma, nonetheless follow their own way of life. Likewise, ethnic groups and folk religion, while mouthing orthodox Confucian values or Communist slogans, have continued to follow customary habits. What political elites called heterodoxy was not necessarily viewed as such by ordinary people, and in fact, much of the so-called heretical beliefs and practices were simply normal parts of everyday folk culture. Even official co-optation and tolerance allowed room for a wide variety of alternative interpretations of popular customs within communities. As argued throughout this book, orthodoxy and heterodoxy not only changed over time and circumstances, but were also interpreted by different people at different times in different ways. Culture wars have been played out largely in terms of civilization versus barbarism or orthodoxy versus heterodoxy, but the battles mainly have been settled in the long run by co-optation, tolerance, compromise, and accommodation. While there is a tendency toward sociocultural integration, it is a process that is ongoing and incomplete, and one in which ordinary men and women, not only political elites, have played remarkable roles in shaping.

I wrote this book not to replace conventional histories, but to explore the possibilities of alternative pasts, to offer different ways to rethink China's history from the people's perspective. My focus has been on several ethnic groups and those individuals that officials considered as rogues and criminals. For the most part, they are the denizens of the nebulous underworld of rivers and lakes, a sociocultural category of people who mainstream society discriminated against and who occupied the lower rungs of the social hierarchy. Besides the standard textual sources found in libraries and archives, to write China's history from below I have had to dig deeper and consult many unconventional sources—folklore, legends, myths, rumors, and hearsay—that most scholars have dismissed as unimportant, unreliable, or just plain nonsense. This endeavor, nonetheless, is worthwhile because it gives voice to the inarticulate and brings to light what has been largely a hidden past. In telling the stories of Righteous Yang, Broken Shoes Chen the Fourth, Golden Dragon Zhao, Zheng Zuxi, and others, we have had to enter the realm of mythohistory. When we listen closely to what they have to say we can reclaim an unfamiliar history.

These glimpses into that invisible history are by no means the last words on the subject but only the start of what I hope will encourage other scholars to delve further into China's past from the native's point of view. I could have traveled different roads; there were other possibilities. As Robert Frost once griped: "No matter which road you take, you'll always sigh, and wish you'd taken another." But like the poet I too have chosen the road less traveled. "And that has made all the difference."[66]

Afterword

THIS BOOK BEGAN LONG BEFORE I COMPLETED MY DOCTORAL DISSERTATION in 1988, and even before I began my formal education. I first learned history as a boy at the dinner table on Sundays from my father, who spent most of his adult life traveling the world as a seaman, and from my maternal grandfather, who was a cabinet maker who had never left New Orleans. Both mentors were self-taught men who enjoyed history and were good storytellers, though the tales they told were largely different from the ones I would learn in school. Their stories came mostly from what they had heard from family, friends, and strangers; they were elements of an oral culture based mainly on rumors, hearsay, and folklore. But to me that didn't make them any less interesting, true, or real.

Many years later when I was finishing my dissertation research in the archives in Beijing, my teacher, Qin Baoqi, suggested that I visit Yunxiao in southern Fujian, a small port town I had been reading about as the purported site of the founding of the Triads. I gladly took up Professor Qin's offer and set off on what would be my first adventure in doing field research on my own in rural south China. The year was 1985. In Yunxiao, I was met by several local cultural experts and history buffs who showed me all the important sites related to the original Triads as recorded in lore. While it was clear to me that my local informants sincerely believed these stories to be real and accurate, what I came away with from this trip was an awareness that ordinary people do not necessarily interpret their own past in the same ways that professional scholars do. And like the stories told to me by my father and grandfather, these stories were no less true or important. Representations of the past do not simply belong to historians and other academics.

By the time I finished my doctorate in 1988, I was hooked on doing field research as an important complement to traditional textual research in libraries and archives. Direct personal encounters with villagers and townspeople have given me important insights about the workings of cultural systems that for the most part otherwise would have remained concealed if I had only relied on standard textual evidence. But it would take me more than three decades to fully realize the potential of fieldwork. In large measure this book is the result of those endeavors.

Along the way I have benefitted from the suggestions, advice, and encouragements of many colleagues, students, and friends. I am indebted to my predecessors from various disciplines with whom I have shared my thoughts, problems, and questions. Intellectually my greatest debts are to Barend ter Haar, David Faure, James Watson, Robert Darnton, Hayden White, Clifford Geertz, and Amitav Ghosh, who have helped to shape my ideas, approaches, and interpretations about the past. Among the many others who over the years have given me more immediate help and encouragement are Wei Qingyuan, Qin Baoqi, Zhuang Jifa, Ye Xianen, Zhou Weimin, Tang Lingling, Harry Lamley, Sue Naquin, David Ownby, Jane Leonard, Xing Hang, Liu Ping, Li Qingxin, Huang Sujuan, Xu Jingjie, Nancy Park, Paul Van Dyke, Thomas DuBois, Nicola Di Cosmo, Zhu Tianshu, Peter Zabielskis, He Xi, Nathan Kwan, Gary Luk, Ma Guang, Susan Schopp, Wong Wei Chin, Patrick Connolly, Odoric Wou, Hyunhee Park, Kobayashi Fumihiko, Joseph Lee, Leng Dong, Ellen Cai, and Vincent Ho. I am indebted to them all.

Over the years the staffs and researchers at the following libraries and archives have furnished me with valuable assistance: Academia Sinica's Fu Sinian Library, Guangdong Provincial Library, Fujian Normal University Library, University of Hong Kong Library, Taiwan Central Library, Library of Congress, New York Public Library, British Library, Harvard-Yenching Library, Princeton University East Asian Library, National Palace Museum in Taipei, First Historical Archives in Beijing, British National Archives, Zhanjiang Museum, Liannan Autonomous Yao County Archives, Leizhou City Museum, Qinzhou Gazetteer Office, and Boluo County Gazetteer Office. In conducting field research I received crucial support from Chen Zhijian and Li Long in Leizhou, Wu Xiaoling in Qinzhou, and Cao Chunsheng and Lu Junfeng in Lianzhou, as well as from many anonymous collaborators and informants. My fieldwork could never have been completed without the support from my students—Liu Jiaqi, He Xingyin, Liang Xiuqing, Huang Meiling, Li Huishi, Kuang Meihua, Xue Qianhui, Chen Bin, and Hei Rei. To them all I owe my sincere gratitude.

Nothing could have been written without the generous support of research grants from the Fulbright Foundation, National Endowment for the Humanities, Committee on Scholarly Communication with the People's Republic of China, and Pacific Cultural Foundation, as well as faculty research grants from Western Kentucky University, Universidade de Macau,

Afterword

and Guangzhou University. Sections of this book were presented during stints as a visiting scholar at Academia Sinica in Taiwan, People's University in Beijing, Beijing Normal University, University of California at Irvine, Pace University, and John Jay College of Criminal Justice in New York City. I wrote and rewrote most of the book between 2019 and 2022, during the coronavirus pandemic, while I was a visiting scholar in the School of Historical Studies at the Institute for Advanced Studies in Princeton and an associate in research in Harvard University's Fairbank Center for Chinese Studies. During the past three years the School of History and Culture at Shandong University has also given me valuable support. I am grateful to each of these institutions for their academic assistance and the intellectual camaraderie of their members. I especially want to thank Marcia Tucker, Librarian at the Historical Studies–Social Science Library in the Institute for Advanced Study, for her steadfast efforts in getting books and articles to me during the pandemic.

Two chapters have been previously published, though updated to include new ideas and information. Chapter 2 appeared online in 2014 as "Righteous Yang: Pirate, Rebel, and Hero on the Sino-Vietnamese Water Frontier, 1644–1684," *Cross-Currents: East Asian History and Culture Review* (University of California, Berkeley); and chapter 4 appeared as "Demons, Gangsters, and Secret Societies in Early Modern South China," *East Asian History*, vol. 27 (June 2004). I wish to thank the respective publishers for permission to reprint the revised articles.

Last but not least is my heartfelt thanks to my wife Lanshin who has stood by my side through thick and thin all these years. She accompanied me and my students on nearly every research trip into the backwoods of rural China. Without her constant encouragements, suggestions, translations, and insights this book could never have been completed.

Appendix 1

Omens, Natural Disasters, and Social Unrest in the Gulf of Tonkin Region, 1644–1683

YEAR	AREA	OMENS	CALAMITIES	SOCIAL UNREST
1644	Gaozhou	solar eclipse		Last Ming emperor commits suicide; Li Zicheng captures Beijing; Qing troops enter China
1646	Guangzhou, Hainan		drought	Qing troops enter Guangdong
1647	Hainan, Leizhou, Gaozhou	blood-colored rain	locusts	Huang Hairu revolts in Leizhou; "righteous uprisings" in Gaozhou
1648	Leizhou, Hainan, Gaozhou		floods, famines, epidemics	fighting between pro-Ming and Qing troops, bandits and pirates
1649	Hainan, Leizhou	sighting of unnatural animal	typhoon	Huang Hairu continues fighting around Leizhou
1650	Guangzhou, Leizhou, Lienzhou	blood-like fluid in Haizhu Temple in Canton		Qing reoccupy Canton followed by massacre of residents; Deng Yao occupies Longmen
1651	Hainan, Gaozhou, Leizhou, Lienzhou		typhoon, drought, famine	continued fighting between pro-Ming and Qing forces, bandits and pirates

YEAR	AREA	OMENS	CALAMITIES	SOCIAL UNREST
1652	Lienzhou, Leizhou, Gaozhou, Hainan	comet	floods, famine, epidemics	pirates loot Hainan; Wang Zhihan active in Leizhou
1653	Zhaoqing, Gaozhou, Lienzhou, Leizhou	comet; strange five-colored vapors	typhoon, floods, famines, epidemics, man-eating tigers	Wuchuan changes hands three times; Deng Yao active around Lienzhou
1654	Hainan, Lienzhou, Gaozhou, Leizhou	blood-colored pool	floods, famine	continued fighting; Wuchuan changes hands four times
1655	Hainan, Gaozhou, Lienzhou, Leizhou		floods, famine	continued fighting; Li uprising in Hainan
1656	Hainan, Gaozhou, Lienzhou	sighting of strange boulder and thunder	famine	continued fighting; Yang Er loots Hainan
1657	Hainan	sighting of strange boulder	drought, famine	continued fighting
1658	Hainan			Yang Er in Hainan; Deng Yao in Qinzhou

YEAR	AREA	OMENS	CALAMITIES	SOCIAL UNREST
1659	Lienzhou, Hainan, Gaozhou	comet, strange white vapors, lightning, and thunder	typhoon	bandits loot villages in Wuchuan; Yang Er loots Hainan
1660	Lienzhou, Leizhou, Hainan	strange thunder and lightning reported at Deng Yao's execution	drought, famine	pirates active in Gulf of Tonkin; Deng Yao executed
1661	Guangzhou, Gaozhou, Leizhou, Hainan	abnormal birth	famine, fire in Canton	Wang Zhihan executed; Yang Er occupies Longmen and loots Hainan
1662	Hainan, Leizhou		famine, typhoon, floods	Yong Li emperor executed; Zheng Chenggong died; Yang Er loots Hainan; Qing navy attacks pirates around Leizhou, Lienzhou, Gaozhou
1663	Lienzhou, Leizhou, Hainan		famine, epidemics	Yang Er plunders Leizhou and Hainan; Qing retakes Longmen and Yang Er flees to Vietnam
1664	Lienzhou, Gaozhou, Hainan, Leizhou	comet		Huang Guolin loots Qinzhou; Huang Mingbiao loots Leizhou

YEAR	AREA	OMENS	CALAMITIES	SOCIAL UNREST
1665	Gaozhou, Lienzhou, Guangzhou	blood-like fluid seen in Haizhu Temple	earthquake, fire in Lienzhou city	mountain bandits in Lienzhou; riots in Wuchuan; Huang Mingbiao active in Gulf of Tonkin
1666	Lienzhou, Leizhou, Gaozhou, Hainan	strange white vapor	typhoon	Yang Er active in Gulf of Tonkin; he flees to Taiwan to join the Zheng camp
1667	Lienzhou, Gaozhou	comet	floods	
1668	Hainan, Leizhou, Lienzhou	strange white and black vapors; moon as bright as sun		
1669	Lienzhou		man-eating tigers	
1671	Lienzhou, Hainan		typhoon, man-eating tigers	
1672	Lienzhou, Gaozhou, Hainan, Leizhou		man-eating tigers, three typhoons, floods, earthquake	bandits loot Wuchuan; pirates loot Hainan and Leizhou
1673	Hainan, Gaozhou		man-eating tigers	pirates loot Hainan and Gaozhou

YEAR	AREA	OMENS	CALAMITIES	SOCIAL UNREST
1674	Hainan, Lienzhou		floods	pirates and bandits loot Qinzhou
1675	Gaozhou, Leizhou, Lienzhou	strange red and white solar halo		pirates and bandits loot Wuchuan; troop mutiny in Gaozhou led by Zu Zeqing; other mutinies in Leizhou and Lienzhou
1676	Gaozhou, Leizhou, Lienzhou			fighting between Zu Zeqing and Qing troops
1677	Lienzhou, Hainan		typhoon, floods	Yang Er reoccupies Longmen and loots Hainan; Li uprisings on Hainan; Qing troops continue fighting pirates
1678	Qinzhou, Gaozhou, Leizhou, Lienzhou, Hainan		floods, dearth	continued fighting with Qing troops; Yang Er loots Leizhou and Hainan; Du Qilong loots Qinzhou
1679	Hainan, Gaozhou			continued fighting with Qing troops; Ye Kechang loots Hainan
1680–1681	Lienzhou, Hainan	comet	drought, famine, epidemics	pirates and bandits active everywhere in Gulf of Tonkin

YEAR	AREA	OMENS	CALAMITIES	SOCIAL UNREST
1681	Lienzhou, Hainan		famine, epidemics, snow in Qinzhou	pirates and bandits active everywhere in Gulf of Tonkin
1682	Hainan, Lienzhou, Leizhou		famine, three typhoons	after losing Longmen, Yang Er flees to Vietnam
1683	Hainan		famine, typhoon	

Appendix 2

Illegal Associations in South China, 1641–1788

DATE	PLACE	REGION	LEADERS	NAME	ATTRIBUTES	SAVIORS	ACTIVITIES
1641–1647	Enping	Guangdong	Tan Yuzhen	Jialanhui	blood oath		banditry, revolt
1645–1658	Kaiping Xinhui Xiangshan Gaoyao Shunde	Guangdong	He Tai Wu Yajiu		blood oath		bondservant revolt
1676	Longchuan	Guangdong	Zheng Jin		blood oath		banditry, revolt
1677	Tongan	Fujian	Cai Yin		messianic	Zhu Santaizi	"sedition"
1702–1703	Zhuluo	Taiwan	Liu Que		blood oath		gangsterism, revolt
1719		Fujian	Xue Yanwen Xue Youlian		messianic (?)	Pusa	gangsterism, "sedition" "swindling"
1720	Huian	Fujian	Chen Ling	Nandouhui Beidouhui			gangsterism
1721	Fengshan	Taiwan	Zhu Yigui		blood oath		revolt
1726–1728	Zhuluo	Taiwan	Tang Wan Zhu Bao	Fumuhui	blood oath		"sedition"

260

DATE	PLACE	REGION	LEADERS	NAME	ATTRIBUTES	SAVIORS	ACTIVITIES
1728		Fujian		Tiebianhui (Fumuhui)	blood oath		gangsterism
1729		Taiwan		Zilonghui			mutual-aid
1729–1743	Enping Kaiping Yangjiang Dong'an Yangchun Xiangshan Xinxing	Guangdong	Li Mei (Li Zantao, Li Shixin)		messianic	Li Kaihua Li Jiukui Zhu Santaizi Chuzhengong Yulong Taizi	"swindling" "sedition"
1730	Xiamen	Fujian	Li Cai	Yiqianhui	sworn oath		revenge, banditry
1731	Raoping Haiyang	Guangdong	Yu Ni	Fumuhui	blood oath		gangsterism, mourning, "sedition"
1732	Fengshan	Taiwan	Wu Fusheng		blood oath		revolt
1733–1734	Haiyang Jieyang	Guangdong	Wang Atong Chen Wurui		messianic		banditry, "swindling"
1734	Zhuluo Fengshan	Taiwan	Wuchifu, Xu Zu, Xiao Quan		messianic (?)	Zhu Sitaizi	"swindling," "sedition"

DATE	PLACE	REGION	LEADERS	NAME	ATTRIBUTES	SAVIORS	ACTIVITIES
1736–1756	Shaowu Ninghua Jianyang Qingliu	Fujian	Du Qi Du Guoxiang Luo Jiaqiu Monk Daoshan	Guansheng-hui Tiechihui (Shisantai Tiechihui)	blood oath messianic	Li Kaihua	gangsterism, "swindling" "sedition"
1736–1759	Lianzhou	Guangdong	Li Boju		messianic		"swindling," "sedition"
1742	Zhanghua	Taiwan	Zhuang Lie Guo Xing		messianic (?)		extortion, "sedition"
1742	Zhangpu Zhaoan Pinghe Raoping	Fujian Guangdong	Cai Huai Chen Zuo	Xiaodaohui Zilonghui	blood oath messianic	Li Kaihua	banditry, homicide "sedition"
1742–1743	Gutian Minqing	Fujian	Huang Tianrui Monk Shanjue		messianic	Li Kaihua Zhu Tianzhu	gangsterism, "sedition"
1747–1748	Jian'an Ouning Gutian	Fujian	Yu Qingfang Pu Shao	Laoguanzhai (Luojiao)	sectarian messianic	Maitreya	vegetarianism, sutra-reading, "sedition," gangsterism
1747	Fuan	Fujian	He Laomei	Bianqianhui	blood oath		
1748	Changtai	Fujian		Fumuhui			
1748	Zhangpu	Fujian		Beidihui			

DATE	PLACE	REGION	LEADERS	NAME	ATTRIBUTES	SAVIORS	ACTIVITIES
1748	Chenghai Haiyang	Guangdong	Li Awan		messianic	Li Tianzhen	banditry, food riot, "sedition"
1749	Ruyuan	Guangdong		Luojiao	sectarian		"sedition"
1752	Nanjing Pinghe	Fujian	Cai Rongzu Feng Heng		sworn oath messianic		"sedition"
1752–1753	Guishan Zengcheng Bouluo Longmen Dongguan	Guangdong	Mo Xinfeng Wang Liangchen		blood oath messianic	Li Kaihua Zhu Hongzhuo	banditry, "swindling" "sedition"
1753	Zhuluo Zhanghua	Taiwan	Shi Tiansi		messianic (?)	Li surname	banditry, "sedition"
1753	Fengshan	Taiwan	Zhang Fengjie		messianic	Li Kaihua	"sedition"
1760	Zhanghua	Taiwan	Shen Fang				"sedition"
1761–1767	Huizhou Raoping Dapu Zhangpu Zhaoan Pinghe	Guangdong Fujian	Monk Hong Er	Tiandihui (?)	blood oath messianic	Li surname Zhu surname	feuds, banditry, "sedition"
1767–1768	Zhangpu	Fujian	Lu Mao		blood oath (?)		banditry, "sedition"

DATE	PLACE	REGION	LEADERS	NAME	ATTRIBUTES	SAVIORS	ACTIVITIES
1767–1768	Ouning Pucheng Shicheng	Fujian Jiangxi	Monk Jueyuan		sworn oath messianic	Wanyuan Santaizi	"swindling"
1768	Guishan	Guangdong	Feng Yajin		sworn oath		gangsterism, theft, gambling, extortion
1768	Fengshan Zhuluo	Taiwan	Huang Jiao Zhu Yide		sworn oath		feud, gangsterism, revolt
1769	Gutian Pingnan	Fujian	Xiao Ri'an		messianic (?)		"swindling," "sedition"
1769–1770	Zhangpu Zhaoan	Fujian	Li Amin		messianic (?) sworn oath	Zhu surname	gangsterism, "sedition"
1770	Fengshun Jieyang Haiyang	Guangdong	Zhu Aijiang		blood oath messianic		banditry, "sedition"
1770–1773	Jieyang	Guangdong	Chen Agao Lin Ayu Mrs. Wang		blood oath sectarian		vegetarianism, sutra-reading, gangsterism, "sedition"
1771	Longxi Anxi	Fujian	Wang Tiansong				"sedition"

DATE	PLACE	REGION	LEADERS	NAME	ATTRIBUTES	SAVIORS	ACTIVITIES
1772–1783	Zhanghua Zhuluo Fengshan	Taiwan	Lin Da Lin Shui	Xiaodaohui (Wangye Xiaodaohui)	blood oath messianic (?)		gangsterism, feuds, "sedition"
1782–1783	Fengshan	Taiwan	Chen Hu		sworn oath messianic (?)		gangsterism, feuds, extortion, "sedition"
1783	Wengyuan Qujiang	Guangdong	Tang Dingxue	sectarian			healing, "swindling"
1783–1788	Zhanghua Zhuluo Zhaoao Zhangpu Longxi Pinghe Raoping Huilai Dapu Chaoyang Jiaying	Taiwan Fujian Guangdong	Lin Shuangwen Yan Yan Lai Abian Liang Abu Zhang Poliangou Chen Mengqin Lin Gongyu	Tiandihui	blood oath messianic	Li Kaihua Li Taohong Zhu Hongde Zhu Juitao Zhu Hongzhu	gangsterism, feuds, banditry "heterodoxy," "sedition," revolt

Appendix 3

Extant Sanpo Temples in Coastal Guangdong and Guangxi

LOCATION	TEMPLE NAME	YEAR TEMPLE BUILT	COMMENTS
Weizhou 涠洲	Sanpo Temple (aka Tianhou Temple) 三婆廟(天后宫)	1738–1739 (Ming?) (Yuan?)	According to local lore Sanpo originated as a water sprite protecting a sacred spring on the island and only later was she transformed into Sanpo; later still, perhaps in the 1840s or 1850s, she was metamorphosed into Tianhou. Sanpo was originally enshrined in a cave and only later in 1738 or 1739 was a temple built; there is some inconclusive evidence that a shrine or temple was built earlier in the Yuan or Ming dynasties.
Nankang, Beihai 北海南康鎮	Sanpo Temple (aka Xiantai Temple, Mazu Temple 三婆廟(冼太廟、媽祖廟)	Qianlong period	Devotees worship three female deities: Mazu, Lady Xian, and Sanpo. According to legend, Mazu had five elder sisters. Her third sister was called Sanpo. The temple has a stone stele dated 1864 that relates how Sanpo used her miraculous powers to help Qing soldiers suppress bandits and pirates.
Yaotou Village, Hepu 合浦縣螯頭村	Sanpo Temple 三婆廟	Qianlong period	
Dangjiang Village, Hepu 合浦縣黨江村	Sanpo Temple 三婆廟		

LOCATION	TEMPLE NAME	YEAR TEMPLE BUILT	COMMENTS
Baishuitang Village, Qinzhou 欽州白水塘村	Sanpo Temple 三婆廟		This is the hometown of the late Qing official and local hero Feng Zicai 馮子材. According to legend he built the Sanpo Temple in his village because at three turning points in his life he had been miraculously helped by an unusual "Old Lady" he came to believe was the deity Sanpo. The temple was destroyed in Cultural Revolution.
Qinzhou 欽州	Kangwang Temple 康王廟		Besides the main deity Kangwang, this temple includes side altars honoring Sanpopo 三婆婆 and Guandi 關帝
Qinzhou 欽州	Sanpopo Temple 三婆婆廟		Devotees worship Sanpopo (Sanpo) and celebrate her festival on the 23rd day of the 3rd lunar month, i.e., Mazu's birthday.
Fangcheng 防城	Ersheng Temple (aka Qinghui or Sanpo Temple) 二聖宮(青慧廟、三婆廟)	1784	This temple, which worshipped Qinghui (Sanpo), was converted into a school after 1949.
Zhushan Village, (Dongxing) 竹山村(東興)	Sansheng Temple (aka Sanpo Temple) 三聖宮(三婆廟)	1876	The original temple was called Sanpo Temple and honored Sanpo, but today villagers venerate three different deities in this temple.

LOCATION	TEMPLE NAME	YEAR TEMPLE BUILT	COMMENTS
Tengxian, Guangxi 藤縣	Longmu Temple (aka Sanpo Temple) 龍母廟(三婆廟)		The three deities worshipped in this temple are called Sanpo; they are the Dragon Mother, Mazu, and the Third Elder Sister Liu.
Shanxin Village, Jiangping (Jing minority) 京族江坪山心村	Sanpo Temple 三婆廟		Vietnamese fishers who settled on the islands off Jiangping brought with them their religious customs, including their deity called Sanpo.
Wutou Village, Jiangping (Jing minority) 京族江坪巫頭村	Sanpo Temple 三婆廟		
Xiajiang, Leizhou 雷州夏江村	Tianhou Temple 天后宮	Song dynasty (repaired in 1446; 1574; 1587)	During the Ming Wanli reign the fishers and pirates forced to leave Weizhou introduced their Qinghui (Sanpo) deity into the Tianhou Temple in Xiajiang.
Shanwei Village, Leizhou 雷州山尾村	Qinghui Temple 菁惠宮	late Ming dynasty?	Devotees worship Qinghui (Sanpo). Introduced into the village by the Cao family.
Wushi Village, Leizhou 雷州烏石村	Qinghui Temple 菁惠宮		Devotees worship Qinghui (Sanpo). Possibly introduced into the village by the Wu family.

LOCATION	TEMPLE NAME	YEAR TEMPLE BUILT	COMMENTS
West Gate, Leizhou City 雷州市西門関	Furen Temple (aka Tianhou Temple) 夫人宮(天后廟)	Song dynasty (?)	Devotees worship Mazu and Qinghui (Sanpo).
Qishui, Leizhou 雷州企水港	Wuwang Temple 鄔王廟		Devotees worship the Black Snake King 鄔蛇大王 and Qinghui (Sanpo).
Qishui, Leizhou 雷州企水港	Wangniang Temple 王娘廟		Devotees worship Lady Wang 王娘 and Qinghui (Sanpo).
Qishui, Leizhou 雷州企水港	Leishou Temple 雷首廟		Devotees worship Deng Tianjun 鄧天君 and Qinghui (Sanpo)
Niukoushan Village, Xiangshan 香山縣牛口山村	Sanpo Temple 三婆廟	1840s	Devotees worshipped Sanpo. Because worshippers practiced unorthodox exorcistic rites and sorcery, the local magistrate destroyed the temple in the 1850s.
Taipa, Macao 澳門氹仔	Sanpo Temple 三婆廟	1843 or 1845	Devotees worship Sanpo, who according to legend is the third elder sister of Tianhou. According to the temple's 1859 stele, the temple was built by fishers after Sanpo helped them defeat pirates in the Gulf of Tonkin. Her festival is celebrated on the 22nd day of the 3rd lunar month, one day before Tianhou's birthday.

LOCATION	TEMPLE NAME	YEAR TEMPLE BUILT	COMMENTS
Dongyong Village, Lantao Island, Hong Kong 香港大嶼山東涌村	Tianhou Temple (Sanpo Temple?) 天后廟(三婆廟?)	Daoguang period	According to local lore, once Zhang Baozai tried to set sail from the island his ships were unable to move because a large stone prevented them from raising the anchor. When sailors removed the stone it turned into Tianhou (i.e., Sanpo) who told the pirates that thereafter they should not rob fishers. Afterward Zhang Baozai erected this temple.

Character List

anchashi 按察使
anchasi zhaomo 按察司照磨
anhao 暗號
Aomen tongzhi 澳門通知

baihu 白虎
Bailongwei 白龍尾
Baimanghua 白芒花
Baise 百色
Baishahu 白沙湖
Baiyanghui 白陽會
Baiyunshan 白雲山
bao 堡
Baochan zhusheng yuanjun
　保產注生元君
baojia 保甲
Bapai Yao 八排猺
bapin jingli 八品經歷
Bayansan 巴延三
Beidi 北帝
Beihai 北海
Beijing wawa 北京娃娃
Beiliu 北流
biaowen 表文
biji 筆記
Boluo 博羅
Botang 柏塘
bushu 卜鼠

Cai Buyun 蔡步云
Cai Jing 蔡景
Cai Qian 蔡牽
Cai Qian Ma 蔡牽媽
Cai Rongzu 蔡榮祖
Cao Risheng 曹日昇
Caoyang 草洋
Cenxi 岑溪

Chang'an 長安
Changle 長樂
Changning 長寧
Changtangping 長塘坪
Chao Gai 晁蓋
Chaoshehui 超社會
Chaozhou 潮州
Chashan 茶山
Chehuang ba 扯謊壩
Chen Acheng 陳阿澄
Chen Biao 陳彪
Chen Fangqi 陳芳奇
Chen Jiaxun 陳家珣
Chen Jingang 陳金鋼/剛/缸
Chen Jinjiang 陳金江
Chen Lanjisi 陳爛屐四
Chen Lanjiwu 陳爛屐五
Chen Maosheng 陳冒生
Chen Shangchuan 陳上川
Chen Shidun 陳士敦
Chen Shizhuang 陳世莊
Chen Shunxi 陳舜系
Chen Weiyan 陳微言
Chen Xingcai 陳興財
Chen Xisi 陳蓆四
Chen Xiwu 陳蓆五
Chen Yaben 陳亞本
Chen Yagui 陳亞桂
Chen Yaqi 陳亞七
Chen Yawu 陳亞五
Chen Zhixi 陳志熙
Chen Zhiyuan 陳志淵
Chen Zhongru 陳仲儒
Chen Zong 陳宗
Chen Zuo 陳作
Cheng Hao 程顥
Cheng Yi 程頤

Character List

Chenghuangye 城隍爺
Chengmai 澄邁
chengxiang 丞相
Chenzhou 郴州
Chitang 池塘
chong 冲
Chongan 崇安
chuanbo yaoyan 傳播謠言
chuanling 穿令
Chunqui fanlu 春秋繁露
Chun Shu 春樹
Chuzhengong 楚震公
ci 詞
Cui Jian 崔健

Da Jiao Sao 大脚嫂
Da Ma 大媽
Da Ming fuxing Zhu Sitaixi san guogong qiyi 大明復興朱四太子三國公起義
Da Ming Zhu Sitaizi 大明朱四太子
Dacheng dajie jing 大乘大戒經
Dacheng Luojiao 大乘羅教
Dacheng zhaitang 大乘齋堂
Dachengjiao 大乘教
Dade 大德
Dagou 打狗
Dai 傣
daitian xingdao 代天行道
dajiang 打降
Dajiaxi 大甲西
dajie fuhu 打劫富戶
Dalong 大龍
Dalongchong 大壠冲
Dan 蛋/蜑/疍
Danjia (Tanka) 蛋家
dao 刀
Daoguang 道光
Daosan 道三
Dasha 大沙
Dashan 達山
Dashi 大石
dawang 大王
dayuanshuai 大元帥

dazai 打仔
Dazhuang 大莊
Deng Chaoxiang 鄧潮相
Deng Yao 鄧耀
Deqing 德慶
di 地
Dianbai 電白
die 牒
diling 地靈
Dingan 定安
Dingsha 盯沙
dingxiong 頂兇
Dong 侗
Dongan 東安
Dongguan 東莞
Donghai Ba 東海八
Dongxiang 東鄉
Dongyong 東涌
Doufu Bagui 豆腐八貴
Du Guoxiang 杜國祥
Du Qi 杜奇
Du Shiming 杜世明
Du Zhen 杜臻
duodao duoshu duoyi 多盜多鼠多蟻

Emeishan 峨眉山
Enben jing 恩本經
Enping 恩平
Er Cheng quanshu 二程全書
Er Ma 二媽
Er Xian niangninag 二仙娘娘
Erlan 二濫

Falungong 法輪功
fan Qing fu Ming 反清復明
fan Qing fu Ming yingxiong 反清復明英雄
Fan Guangxi 范光喜
fandong huidaomen 反動會道門
Fang Dahong 方大洪
Fangcheng 防城
fangshi 方士
Fanhu 氾湖
fantan 番攤

fashi 法師
fashu 法術
fei 匪
Fei Xiaotong 費孝通
feigun 匪棍
Feng Heng 馮珩
Feng Yajin 馮亞金
Feng Yunshan 馮雲山
Fengchuan 封川
Fenghuang 鳳凰
fengjian mixin 封建迷信
Fengjinshan 封禁山
Fengmu 風姆
Fengshan 鳳山
fengshui 風水
fohao 佛號
fu 符
Fu Bilai 傅碧萊
Fuchuan 富川
Fulian ta 浮蓮塔
Fumuhui 父母會
Fuzhou 福州

Gan Runchang 甘潤昌
Gansu 甘肅
Gaogang 高崗
gaoshan 高山
Gaoxin 高辛
Gaoyao 高要
Gaozhou 高州
gepo 歌婆
geta 下駄
gezhou 歌咒
Goutoushan 狗頭山
gu 蠱
Gu Dasao 顧大嫂
Gu Long 古龍
Guan Tiancheng 關天成
Guan Yuelong 官粵瓏
guanbi liangmin 官逼良民
Guandi 關帝
guanggun 光棍
guanggun jie 光棍節

Guanqiao 官橋
Guanshenghui 關聖會
Guanyang 灌陽
Guanyin 觀音
Guanyin laomu 觀音老母
Guanyin zhaitang 觀音齋堂
Guanyinshan 觀音山
guibing 鬼兵
guiguo 鬼國
guihua 歸化
guimen 鬼門
guimenguan 鬼門關
Guishan 歸山
guiwang 鬼王
Guiyang 贵楊
gun 棍
guntu 棍徒
Guo Fei 郭棐
Guo Podai 郭婆帶
Guo Quan 郭全
Guo Run 郭閏
Guo Xiushan 郭秀山
guogong 國公
guohuoshan 過火山
Guoshan bang 過山榜
Guoshan Yao 過山猺
Guoxue 國學
Guweishan 箍圍山

Hải Dương 海陽
Hải Nha 海牙
haidao 海盜
Haikang 海康
haikou 海寇
Hailing'a 海齡阿
Hainan 海南
hainanwang 海南王
haini 海逆
haishui 海水
Haiyang 海陽
haizei 海賊
Han 漢
haohan 好漢

Character List

haoxia 豪俠
He 何
He Deguang 何得廣
He Sanfa 何三發
He Yasi 何亞四
He Zhi 何晢
hefei 河匪
heishui 黑水
Hepu 合浦
Heshan 鶴山
hetong 合同
Hexian 賀縣
hong 紅 (red)
hong 洪 (vast, flood)
Hong Er 洪二
Hong Xiuquan 洪秀全
Hongjiangzhai 洪江寨
hongshui hengliu fanlan yu tianxia 洪水橫流凡濫于天下
Hongxingshe 洪興社
hongzu 洪租
Hu Ermei 胡二妹
Hu Jianglian 胡江連
Hu Jintao 胡錦濤
Hu Sanniang 扈三娘
Huafen furen 花粉夫人
Huagaishan 華蓋山
Huaiji 懷集
Huang Dawan 黃大晚
Huang Dehui 黃德輝
Huang Hairu 黃海如
Huang Kaiguang 黃開廣
Huang Liuhong 黃六鴻
Huang Shengzhang 黃勝長
Huang Tianrui 黃天瑞
Huang Tingchen 黃廷臣
Huang Tongruo 黃烔若
Huang Yongxing 黃永興
Huang Zhenggui 黃正貴
Huang Zuojin 黃佐金
Huangcheng 皇城
Huanggang 黃崗
Huangguachong 黃瓜冲
Huanglian shengmu 黃蓮聖母

Huangtang 黃塘
Huangzhuzhai 黃竹寨
huapo 花婆
Huazhou 化州
hui 會
Huidong 惠東
huifei 會匪
huipu 會簿
huixing 彗星
Huizhou 惠州
Humen 虎門

ji 屐
jian 劍
Jiang Zemin 江澤民
jianghu 江湖
Jianghua 江華
Jianghuliu 江湖流
jiangjun 將軍
Jiangping (Giang Bình) 江坪
jiangshen 降身
jiangun 奸棍
jianmin 賤民 (mean people)
jianmin 奸民 (rascals)
jiansheng 監生
jiao 教
Jiaotang 茭塘
Jiaozhi 交趾
Jiaqing 嘉慶
Jiazi 甲子
jie 劫
jiefu jipin 劫富濟貧
Jieyang 揭陽
jin 斤 (weight)
Jin 金 (gold, surname)
Jin Yong 金庸
Jing (Kinh) 京
jingang 金剛
Jingang Mazu 金剛媽祖
jingang shengdi 金剛聖地
Jinggangshan 井岡山
jingshen wenming 精神文明
jingshen wuran 精神污染
jingshu 經書

Character List

Jingtang 敬堂
jingyuan hou 靖遠侯
Jinhua furen 金華夫人
jinlong 金龍
jinlong wang 金龍王
Jinshan 金山
jinshu 金書
Jintian 錦田
Jinyu 金峪
jiqi 祭旗
jiugui wuren si 舊鬼無人祀
Jiulian jing 九蓮經
Jiuliantang 九蓮堂
jixin 寄信
Jueluo Jiqing 覺羅吉慶
Jueyuan 覺圓
Jumu 颶母
Jushu 桔樹

Kaiping 開平
Kang Youwei 康有為
Kanggong 康公
Kangwang 康王
Kangxi 康熙
kejia (Hakka) 客家
kemin 客民
Kengtou 坑頭
keshang 客商
kezei 客賊
kou 寇
Kunlun 崑崙

Lai Choi San 來財山
Lai Dengyu 賴登愚
Lai Dongbao 賴東保
Lai Enjue 賴恩爵
Lan Xiuwen 藍修文
Lanfenshan 藍汾山
Langbian 朗遍
Lanlong Zhu Tianzi Li Kaihua
  蘭龍朱天子李開花
Lanshan 藍山
lanzai 爛仔
laodawang 老大王

Laoguan zhaihui 老官齋會
Laomujiao 老母教
Laoshushan 老鼠山
Lechang 樂昌
Leidong 雷洞
Leizhou 雷州
li 里 (distance)
Li 狸 (minority)
Li 李 (surname)
Li 黎 (Hainan minority)
Li Amin 李阿閔
Li Awan 李阿萬
Li Boju 李伯舉
Li Chengdong 李成棟
Li Deming 李德明
Li Dexian 李德先
Li Dingguo 李定國
Li Hongzhi 李洪志
Li Jiukui 李九葵
Li Kaihua 李開花
Li Lingkui 李凌魁
Li Mei 李梅
Li Qisheng 李其聖
Li Rong 李榮
Li Shimin 李世民
Li Shixin 李世信
Li Sidi 李色弟
Li Taohong 李桃紅(洪)
Li Tianbao 李天寶(保)
Li Weifeng 李惟鳳
Li Wenmao 李文茂
Li Yao tongzhi 理猺同知
Li Yinhe 李銀河
Li Zantao 李贊韜
Li Zhong 李忠
Li Zicheng 李自成
liang 良 (good)
liang 兩 (taels)
Liang Qichao 梁啓超
Liang Yaxiang 梁亞香
Liang Zibin 梁子賓
Lianghekou 兩河口
liangmin 良民
liangri xiangjiao 兩日相交

Liangshan 梁山
Lianhuashan 蓮花山
Liannan 連南
Lianping 連平
Lianshan 連山
Lianyang ying 連陽營
Lianzhou 連州
Liao 廖
Liao Ganzhou 廖干周
Lienzhou 廉州
Lijing 禮經
Lin Ayu 林阿裕
Lin Daoqian 林道乾
Lin Guniang 林姑娘
Lin Jinlian 林金蓮
Lin Kuan 林寬
Lin Moniang 林默娘
Lin Shuangwen 林爽文
Lin Shuxian 林淑賢
Lin Yongzhao 林永招
ling 靈
Ling Datourong 凌大頭蓉
Lin'gao 臨高
lingchi 凌遲
Linghui furen 靈惠夫人
linglei wenhua 另類文化
lingqi 令旗
Lingshan 靈山
Linhong 臨泓
liu 流
Liu Sanjie 劉三姐
Liu Wencai 劉文才
Liu Zaifu 劉再復
Liucheng 柳城
liumang 流氓
liumin 流民
liuzei 流賊
Longchuan 龍川
Longhua jing 龍華經
Longhuajiao 龍華教
longmai 龍脈
Longmen 龍門
Longmu 龍母
long nü 龍女

Longtan 龍潭
Longwang 龍王
longwen 龍文
Longxue 龍穴
longyin 龍印
lu 路
Lu Dian 陸佃
Lu Mao 盧茂
luan 亂
Lufeng 陸豐
Luo Jiaqiu 羅家球
Luo Ping 羅平
Luo Qi 羅琦
Luo Xingda 羅興達
Luofushan 羅浮山
luohanjiao 羅漢腳
Luojiao 羅教
Luoxi 洛溪
Luoxiying 羅溪營
Luoyong 螺涌

Ma Jiulong 馬九龍
Ma Yuan 馬援
Mai Yarong 麥亞榮
Man 蠻
mao 貓
maogui 貓鬼
maolaoye 貓老爺
Maoming 茂名
Maoshan 貓山
Mazu 媽祖
Mazu *ju* 媽祖颶
Mazupo 媽祖婆
Meizhou shennü 湄洲神女
mengbu 盟布
mengzhu 盟主
Mian Mian 棉棉
Miao 苗
min 民
Mingwang 明王
minjian zongjiao 民間宗教
minzu ronghe 民族融合
mixin 迷信
mixin jiguan 迷信機關

Character List

Mo Mei 莫妹
moyao 莫徭
mu 畝
muchang 木場
Muyangcheng 木楊城
muyin 木印
Muzimei 木子美

Nainiang 奶娘
Nan'ao 南澳
Nanchang 南昌
Nanhai 南海
Nanhaishen 南海神
Nanwan 南灣
nanwu 男巫
Nanxing wang 南興王
Nayancheng 那彥成
Nezha 哪吒
ngok lo 惡佬
ni 逆
niangzi jun 娘子軍
Nie Erkang 聶爾康
Ningyuan 寧遠
niugui sheshen 牛鬼蛇神
Niukoushan 牛口山
Niutouhui 牛頭會
niwu nimen tou zaizai sunsun zuozei tou—laoshu 泥屋泥門頭仔仔孫孫做賊頭—老鼠
nizei 逆賊
nongmin qiyi 農民起義
nü yingxiong 女英雄
Nuhai xiadao 怒海俠盜
nüwu 女巫

Ou Zaitai 區在台

padaoti 爬刀梯
Pai Yao 排猺
Pan Dinggui 潘鼎珪
Pan Junhua 盤均華
Panhu 盤瓠
Pan Wang 盤王
Panyu 番禺

pao jianghu 跑江湖
Paoge 袍哥
Peng 彭
Peng Shangnian 彭尚年
Peng Yasheng 彭亞勝
pengke 朋克
Phan Phú Quốc 潘輔國
pin bu shoufen 貧不受分
pingdi 平地
Pinghuang quandie 評皇券牒
Pingle 平樂
pingmin 平民
Pingnan 平南
Pingshan 平山
Pingyang 平陽
Piya 埤雅
pizi 痞子
po 婆
Pozai 婆仔
Pu 普
Puning 普寧
Puren 普仁
Pusa 菩薩
Pushao 普少
Putian 莆田

qi 氣 (vital force)
qi 旗 (banner)
Qi Jiguang 戚繼光
Qian Yikai 錢以塏
Qianjiadong 千家峒/洞
Qianlong 乾隆
Qianwan bie ba wo dangren 千萬別把我當人
qigong 氣功
Qin Liangyu 秦良玉
qing 青
Qingchun wuhui 青春無悔
Qinghui 青惠
Qinghui jingjuan 青惠經卷
Qinghui Sanpo 清(青)惠三婆
qinglong 青龍
Qingxi 青溪
Qingxishan 清溪山

Character List

Qingyuan 清远
Qinzhou 欽州
Qiongzhou 瓊州
Qishier jing 七十二徑
Qiu Yajiang 邱亞江
Qixing niangniang 七星娘娘
qiyi 起義
Qu Dajun 屈大均
quanrong 犬戎
Quanzhou 泉州
quti 曲蹄
quti po 曲蹄婆

Renmin ribao 人民日報
Renshan 稔山
Rongxian 容縣
Ruyuan 乳源

Sakura Magozō 佐倉孫三
San Ma 三媽
Sanguo yanyi 三國演義
Sanhehui 三合會
Sanhuang shengzujiao 三皇聖祖教
Sanjiang 三江
Sanjiang xieying 三江協營
Sanjiemei 三姐妹
Sanlian 三連
Sanniang 三娘
Sanpo 三婆
Sanpopo 三婆婆
Sanshui 三水
Santaizi 三太子
sha 沙
shafu 沙夫
shagun 沙棍
shahu 下戶
Shalitou 沙利頭
shamin 沙民
shan 善
Shang Kexi 尚可喜
Shang Zhixin 尚之信
Shanghai baobei 上海寶貝
Shangyou 上猶
Shanhaijing 山海經

Shanjue 善覺
shanqi 山氣
Shantou 汕頭
Shanwei 汕尾 (city)
Shanwei 山尾 (village)
Shanxi 山溪
shanxian 山仙
Shanxin 山心
shao bu kan Shuihu lao bu kan Sanguo 少不看水滸老不看三國
Shaolin 少林
Shaolin wuzu 少林五祖
shatian 沙田
Shating 沙亭
Shawan 沙灣
shaxue jiemeng 歃血結盟
shexue 社學
shenbing 神兵
sheng 生
Shengmu 聖母
shenpo 神婆
shenshu 神書
shentan 神壇
shi 士
Shi Xianggu 石香姑
Shi En 施恩
Shidai guniang 時代姑娘
shifu 師父
shigandang 石敢當
shigong 師公
Shiji 石碁
Shijing 詩經
Shili ta 石礪塔
Shilishan 石礪山
Shiqi 石岐
Shiqiao 市橋
Shitou 市頭
Shiwan Dashan 十萬大山
shiwu 師巫
Shiwuzai 十五仔
shu 瘋 (diseases)
shu 書 (books)
shu 熟 (cooked)
Shuangsheng ge 雙聖閣

shubei 鼠輩
Shuihu zhuan 水滸傳
shuiji 水雞
shuikou 水口
shuikoufu 水口符
shuiliuchai 水流柴
shuishang nüren 水上女人
shuishang ren 水上人
Shuiwei shengmu 水尾聖母
Shujing 書經
Shunde 順德
shuntian 順天
shuntian xingdao 順天行道
shuqie goutou 鼠竊狗偷
shuren 庶人
shuxue 鼠穴
shuyi 鼠疫
shuzi 鼠子
Si Ma 四媽
Song Jiang 宋江
Su 蘇
Su Guansheng 蘇觀陞
sui 歲
Sui Yao ying 綏猺營
Suixi 遂溪
Sun Erniang 孫二娘

Taisui 太歲
taibao 泰寶
Taihe 泰和
Taihongguo 太洪國
Taipa (Tanzai) 氹仔
taiping 太平
Tang 糖
Tang Saier 唐賽兒
tangbu 堂簿
Tangong 譚公
Tangxia 塘下
Teng 藤
Tengxian 藤縣
tian 天
Tian Gong 天公
Tian Laoye 天老爺
tian yu dao xing 天與道行

tianbing 天兵
Tiandeng 田橙
Tiandihui 天地會/添弟會
Tianfei 天妃
Tiangou 天狗
Tianhou 天后
Tianlangxing 天狼星
tianshu 天書
tianxian 天仙
Tianyuan taibao 天圓泰寶
tianzhanggong 天長公
Tianzizhang 天字嶂
tiben 題本
Tiecheng 鐵城
Tiechihui 鐵尺會
tiemao 鐵貓
titian xingdao 替天行道
Tixi 提喜
tongpan 通判
toumu 頭目
touren 頭人
ts'oa jio po (daoniaopo) 導溺婆
tuanlian 團練
tudao 土盜
Tudigong 土地公
Tuxi 涂喜
tuzei 土賊

Wan'an 萬安
Wande jiushi xintiao 玩的就是心跳
Wang 王
Wang Atong 王阿童
Wang Conger 王聰兒
Wang Liangchen 王亮臣
Wang Lun 王倫
Wang Shuo 王朔
Wang Tianzu 王添組
Wang Yue 王悦
Wang Zheng 王正
Wang Zhihan 王之瀚
Wangcheng 王城
wangye 王爺
Wangye xiaodaohui 王爺小刀會
Wanli 萬曆

Character List

Wanwei 萬尾
wanshi xianzhi 玩世現實
Wanyuan 萬沅
Wanzhu 頑主
wei 圍
Wei Hui 衛慧
wei renmin fuwu 爲人民服務
Wei Yuan 魏源
Weizhou 潿洲
wen 文
Wen Dengyuan 溫登元
Wen Qiong 溫瓊
Wen Yali 溫亞利
Wen Yashi 溫亞石
wenshen yiren 紋身藝人
wu 巫
Wu Ajiao 吳阿嬌
Wu Fusheng 吳福生
Wu Guniang 吳姑娘
Wu Ma 五媽
Wu Ping 吳平
Wu Qingyuan 吳清遠
Wu Sangui 吳三桂
Wu Song 武松
Wu Tao 吳韜
Wu Wenchun 吳文春
Wu Xinzhi 吳信質
Wu Zixiang 吳子祥
wuchifu 無齒夫
Wuchuan 吳川
Wudi 五帝
wufang 五房
Wugong jing 五公經
wugongjing 蜈蚣精
wuhu 五虎
wulai guntu 無賴棍徒
wulai quangun 無賴拳棍
Wuling 五嶺
Wupanjiao 五盤教
wunü 巫女
wupo 巫婆
Wushan 巫山
Wushen Mazu 五身媽祖
Wusheng Laomu 無生老母

wushi 武士 (warrior)
wushi 巫師 (wizard, ritual specialist)
Wushi Er 烏石二
wushu 五鼠
Wushuntang 五順堂
wusiqi 五色旗
Wutou 巫頭
wuxia 武俠
Wuxian 五顯
wuying 五營
Wuzhou 梧州
wuzu 五祖

Xi Jinping 習近平
xia 俠
xiahu 下戶
Xiajiang 夏江
Xiamen 廈門
Xian Biao 冼彪
Xian furen 冼夫人
xiancheng 縣丞
xiang 鄉
Xiangshan 香山
xiangyue 鄉約
xianpo 仙婆
xianshuige 鹹水歌
xianshuimei 鹹水妹
Xiantiandao 先天道
xiao 孝
Xiao Liangdi 蕭良娣
Xiao Quan 蕭全
Xiaodaohui 小刀會
xiaoqing 小青
xiaoxitian 小西天
Xibian 西邊
xie 邪
Xie Huoying 謝活螢
Xie Xiyuan 謝希元
xiedou 械鬥
xiejiao 邪教
xieshu 邪術
xifeng jihou 蓆豐屐厚
xiha 嘻哈
ximin 細民

Xin'an 新安
Xingning 興寧
Xinhui 新會
Xinjiang 新疆
Xinning 新寧
Xinqiao 新橋
Xintian 新田
xinwei jiangjun 信威將軍
Xinxing 新興
Xinyi 信宜
xiong 凶
Xiong Renlin 熊人霖
xiongdi 兄弟
Xiongmao 熊貓
xiongxing 凶星
xiucai 秀才
Xiwangmu 西王母
Xiyouji 西遊記
Xu Kun 徐崑
Xu Qianjin 徐虔進
Xu Zu 許祖
Xue Youlian 薛有連
xuehai 血海
xun 汛
xunjian 巡檢
xunjiansi 巡檢司

Yaizhou 崖州
Yan Yan 嚴烟
yang 陽
Yang Er 楊二
Yang Er Sanpo 楊二三婆
Yang Daohua 楊道華
Yang Miaozhen 楊妙真
Yang San 楊三
Yang Wang 楊王
Yang Yandi 楊彥迪
Yang Yi 楊義
Yangcheng 楊城
yanggui 洋鬼
Yangjiang 陽江
Yangjingkeng 洋景坑
Yangpan jiao 陽盤教
Yangquan 羊泉

Yangshan 陽山
yangshi 楊市
Yangshishan 羊屎山
Yao 猺/瑤
Yao jiang 猺疆
Yao Lao 猺老
Yao Wang 猺王
yaoping 腰憑
yaoren 妖人
yaoshu 妖書
yaowang 妖王
yaoxing 妖星
Yashan 丫山
Ye 葉
yi 義
Yiguandao 一貫道
yihequan 義和拳
Yijing 易經
yijun 義軍
yin 陰 (female, negative)
yin 淫 (licentious)
yinbing 陰兵
yinci 淫祠
ying 英
Yingde 英德
Yinpanjiao 陰盤教
yiri 一日
Yizhangqing 一丈青
Yizi zhaitang 一字齋堂
yong 勇
Yongan 永安
Yongantang 永安堂
Yongli 永曆
Yongzheng 雍正
You Lihe 游禮和
youxia 游俠
Yu Youxing 余有興
yuan 圓
Yuan Yonglun 袁永綸
Yuandun dachengjiao 圓敦大乘教
yuansou 淵藪
yue 約 (pact)
Yue 越 (ethnic group)
Yue Jun 月君

Yue Min xunshi jilue 粵閩巡視紀略
Yuhong 漁洪
Yulong taizi 玉龍太子
Yuncheng 雲城
Yunxiao 雲霄

zaju 雜劇
Zeng Qinghao 曾清浩
Zengcheng 增城
zha 劄/札
zhai 寨
Zhan 詹
Zhang Baozai 張保仔
Zhang Che 張徹
Zhang Fei 張飛
Zhang Fengjie 張風喈
Zhang Juzheng 張居正
Zhang Poliangou 張破臉狗
Zhang Sichang 張嗣昌
Zhang Yingyu 張應俞
Zhang Yuantong 張元通
Zhanghua 彰化
Zhangpu 漳浦
Zhangzhou 漳州
zhao 兆 (omens)
zhao 照 (certificates)
Zhao 趙 (surname)
Zhao Fucai 趙福才
Zhao Fujin 趙福金
Zhao Jinlong 趙金龍
Zhao Wenfeng 趙文鳳
Zhao Zaiqing 趙仔青
Zhaoan 詔安
Zhaobao 招寶
zhaofu 招撫
Zhaoping 昭平
Zhaoqing 肇慶
zhaoren weifei 招人為匪
Zheng Chenggong (Koxinga) 鄭成功
Zheng Jin 鄭金
Zheng Jing 鄭經
Zheng Qi 鄭七
Zheng Shangpan 鄭上攀
Zheng Wei 鄭為

Zheng Yi 鄭一
Zheng Yi Sao 鄭一嫂
Zheng Zhilong 鄭志龍
Zheng Zuxi 鄭祖禧
Zhenhai dawang 鎮海大王
Zhikai 智開
zhiliting 直隸廳
zhilizhou 直隸州
Zhisan 知叁
zhong 忠 (loyal)
Zhong 鍾 (surname)
Zhongcun 钟村
Zhongguo qingnian bao 中國青年報
Zhongpuwei 中埔圍
Zhongshan 中山
zhongyi tang 忠義堂
zhou 咒
Zhou Caixiong 周才雄
Zhou Shounan 周壽南
Zhou Yan 周延
Zhou Yu 周玉
Zhoushan 周山
zhu 住 (settled)
zhu 主 (master)
Zhu 朱 (surname)
Zhu Ajiang 朱阿姜
Zhu Fen 朱濆
Zhu Hongde 朱洪德
Zhu Hongzhu 朱洪竹
Zhu Hongzhuo 朱洪桌
Zhu Jiutao 朱九桃
Zhu Langsi 朱浪四
Zhu Qigui 朱七桂
Zhu Santaizi 朱三太子
Zhu Sitaizi 朱四太子
Zhu Tianzi 朱天子
Zhu Wo 朱渥
Zhu Yajin 朱亞金
Zhu Yigui 朱一貴
Zhuang 獞
Zhuang Jingyun 莊靜云
zhuanwen 篆文
zhuanying 專營
zhufeng 朱鳳

zhulongshan 主龍山
Zhuluo 諸羅
zhupai 竹牌
zhushan 主山
Zhushan 竹山

Zijingshan 紫荊山
zouzhe 奏摺
Zu Zeqing 祖澤清
zuming 祖名
zuren fanyan fugui 族人繁衍富貴

NOTES

Prelude

1. In this context, North Route referred to the area north of the prefectural city of Tainan, that is Zhuluo and Zhanghua, while South Route referred to the area south of Tainan, that is Fengshan.

2. On Zhu Yigui, see John Shepherd, *Statecraft and Political Economy on the Taiwan Frontier*, 146–148; and David Ownby, *Brotherhoods and Secret Societies in Early and Mid-Qing China*, 95–103. On Wu Fusheng, see John Shepherd, "Taiwan Prefecture in the Eighteenth Century," 90–92. On Dajiaxi, see Shepherd, *Statecraft and Political Economy on the Taiwan Frontier*, 128–132.

3. Yamen refers to a government office and *baojia* was a state-sponsored collective neighborhood watch system of law enforcement and public control; on *baojia*, see Robert Antony, *Unruly People*, 70–77.

4. Only three documents have survived in this case: *Shiliao xunkan*, *tian* series, 173–174; and *Yongzheng zhupi yuzhi*, 27:210–211, 420–421. It is likely that other documents existed but are now lost.

5. See Philip Kuhn, *Soulstealers*, 11, 46–47, 114–118; Alice Bianchi, "Ghost-Like Beggars in Chinese Painting," 223–248; Lu Hanchao, *Street Criers*, 17–18; and James Watson, "Living Ghosts," 454–459.

6. See John McCreery, "The Symbolism of Popular Taoist Magic," 42–43; Avon Boretz, *Gods, Ghosts, and Gangsters*, 230n41; and the discussion in chapter 4 in this book.

7. Natasha Hoare, "The Past Is a Foreign Country."

8. Clifford Geertz, "From the Native's Point of View." In this study "native" refers to the indigenous or local peoples of a community under study and is not meant to imply colonialism's stigma of primitivism and backwardness.

9. On history from below, see Jim Sharpe, "History from Below"; Eric Hobsbawm, "On History from Below"; John Brewer, "Microhistory and the Histories of Everyday Life"; and Andrew Port, "History from Below."

10. Hayden White, *Tropics of Discourse*, 47.

11. Ashis Nandy, "History's Forgotten Doubles," 44; see also Hayden White, *The Practical Past*.

12. Robert Darnton, "The Symbolic Element in History," 219–220; on symbolic anthropology, see Clifford Geertz, *The Interpretation of Cultures*; and on a literary-sociological approach to symbolism, see Kenneth Burke, *On Symbols and Society*.

13. For a wonderful anthology of popular Chinese stories about rats and cats, see Wilt Idema, *Mouse vs. Cat in Chinese Literature*.

14. Barend ter Haar, *Ritual and Mythology of the Triads*, 117.

15. Not coincidentally, according to a purported Falungong apocalyptic prophecy made in 2000, a heroic rider on a white horse will appear to open up Heaven for true believers; see the postlude.

16. Roel Sterckx, *The Animal and the Daemon in Early China*, 3.

17. See Robert Antony, *Like Froth Floating on the Sea* and *Unruly People*, as well as Elizabeth Perry, *Rebels and Revolutionaries in North China*.

18. Stevan Harrell, "Introduction: Civilizing Projects and the Reactions to Them," 10–13.

19. The term Tanka, meaning "egg people," is pejorative; today the preferred term for Dan boat people is *shuishang ren* or "people on the waters."

20. See, for example, Pamela Crossley, "Thinking about Ethnicity in Early Modern China," 23–24; David Faure, "Introduction," 1–5; and Susan Mann, "Presidential Address: Myths of Asian Womanhood."

21. Graham Seal, "The Robin Hood Principle," 84.

22. On Chinese heroes, for example, see Robert Ruhlmann, "Traditional Heroes in Chinese Popular Fiction"; and Ralph Croizer, *Koxinga and Chinese Nationalism*.

23. Sharpe, "History from Below," 31.

24. On the value of archives for understandings of local culture, see Zhuang Jifa, "Gugong dang'an yu Qingdai minsu"; and on the Qing judicial archives, see Nancy Park and Robert Antony, "Archival Research in Qing Legal History."

25. Arlette Farge, *The Allure of the Archives*, 30.

26. On confessions as historical sources, see Susan Naquin, "True Confessions"; Elizabeth Perry, "When Peasants Speak"; and Yasuhiko Karasawa, "From Oral Testimony to Written Records in Qing Legal Cases." On the problems of torture and coerced confessions in today's China, see Zhiyuan Guo, "Torture and Exclusion of Evidence in China."

27. See in particular chapters 4 and 5 for examples of such material evidence.

28. On the importance of field research in Chinese historical studies, see Wang Mingke, *Fansi shixue yu shixue fansi*; and Thomas DuBois and Jan Kiely, eds., *Fieldwork in Modern Chinese History*.

29. On steles as historical sources, see Paul Katz, "Temple Inscriptions and the Study of Taoist Cults"; and Anne Gerritsen, "Visions of Local Culture."

30. For Hong Kong, see David Faure et al., "The Hong Kong Region According to Historical Inscriptions," 51–52; and for Macau, see Daoguang era steles located at the Lord Tam Temple on Coloane island and on the peninsula at the Linfeng Temple.

31. James Hayes, "Specialists and Written Materials in the Village World." For a recent study, with translations of written materials in common use in China between 1850 and 1950, see Ronald Suleski, *Daily Life for the Common People of China*. On genealogies, see David Faure, "Written and the Unwritten." On proverbs, see Nancy Park, "Poverty, Privilege, and Power and Imperial Chinese Proverbs"; and R. David Arkush, "Orthodoxy and Heterodoxy in Twentieth-Century Peasant Proverbs." On rumors, see Barend ter Haar, *Telling Stories*; and Steve Smith, "Fear and Rumour in the People's Republic of China in the 1950s."

32. Douglas Cowan, *Magic, Monsters, and Make-Believe Heroes*, 102.

Notes

33. Jonathan Friedman, "Myth, History, and Political Identity," 195, 207; see also William McNeill, "Mythistory, or Truth, Myth, History, and Historians."

34. See, for example, Mann, "Presidential Address: Myths of Asian Womanhood"; James Watson, "Waking the Dragon"; Arthur Campa, "Folklore and History"; Brynjulf Alver, "Historical Legends and Historical Truths"; Peter Heehs, "Myth, History, and Theory"; and Juwen Zhang, *Oral Traditions in Contemporary China*.

Chapter 1

1. Taisui is a highly respected yet greatly feared cosmic deity or demon, related to Chinese astrology and depicted as a baleful star (see chapter 2), who oversees human fortunes. Because he is easily offended people need to constantly placate him to avoid misfortune. Barend ter Haar ("China's Inner Demons," 35) suggests that it was common practice for ruffians and gangs to adopt the names of stellar deities in expectation that they would absorb their martial skills and power.

2. Huang Liuhong, *Juguan fuhui quanshu*, 11:20a–b; also see a slightly different translation in Huang Liuhong, *A Complete Book Concerning Happiness and Benevolence*, 265.

3. Cited in W. J. F. Jenner, "Tough Guys, Mateship, and Honour," 30.

4. See, for example, Michael Dutton, "Basic Character of Crime in Contemporary China"; Leon Chao, "The Resurgence of Organized Crime in China"; and Deng Xiaogang and Ann Cordilia, "To Get Rich Is Glorious."

5. For a cross-section of studies that discuss the *jianghu*, see Wang Xuetai, *Shuihu jianghu*; Hong Wei, *Tiyan jianghu*; Hsiu-ju Stacy Lo, "Crossing Rivers and Lakes"; Maranatha Ivanova, "Limning the Jianghu"; and Helena Wu, "A Journey across Rivers and Lakes."

6. Christopher Rea and Bruce Rusk, "Translators' Introduction" to Zhang Yingyu, *The Book of Swindles*, xx.

7. Lu Hanchao, *Street Criers*, 14.

8. Avon Boretz, *Gods, Ghosts and Gangsters*, 33–34.

9. Song Geng, "Masculinizing Jianghu Spaces in the Past and Present," 108.

10. Wang Shuo, *Playing for Thrills*, 99.

11. Aspects of the underworld economy are discussed in Robert Antony, "Piracy and the Shadow Economy in the South China Sea"; and in his *Unruly People*, 173–181.

12. See Wang Xuetai, *Shuihu jianghu*.

13. Song Weijie, "Space, Swordsmen, and Utopia," 157.

14. On the theme park, see Lo, "Crossing Rivers and Lakes," 17–22.

15. Antony, *Unruly People*, 118, 182.

16. For the Taiping Rebellion, see Jonathan Spence, *God's Chinese Son*; and for the early Chinese communist movement in Jinggangshan, see Stephen Averill, *Revolution in the Highlands*.

17. *Chinese Repository* 11 (March 1836), 92; and chapter 3 in this volume.

18. Song Geng, "Masculinizing Jianghu Spaces in the Past and Present," 116–117; and Boretz, *Gods, Ghosts and Gangsters*, 176, 183.

19. Ge Liangyan, *Out of the Margins*, 87–90.

20. Song Weijie, "Space, Swordsmen and Utopia," 162.

21. Antony, *Unruly People*, 172–173.
22. Cited in Ge, *Out of the Margins*, 157.
23. Zhang Yingyu, *Book of Swindles*; see also Chen Huiying, "Dangers on the Road," 103–105.
24. Anders Ljungstedt, *An Historical Sketch of the Portuguese Settlements in China*, 108; Rodney Gilbert, "The Lotus Life of Macao"; Benjamim Pires, "The Chinese Quarter One Hundred Years Ago"; and Jonathan Porter, *Macau, The Imagined City*, 94.
25. Frederic Wakeman, *The Shanghai Badlands*, especially chapter 9; on Lucky Jack Riley, see Paul French, *City of Devils*.
26. Wang Di, *Street Culture in Chengdu*, 82–86.
27. Boretz, *Gods, Ghosts and Gangsters*, 33.
28. Yu Yingshi, *Shi yu Zhongguo wenhua*, 8–12, 17–22; James Liu, *The Chinese Knight-Errant*, 1; and Roland Altenburger, *The Sword or the Needle*, 27.
29. Y. W. Ma, "The Knight-Errant in 'hua-pen' Stories," 269.
30. Jenner, "Tough Guys, Mateship, and Honour," 6–8, 20, quote on p. 10.
31. For the history of Chinese *liumang*, see Chen Baoliang, *Zhongguo liumang shi*.
32. Y. Yvon Wang, "Heroes, Hooligans, and Knights-Errant," 338–339.
33. Geremie Barmé, "Wang Shuo and *Liumang* ('Hooligan') Culture," 46.
34. See Li Donghui, "The 'Phenomenon' of Wang Shuo," 103–109; Yao Yusheng, "The Elite Class Background of Wang Shuo and His Hooligan Characters," 432–434; and Barmé, "Wang Shuo and *Liumang* ('Hooligan') Culture," 28–29.
35. See Feng Qing, "Cong Shuihu dao xiha"; and Nathanel Amar, "Do You Freestyle?," 109.
36. Elizabeth Perry, *Rebels and Revolutionaries in North China*, 59–60; Matthew Sommer, *Sex, Law, and Society in Late Imperial China*, 97–99; David Ownby, "Approximations of Chinese Bandits," 244; and Antony, *Unruly People*, 130–131.
37. Today *guanggun* has come to signify Singles Day or Double Eleven Day (*guanggun jie*), a Chinese shopping holiday that originated in the 1990s specifically for singles. On this holiday in 2020, for example, Alibaba reported that consumers spent a record 498.2 billion *yuan* (roughly US$75 billion) on online goods over a four-day sales period, which represented a 26 percent increase from the previous year. The date, November 11 (11/11), was chosen because the number "1" represents a bare stick, which today is a Chinese slang for a lonely man with no significant other (and the four 1s of November 11 simply emphasizes this meaning). The holiday also has become a popular day when thousands of couples marry. See Sherisse Pham, "Singles Day."
38. On China's mean people, see Anders Hansson, *Chinese Outcasts*; and Jing Junjian, *Qingdai shehui de jianmin dengji*; on the Yao see chapter 6; and on the Dan see chapter 7.
39. See chapter 4.
40. For Shaolin monks and martial arts, see Meir Shahar, *The Shaolin Monastery*; for the legends about the connections between Shaolin monks and the founding of the Triads, see Dian Murray, *The Origins of the Tiandihui*; and Barend ter Haar, *Ritual and Mythology of the Chinese Triads*. On Daosan and other monks involved with Triads and other clandestine groups, see chapter 4 in this book.

Notes

41. Ann Lo, "Canton Opera: Folk Heroes, Triads, and Rebels," 47, 49, 51–52. Zhang Fei is one of the key characters in the historical novel *Romance of the Three Kingdoms*, which dramatizes the events before and during that turbulent period. In the novel, Zhang Fei became a sworn brother with Liu Bei and Guan Yu in the Oath of the Peach Garden. Zhang Fei was the subject of many Canton operas in which Li Wenmao played the leading role.

42. For Jin Yong, for example, see John Hamm, *Paper Swordsmen*; and Paul Foster, "Jin Yong and the Kungfu Industrial Complex"; for Gu Long, see Lin Baochun, *Ao shi gu cai gu long*.

43. See Antony, *Unruly People*, 161–165.

44. Huang Liuhong, *Juguan fuhui quanshu*, 11:20b.

45. Antony, *Unruly People*, 147–149, 163.

46. Wang Di, *Street Culture in Chengdu*, 235–238; and his *The Teahouse*, 178–184.

47. Wang, "Heroes, Hooligans, and Knights-Errant," 333.

48. Leon Chao, "The Resurgence of Organized Crime in China," 9, 14. The name Hongxing Society is provocative; it literally means "the Hong (Triad) society is revised."

49. For treatments of the *jianghu* as a homosocial milieu, see Song, "Masculinizing Jianghu Spaces in the Past and Present"; and Boretz, *Gods, Ghosts, and Gangsters*.

50. See the discussion in the postlude.

51. Roland Altenburger, *The Sword or the Needle*, 365; for other studies of female warriors, see Louise Edwards, *Women Warriors and Wartime Spies of China*; and Victoria Cass, *Dangerous Women*, especially chapter 4; for films, see Ngo Sheau-Shi, "*Nüxia*: Historical Depiction and Modern Visuality."

52. Paul Smith, "*Shuihu zhuan* and the Military Subculture of the Northern Song," 408; and Wu Pei-Yi, "Yang Miaozhen: A Woman Warrior in Thirteenth-Century China."

53. Altenburger, *The Sword or the Needle*, 47; and Li Xiaolin, "Women in the Chinese Military," 131.

54. See chapter 7.

55. Paul Cohen, *History in Three Keys*, 126; and Li, "Women in the Chinese Military," 197.

56. Cass, *Dangerous Women*, 70–71; Altenburger, *The Sword or the Needle*, 198–199; and Kenneth Swope, "The Legend of Tang Saier."

57. On Lady Xian, see Li Tiaoyuan, *Yuedong biji*, 4:104; and on Zheng Zuxi, see the first interlude in this book.

58. *Yongzheng zhupi yuzhi*, 10:5988–5989.

59. Ge, *Out of the Margins*, 149; and Ownby, "Approximations of Chinese Bandits," 233.

60. Charles Holcombe, "Theater of Combat," 429, 430.

61. Lo, "Canton Opera: Folk Heroes, Triads, and Rebels," 46; also see Ng Wing Chung, *The Rise of Cantonese Opera*, 17–18; and Barbara Ward, "Regional Operas and Their Audiences," 183.

62. See, for example, Ownby, "Approximations of Chinese Bandits," 233–234; John Fitzgerald, "Continuity within Discontinuity," 380; and Phil Billingsley, *Bandits in Republican China*, 129.

63. Lo, "Crossing Rivers and Lakes," 63; Jean Chesneaux, "The Modern Relevance of Shui-hu chuan," 3; and Jerome Ch'en, "The Nature and Characteristics of the Boxer Movement," 296.
64. Ter Haar, *Ritual and Mythology of the Chinese Triads*, 317, 333, 361; and chapters 4 and 5 in this book.
65. I discuss the concept of righteousness in chapter 2.
66. See C. T. Hsia, *The Classic Chinese Novel*, 80–81; Liu, *The Chinese Knight-Errant*, 195–197; Robert Ruhlmann, "Traditional Heroes in Chinese Popular Fiction,"170–171; Song Weijie, "Space, Swordsmen and Utopia," 157–158; and Jenner, "Tough Guys, Mateship, and Honour," 7–8.
67. Huang Liuhong, *Juguan fuhui quanshu*, 11:20b.
68. Cited in Ge, *Out of the Margins*, 160.
69. See Antony, *Like Froth Floating on the Sea*, 120; and chapter 7 in this volume.
70. Harry Caldwell, *Blue Tiger*, 192, 211.
71. Elizabeth Perry, "Social Banditry Revisited," 359, 369. For a detailed discussion about Bai Lang and banditry in the early twentieth century, see Billingsley, *Bandits in Republican China*.
72. See Robert Antony, "Peasants, Heroes, and Brigands"; and Ruhlmann, "Traditional Heroes in Chinese Popular Fiction," 175–176.
73. Li Donghui, "The 'Phenomenon' of Wang Shuo," 103–110.
74. Cited in Kung-chuan Hsiao, *Rural China*, 457.
75. On pirate brutality and cannibalistic acts, see Robert Antony, "Bloodthirsty Pirates?"
76. *Sunday Journal News* (New York), March 16, 1980, B-11.
77. Wang, "Heroes, Hooligans, and Knights-Errant," 330–333. Altenburger (*The Sword or the Needle*, 366–367) mentions similar cases for an earlier period.
78. Edward Gargan, "Chinese Press Battles 'Surge of Bad Books,'" A-9.
79. See Chesneaux, "The Modern Relevance of *Shui-hu chuan*," 1–2; Ge, *Out of the Margins*, 51; Merle Goldman, "The Media Campaign as a Weapon in Political Struggle," 193; Fitzgerald, "Continuity within Discontinuity," 381–382, 389–392; and Liu Zaifu, *Shuangdian pipan*, 4–6, 203–204.
80. Fan Pen Chen, "Forbidden Fruits," 37, 53, 56–57; see also Fan Pen Chen, "Ritual Roots of the Theatrical Prohibitions of Late-Imperial China," 26–27, 40. For more explicit information on theatrical censorship in imperial China, see Ding Shumei, *Zhongguo gudai jinhui xiju biannian shi*.
81. Ng, *The Rise of Cantonese Opera*, 23.
82. For a discussion on film censorship in China since the 1920s, see Laikwan Pang, "The State Against Ghosts"; and for censorship of traditional theater in the 1950s, see Liu Siyuan, "Theatre Reform as Censorship."
83. Amar, "Do You Freestyle?," 108.
84. See "Zongju tichu jiemu jiabin biaozhun"; and Casey Quackenbush and Aria Chen, "Tasteless, Vulgar and Obscene." On government censorship of music, see Jeroen de Kloet, *China with a Cut*, 180–189.

NOTES

85. Liu, *The Chinese Knight-Errant*, 9; Jenner, "Tough Guys, Mateship, and Honour," 3; and Wang, "Heroes, Hooligans and Knights-errant," 316, 323.

86. On Qing bare sticks laws, see Thomas Buoye, "Bare Sticks and Naked Pity"; and Matthew Sommer, "Dangerous Males, Vulnerable Males, and Polluted Males," 68–72.

87. J. J. M. de Groot, *Sectarianism and Religious Persecution in China*, 268, 284; and chapter 4 in this volume.

88. Jenner, "Tough Guys, Mateship, and Honour," 4.

89. Buoye, "Bare Sticks and Naked Pity," 38.

90. Peter Burke, *The Historical Anthropology of Early Modern Italy*, especially chapters 2 and 6; see also Hayden White, *The Practical Past*, especially chapter 1; Wang Mingke, *Fanshi shixue yu shixue fansi*; and Wang Yuanfei, *Writing Pirates*, 72, 184.

91. Barend ter Haar, *Telling Stories*, 33.

Chapter 2

1. Frederic Wakeman, "Romantics, Stoics, and Martyrs in Seventeenth-Century China," 631.

2. Lynn Struve, *Voices from the Ming–Qing Cataclysm*, 1.

3. Chen Shunxi, *Luanli jianwen lu*, 1–47.

4. The areas that today are coastal Guangxi (Hepu, Qinzhou, Longmen, Fangcheng) were in the seventeenth century a part of Guangdong province.

5. Before 1802 Chinese referred to Vietnam as Annan; for consistency I will use the name Vietnam in this chapter. Some sources say Yang was assassinated in 1687.

6. In order to avoid confusion with another area named Lianzhou (different Chinese characters) on the Guangdong-Hunan border (interlude 2 and chapter 6), I have purposely spelled Lianzhou on the Gulf of Tonkin as Lienzhou in this chapter and chapter 8.

7. *Lienzhou fuzhi*, 63.

8. W. T. Lynn, "First Discovery of the Great Comet of 1680," 437–438.

9. Chen Shunxi, *Luanli jianwen lu*, 18–36; and *Lienzhou fuzhi*, 61.

10. See Hou Ching-lang, "The Chinese Belief in Baleful Stars."

11. *Lin'gao xianzhi*, 32–33; *Yai zhouzhi*, 280–281; *Qin xianzhi*, 890–891; and Chen Shunxi, *Luanli jianwen lu*, 34, 41–42.

12. Cited in Nathan Sivin, "State, Cosmos, and Body in the Last Three Centuries B.C.," 16.

13. See ibid., 5–37; Wolfram Eberhard, "The Political Function of Astronomy and Astronomers in Han China," 33–70; and Tiziana Lippiello, *Auspicious Omens and Miracles in Ancient China*, 28–29, 54, 219.

14. Cited in Sivin, "State, Cosmos, and Body," 27.

15. Hsu Dao-lin, "Crime and Cosmic Order," 115–116.

16. Chen Shunxi, *Luanli jianwen lu*, 24–26; and *Chengmai xianzhi*, 577.

17. Tana Li, "Epidemics, Trade, and Local Worship in Vietnam, Leizhou Peninsula, and Hainan Island," 195–202.

18. Chen Shunxi, *Luanli jianwen lu*, 39.

19. *Lienzhou fuzhi*, 61.

20. For further discussion on this topic, see chapters 4 and 5.

21. For general histories of the Ming–Qing transition, see Lynn Struve, *The Southern Ming, 1644–1662*; Frederick Wakeman, *The Great Enterprise*; Qian Haiyue, *Nan Ming shi*; and Gu Cheng, *Nan Ming shi*.
22. Robert Marks, *Tigers, Rice, Silk, and Silt*, 158–59, tables 4.1 and 4.2.
23. *Qingshi liezhuan*, 80:6689-6690; also see Jiang Zuyuan and Fang Zhiqin, *Jianming Guangdong shi*, 320–321.
24. Chen Shunxi, *Luanli jianwen lu*, 20.
25. *Haikang xianzhi* (1938), 542.
26. *Qingshi liezhuan*, 80:6690; and Jiang and Fang, *Jianming Guangdong shi*, 321–323.
27. Chen Shunxi, *Luanli jianwen lu*, 24; and Marks, *Tigers, Rice, Silk, and Silt*, 149–150.
28. *Fangcheng xianzhi chugao*, 789–791; *Qin xianzhi*, 190; and fieldnotes from Qinzhou and Fangcheng, July 2011.
29. Zheng Guangnan, *Xinbian Zhongguo haidao shi*, 245–246.
30. Pan Dinggui, *Annan jiyou*, 3–4.
31. See, for example, Zhou Qufei, *Lingwai daida*, vol. 1, no pagination.
32. Fieldnotes from Qinzhou, January 2010; Pan Dinggui, *Annan jiyou*, 3–4; and *Qin zhouzhi*, 37; also see Li Qingxin, *Binhai zhi di*, 271–272.
33. Xu Wentang and Xie Qiyi, *Da Nan shilu Qing Yue guanxi shiliao huibian*, 3, 25; and Li Qingxin, *Binhai zhi di*, 276– 277.
34. *Qingdai dang'an shiliao congbian*, 6:248; see also Kenneth Swope, *On the Trail of the Yellow Tiger*, 234–237.
35. Chen Shunxi, *Luanli jianwen lu*, 29–32.
36. *Qin xianzhi*, 190; *Lienzhou fuzhi*, 59–60; *Chengmai xianzhi*, 269, 574, 576–577; and *Lin'gao xianzhi*, 32, 162.
37. Jiang and Fang, *Jianming Guangdong shi*, 327.
38. See the insightful analysis and graphic details of the destructiveness of the forced coastal evacuation policy in Fujian province in Dahpon Ho, "The Empire's Scorched Shore."
39. *Fangcheng xianzhi chugao*, 792; and *Lienzhou fuzhi*, 60–61.
40. Jiang and Fang, *Jianming Guangdong shi*, 330–331.
41. Chen Shunxi, *Luanli jianwen lu*, 34–36.
42. Mio Kishimoto-Nakayama, "The Kangxi Depression and Early Qing Local Markets," 227–256; and Marks, *Tigers, Rice, Silk, and Silt*, 142–143, 153.
43. *Qing shilu Guangdong shiliao*, 1:103, 186, 189; and *Fangcheng xianzhi chugao*, 795, 799.
44. Wu Sangui (1612–1678) was a Chinese general who played a key role in the fall of the Ming dynasty by helping the Manchus enter northern China in 1644. For his efforts in establishing the Qing dynasty, the emperor awarded him a large fiefdom in southwestern China.
45. *Qing shilu Guangdong shiliao*, 1:121–123; and Wakeman, *The Great Enterprise*, 2:1101, 1109.
46. *Qing shilu Guangdong shiliao*, 1:127–128, 132, 135–136, 138–139, 142, 146; *Qingshi liezhuan*, 80:6658-6659; and Chen Shunxi, *Luanli jianwen lu*, 42–46.
47. Wakeman, *The Great Enterprise*, 2:1117, 1119.

48. Struve, *The Southern Ming*, 64.
49. Marks, *Tigers, Rice, Silk, and Silt*, 147.
50. Chen Shunxi, *Luanli jianwen lu*, 45.
51. *Haikang xianzhi* (1812), 149.
52. Chen Shunxi, *Luanli jianwen lu*, 22; and *Lin'gao xianzhi*, 154–155.
53. *Lingshui xianzhi*, 2:39; also see Niu Junkai and Li Qingxin, "Chinese 'Political Pirates' in the Seventeenth-Century Tongking Gulf," 139.
54. *Yai zhouzhi*, 231–232; *Chengmai xianzhi*, 257; and *Fangcheng xianzhi chugao*, 793.
55. *Qin xianzhi*, 190; and Niu and Li, "Chinese 'Political Pirates,'" 139.
56. *Qin xianzhi*, 190–191, 901; and *Fangcheng xianzhi chugao*, 793.
57. *Qing shilu Guangdong shiliao*, 1:96–97; also see Niu and Li, "Chinese 'Political Pirates,'" 139.
58. *Fangcheng xianzhi chugao*, 797–798; and Xing Hang, "Leizhou Pirates and the Making of the Mekong Delta," 125–127.
59. *Qing shilu Guangdong shiliao*, 1:149, 161–162, 165–166; *Leizhou fuzhi*, 3:35b; *Lin'gao xianzhi*, 164, 166; and *Chengmai xianzhi*, 257–258.
60. *Fangcheng xianzhi chugao*, 798; also see Yumio Sakurai, "Eighteenth-Century Chinese Pioneers on the Water Frontier of Indochina," 40; and Hang, "Leizhou Pirates and the Making of the Mekong Delta," 128–129.
61. *Qing shilu Guangdong shiliao*, 1:96–97, 149.
62. *Lienzhou fuzhi*, 60.
63. Chen Shunxi, *Luanli jianwen lu*, 35; see also *Qin xianzhi*, 190; and Qian Haiyue, *Nan Ming shi*, 66:3174.
64. See, for example, *Qin xianzhi*, 901; and *Fangcheng xianzhi chugao*, 797.
65. See, for example, Li Qingxin, *Binhai zhi di*, 273.
66. Hang, "Leizhou Pirates and the Making of the Mekong Delta," 124–127.
67. *Leizhou fuzhi*, 14:14a–b; and Du Zhen cited in Li Qingxin, *Binhai zhi di*, 275.
68. *Leizhou fuzhi*, 3:21a–b; and Qian Haiyue, *Nan Ming shi*, 42:3175.
69. *Yai zhouzhi*, 232, 272–273.
70. *Leizhou fuzhi*, 3:26a; and *Qing shilu Guangdong shiliao*, 1:149, 161–162, 165.
71. *Chengmai xianzhi*, 258; and *Qing shilu Guangdong shiliao*, 1:177–178.
72. Hsieh Kuo Ching, "Removal of Coastal Population," 576.
73. Derk Bodde, "Translating Chinese Philosophical Terms," 238.
74. *Chengmai xianzhi*, 395–96.
75. Interestingly, also in the late nineteenth century in this same area (Qinzhou and Fangcheng) a more recent hero emerged; this was Liu Yongfu, who, like Yang Yandi, was a bandit and rebel who became a patriotic national hero who fought against French imperialism in the region.
76. See, for example, Barend ter Haar, *Ritual and Mythology of the Chinese Triads*; and chapter 4 in this book.
77. Fieldnotes from Longmen, January 2010, and from Qinzhou and Fangcheng, July 2011. See also Deng Yong, "Wangcheng'ao de chuanshuo," 40–41.

Notes

78. Fieldnotes from Longmen, January 2010, and from Qinzhou and Fangcheng, July 2011; for written accounts see *Fangcheng xianzhi chugao*, 1127–1132; and "Fudu niao de chuanshuo," 357–358.

79. Fieldnotes from Longmen, January 2010, and from Qinzhou and Fangcheng, July 2011; and *Qin xianzhi*, 946–947. In an alternate legend, also recorded in the 1946 *Qin xianzhi* (p. 946), Yang constructed the canal not to escape the Qing forces, but to give him easy access to the sea so he could plunder ships and villages. Another legend says the canal was not built by Yang Yandi, but rather by the Eastern Han Fubo General, Ma Yuan, who pacified Nan Yue and northern Vietnam.

80. "Fudu niao de chuanshuo," 358.

81. Thanks to Prof. Xing Hang for this information on the deified Yang Yandi.

82. Fieldnotes from Beihai, December 2010, and from Fangcheng, Dongxing, and Jiangping, July 2011; see also Douglas Stewart, *The Brutal Seas*, 211–247.

83. *Qin xianzhi*, 192, 902.

Interlude 1

1. At the height of pirate disturbances in the early nineteenth century, Longxue island was a pirate nest occupied by Zhang Baozai and his gang. In Chinese geomancy (*fengshui*) the "dragon's lair" is the optimal site for graves or shrines because it has the highest concentration of vital force (*qi*). For these same reasons, it was no coincidence that the pirates selected Longxue as their base. See the discussion on geomancy in chapter 3.

2. Anthropologist Robert Weller has previously discussed other "unorthodox" gods in two essays: "Bandits, Beggars, and Ghosts" and "Matricidal Magistrates and Gambling Gods." For a useful overview on the development of local cults, see Barend ter Haar, "The Genesis and Spread of Temple Cults in Fukien."

3. On Zheng Chenggong's piratical activities, see Wei-chung Cheng, *War, Trade and Piracy in the China Seas*; and on the overall worldwide interconnections between war, trade, and piracy in this period, see Kris Lane and Robert Antony, "Piracy in Asia and the West."

4. See Lynn Struve, "The Southern Ming, 1644–1662," 712–714; Cheng, *War, Trade and Piracy in the China Seas*, 152–154; Xing Hang, *Conflict and Commerce in Maritime East Asia*, 80–81; and Weng Liewei, "Zheng Chenggong zai Shanwei de shishi he chuanshuo," 52–53.

5. Fieldnotes from Baishahu, December 2012; see also Weng Liewei, "Zheng Chenggong zai Shanwei de shishi he chuanshuo," 54; Li Qiaoyin, "Jingang Mazu"; and *Shanwei Ribao*, July 5, 2015.

6. Fieldnotes from Baishahu, December 2012; see also Weng Liewei, "Zheng Chenggong zai Shanwei de shishi he chuanshuo," 54.

7. Fieldnotes from Nan'ao island, July 2005. On Wu Ping, see Chen Chunsheng, "Shiliu shiji Min Yue jiaojie diyu haishang huodong renqun de tezhi."

8. On Lin Daoqian, see Zheng Guangnan, *Xinbian Zhongguo haidao shi*, 190–197; on Lin Jinlian's legend in Taiwan, see Lian Jingchu, "Liuzhuanglou yu banlan baiyin"; and on her legend in Patani, see Cai Peichun, "Taiguo Lin Guniang chuanshuo fenxi."

9. Fieldnotes from Fangcheng, July 2011; Deng Yong, "Wangcheng'ao de chuanshuo," 41; and "Fudu niao de chuanshuo," 358.
10. P. Steven Sangren, "Female Gender in Chinese Religious Symbols," 12.
11. Stevan Harrell, "When a Ghost Becomes a God," 195–196; ter Haar, "The Genesis and Spread of Temple Cults in Fukien," 352–353; and author's fieldnotes from Miaoli, Jiayi, and Wenshui in Taiwan, summer 1986.
12. Fieldnotes from Baishahu, December 2012.
13. See Harrell, "When a Ghost Becomes a God," 193–194, 201; Weller, "Bandits, Beggars, and Ghosts," 46–48; James Watson, "Of Flesh and Bones," 383; Anne Gerritsen, "From Demon to Deity," 20; and Mark Meulenbeld, "Death and Demonization of a Bodhisattva," 691–695.
14. On Zheng's rehabilitation by the Kangxi emperor, see Hang, *Commerce and Conflict in Maritime East Asia*, 238.
15. Gerritsen, "From Demon to Deity," 18–21; see also Harrell, "When a Ghost Becomes a God," 205.
16. In chapter 8 I discuss in more detail how devotees attempted to legitimize another little-known deity called Sanpo.
17. Fieldnotes from Baishahu, December 2012.
18. Fieldnotes from Baishahu, December 2012; see also Weng Liewei, "Zheng Chenggong zai Shanwei de shishi he chuanshuo," 54–55.
19. In these cases the Chinese word "Ma" is short for "Mazu"; thus Da Ma stands for Great Mazu, Er Ma stands for Second Mazu, and so forth.
20. Fieldnotes from Baishahu, Jiazi, and Dade, December 2012.
21. For examples of such unorthodox gods, see Harrell, "When a Ghost Becomes a God," 197, 199; and Weller, "Matricidal Magistrates and Gambling Gods," 117–118.
22. Meulenbeld, "Death and Demonization of a Bodhisattva," 719.
23. See Harrell, "When a Ghost Becomes a God," 193–195, 204; and ter Haar, "The Genesis and Spread of Temple Cults in Fukien," 353, 371–372.

Chapter 3

1. *Panyu xianzhi*, 4:20a.
2. On the development of the sand fields see, for example, Nishikawa Kikuko, "Shindai Shuō deruta no shadan ni tsuite"; and Helen Siu, *Agents and Victims in South China*, especially chapters 2–4; and David Faure, *Emperor and Ancestor*.
3. Robert Antony, *Unruly People*, 19–20.
4. Chen Han-seng, *Landlord and Peasant in China*, 31.
5. See, for example, *Qing shilu Guangdong shiliao*, 1:435–436. On lineage development in the Canton delta, see David Faure, *The Structure of Chinese Rural Society* and his *Emperor and Ancestor*.
6. On the He lineage, see Liu Zhiwei, "Lineage on the Sands."
7. Chen, *Landlord and Peasant in China*, 31.
8. Qu Dajun, *Guangdong xinyu*, 45; and Fan Duanang, *Yue zhong jianwen*, 33.
9. Qu Dajun, *Guangdong xinyu*, 462–463; and Faure, *Emperor and Ancestor*, 179.

Notes

10. Liu, "Lineage on the Sands," 35; see also James Watson, "Hereditary Tenancy and Corporate Landlordism in Traditional China."
11. On floating brothels and Dan prostitution, see chapter 7.
12. Qu Dajun, *Guangdong xinyu*, 51–53, 485–486; and Fan Duanang, *Yue zhong jianwen*, 62. See also Helen Siu and Liu Zhiwei, "Lineage, Market, Pirate, and Dan."
13. Liu, "Lineage on the Sands," 38.
14. Faure, *Emperor and Ancestor*, 275–277; and Antony, *Unruly People*, 96–98.
15. James Watson, "Self Defense Corps, Violence, and the Bachelor Sub-Culture in South China," 252; and Antony, *Unruly People*, 101.
16. *Qing shilu Guangdong shiliao*, 1:87; and *Panyu xianzhi*, 2:12b, 22:7b–8a.
17. *Jiu Guangdong feidao shilu*, 13; also fieldnotes from Shawan and Jiaotang in June 2002 and September 2010. Even in recent years several Shawan and Jiaotang "rural villages" (such as Shitou, Luoxi, Dongxiang, Jushu, Zhongcun, Shiqiao, and Dingsha) are notorious bases for "black gangs" involved in extortion, robbery, assault, and murder, as well as in drug, prostitution, and gambling racketeering; this information was taken from several online Chinese reports in 2018, which since have been removed from the web.
18. *Qing shilu Guangdong shiliao*, 2:462.
19. *Xingke tiben*, QL 44.5.14, and QL 46.8.19.
20. *Gongzhongdang Qianlongchao zouzhe*, 47:756–758; *Junjidang lufu zouzhe*, QL 45.9.18, and QL 45.9.27; and *Panyu xianzhi*, 22:13b, 32:21b.
21. *Shangyudang*, QL 45.8.25; *Junjidang lufu zouzhe*, QL 45.9.18, and QL 45.9.27.
22. For further discussion, see Antony, *Unruly People*, 165–169.
23. *Junjidang lufu zouzhe*, QL 45.10.17; see also *Qing shilu Guangdong shiliao*, 2:446; and *Gongzhongdang Qianlongchao zouzhe*, 52:400–401.
24. *Qing shilu Guangdong shiliao*, 3:22–23.
25. For documentary sources, see *Xingke tiben*, QL 40.r10.4, QL 44.5.14, QL 46.9.25, and DG15.6.27; *Qing shilu Guangdong shiliao*, 2:450; FO 931/1089, dated c. 1850s; and *Jiu Guangdong feidao shilu*, 13, 129, 132. I actually have the names of several other bandit lairs but have been unable to locate them on maps.
26. See the discussion in Antony, *Unruly People*, especially chapter 6.
27. Watson, "Self Defense Corps," 254–256; and Antony, *Unruly People*, 96–101.
28. *Qing shilu Guangdong shiliao*, 1:360, 2:261–262; *Gongzhongdang Qianlongchao zouzhe*, 47:756–758; and *Panyu xianzhi*, 22:13b.
29. *Junjidang lufu zouzhe*, QL 45.9.18.
30. Cited in Siu and Liu, "Lineage, Market, Pirate, and Dan," 299.
31. Qu Dajun, *Guangdong xinyu*, 51–52, 247; see also *Qing shilu Guangdong shiliao*, 2:268–269; and Faure, *Emperor and Ancestor*, 289.
32. *Qing shilu Guangdong shiliao* 2:461–462; *Panyu xianzhi*, 4:20b, 15:12a–13a, 22:13b–14a, and 53:28b. For a detailed discussion of the new law, see Antony, *Unruly People*, 196–202.
33. *Canton Register*, March 15, 1836.
34. Robert Darnton, *The Great Cat Massacre*, 18.
35. Wilt Idema has collected and commented on many of these popular stories and folktales in *Mouse vs. Cat in Chinese Literature*.

Notes

36. Darnton, *The Great Cat Massacre*, 89.
37. For Qing dynasty plagues in Guangdong, see Luo Rulan, *Shuyi huibian*; Lai Wen and Li Yongchen, *Lingnan wenyi shi*; and "Qingmo Yuexi shuyi yu shuyi fangzhi zhuanzhu de bianzhuan."
38. J. J. M. de Groot, *The Religious System of China*, 5:605; 6:1069–1070; Qu Dajun, *Guangdong xinyu*, 526; and fieldnotes from Panyu, July 2010.
39. Liu Wanzhang, *Guangzhou miyu*, 16.
40. Zhang Qu, *Yuedong wenjianlu*, 111.
41. De Groot, *The Religious System of China*, 5:606–607.
42. See the insightful discussion in Idema, *Mouse vs. Cat in Chinese Literature*; and on cats throughout Chinese history, see Timothy Barrett and Mark Strange, "Walking by Itself: The Singular History of the Chinese Cat."
43. Cited in Huang Han, *Mao yuan*, vol. 1, unpaginated text.
44. Rachel Nuwer, "Domestic Cats Enjoyed Village Life in China 5,300 Years Ago." See also Idema's comments on wildcats and the origins of domesticated cats in China in *Mouse vs. Cat in Chinese Literature*, 34–37.
45. Huang Han, *Mao yuan*, vol. 1; see also Derk Bodde, *Festivals in Classical China*, 68–74; and Barrett, *Chinese Cat*, 16.
46. Barrett, *Chinese Cat*, 12–13; and Idema, *Mouse vs. Cat in Chinese Literature*, 38–41.
47. Antony, *Unruly People*, 151.
48. Huang Han, *Mao yuan*, vol. 1; *Chinese Repository* 7 (1839), 598; Nicholas Dennys, *The Folk-Lore of China*, 48; C. A. S. Williams, *Outlines of Chinese Symbolism and Art Motives*, 58–59; and fieldnotes from Panyu, July 2010.
49. De Groot, *The Religious System of China*, 5:820; and Huang Han, *Mao yuan*, vol. 2.
50. Huang Han, *Mao yuan*, vol. 1; for a lengthy discussion of this case, see Rebecca Doran, "The Cat Demon, Gender, and Religious Practice." I would like to thank Barend ter Haar for bringing this article to my attention.
51. De Groot, *The Religious System of China*, 5:610–613, 824. Although the above stories were most common in north China, during my field research in Leizhou (March 2010), a certain Mrs. You, who was eighty-three at the time, told me similar stories that she had heard when she was a child from her grandmother, who came from Dongguan, a suburb of Canton. For other tales of demonic cats, see Idema, *Mouse vs. Cat in Chinese Literature*, 49–52.
52. *Gu*, which was one of the most potent poisons in China, was concocted from a large variety of poisonous insects that are placed in a jar for up to a year; the insects devour each other until only one survives—the survivor becomes the *gu* poison. Cat demons were also believed to be the cause of several ailments related to *gu* poisons; see Doran, "The Cat Demon, Gender, and Religious Practice," 696–697.
53. Huang Han, *Mao yuan*, vol. 1; De Groot, *The Religious System of China*, 5:866; 6:1074; and fieldnotes from Panyu, July 2010. See also Li Shanbao, "The Precious Scroll of the Rat Epidemic," where the Goddess of Mercy expounds on the efficacy of cats in preventing pestilence in China at the end of the nineteenth century.
54. Gu Shujuan, *Ming Qing Guangdong minjian xinyang yanjiu*, 208–209.

55. Wolfram Eberhard, *The Local Cultures of South and East China*, 376. See also Wolfram Eberhard, *A Dictionary of Chinese Symbols*, 152; and Williams, *Outlines of Chinese Symbolism and Art Motives*, 232.

56. For general discussions of Chinese geomancy, see *Fengshui xingqi mingxue mijue*; He Xiaoxin and Luo Jun, *Fengshui shi*; and Ole Bruun, *An Introduction to Feng Shui*.

57. Eitel, *Feng-Shui*, 23.

58. Qu Dajun, *Guangdong xinyu*, 56–57, 78, 80–81, 124–125.

59. Ibid., 125–126, 502; and fieldnotes from Lianhuashan, March 2018. Today the pagoda is better known as Lotus Pagoda.

60. De Groot, *Religious System of China*, 3:958, 978–979, 1041; M. T. Yates, "Ancestral Worship and Fung-Shuy"; and on *fengshui* pagodas in Guangzhou, see Lai Chuanqing, "Guangfu Ming Qing fengshui ta yanjiu."

61. J. H. Stewart Lockhart, "Notes on Chinese Folk-Lore," 361.

62. Daniel McMahon, "Geomancy and Walled Fortifications in Late Eighteenth Century China," 376.

63. De Groot, *Religious System of China*, 3:1006; also see McMahon, "Geomancy and Walled Fortifications," 390.

64. On geomancy in the Song dynasty, see Zhou Bei, "Songdai fengshui yanjiu."

65. Jiang Yonglin, *The Mandate of Heaven and the Great Ming Code*, 79.

66. De Groot, *Religious System of China*, 3:1028. In some areas of south China, particularly the Canton delta, there was the custom of temporary or double burials, which allowed family members time to find good *fengshui* sites before permanently burying the deceased; on Cantonese burials, see James Watson, "Of Flesh and Bones."

67. See McMahon, "Geomancy and Walled Fortifications."

68. Eitel, *Feng-Shui*, 80. During the military campaigns against the Hakka-Triad rebels in 1802 and against the Yao rebels in 1832, Qing officials made it a point to locate and destroy the ancestral graves of rebel leaders; see interlude 2 and chapter 6.

69. De Groot, *Religious System of China*, 3:951; and Williams, *Outlines of Chinese Symbolism and Art Motives*, 398–399.

70. McMahon, "Geomancy and Walled Fortifications," 384.

71. Jack Potter, "Wind, Water, Bones and Souls," 141–142.

72. Darnton, *The Great Cat Massacre*, 64.

Chapter 4

1. In the 1820s the missionary William Milne coined the term "Triad" to stand for the Sanhehui, which he translated as the "Society of the Three United, or Triad Society." The Sanhehui was one of the alternate names of the Tiandihui; see William Milne, "Some Account of the Secret Association in China, Entitled the Triad Society."

2. *Tiandihui*, 1:110–112. For a translation of Yan Yan's testimony, see Dian Murray, *The Origins of the Tiandihui*, 184–190.

3. On the historiography of the Triads, see Murray, *The Origins of the Tiandihui*; and David Ownby, "Recent Chinese Scholarship on the History of Chinese Secret Societies."

4. See, for example, Zhuang Jifa, *Qingdai tiandihui yuanliu kao* and *Qingdai mimi huidang shi yanjiu*; and Qin Baoqi, *Qing qianqi tiandihui yanjiu*.

Notes

5. See He Zhiqing, *Tiandihui qiyuan yanjiu*; He Zhiqing and Wu Zhaoqing, *Zhongguo banghui shi*; and Weng Tongwen, "Tiandihui yinyu 'mulidoushi' xinyi."

6. See, for example, Ma Shichang, "Ming dai tiandihui ziliao de xin faxian"; and Chen Baoliang, *Zhongguo de she yu hui*.

7. See, for example, Xiao Yishan, *Jindai mimi shehui shiliao*; Luo Ergang, *Tiandihui wenxianlu*; and Jean Chesneaux, *Popular Movements and Secret Societies in China*.

8. David Ownby, *Brotherhoods and Secret Societies in Early and Mid-Qing China*; and Barend ter Haar, *Ritual and Mythology of the Chinese Triads*. Among the earlier generation of scholars who pointed out links between the Triads and popular religion, see Dai Xuanzhi, "Tiandihui yu daojiao."

9. For background, see Harry Lamley, "*Hsieh-tou*: The Pathology of Violence in Southeastern China"; Ownby, *Brotherhoods and Secret Societies*; and Robert Antony, *Like Froth Floating on the Sea*.

10. Rolf Stein, "Religious Taoism and Popular Religion," 62–66.

11. See, for example, the discussions on anxiety and violence in the eighteenth century in Antony, *Like Froth Floating on the Sea* and *Unruly People*; on the Yongzheng suppression campaigns, see Jonathan Spence, *Treason by the Book*; and for the Qianlong period, see Philip Kuhn, *Soulstealers*.

12. *Shiliao xunkan*, *tian* series, 20b; J. J. M. de Groot, *Sectarianism and Religious Persecution in China*, 268, 284; and Robert Antony, "Brotherhoods, Secret Societies, and the Law in Qing-Dynasty China."

13. Ter Haar, *Ritual and Mythology of the Chinese Triads*, 224–262; on the Daoist demonological tradition, see Kristofer Schipper, "Demonologie chinoise," 405–427; and on Daoist views of the apocalypse, see Christine Mollier, *Une Apocalypse taoiste du Ve siecle*.

14. J. J. M. de Groot, *The Religious System of China*, 5:476.

15. Wu Junqing, *Mandarins and Heretics*, 64.

16. Richard Strassberg, *A Chinese Bestiary*, 197–198. Although an ancient text, Strassberg explains that stories from the *Shanhaijing* continued to pervade Chinese consciousness well into the twentieth century (pp. 26–28).

17. Stein, "Religious Taoism and Popular Religion," 63.

18. It is noteworthy to recall that as late as the twentieth century some Chinese still referred to Westerners as "ocean devils" (*yanggui*).

19. *Gongzhongdang Kangxichao zouzhe*, 7:614–617; *Sihui xianzhi*, 1:68; and Qu Dajun, *Guangdong xinyu*, 302.

20. *Kang Yong Qian shiqi chengxiang fankang douzheng ziliao*, 2:653–654.

21. Zhuang Jifa, *Qingdai mimi huidang shi yanjiu*, 19–20; and ter Haar, *Ritual and Mythology of the Chinese Triads*, 77, 287.

22. See de Groot, *The Religious System of China*, 6:1277–1278, 1291, 1316; Kristofer Schipper, "Vernacular and Classical Ritual," 28; and ter Haar, *Ritual and Mythology of the Chinese Triads*, 284. See also the discussion in the prelude about the Toothless Man.

23. Kristofer Schipper, *The Taoist Body*, 62–63; see also Hubert Seiwert, *Popular Religious Movements and Heterodox Sects in Chinese History*, 38, 50.

24. *Tiandihui*, 1:18, 6:340; see also ter Haar, *Ritual and Mythology of the Chinese Triads*, 281–282.

Notes

25. On various surnames used as saviors in China, see Mollier, *Une Apocalypse taoiste du Ve siècle*, 10–12, 22–23; ter Haar, *Ritual and Mythology of the Chinese Triads*, 313–314; and Seiwert, *Popular Religious Movements and Heterodox Sects*, 88, 407.

26. See *Shiliao xunkan, tian* series, 324a–325b; *Kang Yong Qian shiqi chengxiang fankang douzheng ziliao*, 2:626–627; *Qing Gaozong shilu xuanji*, 100; and *Zhupi zouzhe*, QL 7.6.22, QL 7.8.2, and QL 7.8.25.

27. Sasaki Masaya, *Shinmatsu no himitsu kessha*, 187–188.

28. Ter Haar, *Ritual and Mythology of the Chinese Triads*, 255–256.

29. What is more, as Barend ter Haar (*Ritual and Mythology of the Chinese Triads*) and Suzuki Chusei ("Shincho chuki") have shown, the names of such saviors were found not only in southern China but also in many other regions of China during the early and mid-Qing periods.

30. De Groot, *The Religious System of China*, 6:980, 985, 1195; Qu Dajun, *Guangdong xinyu*, 216; and Barend ter Haar, "China's Inner Demons," 40.

31. De Groot, *The Religious System of China*, 6:962, 1264–1266; Justus Doolittle, *Social Life of the Chinese*, 2:308; Gerald Willoughby-Meade, *Chinese Ghouls and Goblins*, 33; and ter Haar, *Ritual and Mythology of the Chinese Triads*, 257.

32. Ter Haar, "China's Inner Demons," 37.

33. *Kang Yong Qian shiqi chengxiang fankang douzheng ziliao*, 2:613–616; and *Shiliao xunkan, tian* series, 20b–25a.

34. De Groot, *Sectarianism and Religious Persecution*, 266.

35. Paul Katz, *Demon Hordes and Burning Boats*, 62. Also see the important study by Michel Strickmann, *Chinese Magical Medicine*.

36. Among the many popular handbooks on amulets, see *Sanxing leitan*; and Xu Zhenghong, *Fuzhou mixin fengyun*. Both books have been helpful in writing this section on amulets.

37. Schipper, "Vernacular and Classical Ritual," 46.

38. Cited in Willoughby-Meade, *Chinese Ghouls and Goblins*, 119.

39. Xu Zhenghong, *Fuzhou mixin fengyun*, 38–45; Henry Doré, *Researches into Chinese Superstitions*, 2:162; John McCreery, "The Symbolism of Popular Taoist Magic," 86, 107; and Robert Antony, "Spectacles of Violence in China," 624–625.

40. On the use of charms and spells in messianic movements, see Suzuki, "Shincho chuki," 163–164.

41. *Shiliao xunkan, tian* series, 20b–23a, and *di* series, 441a–451b.

42. *Kang Yong Qian shiqi chengxiang fankang douzheng ziliao*, 2:686–688.

43. Willoughby-Meade, *Chinese Ghouls and Goblins*, 28, 45.

44. Gustave Schlegel, *Thian Ti Hwui*, 148, 222–224; and Xiao Yishan, *Jindai mimi shehui shiliao*, 4:21b.

45. *Tiandihui*, 3:124–125.

46. Ownby, *Brotherhoods and Secret Societies*, 4; see also chapter 5 in this book.

47. De Groot, *The Religious System of China*, 6:1019, 1048; and ter Haar, *Ritual and Mythology of the Chinese Triads*, 230, 247.

48. *Yongzheng zhupi yuzhi*, 10:5988–5989.

49. Anna Seidel, "Imperial Treasures and Taoist Sacraments," 301.

50. *Shiliao xunkan, tian* series, 673a–677a.
51. De Groot, *The Religious System of China*, 6:1026; and Xu Zhenghong, *Fuzhou mixin fengyun*, 260.
52. *Kang Yong Qian shiqi chengxiang fankang douzheng ziliao*, 2:686–688.
53. Willoughby-Meade, *Chinese Ghouls and Goblins*, 177–178.
54. See de Groot, *The Religious System of China*, 5:819, and 6:958, 960, 991, 995–997.
55. *Shiliao xunkan, tian* series, 20b–25a.
56. *Kang Yong Qian shiqi chengxiang fankang douzheng ziliao*, 2:667–668; and *Yongzheng zhupi yuzhi*, 10:5989.
57. *Gongzhongdang*, JQ 7.9.24, and JQ 7.11.17; see also William Stanton, *The Triad Society*, 40–41.
58. *Tiandihui*, 1:18; and Xiao Yishan, *Jindai mimi shehui shiliao*, 2:8a–10a.
59. De Groot, *The Religious System of China*, 6:1000–1005, 1096; Willoughby-Meade *Chinese Ghouls and Goblins*, 67; Nicholas Dennys, *Folk-Lore of China*, 45; and ter Haar, *Ritual and Mythology of the Chinese Triads*, 65, 69–71.
60. Ter Haar, *Ritual and Mythology of the Chinese Triads*, 63, 82–83, 94–95, 225; see also Seiwert, *Popular Religious Movements and Heterodox Sects*, 282–284.
61. Ter Haar, *Ritual and Mythology of the Chinese Triads*, 250.
62. See *Shiliao xunkan, tian* series, 20b; and *Zhupi zouzhe*, QL 7.8.25; see also ter Haar, "China's Inner Demons," 39.
63. *Kang Yong Qian shiqi chengxiang fankang douzheng ziliao*, 2:626–627; and *Qingdai mimi jieshe dang'an jiyin*, 1:236–239.
64. For a non-messianic case uncovered in 1708 concerning the Third Prince Zhu as a Ming pretender, see *Shiliao xunkan, tian* series, 33a–37b. In at least one instance, Li Mei reportedly told one of his followers that the Third Prince Zhu referred to a son of the Taiwan rebel Zhu Yigui.
65. *Ming Qing shiliao, wu* series, 1:21a.
66. *Kang Yong Qian shiqi chengxiang fankang douzheng ziliao*, 2:615; for other examples see chapters 5 and 6 in this book.
67. *Shiliao xunkan, di* series, 441b–442b.
68. See Seidel, "Imperial Treasures and Taoist Sacraments," 298–299.
69. *Kang Yong Qian shiqi chengxiang fankang douzheng ziliao*, 2:614–615, 672; and *Zhupi zouzhe*, QL 7.8.25.
70. See, for example, the discussions on blood oaths in Suzuku, "Shincho chuki," 162–163; and ter Haar, *Ritual and Mythology of the Chinese Triads*, 151–179; on ritual human sacrifice among Chinese pirates, see Robert Antony, "Bloodthirsty Pirates?"
71. Mark Lewis, *Sanctioned Violence in Early China*, 43–46.
72. Ownby, *Brotherhoods and Secret Societies*, 41.
73. Ter Haar, *Ritual and Mythology of the Chinese Triads*, 156; and Chen Baoliang, *Zhongguo de she yu hui*, 94–126.
74. See Antony, "Brotherhoods, Secret Societies, and the Law in Qing-Dynasty China," 193–194, 207.

75. See de Groot, *The Religious System of China*, 6:968–969, 1178–1179; Willoughby-Meade, *Chinese Ghouls and Goblins*, 156; Schipper, "Vernacular and Classical Ritual," 30–31; and ter Haar, *Ritual and Mythology of the Chinese Triads*, 154, 246.
76. *Shiliao xunkan*, *di* series, 441a–451b.
77. Seidel, "Imperial Treasures and Taoist Sacraments," 294–295.
78. For example, see de Groot, *The Religious System of China*, vol. 6, part 5; McCreery, "The Symbolism of Popular Taoist Magic," 18, 25–57; and Schipper, "Vernacular and Classical Ritual," 27–32.
79. *Shiliao xunkan*, *tian* series, 20b–25a, 673a–677b; *Yongzheng zhupi yuzhe*, 10:5989; and *Qingdai mimi jieshe dang'an jiyin*, 1:176.
80. *Shiliao xunkan*, *tian* series, 673a–677b; and *Kang Yong Qian shiqi chengxiang fankang douzheng ziliao*, 2:653.
81. Seiwert, *Popular Religious Movements and Heterodox Sects*, 107, 155–156, 211–212.
82. See Ownby, *Brotherhoods and Secret Societies*, 21, 62–66.
83. *Zhupi zouzhe*, QL 7.6.8 and QL 7.6.22; and *Kang Yong Qian shiqi chengxiang fankang douzheng ziliao*, 2:667.
84. *Shiliao xunkan*, *di* series, 445b–447b; and *Qingdai mimi jieshe dang'an jiyin*, 1:213, 236.
85. *Shiliao xunkan*, *tian* series, 964b–966b; and Barend ter Haar, *Practicing Scripture*, 164–166. This group was related to the Dachengjiao discussed in the next chapter.
86. *Gongzhongdang Qianlongchao zouzhe*, 34:223–228.
87. *Shiliao xunkan*, *tian* series, 23b.
88. See, for example, Antony, *Like Froth Floating on the Sea* and *Unruly People*.
89. For examples, see the Xue Yanwen, Wang Atong, Huang Tianrui, Li Awan, Lu Mao, and Li Amin cases listed in appendix 2.
90. *Taiwan tongzhi*, 140:553; *Zhupi zouzhe*, QL 7.8.6, QL 7.8.10, and QL 7.8.2; and Sasaki, *Shinmatsu no himitsu kessha*, 145.
91. *Shiliao xunkan*, *di* series, 443b–449b.
92. Paul Katz, "Demons or Deities?," 203–204.
93. *Qingdai mimi jieshe dang'an jiyin*, 2:444–446; and *Zhanghua xianzhi*, 158.
94. De Groot, *The Religious System of China*, 6:991, 995.
95. On Chen and the early Triads in Guangdong, see Robert Antony, "Pirates, Bandits, and Brotherhoods," 280–292; on the predatory activities of secret societies, see Antony, *Unruly People*, 161–165.
96. Elizabeth Perry, *Challenging the Mandate of Heaven*, 282.
97. Ibid., 298; for other post-1949 cases, see also Ann Anagnost, "The Beginning and End of an Emperor"; Steve Smith, "Fear and Rumour in the People's Republic of China in the 1950s"; and Wu Junqing, *Mandarins and Heretics*, 147.

Chapter 5
1. Official sources also use the homonym Tiandihui (meaning Adding Brothers Society).
2. Sow-Theng Leong, *Migration and Ethnicity in Chinese History*, 45, 47, 64–65, 70–71; and *Boluo xianzhi* (1988), 184.

Notes

3. *Chen shi zupu*; "Guangdong sheng Huiyang dichu diming zhi," 280–281; and fieldnotes from Chashan village, Boluo county, June 2002.
4. *Chen shi zupu*; and Leong, *Migration and Ethnicity in Chinese History*, 70–71.
5. See Myron Cohen, "The Hakka or 'Guest People.'"
6. Leong, *Migration and Ethnicity in Chinese History*, 51, 72. On community pacts, see Robert Antony, *Unruly People*, 95.
7. *Boluo xianzhi* (1988), 30–31.
8. Leong, *Migration and Ethnicity in Chinese History*, 61–62.
9. *Yongan xian sanzhi*, 167; and *Boluo xianzhi* (2001), 74–75.
10. *Yongan xian sanzhi*, 167–170, 526–527.
11. *Nawenyigong zouyi*, 724–727; *Lufu zouzhe*, JQ 8.1.3; and *Shangyudang*, JQ 8.2.6.
12. See, for example, *Huizhou fuzhi* (1688), 5:14.
13. Leong, *Migration and Ethnicity in Chinese History*, 45.
14. *Huizhou fuzhi* (1881), 17:45a; and *Boluo xianzhi* (1988), 28.
15. *Boluo xianzhi* (1988), 31–32; and *Yongan xian sanzhi*, 496.
16. *Chen shi zupu*; and fieldnotes from Yangjingkeng village, Boluo county, June 2002.
17. *Kang Yong Qian shiqi chengxiang renmin fankang douzheng ziliao*, 2:669–671; *Qingshilu Guangdong shiliao*, 2:109–110, 119–120; and *Boluo xianzhi* (1988), 42.
18. *Qing shilu Guangdong shiliao*, 2:203, 230, 368, 483.
19. *Boluo xianzhi* (1988), 42–44; and *Huizhou shigao*, 162–163. In 1795, for instance, a severe famine, with concurrent rising food costs, occurred across Guangdong, Fujian, and Taiwan (see *Tiandihui* 6:41–42).
20. *Tiandihui*, 1:96–98.
21. *Nawenyigong zouyi*, 724–725.
22. On the spread of the Triads in Guangdong, see Qin Baoqi, *Qing qianqi Tiandihui yanjiu*, 169–179; and Robert Antony, "Pirates, Bandits, and Brotherhoods," 280–292.
23. *Gongzhongdang* (enclosure), JQ 7.7.29.
24. *Gongzhongdang*, JQ 7.8.4; and *Nawenyigong zouyi*, 724–727.
25. *Gongzhongdang*, JQ 7.8.11; and fieldnotes from Huidong county, which includes Renshan, Baimanghua, Pingshan, in May 2011.
26. *Waijidang*, JQ 8.12.21.
27. See the following interlude on Broken Shoes Chen the Fourth.
28. It may be no coincidence that Chen's mountain refuge was named "Goat Dung"; its homonym written with different characters (*yangshi*) means City of Willows, which as noted in the previous chapter symbolized an important safe haven in Triad lore.
29. *Lufu zouzhe*, JQ 7.9.20; *Shangyudang*, JQ 7.10.1; *Gongzhongdang*, JQ 7.10.3; and *Boluo xianzhi* (1988), 120.
30. *Gongzhongdang*, JQ 7.9.3 and JQ 7.10.3; *Guangdongsi xingbu dang'an*, JQ 8.7.28 and JQ 8.8.4; *Nawenyigong zouyi*, 793–798, 908; and *Yongan xian sanzhi*, 522–538. On human sacrifices to banners in Chinese history, see Paul Katz, "Banner Worship and Human Sacrifice in Chinese Military History."
31. *Nawenyigong zouyi*, 724–727; *Chen shi zupu*; and fieldnotes from Yangjingkeng village, Boluo county, June 2002, from Renshan township, Huidong county, May 2011, and from Tiandeng village, Lianzhou, November 2015.

Notes

32. *Shangyudang*, JQ 7.11.19 and JQ 7.12.9; and *Gongzhongdang*, JQ 7.11.21. On Jueluo Jiqing's case, see Tang Ruiyu, *Qingdai lizhi tanwei*, 87–111.
33. *Nawenyigong zouyi*, 840. Similarly, in 1886 in Huizhou several thousand Hakka formed a Triad society and rose up in revolt due to "the oppressive acts of Government officials" (Stanton, *The Triad Society*, 23).
34. Lian Lichang, *Fujian mimi shehui*, 66–68.
35. *Chen shi zupu*; and fieldnotes from Yangjingkeng village, Boluo county, June 2002.
36. Zhuang Jifa, *Qingdai tiandihui yuanliu kao*, 82–83; and David Ownby, "The Heaven and Earth Society as Popular Religion," 1034–1035.
37. *Kang Yong Qian shiqi chengxiang renmin fankang douzheng ziliao*, 2:648–652, 656; *Qing shilu Guangdong shiliao*, 2:61–62; de Groot, *Sectarianism and Religious Persecution in China*, 267, 284–287; also see Sasaki Masaya, *Shinmatsu no himitsu kessha*, 183–186; and Daniel Overmyer, *Folk Buddhist Religion*, 120–122.
38. Wu Zixiang, who was one of the most important lay religious leaders in south China in the mid-Qing period, followed a variant of the Luo Teaching referred to as Dachengjiao that he later developed into the Wupanjiao. See Ma and Han, *Zhongguo minjian zongjiao shi*, 368–379.
39. *Tiandihui*, 6:245–246.
40. *Lufu zouzhe*, JQ 8.8.8; and *Tiandihui*, 6:246–248, 253, 273, 276–277.
41. *Lufu zouzhe*, JQ 8.12.8; and *Tiandihui*, 6:259–261, 269–274, 276–278.
42. *Tiandihui*, 6:283–285; also see Lian, *Fujian mimi shehui*, 68–69; ter Haar, *Ritual and Mythology of the Chinese Triads*, 290–296; and Ownby, "The Heaven and Earth Society as Popular Religion," 1034–1036.
43. On Wu Qingyuan, see Ma and Han, *Zhongguo minjian zongjiao shi*, 378.
44. *Gongzhongdang*, JQ 5.3.27. After Wu Qingyuan died his wife, neé Zhang, continued to spread the Wupanjiao and in 1821 it was revived in Guangdong by Peng Yasheng (Ma and Han, *Zhongguo minjian zongjiao shi*, 378–379).
45. *Gongzhongdang*, JQ 7.10.24.
46. *Gongzhongdang*, JQ 7.8.16, JQ 7.8.2, and JQ 7.10.24; and *Chen shi zupu*.
47. *Yongan xian sanzhi*, 522. Actually members of this latter group were followers of the Dachengjiao tradition and not associated with the so-called White Lotus tradition.
48. *Gongzhongdang*, JQ 7.8.16, JQ 7.8.23, and JQ 7.10.24; and *Tiandihui*, 7:45, 86, 141, 151.
49. Ter Haar, *Ritual and Mythology of the Triads*, 115.
50. Hubert Seiwert, *Popular Religious Movements and Heterodox Sects in Chinese History*, 116, 151, 154.
51. Ter Haar, *Ritual and Mythology of the Triads*, 116. William Stanton (*The Triad Society*, 117), writing in 1900, explained that during times of disorders Triad members, "in order to protect their families from violence, nail a square piece of red cloth over the door-ways of their dwellings, with the character *hung* (vast), written on the outside and the character *ying* on the inside of it."
52. Ownby, "The Heaven and Earth Society as Popular Religion," 1024.
53. See, for example, Seiwert, *Popular Religious Movements and Heterodox Sects*, 435–436; and Barend ter Haar, *Practicing Scripture*, 6.

54. The history of China's popular religious movements is complex and complicated and beyond the scope of this study. The Luo Teaching, for instance, is discussed in detail in Ma and Han, *Zhongguo minjian zongjiao shi*, 165–405; Suzuki Chusei, "Shincho chuki," 166–192; Seiwert, *Popular Religious Movements and Heterodox Sects*, 214–267; and ter Haar, *Practicing Scripture*.

55. See Ma and Han, *Zhongguo minjian zongjiao shi*, 1104–1108; and Wang Jianchuan, *Taiwan de zhaijiao yu luantang*, 89–94. On the Yiguandao tradition, see David Jordan and Daniel Overmyer, *The Flying Phoenix*, 213–266; Seiwert, *Popular Religious Movements and Heterodox Sects*, 427–437; and Ma and Han, *Zhongguo minjian zongjiao shi*, 1092–1168.

56. Ma and Han, *Zhongguo minjian zongjiao shi*, 1100–1104.

57. *Lufu zouzhe*, JQ 19.5.22; *Tiandihui*, 6:267, 287; Ma and Han, *Zhongguo minjian zongjiao shi*, 1107–1108; and Seiwert, *Popular Religious Movements and Heterodox Sects*, 281–293, 432–433.

58. *Tiandihui*, 6:267, 276–277.

59. Ibid., 6:282–288; ter Haar, *Ritual and Mythology of the Triads*, 205–206, 292–295; and Ma and Han, *Zhongguo minjian zongjiao shi*, 1103.

60. *Gongzhongdang*, JQ 7.8.16, JQ 7.8.23, JQ 7.10.3, JQ 7.10.24, and JQ 7.11.17.

61. *Gongzhongdang*, JQ 5.3.27.

62. On the *Longhua jing*, see Seiwert, *Popular Religious Movements and Heterodox Sects*, 366–402; on the *Wugong jing*, see Barend ter Haar, "The Sutra of the Five Lords"; and on its influence on Li Lingkui, see ter Haar, *Ritual and Mythology of the Triads*, 291.

63. *Lufu zouzhe*, JQ 7.9.20 (enclosure). This or similar couplets became common in later Triad manuals.

64. Gustave Schlegel, *Thian Ti Hwui*, 225n2; and ter Haar, *Ritual and Mythology of the Triads*, 278–279.

65. Kristofer Schipper, "Vernacular and Classical Taoist Ritual," 30.

66. See Seiwert, *Popular Religious Movements and Heterodox Sects*, 471; and ter Haar, *Ritual and Mythology of the Triads*, 295.

67. On macroregions, see G. William Skinner, "Cities and the Hierarchy of Local Systems."

68. Ownby, "The Heaven and Earth Society as Popular Religion," 1028; Wen-hsiung Hsu, "The Triads and Their Ideology up to the Early Nineteenth Century," 332–334. On the laboring poor and their underworld culture, see Antony, *Unruly People*, 183–189.

69. Cited in Wing-hoi Chan, "Ethnic Labels in a Mountainous Region," 275.

70. *Shangyudang*, JQ 7.10.28. Earlier, in 1791, there was the case involving Peng Shangnian from Fujian, Zhu Langsi from Guangdong, and Huang Zuojin from Jiangxi who formed an Adding Brothers Society in Nankang county in northern Jiangxi (*Tiandihui*, 6:365–366).

71. *Chen shi zupu*; according to interviews I conducted in June 2002, the Boluo Chens still have contacts with family members across Guangdong, Jiangxi, and Guangxi.

72. Sasaki Masaya, *Shinmatsu no himitsu kessha*, 172. When neophytes entered the Tiandihui, they took Hong as their new surname; the word Hong was also invoked on protective talismans by members.

73. Leong, *Migration and Ethnicity in Chinese History*, 63, 69, 75; also see ter Haar, *Ritual and Mythology of the Chinese Triads*, 402.

74. Two important anthropological studies on Hakka ethnicity in the Hong Kong setting are C. Fred Blake, *Ethnic Groups and Social Change in a Chinese Market Town*; and Nicole Constable, "Christianity and Hakka Identity."

75. Daniel Overmyer, *Folk Buddhist Religion*, 21.

76. Seiwert, *Popular Religious Movements and Heterodox Sects*, 80–83.

Interlude 2

1. *Gongzhongdang*, JQ 7.11.17.
2. *Lufu zouzhe* (enclosure), JQ 7.9.20.
3. *Shangyudang*, JQ 7.10.1; and *Tiandihui*, 7:26.
4. There is also a tradition of giving children demeaning nicknames to make the disease-bearing demons overlook them; however, this was not mentioned in my interviews.
5. *Lufu zouzhe* (enclosure), JQ 7.9.20.
6. *Chen shi zupu*.
7. *Shangyudang*, JQ 7.10.5.
8. *Chen shi zupu*; and fieldnotes from Yangjingkeng village, Boluo county, June 2002.
9. *Chen shi zupu*.
10. Fieldnotes from Yangjingkeng village, Boluo county, June 2002.
11. *Chen shi zupu*; and fieldnotes from Yangjingkeng and Botang, Boluo county, June 2002. See also chapter 3 for further discussion of grave desecrations as related to Chinese geomancy.
12. *Nawenyigong zouyi*, 856–857.
13. William Hunter, *Bits of Old China*, 165–166.
14. Harry Lamley, "*Hsieh-tou*: The Pathology of Violence in Southeastern China," 9, 19; and David Ownby, "Approximations of Chinese Bandits," 230.
15. John Scarth, *Twelve Years in China*, 239. See also John Slade, *Notices on the British Trade to the Port of Canton*, 53; and S. Wells Williams, *The Middle Kingdom*, 1:485.
16. Chen Weiyan, *Nanyue youji*, 171–172.
17. *Qiu shi da zongpu*, 14.
18. *Chen shi zupu Lianzhou Longtan Tiandeng Xisi xi*; and fieldnotes from Tiandeng village, Lianzhou, and from Liannan Yao Autonomous County, November 2015. On the economic development and trading networks in this mountainous borderland, see Robert Antony, "Mountains, Rivers, and Sea."
19. *Chen shi zupu fuben*; and fieldnotes from Tiandeng village, Lianzhou, November 2015. On Hong Xiuquan and the Taipings in Guangdong, see Jonathan Spence, *God's Chinese Son*, 69–79, and Frederic Wakeman, *Strangers at the Gate*, 126, 132–133.
20. Based on family records and interviews, Chen Jinjiang was twenty-one *sui* at the time of the Boluo uprising in 1802 (not twenty-six as stated in the confession), which meant that he would have been born in 1781 or 1782. If this is correct, then he would have been seventy-two or seventy-three in 1854.

21. *Chen shi zupu fuben*; Chen Fangqi, "Chen Jinjiang lingdao de tiandihui yu hongbing qiyi shiji"; and fieldnotes from Tiandeng village, Lianzhou, November 2015. See also *Lianzhou ribao*, June 7, 2009.

22. *Foshan ribao*, August 22, 2018; *Maoming wang*, April 14, 2017; and fieldnotes from my student, Liu Jiaqi, from Sanshui county, January 2016. According to historian Liu Ping (*Bei yiwang de zhanzheng*, 223–226), Chen Jingang came from Sanshui, established a short-lived kingdom on the Guangdong-Guangxi border, and took the title Southern Efflorescent King. It is interesting to note, as discussed in the first interlude, that the name Jingang refers to the warrior guardians of the Buddha, and therefore the name would indicate a person of great martial prowess.

23. *Xinning xianzhi*, 12:14a, 18b–21b; *Kaiping xianzhi*, 21:3a; and Scarth, *Twelve Years in China*, 232–238; see also Liu Ping, *Bei yiwang de zhanzheng*; Harry Lamley, "Hsieh-tou: The Pathology of Violence in Southeastern China," 13; Zheng Dehua, "Guangdong zhonglu tuke xiedou yanjiu," 239–242, 281–282, 289–292, 296–297, 314; and Jaeyoon Kim, "The Heaven and Earth Society and the Red Turban Rebellion in Late Qing China," 17–21. During the turmoil a large group of Hakkas fled Enping and Kaiping and resettled in Leizhou; others who had converted to Catholicism resettled on Weizhou island, where, together with a French priest, they build a church that was completed in 1863 (fieldnotes from Weizhou island, January 2010).

24. *Chen shi zupu Lianzhou Longtan Tiandeng Xisi xi*; Chen Fangqi, "Chen Jinjiang lingdao de tiandihui yu hongbing qiyi shiji"; and fieldnotes from Tiandeng village, Lianzhou, November 2015.

25. For example, see *Lianzhou ribao*, June 7, 2009; *Nanfang ribao*, September 5, 2016; and "Minzu yingxiong jiazu zuiren."

26. James Harrison, *The Communists and Chinese Peasant Rebellions*, 120, 248, 271.

27. While it is true that since the 1980s, many professional historians in China have turned away from the strictures of Marxist rhetoric emphasizing class conflict and righteous peasant uprisings, nonetheless the Chens and their neighbors are not academics and they continue to adhere to popular versions of Maoist era historiography. Put simply, their representations of the past are different from those of most historians.

Chapter 6

1. *Hunan difangzhi shaoshu minzu shiliao*, 2:549, 557.
2. *Shangyudang*, DG 12.3.8.
3. On the Great Yao Wars in the mid-Ming, see David Faure, "The Yao Wars in the Mid-Ming and their Impact on Yao Ethnicity," 172–178; and his chapter on the Yao Wars in *Emperor and Ancestor*, 93–108; and for the Yao disturbances in the early Qing, see *Qing shilu yu Qing dang'an*, 1–33; and *Guangdong Yaozu lishi ziliao*, 1:358–366.
4. Although not dealing specifically with the Yao, Thomas Mullaney's *Coming to Terms with the Nation* is the best study on the ethnic classification system in Communist China.
5. Ralph Litzinger, "Making Histories," 126.
6. In other versions the emperor is named Gaoxin and his enemy is King Wu. The storyline, nonetheless, is basically the same.

7. In some versions, the emperor betrayed the Yao who were forced to leave their idyllic home; on their perilous journey across rivers and seas the Yao were saved only by the divine assistance of King Pan and his spirit armies, and eventually the Yao reached the southern regions where they now live (in south China and Southeast Asia, depending on the source of the story).

8. On Yao charters, see Huang Yu, "Yaozu 'pinghuang quandie' chutan"; Eli Alberts, "Commemorating the Ancestors' Merit"; and Barend ter Haar, "A New Interpretation of Yao Charters." This version of the Panhu myth is a composite drawn from several sources: *Hunan Yaozu shehui lishi diaocha*, 7–8, 10–13; Pu Chaojun, *Zhongguo Yaozu fengtu zhi*, 316–318; Hans Stübel, "The Yao of the Province of Kuangtung," 411–412; Chungshee Liu, "The Dog-Ancestor Story," 361–364; and Victor Mair, "Canine Conundrums," 5–6. Zheng Hui has made a detailed study of extant Yao literary documents relating to the Panhu myth in his *Yaozu wenshu dang'an yanjiu*, 79–90, 151–174.

9. *Chinese Repository* 1 (May 1832), 29; and E. W. Thwing, "A Legend of the Ius," 781. Even today some Hakka villagers in Lianzhou that I interviewed in 2015 regard the Yao as an inferior race because of their "dog ancestry."

10. Richard Cushman, "Rebel Haunts and Lotus Huts," 71, 146; and Eli Alberts, *A History of Daoism and the Yao People of South China*, 142–143. Up until today the most important Yao festival celebrates their primal ancestor, Panhu or King Pan, which occurs each year on the sixteenth day of the tenth lunar month. Today the Chinese government recognizes the Pan Wang festival as an intangible cultural heritage. For the Yao communities in Liannan the festival is an important tourist attraction, which gives the Yao people an opportunity to display their culture and earn extra money.

11. Leo Shin, *The Making of the Chinese State*, 9; quote on p. 4.

12. Alberts, *A History of Daoism and the Yao People*, 23, 30–46; Ralph Litzinger, *Other Chinas*, 54, 57–59; Faure, "The Yao Wars in the Mid-Ming," 186; and Shin, *The Making of the Chinese State*, 111.

13. Jacques Lemoine, "Yao Culture and Some Other Related Problems," 596–597.

14. Qu Dajun, *Guangdong xinyu*, 237–238.

15. Hjorleifur Jonsson, *Mien Relations*, 150.

16. Cited in Cushman, "Rebel Haunts and Lotus Huts," 154.

17. Li Laizhang, *Lianyang Bapai fengtu ji*, 48; Qian Yikai, *Linghai jianwen*, 55–56; and Alberts, *A History of Daoism and the Yao People*, 24, 28.

18. See Magnus Fiskesjö, "On the 'Raw' and 'Cooked' Barbarians of Imperial China."

19. *Hunan difangzhi shaoshu minzu shiliao*, 2:292, 339, 479–480; and Kuang Meihua, "The Yao Rebellion in the 11th-12th Years of Daoguang Reign," 84–85.

20. Cushman, "Rebel Haunts and Lotus Huts," 106.

21. R. Brian Ferguson and Neil Whitehead, *War in the Tribal Zone*, xxii–xxiii.

22. Cushman, "Rebel Haunts and Lotus Huts," 233.

23. *Hunan difangzhi shaoshu minzu shiliao*, 2:466; and Fei Xiaotong, "Fifty Years Investigation in Yao Mountains," 27.

24. Kuang, "The Yao Rebellion," 26–27.

25. See, for example, Rao Zongyi, "Taiguo 'Yaoren wenshu' du houji"; and Huang Yu, "Yaozu 'pinghuang quandie' chutan."

Notes

26. Ter Haar, "A New Interpretation of Yao Charters," 4–5; see also Alberts, "Commemorating the Ancestors' Merit," 19, 24; Jonsson, "Shifting Social Landscape," 9, 110–111; and Litzinger, *Other Chinas*, 9–10, 58.

27. Pu Chaojun, *Zhongguo Yaozu fengtu zhi*, 352–353; ter Haar, "A New Interpretation of Yao Charters," 4, 8–9; and Alberts, *A History of Daoism and the Yao People*, 47, 69, 132–133, 143.

28. *Qing shilu yu Qing dang'an*, 51.

29. Kuang, "The Yao Rebellion," 19–21; see also Robert Antony, "Mountains, Rivers, and Sea," for the web of marketing networks that stitched the region together and linked it with the outside world.

30. *Zhupi zouzhe*, DG 12.2.19.

31. Fieldnotes from Yao villages of Nangang and Youling in Liannan, July 2014 and May and November 2015.

32. *Guangdong sheng Yaozu shehui lishi qingkuang*, 2–3; see also the discussions in C. Pat Giersch, "A Motley Throng," 72–73; and Richard White, *The Middle Ground*.

33. See James Scott, *The Art of not Being Governed*.

34. Fieldnotes from Yao villages of Nangang and Youling in Liannan, July 2014 and May 2015; Li Laizhang, *Lianyang Bapai fengtu ji*; Cushman, "Rebel Haunts and Lotus Huts," 198; and for comparison with the Miao, see Donald Sutton, "Violence and Ethnicity on a Qing Colonial Frontier," 45.

35. Fieldnotes from Shanxi village, Liannan, May 2015.

36. Li Laizhang, *Lianyang Bapai fengtu ji*, 133–136; *Lianzhou zhi*, 9:9a; and *Guangdong Yaozu lishi ziliao*, 1:65, 366–367.

37. Kuang, "The Yao Rebellion," 22–25.

38. *Guangdong Yaozu lishi ziliao*, 1:365.

39. Fieldnotes from Lianzhou and Liannan, November 2015; and *Qiushi da zongpu*, 44–45; also see the interlude preceding this chapter.

40. Fieldnotes from Bapai Yao and Guoshan Yao villages in Lianzhou, Liannan, and Yangshan, May and November 2015 and August 2017.

41. *Lianshan sui Yao tingzhi*, 19a.

42. *Hunan difangzhi shaoshu minzu shiliao*, 2:335. In both cases, of course, these figures are only for the registered populations; the number of unregistered Yao likely exceeded the Chinese population.

43. Qian Yikai, *Linghai jianwen*, 55; *Guangdong shangyu zouzhe*, vol. 1, dated DG 12.7. The Bapai Yao belonged to the Pai Yao group.

44. Kuang, "The Yao Rebellion," 27–28; and fieldnotes from Youling in Liannan, May 2015, and from Tiandeng in Lianzhou, November 2015. Of course, over the centuries of contact, the Yao also had been embracing aspects of Chinese culture, most notably the adoption of Daoism.

45. On the Miao, see Sutton, "Violence and Ethnicity on a Qing Colonial Frontier."

46. Li Laizhang, *Lianyang Bapai fengtu ji*, 225; and Kuang, "The Yao Rebellion," 35.

47. Wei Yuan, *Shengwu ji*, 325; and *Hunan difangzhi shaoshu minzu shiliao*, 2:577; also see Cai Tun, "Luelun Daoguang Jianghua Yaomin baodong zhi qiyin," 70.

48. *Hunan difangzhi shaoshu minzu shiliao*, 2:294.

Notes

49. *Hunan Yaozu shehui lishi diaocha*, 41; and *Guangdong sheng Yaozu shehui lishi qingkuang*, 8, 29–30.
50. Li Laizhang, *Lianyang Bapai fengtu ji*, 210.
51. *Zhupi zouzhe*, DG 12.9.3.
52. Wei Yuan, *Shengwu ji*, 325.
53. *Qing shilu yu Qing dang'an*, 214–217; see also *Zhupi zouzhe*, DG 12.r9.2; and *Hunan Yaozu shehui lishi diaocha*, 41.
54. See the discussion in Brian Sandberg, "Beyond Encounters," 12; and on millenarian uprisings of the Miao minority, see Cheung Siu-woo, "Millenarianism, Christian Movements, and Ethnic Change among the Miao in Southwest China"; and Paul Katz, *Religion, Ethnicity, and Gender in Western Hunan,* especially chapter 5.
55. Jonsson, "Shifting Social Landscape," 100, 222.
56. *Shangyudang*, DG 12.8; *Qing shilu yu Qing dang'an*, 147, 175; and Wei Yuan, *Shengwu ji*, 325.
57. *Hunan Yaozu shehui lishi diaocha*, 1, 67; Pu Chaojun, *Zhongguo Yaozu fengtu zhi*, 434–436; and Gong Zhebing, *Qianjiadong yundong yu Yaozu faxiangdi*, 167–169, 185.
58. *Hunan Yaozu shehui lishi diaocha*, 36–37, 123; and ter Haar, "A New Interpretation of the Yao Charters," 9–10; see also the extended discussion in Gong Zhebing, *Qianjiadong yundong yu Yaozu faxiangdi*.
59. *Shangyudang*, DG 12.8; *Qing shilu Guangdong shiliao*, 4:49; and *Qing shilu yu Qing dang'an*, 174–176, 180.
60. *Hunan Yaozu shehui lishi diaocha*, 40–41; and Yao Shun'an, "Zhao Jinlong lingdao de Yaomin qiyi," 63.
61. Stübel, "The Yao of the Province of Kuangtung," 373.
62. Fieldnotes from Yao villages of Nangang and Youling in Liannan, May 2015 and August 2017; Ma Jianzhao, *Pai Yao yanjiu lunwen xuanji*, 129; and ter Haar, "A New Interpretation of Yao Charters," 11. See also Wong Sik-ling, "In Search of a Forgotten Tribe," 479, and "More Notes on the Ruler of the Yao of Loh-Fah Mountains," 123–125.
63. Sutton, "Violence and Ethnicity on a Qing Colonial Frontier," 119. See also Katz, *Religion, Ethnicity, and Gender in Western Hunan*, 134, 142–147.
64. See the discussions in Pu Chaojun, *Zhongguo Yaozu fengtu zhi*, 438; and Xu Wenqing, "Lun Liannan Pai Yao de shenhua gushi," 183, 186–188.
65. *Shangyudang*, DG 12.8; and on Panhu as the Yao savior, see Alberts, "Commemorating the Ancestors' Merit," 54; Peter Kandre, "Yao (Iu Mien) Supernaturalism, Language, and Ethnicity," 175; and ter Haar, "A New Interpretation of Yao Charters," 11.
66. *Shangyudang*, DG 12.2.2; and *Qing shilu yu Qing dang'an*, 180.
67. Cushman, "Rebel Haunts and Lotus Huts," Appendix 2, pp. 15, 22; Pu Chaojun, *Zhongguo Yaozu fengtu zhi*, 317; and Wolfram Eberhard, *Studies in Chinese Folklore and Related Essays*, 138.
68. *Shangyudang*, DG 12.8; *Qing shilu Guangdong shiliao*, 4:46–49; and *Qing shilu yu Qing dang'an*, 180. This, of course, was typical of Daoist ritual specialists and, as discussed in chapters 4 and 5, a major source for the Triads demonological messianic teachings.
69. Jonsson, "Moving House," 627–28, 631–632.
70. *Shangyudang*, DG 12.2.2; and *Chinese Repository* 1 (May 1832), 39.

71. *Qing shilu yu Qing dang'an*, 148.
72. Gong Zhebing, *Qianjiadong yundong yu Yaozu faxiangdi*, 12–14; and Litzinger, *Other Chinas*, 73–74.
73. Pu Chaojun, *Zhongguo Yaozu fengtu zhi*, 437–438; *Hunan Yaozu shehui lishi diaocha*, 40; and fieldnotes from Youling, Liannan, May 2015.
74. *Shangyudang*, DG 12.7.8, and DG 12.10.3.
75. See Cai Tun, "Luelun Daoguang Jianghua Yaomin baodong zhi qiyin," 69–70; and Yang Yiqing, "Guanyu Zhao Jinlong qiyi jige wenti de shangque," 34–35.
76. Wei Yuan, *Shengwu ji*, 328.
77. *Shangyudang*, DG 12.5.10, and DG 12.8.
78. *Shangyudang*, DG 12.2.2; *Hunan difangzhi shaoshu minzu shiliao*, 2:577; and Wei Yuan, *Shengwu ji*, 2:325; also see Yang Yiqing, "Guanyu Zhao Jinlong qiyi jige wenti de shangque," 34.
79. *Chinese Repository* 1 (May 1832), 30; Wei Yuan, *Shengwu ji*, 325–326; and Yang Yiqing, "Guanyu Zhao Jinlong qiyi jige wenti de shangque," 37.
80. *Shangyudang*, DG 12.2.2, DG 12.2.20; *Zhupi zouzhe*, DG 12.6.18, DG 12.7.2; and Wei Yuan, *Shengwu ji*, 326. On the custom of Yao Daoist masters leading soldiers into battle, see Li Laizhang, *Lianyang Bapai fengtu ji*, 144.
81. *Zhupi zouzhe*, DG 12.1.28; *Shangyudang*, DG 12.2.1, DG 12.4.14, and DG 12.8.16; and *Qing shilu Guangdong shiliao*, 4:46–49.
82. *Shangyudang*, DG 12.4.8, DG 12.8; Wei Yuan, *Shengwu ji*, 326–327; and Yang Yiqing, "Guanyu Zhao Jinlong qiyi jige wenti de shangque," 34. On the use of *fengshui* in warfare see chapter 3.
83. *Qing shilu yu Qing dang'an*, 162, 197; *Guangdong shangyu zouzhe*, vol. 2, dated DG 12.8.3.
84. *Zhupi zouzhe*, DG 12.5.7; *Lufu zouzhe*, DG 12.9.20; and *Shangyudang*, DG 12.5.25, DG 12.7.6, DG 12.9.15, and DG 12.10.3.
85. *Shangyudang*, DG 12.7.21; Wei Yuan, *Shengwu ji*, 327; and *Yangshan xianzhi*, 716–717.
86. *Shangyudang*, DG 12.3.8, DG 12.8.23; *Qing shilu Guangdong shiliao*, 4:74–75; Wei Yuan, *Shengwu ji*, 327; and *Qing shilu yu Qing dang'an*, 242–244.
87. *Qing shilu Guangdong shiliao*, 4:48, 51, 53; *Chinese Repository* 1 (August 1832), 158; and Kuang, "The Yao Rebellion," 54–57.
88. *Lufu zouzhe*, DG 12.8.23; and *Chinese Repository* 1 (May 1832), 31.
89. *Shangyudang*, DG 12.4.9, DG 12.4.14, DG 12.9.15; and *Qing shilu yu Qing dang'an*, 192–195.
90. Douglas Cowan, *Magic, Monsters, and Make-Believe Heroes*, 103.

Chapter 7

1. I should start with a disclaimer. One could easily argue that south China's water world was a masculine space. There were certainly as many male sailors and pirates as there were female sailors and pirates, and certainly many male sea deities, such as the God of the Southern Seas (Nanhaishen), Lord Tam (Tangong), and the Dragon King (Longwang). But in this chapter, I would like to indulge a bit in my historical imagination to discuss

the more pronounced feminine features of maritime south China in the early modern and modern eras.

2. Studies on women from elite families in late imperial China by Dorothy Ko and Susan Mann have shown that under their privileged circumstances some of them were able to obtain a degree of independence outside the patriarchal system, but without openly challenging it. Paola Paderni has likewise argued that some non-elite women were able to overcome difficult social and economic circumstances to express some degree of independence, but also without directly challenging orthodox family values. In the present study I argue that Dan boat women and female pirates not only obtained a large degree of independence but did so by consciously challenging the orthodox values and the prevailing patriarchal system on land. On elite women, see Dorothy Ko, *Teachers of the Inner Chambers*, and Susan Mann, *Precious Records*; on non-elite women, see Paola Paderni, "Between Constraints and Opportunities."

3. See, for example, Robert Antony, "Mountains, Rivers, and Sea."

4. Anders Hansson, *Chinese Outcasts*, 109–110; and He Xi and David Faure, "Introduction: Boat and Shed Living in Land-Based Society," 1–2. Although in the PRC the Dan are classified as Han, not as a minority nationality, they are still treated as an outcast ethnic group by society at large; for an authoritative study on the racial and ethnic classification of the Dan in the Republican period, see by Gary Luk, "The Making of a Littoral Minzu."

5. Chen Xujing, *Danmin de yanjiu*, 9–10; Luk, "The Making of a Littoral *Minzu*," 3–4; Grant Alger, "The Floating Community of the Min," 241–243; Hansson, *Chinese Outcasts*, 107; and Huang Xiangchun, "Going Beyond Pariah Status," 145. Another group of Fujianese boat people were the Hoklo, who originally hailed from Zhangzhou and Quanzhou prefectures, and later spread into neighboring Guangdong, Taiwan, and Southeast Asia. However, not all Hoklo lived on boats or went to sea. In this chapter my focus is on Dan boat people, and in my discussions about "boat women" I am specifically referring to Dan boat women.

6. Qu Dajun, *Guangdong xinyu*, 130–133. Qu goes on to describe fresh water as *yang*, but most other writers depict all bodies of water as *yin*.

7. Edward Schafer, *The Divine Woman*, 9.

8. Lee Irwin, "Divinity and Salvation," 65.

9. John Barrow, *Travels in China*, 595.

10. Cited in Michael Wise, *Travellers Tales of the South China Coast*, 219.

11. Wu Ruilin, *Sanshui Danmin diaocha*, 48.

12. Cited in Alger, "The Floating Community of the Min," 227.

13. Hiroaki Kani, *A General Survey of the Boat People in Hong Kong*, 58.

14. Zhang Qu, *Yuedong wenjianlu*, 59.

15. Eugene Anderson, *Floating World Lost*, 51, 73–74, 181; see also Wu Ruilin, *Sanshui Danmin diaocha*, 52, 58–60; *Guangdong fengsu zhuilu*, 131–132, 420–424; and Luk, "The Making of a Littoral Minzu," 7–8. It is not that other women on shore did not engage in premarital or extramarital sex—they certainly did—but rather what stands out in marked contrast is that Dan females did so quite openly.

16. On Dan folksongs, see Zhong Jingwen, *Dan ge*; and Eugene Anderson, "The Folksongs of the Hong Kong Boat People." Certainly Dan boat people were not the only

Chinese to sing erotic folk songs; see, for example, Hung Chang-tai, *Going to the People*, 75–79.

17. Wu Ruilin, *Sanshui Danmin diaocha*, 51–52. For a recent revisionist evaluation that downplays Dan prostitution, see *Guangdong Danmin shehui diaocha*, 44–45.

18. Cited in Virgil Ho, "Selling Smiles in Canton," 124.

19. Isabel Nunes, "Singing and Dancing Girls of Macao," 67, 70; and Ho, "Selling Smiles in Canton," 106.

20. Gail Hershatter, "Sex Work and Social Order," 1103.

21. Wu Ruilin, *Sanshui Danmin diaocha*, 51–52.

22. Cited in Nunes, "Singing and Dancing Girls of Macao," 70.

23. Cited in Paul Van Dyke, *Whampoa and the Canton Trade*, 221.

24. Hansson, *Chinese Outcasts*, 130.

25. Alger, "The Floating Community of the Min," 241.

26. Charles Gutzlaff, *Journal of Three Voyages*, 88; *Gongzhongdang*, JQ 2.11.12; Dian Murray, *Pirates of the South China Coast*, 78; and Van Dyke, *Whampoa and the Canton Trade*, 226–228.

27. For a firsthand account of Canton flower boats by a late nineteenth-century Chinese scholar, see Shen Fu, *Six Records of a Floating Life*, 118–125. For useful surveys about flower boats, see Nunes, "Singing and Dancing Girls of Macao"; Van Dyke, *Whampoa and the Canton Trade*, 229–234; and Virgil Ho, "Selling Smiles in Canton."

28. Hansson, *Chinese Outcasts*, 129; and Van Dyke, "Floating Brothels," 113–116.

29. Fieldnotes from Yunxiao, August 1985.

30. Fieldnotes from Kaiping (on the Tan River), May 2011; and from Baitenghu (on the coast in Zhuhai), October 2018.

31. Anderson, *Floating World Lost*, 175.

32. Sakura Magozō, *Minfeng zaji*, 4a.

33. Fieldnotes from the Dan anchorage on the Tan River in Kaiping, Guangdong, April 2007; Wu Ruilin, *Sanshui Danmin diaocha*, 16; and Anderson, *Floating World Lost*, 171–176.

34. Chen Xujing, *Danmin de yanjiu*, 153–155; Kani, *A General Survey of the Boat People in Hong Kong*, 58–59, Anderson, *Floating World Lost*, 26–27, 48, 62, 71, 171; and *Guangdong Danmin shehui diaocha*, 45.

35. Wu Gaozi, "Fuzhou Danmin diaocha," 144–145.

36. Kani, *A General Survey of the Boat People in Hong Kong*, 59.

37. Fanny Loviot, *A Lady's Captivity among Chinese Pirates in the Chinese Seas*, 78.

38. *Ming Qing shiliao*, wu series, 465.

39. *Shangyudang*, JQ 12.4.1, JQ 14.5.11, and JQ 14.11.28; *Ming Qing shiliao*, wu series, 579, 585; see also Robert Antony, *Like Froth Floating on the Sea*, 47–48.

40. *Gongzhongdang*, JQ 6.9.29.

41. *Gongzhongdang*, JQ 1.8.19.

42. Yuan Yonglun, *Jing haifen ji*, 1:10b.

43. *Gongzhongdang*, JQ 14.2.10 and JQ 14.5.28.

44. Beresford Scott, *An Account of the Destruction of the Fleets of the Celebrated Pirate Chieftains Chui-Apoo and Shap-ng Tsai*, 234–239; and C. Nathan Kwan, "In the Business of Piracy," 202–211.

45. Dian Murray, "One Woman's Rise to Power: Cheng I's Wife and the Pirates," 149. See also Kwan, "In the Business of Piracy," 197–202.

46. Antony, *Like Froth Floating on the Sea*, 48–52.

47. Murray, "One Woman's Rise to Power," 158.

48. Kwan, "In the Business of Piracy," 204.

49. Some online articles claim that she was surnamed Lü, but this is not substantiated in other sources. See, for example, Academia Sinica Digital Archives at sinica.digitalarchives.tw/subject_2062.html (accessed September 9, 2019).

50. *Pingyang xianzhi*, 59:22a–23b.

51. *Maxiang tingzhi*, addendum 1:56b–57a.

52. See Antony, *Like Froth Floating on the Sea*, 46, 147; and fieldnotes from Fuzhou and Amoy, August 1985.

53. Aleko E. Lilius, *I Sailed with Chinese Pirates*.

54. Ibid., 37–57; and author's interviews with residents in Shalitou district of Macau, summer 2011.

55. Lilius, *I Sailed with Chinese Pirates*, 53–54.

56. See Milton Caniff, *Terry and the Pirates*; and Marlon Brando, *Fantan*.

57. Jason Wordie, "Lai Choi San, All Woman, All Pirate"; and author's interviews with residents in Shalitou district of Macau, summer 2011.

58. J. J. M. de Groot, *The Religious System of China*, 5:532–533.

59. Niu Junkai, "Hai wei wubo," 49–60.

60. Hugh Clark, *The Sinitic Encounter*, 143.

61. Barend ter Haar, "The Genesis and Spread of Temple Cults in Fukien," 356–357, 373–376; Clark, *The Sinitic Encounter*, 138–147; and Luo Chunrong, "Tianfei heshi feng Tianhou," 271–284.

62. *Lianjiang xianzhi*, 2:34–35.

63. Justus Doolittle, *Social Life of the Chinese*, 1:264.

64. James Watson, "Standardizing the Gods," 302.

65. Clark, *The Sinitic Encounter*, 144.

66. Qu Dajun, *Guangdong xinyu*, 201–202; Qian Yikai, *Linghai jianwen*, 38; and fieldnotes from Leizhou and Hainan, June 2011.

67. Brigitte Baptandier, *The Lady of Linshui*, 162–164.

68. Zeng Huijuan, "From Sheds to Houses," 165, 171n13; and Huang Xiangchun, "Going Beyond Pariah Status," 147. See also Baptandier, *The Lady of Linshui*, on other female deities who assisted women in childbirth.

69. Keith Stevens, "The Popular Religion Gods of the Hainanese," 54–56.

70. Irwin, "Divinity and Salvation," 59.

71. Fieldnotes from Leizhou, June 2011, and December 2013.

Chapter 8

1. *Gongzhongdang*, JQ 13.5.25.

2. Fieldnotes from Weizhou, January 2010; Guo Fei, *Yue daji*, 32:529; and Chen Xujing, *Danmin de yanjiu*, 111.

3. Chen Xianbo, "Ming Qing Huanan haidao de jingying yu kaifa," 91.

Notes

4. Fieldnotes from Weizhou, January 2010; and Chen Xianbo, "Ming Qing Huanan haidao de jingying yu kaifa," 90–91.

5. The history of this stele is interesting. During the Cultural Revolution, it was removed from its original site to the nearby fish market where it was used as a cutting board. Only later in the 1980s did local cadre rediscover the stele and move it back to the Sanpo Temple.

6. Chen Xujing, *Danmin de yanjiu*, 112, 115; and *Guangdong shengzhi dashiji*, 103.

7. See Chen Xianbo, "Ming Qing Huanan haidao de jingying yu kaifa," 96–97; and Robert Antony, "Violence and Predation on the Sino-Vietnamese Maritime Frontier," 105–107.

8. Fieldnotes from the Xiajiang Tianhou Temple, April 2012, and from Shanwei village, January 2009.

9. Fieldnotes from the Shanwei village and Xiajiang Tianhou Temple, Leizhou, January 2009.

10. *Xu Xiu Siku Quanshu*, 20:30a–b.

11. See, for example, Weng Kuan, "Qinzhou San Niang wan shihua."

12. Fieldnotes from Qinzhou, Fangcheng, Jiangping, and Dongxing, June 2011. See also the discussion about the Jing minority in the postlude.

13. On the relationship between pirates and fishers, see Robert Antony, *Like Froth Floating on the Sea*, chapter 4.

14. Wushi Er and members of his family had settled on Weizhou island probably in the late eighteenth century and his father was buried on the island. Incidentally, in 1808 Qing soldiers desecrated his father's grave when they drove the pirates away. Also, in their home village, named Wushi, on the west side of the Leizhou peninsula, there is a Qinghui (Sanpo) Temple, but its date of origin is unknown. Villagers simply told me that it was several centuries old. It is possible that Wushi Er or other members of his family brought the Sanpo cult to their home village in Leizhou.

15. Yuan Yonglun, *Jing haifen ji*, 1:6b. The author's mention of Huizhou as the site of a Sanpo Temple, however, may have been a mistake, as there is no evidence of the Sanpo cult in that area. Perhaps Yuan confused the name Huizhou with Weizhou, which in Cantonese have remarkably similar pronunciations.

16. In Fujian, according to Judith Boltz ("In Homage to T'ien-fei," 211n1), Mazu was the shortened form of Mazupo, in which *po* means "grandmother," and therefore a term of familiarity, not disrespect.

17. Fieldnotes from Taipa, Macau, March 2009, and from Lantao, Hong Kong, October 2009; on Xiangshan, see *Xiangshan xianzhi*, 22:80a–b.

18. While much of the same can be said about Tianhou, the major difference was that Sanpo never had a large multi-province or overseas following; Sanpo remained very much a local deity in only a few communities in coastal Guangdong.

19. *Xiangshan xianzhi*, 22:80a–b.

20. When I interviewed Ms. Liu she was in her eighties and frail, but her mind was still sharp and she willingly told me a great deal about her life and sufferings during the Cultural Revolution; fieldnotes from Shanwei village, March 2010.

21. Fieldnotes from Caoyang village, April 2009; Shanwei village and Xiajiang Tianhou Temple, August 2010; and Xibian village and Leizhou City, February 2010.

22. Fieldnotes from the Sanpo Temple on Weizhou island, January 2010. On the preservation of local beliefs as intangible cultural heritage, see Gao Bingzhong, "The Social Movement of Safeguarding Intangible Cultural Heritage and the End of Cultural Revolutions in China"; and You Ziying, *Folk Literati, Contested Tradition, and Heritage in Contemporary China*, especially chapter 6.

23. For background on the turmoil in Guangdong between the 1840s and 1860s, see Laai Yi-Faai, "The Part Played by the Pirates of Kwangtung and Kwangsi Provinces in the Taiping Insurrection"; Frederic Wakeman, *Strangers at the Gate*; and Liu Ping, *Bei yiwang de zhanzheng*. See also my discussion in the second interlude about the Red Turban uprising and the Hakka-Punti War.

24. Information taken from the 1859 stone inscription, Taipa Sanpo Temple, Macau, recorded in May 2013. See also He Weijie, "Miaoyu, zujun shenfen yu shequ fazhan de shehui huayu," 63–64. This inscription had been commissioned by Dan fishers belonging to the Wing On Hall (Yongantang), a local fishing guild.

25. On the British navy's expedition against pirates, see Beresford Scott, *An Account of the Destruction of the Fleets of the Celebrated Pirate Chieftains Chui-Apoo and Shap-ng Tsai*.

26. Fieldnotes from Weizhou, January 2010.

27. In another story from Weizhou, Sanpo aided the Qing navy to suppress the pirate Wushi Er in 1810.

28. Fieldnotes from Weizhou, January 2010; from Qinzhou and Dongxing, June 2011; and from Lantao island, Hong Kong, October 2009.

29. See further discussion in the postlude.

30. Fieldnotes from Taipa, April 2015; and He Weijie, "Miaoyu, zujun shenfen yu shequ fazhan de shehui huayu," 71. Today in Taipa there still is a Sanpo temple but no Sanpo cult associated with it.

31. Fieldnotes from Shanwei village and Leizhou City, March and August 2010.

Postlude

1. See, for example, Maighna Nanu, "Chinese Government Tells People to Stop Sharing Food Over Outbreak Fears"; Andy Boreham, "Chopstick Revolution"; and Amy Qin, "Coronavirus Threatens China's Devotion to Chopsticks." On the history and culture of chopsticks, see Q. Edward Wang, *Chopsticks*.

2. See, for example, Daniel Bell, *China's New Confucianism*; and on the recent popularization of Confucianism in China, see Sebastien Billioud and Joel Thoraval, *The Sage and the People*.

3. Damien Ma, "Beijing's 'Culture War.'"

4. James Hunter, *Culture Wars*, 52.

5. Taking the long view of China's history, Hugh Clark has persuasively argued that what we call Chinese civilization actually resulted from thousands of years of accommodation, assimilation, and cross-cultural encounters with indigenous non-Sinitic peoples and cultures; see Clark, *The Sinitic Encounter*.

Notes

6. Yiching Wu, *The Cultural Revolution at the Margins*, 48. On the slogan "ox-demons and snake-spirits," see Michael Schoenhals, "Demonizing Discourse in Mao Zedong's China"; and Yang Xiguang, *Niugui sheshen lu*.

7. Barend ter Haar, "China's Inner Demons," 57–58.

8. Robert Antony, "Spectacles of Violence in China," 626.

9. Donald Sutton, "From Credulity to Scorn," 16, 18, 25, 36; and Ann Anagnost, "Politics and Magic in Contemporary China," 44–45; see also chapter 4 in this book.

10. See Sarah Schneewind, "Competing Institutions."

11. J. J. M. de Groot, *Sectarianism and Religious Persecution in China*, 268, 283.

12. Qu Dajun, *Guangdong xinyu*, 208–209, 215–219, 302–303; and Zhang Qu, *Yuedong wenjianlu*, 49, 68–69.

13. See Geremie Barmé, "Spiritual Pollution Thirty Years On"; and Kevin Carrico, "Eliminating Spiritual Pollution."

14. See "Religious Faith Is Protected by Law."

15. Anagnost, "Politics and Magic in Contemporary China," 59n3; and Eleanor Albert and Lindsay Maizland, "The State of Religion in China."

16. See the discussions in David Ownby, "Redemptive Societies in China's Long Twentieth Century"; and David Palmer, "Heretical Doctrines, Reactionary Secret Societies, Evil Cults."

17. Palmer, "Heretical Doctrines, Reactionary Secret Societies, Evil Cults," 119–120, 124–125.

18. Ibid., 127; and on the Falungong, see David Ownby, *Falun Gong and the Future of China*.

19. *Qigong* (life energy cultivation) is a traditional Chinese system of breathing control, physical exercise, and meditation used for the purposes of health, spirituality, and martial-arts training. See David Palmer, *Qigong Fever*.

20. Benjamin Penny, "Falun Gong, Prophesy and Apocalypse," 150–151, 157, 165–168; and on toads and crocodiles, see Henry Doré, *Researches into Chinese Superstitions*, 5:646.

21. See Li Geng, "Divination, *Yijing*, and Cultural Nationalism"; William Matthews, "Making 'Science' from 'Superstition,'" 176–178; Jean DeBernardi, "The God of War and the Vagabond Buddha," 326–327; and Avon Boretz, "Martial Gods and Magic Swords," 103.

22. P. Steven Sangren, "Orthodoxy, Heterodoxy, and the Structure of Value in Chinese Rituals," 83; see also DeBernardi, "The God of War and the Vagabond Buddha," 310–311.

23. Michael Szonyi, "Making Claims about Standardization and Orthopraxy in Late Imperial China," 49–53; and Qu Dajun, *Guangdong xinyu*, 208–209.

24. Qu Dajun, *Guangdong xinyu*, 215; David Faure, "The Emperor in the Village," 92–94; Sutton, "From Credulity to Scorn," 22; and fieldnotes from the Jinhua Ancient Temple in the Huangpu district of Guangzhou, March 2017.

25. Terry Kleeman, "Licentious Cults and Bloody Victuals," 197, 205–206; Schneewind, "Competing Institutions," 100–101; Boretz, "Martial Gods and Magic Swords," 103–104; and Szonyi, "Making Claims about Standardization and Orthopraxy in Late Imperial China," 62–64.

26. Megan Ferry, "Marketing Chinese Women Writers in the 1990s," 655–666, 672–673.
27. On the sexual revolution in Shanghai in the 1990s, see James Farrer, *Opening Up*.
28. See Xiao Zhiwen, Purnima Mehrotra, Rick Zimmerman, "Sexual Revolution in China"; Kristina Sivelle, "Chinese Women and Their Contraceptive Choices"; and "Chinese Women Change Attitudes Towards Sexual Life."
29. Quoted in Alyssa Abkowitz, "More and More Chinese People Are Having Pre-Marital Sex."
30. Xu Anqi, "Beidongxing juezequan he di manyidu," 105–108; Shelley Chan, "Sex for Sex's Sake?," 55; Ferry, "Marketing Chinese Women Writers in the 1990s," 666; and Lin Zhongxuan, "Individualizing the Sexual Revolution in China," 448.
31. Paola Paderni, "I Thought I Would Have Some Happy Days"; and Janet Theiss, *Disgraceful Matters*. See also Matthew Sommer, *Sex, Law, and Society in Late Imperial China* and *Polyandry and Wife-Selling in Qing Dynasty China*.
32. Zhang Yingjin, *The City in Modern Chinese Literature and Film*, 212–217; see also Lisa Snowden, "Chinese Déjà Vu."
33. Ferry, "Marketing Chinese Women Writers in the 1990s," 671, 673; Lin Zhongxuan, "Individualizing the Sexual Revolution in China," 449; Snowden, "Chinese Déjà Vu," 61–62, 97; Kay Schaffer and Xianlin Song, "Unruly Spaces," 21–24; James Farrer, "China's Women Sex Bloggers," 10–14, 23–24; and Jeroen de Kloet, *China with a Cut*, 112–118.
34. Chan, "Sex for Sex's Sake?," 56; and Farrer, "China's Women Sex Bloggers," 14–19.
35. See "Chinese President Xi Jinping Warns against 'Immoral' Art."
36. Mary Douglas, *Purity and Danger*, 36–37, 100.
37. See Theiss, *Disgraceful Matters*, 133, 142.
38. See Gail Hershatter, "Sex Work and Social Order"; and chapter 7 in this book.
39. Charlotte Furth, "Blood, Body and Gender," 43.
40. See Emily Ahern, "The Power and Pollution of Chinese Women"; Patricia Shih, "Female Pollution in Chinese Society"; and Cordia Chu, "Menstrual Beliefs and Practices of Chinese Women." On death pollution in Cantonese society, see James Watson, "Of Flesh and Bones."
41. Ahern, "The Power and Pollution of Chinese Women," 278.
42. For a useful overview of the magical properties of menstrual blood, see Shih, "Female Pollution in Chinese Society," 90–99.
43. Paul Cohen, *History in Three Keys*, 130–132, 138–144. On the Wang Lun Rebellion, see Susan Naquin, *Shantung Rebellion*.
44. See Hyeon Jung Lee, "Fearless Love, Death for Dignity"; Joseph Lau, "The Courage to Be: Suicide as Self-Fulfillment in Chinese History and Literature"; and Margery Wolf, "Women and Suicide in China."
45. Ferry, "Marketing Chinese Women Writers in the 1990s," 668, 670.
46. Lena Scheen, *Shanghai Literary Imaginings*, 204–205.
47. C. Zhao, "From Punk to Environmentalist: The Return of Chun Shu."
48. Schaffer and Song, "Unruly Spaces," 25–26.
49. Kloet, *China with a Cut*, 111–113.

50. Fieldnotes from Wanwei, Guangxi, July 2011; for printed versions of this story, see Cheung Siu-woo, "Regional Development and Cross-Border Cultural Linkages," 281–282; "Sandao de laili"; and "Guanyu Jingzu Sandao youzhao zenyang de chuanshuo."

51. Cheung, "Regional Development and Cross-Border Cultural Linkages," 282.

52. Ma Muchi, "Bianyuan qunti de renting," 41–42; also see Cheung, "Regional Development and Cross-Border Cultural Linkages," 287.

53. Ma Muchi, "Bianyuan qunti de renting," 42.

54. On the PRC's ethnic classification campaign, see Thomas Mullaney, *Coming to Terms with the Nation*.

55. Fieldnotes from Wutou, Wanwei, and Shanxin in Guangxi, July and August 2011.

56. See, for example, Norma Diamond, "The Miao and Poison," 19–20; Anne Csete, "A Frontier Minority in the Chinese World," 170–173; Vanessa Frangville, "The Non-Han in Socialist Cinema and Contemporary Films in the People's Republic of China," 63–64; and James Leibold, *Ethnic Policy in China*, 38–39. On the Yao, see chapter 6. Much of what I have to say in this section about ethnic relations, of course, does not apply to the current situation in Xinjiang and Tibet; however, discussion on this important topic is beyond the scope of this book, which mainly concerns southern China.

57. Stevan Harrell, "Introduction: Civilizing Projects and the Reactions to Them," 10–13; Diamond, "The Miao and Poison," 18–19; Yujie Zhu, *Heritage and Romantic Consumption in China*, 50–53; Anouska Komlosy, "Feminization, Recognition, and the Cosmological in Xishuangbanna," 129–130; and Ma Muchi, "Bianyuan qunti de renting," 34–35. On the Dan, see chapter 7.

58. Harrell, "Introduction: Civilizing Projects and the Reactions to Them," 4.

59. See, for example, Fiskesjö, "On the 'Raw' and 'Cooked' Barbarians of Imperial China," 141, 151; C. Pat Giersch, "A Motley Throng," 86; and Harrell, "Introduction: Civilizing Projects and the Reactions to Them," 18–19, 26.

60. Harrell, "Introduction: Civilizing Projects and the Reactions to Them," 23–24; Chen Meiwen, "Constructed History: Ethnic Yao in Modern China," 93, 96–97; Anne-Marie Brady, "We Are All Part of the Same Family," 162; Leibold, *Ethnic Policy in China*, 3–6, 47; Leibold, "Planting the Seeds"; and Xi Jinping, "Zai quanguo minzu tuanjie jinbu biaozhang dahuishang de jianghua."

61. Giersch, "A Motley Throng," 73, 85–88; Csete, "A Frontier Minority in the Chinese World," 218–221; and Diamond, "The Miao and Poison," 20–21. See also chapter 6 in this book.

62. Juwen Zhang, *Oral Traditions in Contemporary China*, 49.

63. See, for example, Yujie Zhu, *Heritage and Romantic Consumption in China*, 29–31.

64. Harriet Evans, "Threads of Time in a Small Naxi Village," 198.

65. Timothy Oakes, "Ethnic Tourism in Rural Guizhou," 36, 42; quote on p. 65. On the Jing, see Cheung, "Regional Development and Cross-Border Cultural Linkages," 285–286. See also Gao Bingzhong, "The Social Movement of Safeguarding Intangible Cultural Heritage and the End of Cultural Revolutions in China."

66. See Katherine Robinson, "Robert Frost: 'The Road Not Taken.'"

Bibliography

Abkowitz, Alyssa. "More and More Chinese People Are Having Pre-Marital Sex." *Wall Street Journal*, April 16, 2015. https://blogs.wsj.com/chinarealtime/2015 04 16/more-and-more-chinese-people-are-having-pre-marital-sex.

Ahern, Emily M. "The Power and Pollution of Chinese Women." In *Studies in Chinese Society*, edited by Arthur P. Wolf, 269–290. Stanford: Stanford University Press, 1978.

Albert, Eleanor, and Lindsay Maizland. "The State of Religion in China." Council on Foreign Relations, September 25, 2020. https://www.cfr.org/backgrounder/religion-china.

Alberts, Eli. "Commemorating the Ancestors' Merit: Myth, History, and Schema in the Charter of Emperor Ping." *Taiwan Journal of Anthropology* 9, no.1 (2011): 19–65.

———. *A History of Daoism and the Yao People of South China*. Youngstown, NY: Cambria Press, 2006.

Alger, Grant A. "The Floating Community of the Min: River Transport, Society and the State in China, 1758–1889." PhD diss., Johns Hopkins University, 2002.

Altenburger, Roland. *The Sword or the Needle: The Female Knight-Errant (xia) in Traditional Chinese Narrative*. Bern: Peter Lang, 2009.

Alver, Brynjulf. "Historical Legends and Historical Truths." In *Nordic Folklore: Recent Studies*, edited by Reimund Kvideland and Henning Schmsdorf, 137–149. Bloomington: Indiana University Press, 1989.

Amar, Nathanel. "'Do You Freestyle?' The Roots of Censorship in Chinese Hip-hop." *China Perspectives* 1–2, no. 113 (2018): 107–114.

Anagnost, Ann. "Politics and Magic in Contemporary China." *Modern China* 13, no. 1 (1987): 40–61.

———. "The Beginning and End of an Emperor: A Counterrepresentation of the State." *Modern China* 11, no. 2 (1985): 147–176.

Anderson, Eugene N. *Floating World Lost: A Hong Kong Fishing Community*. New Orleans: University Press of the South, 2007.

———. "The Folksongs of the Hong Kong Boat People." *Journal of American Folklore* 80, no. 317 (1967): 285–296.

Antony, Robert J. "Spectacles of Violence in China." In *Cambridge World History of Violence, Vol. 3 (1500–1800)*, edited by Robert Antony, Stuart Carroll, and Caroline Pennock, 612–633. Cambridge: Cambridge University Press, 2020.

———. "Mountains, Rivers, and Sea: Canton and the Lianyang Trading System in Historical Perspective." *Journal of the Hong Kong Branch of the Royal Asiatic Society* 59 (2019): 51–75.

———. *Unruly People: Crime, Community, and State in Late Imperial South China*. Hong Kong: Hong Kong University Press, 2016.

———. "Violence and Predation on the Sino-Vietnamese Maritime Frontier, 1450–1850." *Asia Major*, Third Series, 27, no. 2 (2014): 87–114.

———. "Bloodthirsty Pirates? Violence and Terror on the South China Sea in Early Modern Times," *Journal of Early Modern History* 16, no. 6 (2012): 481–501.

———. "Piracy and the Shadow Economy in the South China Sea, 1780–1810." In *Elusive Pirates, Pervasive Smugglers: Violence and Clandestine Trade in the Greater China Seas*, edited by Robert Antony, 99–114. Hong Kong: Hong Kong University Press, 2010.

———. *Like Froth Floating on the Sea: The World of Pirates and Seafarers in Late Imperial South China*. Berkeley: University of California, Institute of East Asian Studies, China Research Monograph, no. 56, 2003.

———. "Brotherhoods, Secret Societies, and the Law in Qing-Dynasty China." In *Secret Societies Reconsidered: Studies in the Social History of Early Modern China and Southeast Asia*, edited by David Ownby and Mary Somers Heldhues, 190–211. Armonk, NY: M. E. Sharpe, 1993.

———. "Peasants, Heroes, and Brigands: The Problems of Social Banditry in Early Nineteenth-Century South China." *Modern China* 15, no. 2 (1989): 123–148.

———. "Pirates, Bandits, and Brotherhoods: A study of Crime and Law in Kwangtung Province, 1796–1839," PhD diss., University of Hawai'i, 1988.

Arkush, R. David. "Orthodoxy and Heterodoxy in Twentieth-Century Peasant Proverbs." In *Orthodoxy in Late Imperial China*, edited by Kwang-ching Liu, 311–331. Berkeley: University of California Press, 1990.

Averill, Stephen C. *Revolution in the Highlands: China's Jinggangshan Base Area*. Lanham, MD: Rowman and Littlefield, 2006.

Baptandier, Brigitte. *The Lady of Linshui: A Chinese Female Cult*. Translated by Kristin Ingrid Fryklund. Stanford: Stanford University Press, 2008.

Barmé, Geremie. "Spiritual Pollution Thirty Years On." *The China Story Journal* 17 (2013). http://chinaheritage.net/archive/spiritual-pollution-thirty-years-on.

———. "Wang Shuo and *Liumang* ('Hooligan') Culture." *Australian Journal of Chinese Affairs* 28 (July 1992): 23–64.

Barrett, Timothy H. "The Religious Affiliations of the Chinese Cat: An Essay Towards an Anthropozoological Approach to Comparative Religion." London: London School of Oriental and African Studies, 1998.

Barrett, Timothy H., and Mark Strange. "Walking by Itself: The Singular History of the Chinese Cat." In *Animals through Chinese History: Earliest Times to 1911*, edited by Roel Sterckx, Martina Siebert, and Dagmar Schäfer, 84–98. New York: Cambridge University Press, 2019.

Barrow, John. *Travels in China: Containing Descriptions, Observations and Comparisons, Made and Collected in the Course of a Short Residence at the Imperial Palace of Yuen-Min-Yuen, and on a Subsequent Journey through the Country from Pekin to Canton*. First published 1804. Cambridge: Cambridge University Press, 2010.

Bell, Daniel. *China's New Confucianism: Politics and Everyday Life in a Changing Society*. Princeton: Princeton University Press, 2010.

Bianchi, Alice. "Ghost-Like Beggars in Chinese Painting: The Case of Zhou Chen." In *Fantômes dans l'Extrême-Orient d'hier et d'aujourd'hui*, tome 1, edited by Marie Laureillard and Vincent Durand-Dastès, 223–248. Paris: Presses de l'Inalco, 2017.
Billingsley, Phil. *Bandits in Republican China*. Stanford: Stanford University Press, 1988.
Billioud, Sebastien, and Joel Thoraval. *The Sage and the People: The Confucian Revival in China*. New York: Oxford University Press, 2015.
Blake, C. Fred. *Ethnic Groups and Social Change in a Chinese Market Town*. Honolulu: University Press of Hawai'i, 1981.
Bodde, Derk. *Festivals in Classical China*. Princeton: Princeton University Press, 1975.
———. "Translating Chinese Philosophical Terms." *The Far Eastern Quarterly* 14, no. 2 (1955): 231–244.
Boltz, Judith. "In Homage to T'ien-fei." *Journal of the American Oriental Society* 106 (1986): 211–132.
Boluo xianzhi 博羅縣志 [Gazetteer of Boluo county, Guangdong]. Beijing: Zhonghua shuju, 2001.
Boluo xianzhi 博羅縣志 [Gazetteer of Boluo county, Guangdong]. Boluo: Boluo yinshuachang, 1988.
Boreham, Andy. "Chopstick Revolution: How COVID-19 Might Change China's Eating Habits." *Shanghai Daily*, May 31, 2020. https://www.shine.cn/opinion/2005319260.
Boretz, Avon. *Gods, Ghosts, and Gangsters: Ritual Violence, Martial Arts, and Masculinity on the Margins of Chinese Society*. Honolulu: University of Hawai'i Press, 2011.
———. "Martial Gods and Magic Swords: Identity, Myth, and Violence in Chinese Popular Religion." *Journal of Popular Culture* 29, no. 1 (1995): 93–109.
Brady, Anne-Marie. "We Are All Part of the Same Family: China's Ethnic Propaganda." *Journal of Current Chinese Affairs* 41, no. 4 (2012): 159–181.
Brando, Marlon, with David Cammell. *Fantan*. New York: Alfred A. Knopf, 2007.
Brewer, John. "Microhistory and the Histories of Everyday Life." *Cultural and Social History* 7, no. 1 (2010): 87–109.
Bruun, Ole. *An Introduction to Feng Shui*. New York: Cambridge University Press, 2008.
Buoye, Thomas. "Bare Sticks and Naked Pity: Rhetoric and Representation in Qing Dynasty (1644–1911) Capital Case Records." *Crime, Histoire & Sociétés* 18, no. 2 (2014): 27–47.
Burke, Kenneth. *On Symbols and Society*. Edited by Joseph Gusfield. Chicago: University of Chicago Press, 1989.
Burke, Peter. *The Historical Anthropology of Early Modern Italy: Essays on Perception and Communication*. Cambridge: Cambridge University Press, 1987.
Cai Peichun 蔡佩春. "Taiguo Lin Guniang chuanshuo fenxi" 泰國林姑娘傳說分析 [A study of the Lin Guniang legend in Thailand]. *Journal of Changshu Institute of Technology (Philosophy and Social Sciences)* 6 (November 2019): 10–19.
Cai Tun 蔡屯. "Luelun Daoguang Jianghua Yaomin baodong zhi qiyin" 略論道光江華瑤民暴動之起因 [Causes of the Yao uprising in Jianghua in the Daoguang period]. *Minzu xuetan* 民族学探 4 (1992): 69–70.
Caldwell, Harry R. *Blue Tiger*. New York and Cincinnati: Abingdon Press, 1924.

Campa, Arthur L. "Folklore and History." *Western Folklore* 24, no. 1 (1965): 1–5.
Caniff, Milton. *Terry and the Pirates: Enter the Dragon Lady*. New York: Crown, 1976.
Canton Register. Macau and Canton, 1827–1843.
Cao shi zupu 曹氏族譜 [Cao family genealogy]. Shanwei village, Leizhou; unpaginated handwritten copy, dated 1894.
Cao sifang zhanbu 曹四房展簿 [Register of ancestral rites for the fourth branch of the Cao family]. Shanwei village, Leizhou; unpaginated handwritten copy, dated 1998.
Carrico, Kevin. "Eliminating Spiritual Pollution: A Genealogy of Closed Political Thought in China's Era of Opening." *The China Journal* 78 (2017): 100–119.
Cass, Victoria. *Dangerous Women: Warriors, Grannies, and Geishas of the Ming*. Lanham, MD: Rowman and Littlefield, 1999.
Chan, Shelley W. "Sex for Sex's Sake? The 'Genital Writings' of the Chinese Bad-Girl Writers." In *Asian Literary Voices: From Marginal to Mainstream*, edited by Philip F. Williams, 53–62. Amsterdam: Amsterdam University Press, 2010.
Chan, Wing-hoi. "Ethnic Labels in a Mountainous Region: The Case of She 'Bandits.'" In *Empire at the Margins: Culture, Ethnicity, and Frontier in Early Modern China*, edited by Pamela Crossley, Helen Siu, and Donald Sutton, 255–284. Berkeley: University of California Press, 2006.
Chao, Leon. "The Resurgence of Organized Crime in China." *Chinascope* (June 2006): 8–17.
Chen Baoliang 陳寶良. *Zhongguo de she yu hui* 中國的社與會 [On Chinese *she* and *hui*]. Taibei: Nantian shuju, 1998.
———. *Zhongguo liumang shi* 中國流氓史 [History of Chinese hooligans]. Beijing: Zhongguo shehui kexue chubanshe, 1993.
Chen Chunsheng 陳春生. "Shiliu shiji Min Yue jiaojie diyu haishang huodong renqun de tezhi: yi Wu Ping de yanjiu wei zhongxin" 十六世紀閩粵交界地域海上活動人群的特質: 以吳平的研究為中心 [Characteristics of people's activities on the seas on the border of Fujian and Guangdong in the sixteenth century: The case of Wu Ping]. *Haiyang shi yanjiu* 海洋史研究 1 (October 2010): 129–152.
Chen, Fan Pen. "Ritual Roots of the Theatrical Prohibitions of Late-Imperial China." *Asia Major*, Third Series, 20, no. 1 (2007): 25–44.
———. "Forbidden Fruits: Ethnicity and Gender in Prohibitions on Performances in Late Imperial China." *CHINOPERL* 25, no. 1 (2004): 35–85.
Chen Fangqi 陳芳奇. "Chen Jinjiang lingdao de tiandihui yu hongbing qiyi shiji" 陳金江領導的天地會與洪兵起義史記 [Historical records on Chen Jinjiang leading the Tiandihui and Hongbing uprisings]. Lianzhou, photocopy, dated 2000.
Chen, Han-seng. *Landlord and Peasant in China: A Study of the Agrarian Crisis in South China*. New York: International Publishers, 1936.
Chen, Huiying. "Dangers on the Road: Travelers, *Laoguazei*, and the State in Eighteenth-Century North China." *Late Imperial China* 40, no. 1 (2019): 87–132.
Ch'en, Jerome. "The Nature and Characteristics of the Boxer Movement: A Morphological Study." *Bulletin of the School of Oriental and African Studies* 23, no. 2 (1960): 287–308.

Chen, Meiwen. "Constructed History: Ethnic Yao in Modern China." *Leidschrift* 26, no. 1 (2011): 93–108.

Chen shi zupu 陳氏族譜 [Chen family genealogy]. Boluo, written in 1833, unpaginated handwritten copy with additional notes, dated 1999.

Chen shi zupu Lianzhou Longtan Tiandeng Xisi xi 陳氏族譜連州龍潭田橙蓆四系 [Chen family genealogy of descendants of Xisi in Tiandeng village, Longtan, Lianzhou], photocopy, dated 1999.

Chen shi zupu fuben 陳氏族譜副本 [Addendum to the Chen family genealogy]. Lianzhou, photocopy, dated 2000.

Chen Shunxi 陳舜系. *Luanli jianwen lu* 亂離見聞錄 [A record of the chaos and abandonment seen and heard]. In *Ming Qing Guangdong xijian biji qizhong* 明清廣東稀見筆記七種 [Seven types of rare miscellaneous writings from Guangdong in the Ming and Qing periods], edited by Li Longqian 李龍潛 et al., 1–47. Guangzhou: Guangdong renmin chubanshe, 2010.

Chen Weiyan 陳微言. *Nanyue youji* 南越游記 [A record of travels in southern Guangdong]. Preface dated 1850. Guangzhou: Guangdong gaodeng jiaoyu chubanshe, 1990.

Chen Xianbo 陳賢波. "Ming Qing Huanan haidao de jingying yu kaifa: yi Beibuwan Weizhou dao weili" 明清華南海島的經營與開發:以北部灣潿洲島為例 [The management of south China islands from the Ming to the Qing: A case study of Weizhou island in the Gulf of Tonkin]. *Mingdai yanjiu* 明代研究 15 (2010): 85–117.

Chen Xujing 陳序經. *Danmin de yanjiu* 蛋民的研究 [A study of the Dan boat people]. First published 1948. Taipei: Dongfang wenhua shuju, 1971.

Cheng, Wei-chung. *War, Trade and Piracy in the China Seas, 1622–1683*. Leiden: Brill, 2013.

Chengmai xianzhi 澄邁縣志 [Gazetteer of Chengmai county]. Qing Guangxu edition. Haikou: Hainan chubanshe, 2004.

Chesneaux, Jean, ed. *Popular Movements and Secret Societies in China, 1840–1950*. Stanford: Stanford University Press, 1972.

———. "The Modern Relevance of *Shui-hu chuan*: Its Influence on Rebel Movements in Nineteenth- and Twentieth-Century China." *Papers on Far Eastern History* 3 (1971): 1–26.

Cheung, Siu-woo. "Regional Development and Cross-Border Cultural Linkages: The Case of a Vietnamese Community in Guangxi, China." In *Where China Meets Southeast Asia: Social and Cultural Change in the Border Regions*, edited by Grant Evans, Christopher Hutton, Kuah Khun Eng, 277–311. New York: St. Martin's Press, 2000.

———. "Millenarianism, Christian Movements, and Ethnic Change among the Miao in Southwest China." In *Cultural Encounters on China's Ethnic Frontiers*, edited by Stevan Harrell, 217–247. Hong Kong: Hong Kong University Press, 1996.

"Chinese President Xi Jinping Warns against 'Immoral' Art." *BBC News*, October 16, 2014. https://www.bbc.com/news/entertainment-arts-29645574.

Chinese Repository. Macau and Canton, 1832–1851.

Bibliography

"Chinese Women Change Attitudes Towards Sexual Life: Survey." *People's Daily*, September 21, 2003. https://www.china.org.cn/english/2003/Sep/75623.htm.

Chu, Cordia Ming-Yeuk. "Menstrual Beliefs and Practices of Chinese Women." *Journal of the Folklore Institute* 17, no. 1 (1980): 38–55.

Clark, Hugh R. *The Sinitic Encounter in Southeast China through the First Millennium CE.* Honolulu: University of Hawai'i Press, 2016.

Cohen, Myron. "The Hakka or 'Guest People': Dialect as a Sociocultural Variable in Southeastern China." *Ethnohistory* 15, no. 3 (1968): 237–292.

Cohen, Paul A. *History in Three Keys: The Boxers as Event, Experience, and Myth.* New York: Columbia University Press, 1997.

Constable, Nicole. "Christianity and Hakka Identity." In *Christianity in China from the Eighteenth Century to the Present*, edited by Daniel Bays, 158–174. Stanford: Stanford University Press, 1996.

Cowan, Douglas. *Magic, Monsters, and Make-Believe Heroes: How Myth and Religion Shape Fantasy Culture.* Berkeley: University of California Press, 2019.

Croizer, Ralph C. *Koxinga and Chinese Nationalism: History, Myth, and the Hero.* Cambridge, MA: Harvard University Press, 1977.

Crossley, Pamela. "Thinking about Ethnicity in Early Modern China." *Late Imperial China* 11, no. 1 (1990): 1–35.

Csete, Anne Alice. "A Frontier Minority in the Chinese World: The Li People of Hainan Island from the Han through the High Qing." PhD diss., University of New York at Buffalo, 1995.

Cushman, Richard D. "Rebel Haunts and Lotus Huts: Problems in the Ethnohistory of the Yao." PhD diss., Cornell University, 1970.

Dai Xuanzhi 戴玄之. "Tiandihui yu daojiao" 天地會與道教 [The Heaven and Earth Society and Daoism]. *Nanyang daxue xuebao* 南洋大學學報 6 (1972): 156–161.

Darnton, Robert. "The Symbolic Element in History." *Journal of Modern History* 58, no. 1 (1986): 218–234.

———. *The Great Cat Massacre and Other Episodes in French Cultural History.* New York: Vintage Books, 1985.

DeBernardi, Jean. "The God of War and the Vagabond Buddha." *Modern China* 13, no. 3 (1987): 310–332.

Deng, Xiaogang, and Ann Cordilia. "To Get Rich Is Glorious: Rising Expectations, Declining Control, and Escalating Crime in Contemporary China." *International Journal of Offender Therapy and Comparative Criminology* 43, no. 2 (1999): 211–229.

Deng Yong 鄧永. "Wangcheng'ao de chuanshuo" 王城坳的傳說 [The legends of the King's City]. In *Fangcheng gang wenhua yichan congshu: lishi wenhua yichan bufen* 防城港文化遺產叢書:歷史文化遺產部分 [Anthology on the cultural heritage of the port of Fangcheng: Section on history and cultural heritage], edited by Zhu Haiyan 朱海燕, 40–41. Nanning: Guangxi renmin chubanshe, 2009.

Dennys, Nicholas B. *The Folk-Lore of China.* London: Trubner and Co., 1876.

Diamond, Norma. "The Miao and Poison: Interactions on China's Southwest Frontier." *Ethnology* 27, no. 1 (1988): 1–25.

Ding Shumei 丁淑梅. *Zhongguo gudai jinhui xiju biannian shi* 中国古代禁毁戲劇编年史 [History of ancient Chinese banned and destroyed dramas]. Chongqing: Chongqing daxue chubanshe, 2014.

Doolittle, Justus. *Social Life of the Chinese.* 2 vols. New York: Harper and Bros., 1865.

Doran, Rebecca. "The Cat Demon, Gender, and Religious Practice: Towards Reconstructing a Medieval Chinese Cultural Pattern." *Journal of the American Oriental Society* 135, no. 4 (2015): 689–707.

Doré, Henry. *Researches into Chinese Superstitions.* Translated by M. Kennelly. 13 vols. Shanghai: T'usewei Printing Press, 1914–1938.

Douglas, Mary. *Purity and Danger: An Analysis of Concepts of Pollution and Taboo.* London: Routledge and K. Paul, 1966.

DuBois, Thomas D., and Jan Kiely, eds., *Fieldwork in Modern Chinese History: A Research Guide.* New York: Routledge, 2020.

Dutton, Michael. "Basic Character of Crime in Contemporary China." *China Quarterly* 149 (1997): 160–177.

Eberhard, Wolfram. *A Dictionary of Chinese Symbols: Hidden Symbols in Chinese Life and Thought.* Translated by G. L. Campbell. New York: Routledge, 1993.

———. *Studies in Chinese Folklore and Related Essays.* Bloomington: Indiana University Research Center for the Language Sciences, 1970.

———. *The Local Cultures of South and East China.* Translated by Alide Eberhard. Leiden: E. J. Brill, 1968.

———. "The Political Function of Astronomy and Astronomers in Han China." In *Chinese Thought and Institutions*, edited by John Fairbank, 33–70. Chicago: University of Chicago Press, 1957.

Edwards, Louise. *Women Warriors and Wartime Spies of China.* Cambridge: Cambridge University Press, 2016.

Eitel, Ernest J. *Feng-Shui, or the Rudiments of Natural Science in China.* Hong Kong: Lane, Crawford and Co., 1873.

Evans, Harriet. "Threads of Time in a Small Naxi Village: Women, Weaving and Gendered Dimensions of Local Cultural Heritage." In *Grassroots Values and Local Cultural Heritage in China*, edited by Harriet Evans and Michael Rowlands, 183–207. Lanham, MD: Lexington Books, 2021.

Fan Duanang 范端昂. *Yue zhong jianwen* 粵中見聞 [Things seen and heard in Guangdong]. Preface dated 1777. Guangzhou: Guangdong gaodeng jiaoyu chubanshe, 1988.

Fangcheng xianzhi chugao 防城縣志初稿 [Draft gazetteer of Fangcheng county, Guangdong]. Minguo edition. Guangzhou: Guangzhou chubanshe, 2000.

Farge, Arlette. *The Allure of the Archives.* Translated by Thomas Scott-Railton. New Haven: Yale University Press, 2013.

Farrer, James. "China's Women Sex Bloggers and Dialogic Sexual Politics on the Chinese Internet." *Journal of Current Chinese Affairs* 4 (2007): 1–36.

———. *Opening Up: Youth Sex Culture and Market Reform in Shanghai.* Chicago: University of Chicago Press, 2002.

Faure, David. "Introduction." In *Chieftains into Ancestors: Imperial Expansion and Indigenous Society in Southwest China*, edited by David Faure and Ho Ts'ui-p'ing, 1–21. Vancouver: University of British Columbia Press, 2013.

———. *Emperor and Ancestor: State and Lineage in South China*. Stanford: Stanford University Press, 2007.

———. "The Yao Wars in the Mid-Ming and Their Impact on Yao Ethnicity." In *Empire at the Margins: Culture, Ethnicity, and Frontier in Early Modern China*, edited by Pamela Crossley, Helen Siu, and Donald Sutton, 171–189. Berkeley: University of California Press, 2006.

———. "The Emperor in the Village: Representing the State in South China." *Journal of the Hong Kong Branch of the Royal Asiatic Society* 35 (1995): 75–112.

———. "Written and the Unwritten: The Political Agenda of the Written Genealogy." In *Family Process and Political Process in Modern Chinese History*, edited by the Institute of Modern History, Academia Sinica, 259–296. Nangang: Academia Sinica, 1992.

———. *The Structure of Chinese Rural Society: Lineage and Village in the Eastern New Territories*. Hong Kong: Oxford University Press, 1986.

Faure, David, Bernard H. K. Luk, and Alice Ngai-ha Lun Ng. "The Hong Kong Region According to Historical Inscriptions." In *From Village to City: Studies in the Traditional Roots of Hong Kong Society*, edited by David Faure, James Hayes, and Alan Birch, 43–54. Hong Kong: Centre of Asian Studies, University of Hong Kong, 1984.

Fei, Xiaotong. "Fifty Years Investigation in Yao Mountains." In *The Yao of South China: Recent International Studies*, edited by Jacques Lemoine and Chiao Chien, 17–36. Paris: Pangu, 1991.

Feng Qing 馮慶. "Cong Shuihu dao xiha: shuochang wenhua yu Zhongguo jianghu" 從水滸到嘻哈:說唱文化與中國江湖 [From *Water Margin* to hip-hop: Rap culture and China's *jianghu*]. *Jiemian wenhua* 界面文化 2 (2017). https://www.sohu.com/a/169030139_99897611.

Fengshui xingqi mingxue mijue 風水形氣命學秘訣 [Secret arts of geomantic motifs for determining ones fate]. Guangdong, handwritten copy, dated 1875.

Ferguson, R. Brian, and Neil L. Whitehead. *War in the Tribal Zone: Expanding States and Indigenous Warfare*, Second printing. Santa Fe: School of American Research Press, 2000.

Ferry, Megan M. "Marketing Chinese Women Writers in the 1990s, or the Politics of Self-Fashioning." *Journal of Contemporary China* 12, no. 37 (2003): 655–675.

Fiskesjö, Magnus. "On the 'Raw' and 'Cooked' Barbarians of Imperial China." *Inner Asia* 1 (1999): 139–168.

Fitzgerald, John. "Continuity within Discontinuity: The Case of *Water Margin* Mythology." *Modern China* 12, no. 3 (1986): 361–400.

FO 931/1089. "List of 45 bandits known to be active in the district subdivisions of Shawan and Chiao-t'ang in P'an-yü district," dated c. 1850s. Foreign Office Records, British National Archives, Kew, London.

Foshan ribao 佛山日報 [Foshan Daily], August 22, 2018.

Foster, Paul B. "Jin Yong and the Kungfu Industrial Complex." *Chinese Literature Today* 8, no. 2 (2019): 68–76.
Frangville, Vanessa. "The Non-Han in Socialist Cinema and Contemporary Films in the People's Republic of China." *China Perspectives* 2 (June 4, 2012): 61–69.
French, Paul. *City of Devils: The Two Men Who Ruled the Underworld of Old Shanghai.* New York: Picador, 2018.
Friedman, Jonathan. "Myth, History, and Political Identity." *Cultural Anthropology* 7, no. 2 (1992): 194–210.
"Fudu niao de chuanshuo" 夫毒鳥的傳說 [The legend of the *fudu* bird]. In *Fangcheng xian minjian gushiji* 防城縣民間故事集 [Anthology of folk stories from Fangcheng county, Guangxi], edited by Zhou Minsheng 周民生 et al., 357–358. Nanning: Fangcheng xian minjian wenxue, 1988.
Furth, Charlotte. "Blood, Body and Gender: Medical Images of the Female Condition in China, 1600–1850." *Chinese Science* 7 (1986): 43–66.
Gao, Bingzhong. "The Social Movement of Safeguarding Intangible Cultural Heritage and the End of Cultural Revolutions in China." *Western Folklore* 76, no. 2 (2017): 167–80.
Gargan, Edward. "Chinese Press Battles 'Surge of Bad Books.'" *The Globe and Mail* (Canada), August 3, 1987.
Ge, Liangyan. *Out of the Margins: The Rise of Chinese Vernacular Fiction*. Honolulu: University of Hawai'i Press, 2001.
Geertz, Clifford. "'From the Native's Point of View': On the Nature of Anthropological Understanding." *Bulletin of the American Academy of Arts and Sciences* 28, no. 1 (1974): 26–45.
———. *The Interpretation of Cultures: Selected Essays*. New York: Basic Books, 1973.
Gerritsen, Anne. "From Demon to Deity: Kang Wang in Thirteenth-Century Jizhou and Beyond." *T'oung Pao*, Second Series, 90, nos. 1–3 (2004): 1–31.
———. "Visions of Local Culture: Tales of the Strange and Temple Inscriptions from Song-Yuan Jizhou." *Journal of Chinese Religions* 28 (2000): 69–92.
Giersch, C. Pat. "'A Motley Throng': Social Change on Southwest China's Early Modern Frontier, 1700–1800." *Journal of Asian Studies* 60, no. 1 (2001): 67–94.
Gilbert, Rodney. "The Lotus Life of Macao." *The North-China Herald*, May 6, 1922.
Goldman, Merle. "The Media Campaign as a Weapon in Political Struggle: The Dictatorship of the Proletariat and *Water Margin* Campaigns." In *Moving a Mountain: Cultural Change in China*, edited by Godwin C. Chu and Francis L. K. Hsu, 179–206. Honolulu: University Press of Hawai'i, 1979.
Gong Zhebing 宮哲兵. *Qianjiadong yundong yu Yaozu faxiangdi* 千家峒運動與瑤族發祥地 [The thousand family grotto movement and the birthplace of the Yao minority]. Wuhan: Wuhan chubanshe, 2001.
Gongzhongdang 宮中檔 [Unpublished palace memorials]. National Palace Museum, Taibei.
Gongzhongdang Kangxichao zouzhe 宮中檔康熙朝奏摺 [Published palace memorials of the Kangxi reign]. Taibei: Guoli gugong bowuyuan, 1976.

Bibliography

Gongzhongdang Qianlongchao zouzhe 宮中檔乾隆朝奏摺 [Published palace memorials of the Qianlong reign]. Taibei: Guoli gugong bowuyuan, 1986.
Groot, J. J. M. de. *The Religious System of China*. 6 vols. Leiden: Brill, 1892–1910.
———. *Sectarianism and Religious Persecution in China*. Leiden: Brill, 1901.
Gu Cheng 顧誠. *Nan Ming shi* 南明史 [History of the Southern Ming]. 2 vols. Beijing: Guangming ribao chubanshe, 2011.
Gu Shujuan 顧書娟. *Ming Qing Guangdong minjian xinyang yanjiu* 明清廣東民間信仰研究 [A study of popular beliefs in Guangdong in the Ming and Qing periods]. Guangzhou: Nanfang ribao chubanshe, 2015.
Guangdong Danmin shehui diaocha 廣東蛋民社會調查 [Investigation of Guangdong's Danmin society]. Edited by the Guangdong Institute for Minority Studies. Guangzhou: Zhongshan daxue chubanshe, 2001.
Guangdong fengsu zhuilu 廣東風俗綴錄 [Record of Guangdong customs]. Compiled by Zhou Kangxie 周康燮. Hong Kong: Chongwen shudian, 1972.
Guangdong shangyu zouzhe 廣東上諭奏摺 [Edicts and memorials from Guangdong]. Three vols., Qing dynasty, undated and unpaginated. Academia Sinica, Nangang, Taiwan.
"Guangdong sheng Huiyang dichu diming zhi" 廣東省惠陽地處地名志 [Gazetteer of place names from Huiyang in Guangdong province]. Unpublished typescript, dated 1988. Boluo County Gazetteer Office.
Guangdong sheng Yaozu shehui lishi qingkuang 廣東省瑤族社會歷史情況 [The condition of society and history of the Yao in Guangdong]. Beijing: Zhongguo kexueyuan minzu yanjiusuo and Guangdong shaoshu minzu shehui lishi diaochazu, 1963.
Guangdong shengzhi dashiji 廣東省志大事記 [Record of major events in the Guangdong gazetteer]. Guangzhou: Guangdong renmin chubanshe, 2005.
Guangdong Yaozu lishi ziliao 廣東瑤族歷史資料 [Historical sources on the Yao of Guangdong]. Compiled by Huang Chaozhong 黃朝中 and Liu Yaoquan 劉耀荃. 2 vols. Nanning: Guangxi minzu chubanshe, 1984.
Guangdongsi xingbu dang'an 廣東司刑部檔案. [Guangdong's judicial archives]. Qing dynasty. First Historical Archives, Beijing.
"Guanyu Jingzu Sandao youzhao zenyang de chuanshuo" 關於京族三島有着怎樣的傳說 [On the legends about the Three Islands of the Jing minority]. Posted August 8, 2014. https://www.fqsjw.com/zh-mo/gxbk/ctwh/21545.html.
Guo Fei 郭棐. *Yue daji* 粵大記 [*Great record of Guangdong*]. First published 1598. Guangzhou: Zhongshan daxue chubanshe, 1998.
Guo Zhiyuan. "Torture and Exclusion of Evidence in China." *China Perspectives* 1 (March 2019): 45–53.
Gutzlaff, Charles. *Journal of Three Voyages along the Coast of China in 1831, 1832, and 1833, with Notices of Siam, Corea, and the Loo-Choo Islands*. London: Frederick Westley and A. H. Davis, 1834.
Haar, Barend ter. "The Sutra of the Five Lords: Manuscript and Oral Tradition," *Studies in Chinese Religions* 1, no. 2 (2015): 172–197.
———. *Practicing Scripture: A Lay Buddhist Movement in Late Imperial China*. Honolulu: University of Hawai'i Press, 2014.
———. *Telling Stories: Witchcraft and Scapegoating in Chinese History*. Leiden: Brill, 2006.

———. "China's Inner Demons: The Political Impact of the Demonological Paradigm." In *China's Great Proletarian Cultural Revolution: Master Narratives and Post-Mao Counternarratives*, edited by Woei Lien Chong, 27–68. Lanham, MD: Rowman and Littlefield, 2002.

———. *Ritual and Mythology of the Chinese Triads: Creating an Identity*. Leiden: Brill, 1998.

———. "A New Interpretation of the Yao Charters." In *New Developments in Asian Studies*, edited by Paul van der Velde and Alex McKay, 3–19. London: Kegan Paul International, 1998.

———. "The Genesis and Spread of Temple Cults in Fukien." In *Development and Decline of Fukien Province in the 17th and 18th Centuries*, edited by E. B. Vermeer, 349–396. Leiden: E. J. Brill, 1990.

Haikang xianzhi 海康縣志 [Gazetteer of Haikang county, Guangdong]. 1938 edition. Shanghai: Shanghai shudian chubanshe, 2003.

Haikang xianzhi 海康縣志 [Gazetteer of Haikang county, Guangdong]. 1812 edition. Harvard-Yenching Library.

Hamm, John Christopher. *Paper Swordsmen: Jin Yong and the Modern Chinese Martial Arts Novel*. Honolulu: University of Hawai'i Press, 2005.

Hang, Xing. "Leizhou Pirates and the Making of the Mekong Delta." In *Beyond the Silk Roads: New Discourses on China's Role in East Asian Maritime History*, edited by Robert Antony and Angela Schottenhammer, 115–131. Wiesbaden: Harrassowitz Verlag, 2017.

———. *Conflict and Commerce in Maritime East Asia: The Zheng Family and the Shaping of the Modern World, c. 1620–1720*. Cambridge: Cambridge University Press, 2015.

Hansson, Anders. *Chinese Outcasts: Discrimination and Emancipation in Late Imperial China*. Leiden and New York: E. J. Brill, 1996.

Harrell, Stevan. "Introduction: Civilizing Projects and the Reactions to Them." In *Cultural Encounters on China's Ethnic Frontiers*, edited by Stevan Harrell, 3–36. Hong Kong: Hong Kong University Press, 1996.

———. "When a Ghost Becomes a God." In *Religion and Ritual in Chinese Society*, edited by Arthur Wolf, 193–206. Stanford: Stanford University Press, 1974.

Harrison, James P. *The Communists and Chinese Peasant Rebellions: A Study in the Rewriting of Chinese History*. New York: Atheneum, 1969.

Hayes, James. "Specialists and Written Materials in the Village World." In *Popular Culture in Late Imperial China*, edited by David Johnson, Andrew Nathan, Evelyn Rawski, 75–111. Berkeley: University of California Press, 1985.

He Weijie 何偉傑. "Miaoyu, zujun shenfen yu shequ fazhan de shehui huayu: cong beiming wenwu he yingbian chonggou Qingdai de Danzai" 廟宇、族郡身份與社區發展的社會話語: 從碑銘文物和梘區重構清代的疍仔 [Social discourse on temples, ethnic identity and community development: reconstruction of Taipa in the Qing period from steles and tablets]. *Aomen lishi yanjiu* 澳門歷史研究 6 (2007): 63–74.

He, Xi, and David Faure. "Introduction: Boat and Shed Living in Land-Based Society." In *The Fisher Folk of Late Imperial and Modern China: An Historical Anthropology of*

Boat-and-Shed Living, edited by He Xi and David Faure, 1–29. London and New York: Routledge, 2016.

He Xiaoxin 何曉昕 and Luo Jun 羅雋. *Fengshui shi* 風水史 [A history of *fengshui*]. Taibei: Huacheng tushu, 2004.

He Zhiqing 赫治清. *Tiandihui qiyuan yanjiu* 天地會起源研究 [A study of the origins of the Heaven and Earth Society]. Beijing: Shehui kexue wenxian, 1996.

He Zhiqing 赫治清 and Wu Zhaoqing 吳兆清. *Zhongguo banghui shi* 中國幫會史 [A history of Chinese secret societies]. Taibei: Wenjing chubanshe, 1996.

Heehs, Peter. "Myth, History, and Theory." *History and Theory* 33, no. 1 (1994): 1–19.

Hershatter, Gail. "Sex Work and Social Order: Prostitutes, Their Families, and the State in Twentieth-Century Shanghai." In *Family Process and Political Process in Modern Chinese History*, edited by the Institute of Modern History, Academia Sinica, 1083–1123. Taibei: Academia Sinica, 1992.

Ho, Dahpon David. "The Empire's Scorched Shore: Coastal China, 1633–1683." *Journal of Early Modern History* 17, no. 1 (2013): 53–74.

Ho, Virgil Kit-yiu. "Selling Smiles in Canton: Prostitution in the Early Republic." *East Asian History* 5 (June 1993): 101–132.

Hoare, Natasha. "The Past Is a Foreign Country." *The White Review*, November 2013. https://www.thewhitereview.org/feature/the-past-is-a-foreign-country.

Hobsbawm, Eric. "On History from Below." In *On History*, edited by Eric Hobsbawm, 201–216. London: Weidenfeld and Nicolson, 1997.

Holcombe, Charles. "Theater of Combat: A Critical Look at the Chinese Martial Arts." *The Historian* 52, no. 3 (1990): 411–431.

Hong Wei 紅葦. *Tiyan jianghu* 體驗江湖 [Experiencing the rivers and lakes]. Shanghai: Shanghai sanlian, 2003.

Hou, Ching-lang. "The Chinese Belief in Baleful Stars." In *Facets of Taoism: Essays in Chinese Religion*, edited by Holmes Welch and Anna Seidel, 193–228. New Haven: Yale University Press, 1979.

Hsia, C. T. *The Classic Chinese Novel*. New York: Columbia University Press, 1968.

Hsiao, Kung-chuan. *Rural China: Imperial Control in the Nineteenth Century*. Seattle: University of Washington Press, 1960.

Hsieh, Kuo Ching. "Removal of Coastal Population in Early Tsing Period." *Chinese Social and Political Science Review* 15 (1932): 559–596.

Hsu, Dao-lin. "Crime and Cosmic Order." *Harvard Journal of Asiatic Studies* 30 (1970): 111–125.

Hsu, Wen-hsiung. "The Triads and Their Ideology up to the Early Nineteenth Century." In *Heterodoxy in Late Imperial China*, edited by K. C. Liu and Richard Shek, 323–364. Honolulu: University of Hawai'i Press, 2004.

Huang Han 黃漢. *Mao yuan* 貓苑 [An anthology on cats]. 2 vols. Preface dated 1852. Accessed April 14, 2018. https://www.guoxuedashi.com/a/9679y/79548r.html. Unpaginated.

Huang Liuhong 黃六鴻. *Juguan fuhui quanshu* 居官福惠全書 [A complete book concerning happiness and benevolence for officials in office]. Preface dated 1694. Shanghai: Taoyuan shuwu, undated late Qing edition.

———. [Huang Liu-hung]. *A Complete Book Concerning Happiness and Benevolence: A Manual for Local Magistrates in Seventeenth-Century China*, edited and translated by Djang Chu. Tucson: University of Arizona Press, 1984.

Huang, Xiangchun. "Going Beyond Pariah Status: The Boat People of Fuzhou in the Chinese People's Republic." In *The Fisher Folk of Late Imperial and Modern China: An Historical Anthropology of Boat-and-Shed Living*, edited by He Xi and David Faure, 142–158. London and New York: Routledge, 2016.

Huang Yu 黃鈺. "Yaozu 'pinghuang quandie' chutan" 瑤族'評皇券牒'初談 [Preliminary discussion on the Yao minority's 'Charter from Emperor Ping']. In *Yaozu yanjiu lunwen ji: 1986 nian Yaozu yanjiu guoji yantaohui* 瑤族研究論文集: 1986年瑤族研究國際研討會 [Collected essays on the Yao from the 1986 international conference on Yao studies], edited by Qiao Jian 喬健, Xie Jian 謝劍, and Hu Qiwang 胡起望, 89–123. Beijing: Minzu chubanshe, 1988.

Huizhou fuzhi 惠州府志 [Gazetteer of Huizhou prefecture, Guangdong]. 1881 edition. Taibei: Chengwen chubanshe, 1966.

Huizhou fuzhi 惠州府志 [Gazetteer of Huizhou prefecture, Guangdong]. 1688 edition. Guangdong Provincial Library.

Huizhou shigao 惠州史稿 [Draft history of Huizhou]. Huizhou: Huiyang dichu xingzheng gongshu yinshuachang, 1982.

Hunan difangzhi shaoshu minzu shiliao 湖南地方志少數民族史料 [Historical materials on minorities in Hunan gazetteers]. Compiled by Hunan sheng shaoshu minzu guji bangong shi 湖南省少數民族古籍辦公室. 2 vols. Changsha: Yuelu shushe, 1992.

Hunan Yaozu shehui lishi diaocha 湖南瑤族社會歷史調查 [Survey of the social history of the Yao minority in Hunan]. Edited by Guangxi Zhuangzu Zizhiqu bianjizu 廣西壯族自治區編輯組. Nanning: Guangxi minzu chubanshe, 1986.

Hung, Chang-tai. *Going to the People: Chinese Intellectuals and Folk Literature, 1918–1937*. Cambridge, MA: Harvard University Press, 1985.

Hunter, James. *Culture Wars: The Struggle to Define America*. New York: Basic Books, 1991.

Hunter, William C. *Bits of Old China*. London: K. Paul, Trench, and Co., 1855.

Idema, Wilt L. *Mouse vs. Cat in Chinese Literature: Tales and Commentary*. Seattle: University of Washington Press, 2019.

Irwin, Lee. "Divinity and Salvation: The Great Goddesses of China." *Asian Folklore Studies* 49, no. 1 (1990): 53–68.

Ivanova, Maranatha C. "Limning the *Jianghu*: Spaces of Appearance and the Performative Politics of the Chinese Cultural Underground." PhD diss., University of California, Berkeley, 2009.

Jenner, W. J. F. "Tough Guys, Mateship, and Honour: Another Chinese Tradition." *East Asian History* 12 (December 1996): 1–34.

Jiang Yonglin. *The Mandate of Heaven and the Great Ming Code*. Seattle: University of Washington Press, 2013.

Jiang Zuyuan 蔣祖緣 and Fang Zhiqin 方志欽. *Jianming Guangdong shi* 簡明廣東史 [Concise history of Guangdong]. Guangzhou: Guangdong renmin chubanshe, 1993.

Jing Junjian 經君健. *Qingdai shehui de jianmin dengji* 清代社會的賤民等級 [The status of mean people in Qing society]. Beijing: Zhongguo renmin daxue chubanshe, 2009.

Jiu Guangdong feidao shilu 舊廣東匪盜實錄 [True record of banditry in old Guangdong]. Compiled by Guangdong wenshi ziliao bianjibu 廣東文史資料編輯部. Guangzhou: Guangzhou chubanshe, 1997.

Jonsson, Hjorleifur. *Mien Relations: Mountain People and State Control in Thailand*. Ithaca: Cornell University Press, 2005.

———. "Moving House: Migration and the Place of the Household on the Thai Periphery." *Journal of the Siam Society* 87, nos. 1–2 (1999): 99–118.

———. "Shifting Social Landscape: Mien (Yao) Upland Communities and Histories in State-Client Settings." PhD diss., Cornell University, 1996.

Jordan, David, and Daniel Overmyer. *The Flying Phoenix: Aspects of Chinese Sectarianism in Taiwan*. Princeton: Princeton University Press, 1986.

Junjidang lufu zouzhe 軍機檔錄副奏摺 [Grand Council copies of palace memorials]. National Palace Museum, Taibei.

Kaiping xianzhi 開平縣志 [Gazetteer of Kaiping county, Guangdong]. First published 1823. Taibei: Chengwen chubanshe, 1966.

Kandre, Peter. "Yao (Iu Mien) Supernaturalism, Language, and Ethnicity." In *Changing Identities in Modern Southeast Asia*, edited by David J. Banks, 171–197. The Hague: Mouton, 1976.

Kang Yong Qian shiqi chengxiang renmin fankang douzheng ziliao 康永乾時期城鄉人民反抗鬥爭資料 [Source materials on opposition and struggles by urban and rural people in the Kangxi, Yongzheng, and Qianlong reigns]. 2 vols. Edited by the Institute for Qing Studies and the Department of State Archives, People's University. Beijing: Zhonghua shuju, 1979.

Kani, Hiroaki. *A General Survey of the Boat People in Hong Kong*. Hong Kong: Chinese University of Hong Kong, New Asia Research Institute, Monograph Series, no. 5, 1967.

Karasawa, Yasuhiko. "From Oral Testimony to Written Records in Qing Legal Cases." In *Thinking with Cases: Specialist Knowledge in Chinese Cultural History*, edited by Charlotte Furth, Judith T. Zeitlin, Ping-chen Hsiung, 101–122. Honolulu: University of Hawai'i Press, 2007.

Katz, Paul R. *Religion, Ethnicity, and Gender in Western Hunan during the Modern Era: The Dao among the Miao?* New York: Routledge, 2022.

———. "Banner Worship and Human Sacrifice in Chinese Military History." In *The Scholar's Mind: Essays in Honor of Frederick W. Mote*, edited by Perry Link, 207–227. Hong Kong: Chinese University Press, 2009.

———. "Temple Inscriptions and the Study of Taoist Cults: A Case Study of Inscriptions at the Palace of Eternal Joy." *Taoist Resources* 7, no. 1 (1997): 1–22.

———. *Demon Hordes and Burning Boats: The Cult of Marshal Wen in Late Imperial Chekiang*. Albany: State University of New York Press, 1995.

———. "Demons or Deities?—The 'Wangye' of Taiwan." *Asian Folklore Studies* 46, no. 2 (1987): 197–215.

Kim, Jaeyoon. "The Heaven and Earth Society and the Red Turban Rebellion in Late Qing China." *Journal of Humanities and Social Sciences* 9, no. 1 (2009): 1–35.
Kishimoto-Nakayama, Mio. "The Kangxi Depression and Early Qing Local Markets." *Late Imperial China* 10, no. 2 (1984): 227–256.
Kleeman, Terry. "Licentious Cults and Bloody Victuals: Sacrifice, Reciprocity, and Violence in Traditional China." *Asia Major* 7, no. 1 (1994): 185–211.
Kloet, Jeroen de. *China with a Cut: Globalisation, Urban Youth and Popular Music*. Amsterdam: Amsterdam University Press, 2008.
Ko, Dorothy. *Teachers of the Inner Chambers: Women and Culture in Seventeenth-Century China*. Stanford: Stanford University Press, 1994.
Komlosy, Anouska. "Feminization, Recognition, and the Cosmological in Xishuangbanna." In *Marginalization in China: Recasting Minority Politics*, edited by Siu-Keung Cheung, Joseph Tse-Hei Lee, and Lida Nedilsky, 123–143. New York: Palgrave Macmillan, 2009.
Kuang, Meihua. "The Yao Rebellion in the 11th–12th Years of Daoguang Reign (1831–1832): Interaction and Confrontation in China's Middle Ground." MA thesis, University of Macau, 2015.
Kuhn, Philip. *Soulstealers: The Chinese Sorcery Scare of 1768*. Cambridge, MA: Harvard University Press, 1990.
Kwan, C. Nathan. "In the Business of Piracy: Entrepreneurial Women Among Chinese Pirates in the Mid-Nineteenth Century." In *Female Entrepreneurs in the Long Nineteenth Century*, edited by Jennifer Aston and Catherine Bishop, 195–218. London: Palgrave Macmillan, 2020.
Laai, Yi-Faai. "The Part Played by the Pirates of Kwangtung and Kwangsi Provinces in the Taiping Insurrection." PhD diss., University of California, Berkeley, 1950.
Lai Chuanqing 賴傳青. "Guangfu Ming Qing fengshui ta yanjiu" 廣府明清風水塔研究 [Research about fengshui pagodas in the Ming and Qing dynasties in Guangzhou]. PhD diss., South China University of Technology, 2007.
Lai Wen 賴文 and Li Yongchen 李永宸. *Lingnan wenyi shi* 嶺南瘟疫史 [History of plagues in Guangdong]. Guangzhou: Guangdong renmin chubanshe, 2004.
Lamley, Harry. "*Hsieh-tou*: The Pathology of Violence in Southeastern China." *Ch'ing-shih wen-t'i* 3, no. 7 (1977): 1–39.
Lane, Kris, and Robert Antony. "Piracy in Asia and the West." In *Cambridge World History of Violence, Vol. 3 (1500–1800)*, edited by Robert Antony, Stuart Carroll, and Caroline Pennock, 449–471. Cambridge: Cambridge University Press, 2020.
Lau, Joseph S. M. "The Courage to Be: Suicide as Self-Fulfillment in Chinese History and Literature." *Tamkang Review* 19 (1989): 715–734.
Lee, Hyeon Jung. "Fearless Love, Death for Dignity: Female Suicide and Gendered Subjectivity in Rural North China." *China Journal* 71 (2014): 25–42.
Leibold, James. "Planting the Seed: Ethnic Policy in Xi Jinping's New Era of Cultural Nationalism." *China Brief* 19, no. 22 (2019). https://jamestown.org/program/planting-the-seed-ethnic-policy-in-xi-jinpings-new-era-of-cultural-nationalism.
———. *Ethnic Policy in China: Is Reform Inevitable?* Honolulu: East-West Center, Policy Studies, no. 68, 2013.

Leizhou fuzhi 雷州府志 [Gazetteer of Leizhou prefecture, Guangdong]. 1811 edition. Leizhou City Museum.

Lemoine, Jacques. "Yao Culture and Some Other Related Problems." In *The Yao of South China: Recent International Studies*, edited by Jacques Lemoine and Chiao Chien, 591–612. Paris: Pangu, 1991.

Leong, Sow-Theng. *Migration and Ethnicity in Chinese History: Hakkas, Pengmin, and Their Neighbors*. Edited by Tim Wright. Stanford: Stanford University Press, 1997.

Lewis, Mark. *Sanctioned Violence in Early China*. Albany: State University of New York Press, 1990.

Li, Donghui. "The 'Phenomenon' of Wang Shuo: A Historico-Literary Consideration." PhD diss., University of Wisconsin-Madison, 1998.

Li, Geng. "Divination, *Yijing*, and Cultural Nationalism: The Self-Legitimation of Divination as an Aspect of 'Traditional Culture' in Post-Mao China." *China Review* 18, no. 4 (2018): 63–84.

Li Laizhang 李來章. *Lianyang Bapai fengtu ji* 連陽八排風土記 [Record of the customs of the Bapai in Lianyang]. Preface dated 1708. Guangzhou: Zhongshan daxue chubanshe, 1990.

Li Qiaoyin 李俏銀. "Jingang Mazu" 金剛媽祖 [Warrior Mazu], *Zhongguo minzu zongjiao wang* 中國民族宗教罔. Posted October 30, 2011. https://www.mzb.com.cn/html/report/246801-1.htm.

Li Qingxin 李慶新. *Binhai zhi di: Nanhai maoyi yu Zhongwai guanxishi yanjiu* 瀕海之地:南海貿易與中外關係史研究 [The seaside world: Studies on the history of trade in the South China Sea and Sino-foreign relations]. Beijing: Zhonghua shuju, 2010.

Li, Shanbao. "The Precious Scroll of the Rat Epidemic." First published 1910. Translated by Will Idema. *Sino-Platonic Papers* 313 (April 2021): Unpaginated.

Li, Tana. "Epidemics, Trade, and Local Worship in Vietnam, Leizhou Peninsula, and Hainan Island." In *Imperial China and its Southern Neighbours*, edited by Victor H. Mair and Liam C. Kelley, 194–213. Singapore: Institute of Southeast Asian Studies, 2015.

Li Tiaoyuan 李調元. *Yuedong biji* 粵東筆記 [Miscellaneous jottings on Guangdong]. Preface dated 1774. Taibei: Xinwenfeng chuban gongsi, 1979.

Li, Xiaolin. "Women in the Chinese Military." PhD diss., University of Maryland, 1995.

Lian Jingchu 連景初. "Liuzhuanglou yu banlan baiyin" 梳粧樓與半籃白銀 [The Liuzhuang tower and the half basket of silver]. *Tainan wenhua* 臺南文化 9, no. 1 (1969): 24–25.

Lian Lichang 連立昌. *Fujian mimi shehui* 福建秘密社會 [Secret societies in Fujian]. Fuzhou: Fujian renmin chubanshe, 1989.

Lianjiang xianzhi 連江縣志 [Gazetteer of Lianjiang county, Fujian]. First published 1927. Taibei: Chengwen chubanshe, 1967.

Lianshan sui Yao tingzhi 連山綏瑤廳志 [Gazetteer on Suppressing the Yao of Lianshan subprefecture, Guangdong]. Liannan Archive, Liannan Yao Autonomous County, Guangdong, dated 1876.

Bibliography

Lianshan zhi 連山志 [Gazetteer of Lianshan, Guangdong]. Liannan Archive, Liannan Yao Autonomous County, Guangdong, dated 1928.
Lianzhou ribao 連州日報 [Lianzhou Daily], June 7, 2009.
Lianzhou zhi 連州志 [Gazetteer of Lianzhou, Guangdong]. Liannan Archive, Liannan Yao Autonomous County, Guangdong, dated 1771.
Lienzhou fuzhi 廉州府志 [Gazetteer of Lienzhou prefecture, Guangdong]. First published 1721. Haikou: Hainan chubanshe, 2001.
Lilius, Aleko E. *I Sailed with Chinese Pirates*. First published 1930. Hong Kong: Oxford University Press, 1991.
Lin Baochun 林保淳. *Ao shi gu cai gu long: Gulong yu wuxia shaoshuo guoji xueshu yantaohui lunwenji* 傲世鬼才一古龍:古龍與武俠小說國際學術研討會論文集 [The ghost of the world is an old dragon: A collection of essays from an international conference on Gu Long and martial arts novels]. Taibei: Xuesheng shuju chuban, 2006.
Lin, Zhongxuan. "Individualizing the Sexual Revolution in China: Staging, Enjoying, and Experiencing Sexuality." *Asian Journal of Women's Studies* 24, no. 4 (2018): 446–462.
Lin'gao xianzhi 臨高縣志 [Gazetteer of Lin'gao county, Guangdong]. Qing Kangxi edition. Haikou: Hainan chubanshe, 2004.
Lingshui xianzhi 陵水縣志 [Gazetteer of Lingshui county, Guangdong]. 1673 edition. Shanghai: Shanghai shudian chubanshe, 2001.
Lippiello, Tiziana. *Auspicious Omens and Miracles in Ancient China: Han, Three Kingdoms, and Six Dynasties*. Sankt Augustin, Germany: Monumenta Serica Institute, 2001.
Litzinger, Ralph A. *Other Chinas: The Yao and the Politics of National Belonging*. Durham: Duke University Press, 2000.
———. "Making Histories: Contending Conceptions of the Yao Past." In *Cultural Encounters on China's Ethnic Frontiers*, edited by Stevan Harrell, 117–139. Hong Kong: Hong Kong University Press, 1996.
Liu, Chungshee Hsien. "The Dog-Ancestor Story of the Aboriginal Tribes of Southern China." *Journal of the Royal Anthropological Institute of Great Britain and Ireland* 62 (July–December 1932): 361–368.
Liu, James J. Y. *The Chinese Knight-Errant*. Chicago: University of Chicago Press, 1967.
Liu Ping 劉平. *Bei yiwang de zhanzheng: Xianfeng Tongzhi nianjian Guangdong tuke xiedou yanjiu* 被遺忘的战争: 咸豐同治年間廣東土客大械鬥研究 [The Hakka-Punti War in Guangdong, 1854–1867]. Beijing: Shangwu yinshuguan, 2003.
Liu, Siyuan. "Theatre Reform as Censorship: Censoring Traditional Theatre in China in the Early 1950s." *Theatre Journal* 61, no. 3 (2009): 387–406.
Liu Wanzhang 劉萬章, ed. *Guangzhou miyu* 廣州謎語 [Cantonese riddles]. Taibei: Dongfang wenhua gongyingshe, 1970.
Liu Zaifu 劉再復. *Shuangdian pipan: dui Shuihu zhuan he Sanguo yanyi de wenhua pipan* 雙典批判: 對水滸傳和三國演義的文化批判 [A critique of two classics: cultural critique of *Water Margin* and *Romance of the Three Kingdoms*]. Beijing: Sanlian shudian, 2010.

Liu, Zhiwei. "Lineage on the Sands: The Case of Shawan." In *Down to Earth: The Territorial Bond in South China*, edited by David Faure and Helen Siu, 21–43. Stanford: Stanford University Press, 1995.

Ljungstedt, Anders. *An Historical Sketch of the Portuguese Settlements in China*. Boston: J. Munroe, 1835.

Lo, Ann L. Hsu. "Canton Opera: Folk Heroes, Triads, and Rebels." *Southeast Review of Asian Studies* 18 (1996): 39–57.

Lo, Hsiu-ju Stacy. "Crossing Rivers and Lakes: The Art of Everyday Life in Contemporary China." PhD diss., Columbia University, 2018.

Lockhart, J. H. Stewart. "Notes on Chinese Folk-Lore." *Folk-lore* 1 (1890): 359–368.

Loviot, Fanny. *A Lady's Captivity among Chinese Pirates in the Chinese Seas*. Translated by Amelia Edwards. London: Geo. Routledge and Co., 1856.

Lu, Hanchao. *Street Criers: A Cultural History of Chinese Beggars*. Stanford: Stanford University Press, 2005.

Lufu zouzhe 錄副奏摺 [Copies of palace memorials]. First Historical Archives, Beijing.

Luk, Gary Chi-hung. "The Making of a Littoral *Minzu*: The Dan in Late Qing-Republican Intellectual Writings." *International Journal of Asian Studies* (2021): 1–17.

Luo Ergang 羅爾綱. *Tiandihui wenxianlu* 天地會文獻錄 [Records on the Tiandihui]. Hong Kong: Shiyong shuju, 1965.

Luo Chunrong 羅春榮. "Tianfei heshi feng Tianhou—hai lishi benlai mianmu" 天妃何時封天后—還歷史本來面目 [When the Heavenly Concubine became Empress of Heaven—in history's original appearance]. In *Mazu wenhua yanjiu* 媽祖文化研究 [A study of Mazu culture], edited by Luo Chunrong, 271–284. Tianjin: Tianjin guji chubanshe, 2006.

Luo Rulan 羅汝蘭. *Shuyi huibian* 鼠疫彙編 [A compilation on plagues]. Preface dated 1901. Guangzhou: Guangdong keji chubanshe, 2008.

Lynn, W. T. "First Discovery of the Great Comet of 1680." *The Observatory* 11 (1888): 437–438.

Ma, Damien. "Beijing's 'Culture War' Isn't About the U.S.—It's About China's Future." *Atlantic*, January 5, 2012. https://www.theatlantic.com/international/archive/2012/01/beijings-culture-war-isnt-about-the-us-its-about-chinas-future/250900.

Ma Jianzhao 馬建昭, ed. *Pai Yao yanjiu lunwen xuanji* 排瑤研究論文選集 [Collected research on the Pai Yao]. Guangzhou: Guangdong renmin chubanshe, 2013.

Ma Muchi 馬木池. "Bianyuan qunti de rentong: shijiu shiji yilai Guangxi bianjingshang de Jingzu shequ" 邊緣群體的認同：十九世紀以來廣西邊境上的京族社區 [The identity of marginal groups: the Jing minority community on the Guangxi border in the nineteenth century]. *Lishi renleixue xuekan* 歷史人類學學刊 12, no. 1 (2014): 31–52.

Ma Shichang 馬世張. "Ming dai tiandihui ziliao de xin faxian" 明代天地會資料的發現 [Newly discovered materials on the Tiandihui in the Ming period]. *Wenwu* 文物 8 (1996): 59–61.

Ma, Y. W. "The Knight-Errant in 'hua-pen' Stories." *T'oung Pao*, Second Series, 61, nos. 4–5 (1975): 266–300.

Ma Xisha 馬西沙 and Han Bingfang 韓秉方. *Zhongguo minjian zongjiao shi* 中國民間宗教史 [A history of Chinese popular religion]. Shanghai: Shanghai renmin chubanshe, 1998.

Mair, Victor H. "Canine Conundrums: Eurasian Dog Ancestor Myths in Historical and Ethnic Perspective." *Sino-Platonic Papers* 87 (October 1998): Unpaginated.

Mann, Susan. "Presidential Address: Myths of Asian Womanhood." *Journal of Asian Studies* 59, no. 4 (2000): 835–862.

———. *Precious Records: Women in China's Long Eighteenth Century*. Stanford: Stanford University Press, 1997.

McCreery, John. "The Symbolism of Popular Taoist Magic." PhD diss., Cornell University, 1973.

McMahon, Daniel. "Geomancy and Walled Fortifications in Late Eighteenth-Century China." *Journal of Military History* 76, no. 2 (2012): 373–393.

McNeill, William. "Mythistory, or Truth, Myth, History, and Historians." *American Historical Review* 91, no. 1 (1986): 1–10.

Maoming wang 茂名網 [*Maoming online news*]. Accessed May 17, 2020. https://kknews.cc/history/6nre4pm.html.

Marks, Robert. *Tigers, Rice, Silk, and Silt: Environment and Economy in Late Imperial South China*. Cambridge: Cambridge University Press, 1998.

Matthews, William. "Making 'Science' from 'Superstition': Conceptions of Knowledge Legitimacy among Contemporary *Yijing* Diviners." *Journal of Chinese Religions* 45, no. 2 (2017): 173–196.

Maxiang tingzhi 馬巷廳志 [Gazetteer of Maxiang subprefecture, Fujian]. Dated 1893. Taibei: Chengwen chubanshe, 1967.

Meulenbeld, Mark. "Death and Demonization of a Bodhisattva: Guanyin's Reformulation within Chinese Religion." *Journal of the American Academy of Religion* 84, no. 3 (2016): 690–726.

Mian Mian. *Candy: A Novel*. Translated by Andrea Lingenfelter. New York: Little, Brown and Co., 2003.

Milne, William. "Some Account of the Secret Association in China, Entitled the Triad Society." *Transactions of the Royal Asiatic Society of Great Britain and Ireland* 1 (1827): 240–250.

Ming Qing shiliao 明清史料 [Historical materials on the Ming and Qing periods], *wu* 戊 series. Taibei: Academia Sinica, 1972.

"Minzu yingxiong jiazu zuiren" 民族英雄家族罪人 [People's hero, family's criminal]. Accessed May 17, 2020. https://kknews.cc/history/opbg2p.html.

Mollier, Christine. *Une Apocalypse taoiste du Ve siecle: Le Livre des incantations divines des grottes abyssales*. Paris: Institut des Hautes Etudes Chinoises, 1990.

Mullaney, Thomas. *Coming to Terms with the Nation: Ethnic Classification in Modern China*. Berkeley: University of California Press, 2011.

Murray, Dian. *Pirates of the South China Coast, 1790–1810*. Stanford: Stanford University Press, 1987.

———. "One Woman's Rise to Power: Cheng I's Wife and the Pirates." *Historical Reflections* 8, no. 3 (1981): 147–162.

Murray, Dian, with Qin Baoqi. *The Origins of the Tiandihui: The Chinese Triads in Legend and History*. Stanford: Stanford University Press, 1994.

Nandy, Ashis. "History's Forgotten Doubles." *History and Theory* 34, no. 2 (1995): 44–66.

Nanfang ribao 南方日報 [Southern Daily]. September 5, 2016.

Nanu, Maighna. "Chinese Government Tells People to Stop Sharing Food Over Outbreak Fears." *The Independent*, March 5, 2020. https://www.independent.co.uk/news/world/coronavirus-china-food-outbreak-chopsticks-restaurant-a9379266.html.

Naquin, Susan. *Shantung Rebellion: The Wang Lun Uprising of 1774*. New Haven: Yale University Press, 1981.

———. "True Confessions: Criminal Interrogations as Sources for Ch'ing History." *National Palace Museum Bulletin* (Taiwan) 11, no. 1 (1976): 1–17.

Nawenyigong zouyi 那文毅公奏議 [Collected memorials of Nayancheng]. 2 vols. Compiled by Rongan 容安. First published 1834. Taibei: Wenhai chubanshe, 1968.

Ng, Wing Chung. *The Rise of Cantonese Opera*. Champaign: University of Illinois Press, 2015.

Ngo, Sheau-Shi. "*Nüxia:* Historical Depiction and Modern Visuality." *Asian Journal of Women's Studies* 20, no. 3 (2014): 7–26.

Nishikawa Kikuko 西川喜久子. "Shindai Shuō deruta no shadan ni tsuite" 清代珠江下流域の沙田について [Study of the sand fields in the Pearl River delta in the Qing period]. *Tōyō gakuho* 東洋學報 63, nos. 1–2 (1981): 93–135.

Niu Junkai 牛軍凱. "Hai wei wubo: Yuenan haishen Nanhai siwei shengniang de chuanshuo yu xinyang" 海為無波: 越南海神南海四位聖娘的傳說與信仰 [Seas without waves: the spread and beliefs in four female deities of the Southern Seas in Vietnam]. *Haijiao shi yanjiu* 海交史研究 1 (2011): 49–60.

Niu, Junkai, and Li Qingxin. "Chinese 'Political Pirates' in the Seventeenth-Century Tongking Gulf." In *The Tongking Gulf Through History*, edited by Nola Cooke, Tana Li, and James Anderson, 133–142. Philadelphia: University of Pennsylvania Press, 2011.

Nunes, Isabel. "Singing and Dancing Girls of Macau: Aspects of Prostitution in Macau." *Review of Culture* 18 (1994): 61–84.

Nuwer, Rachel. "Domestic Cats Enjoyed Village Life in China 5,300 Years Ago." Accessed April 7, 2018. https://www.smithsonianmag.com/science-nature/domestic-cats-enjoyed-village-life-in-china-5300-years-ago-180948065.

Oakes, Timothy. "Ethnic Tourism in Rural Guizhou: Sense of Place and the Commerce of Authenticity." In *Tourism, Ethnicity, and the State in Asian and Pacific Societies*, edited by Michel Picard and Robert Wood, 35–70. Honolulu: University of Hawai'i Press, 1997.

Overmyer, Daniel. *Folk Buddhist Religion: Dissenting Sects in Late Traditional China*. Cambridge: Harvard University Press, 1976.

Ownby, David. "Redemptive Societies in China's Long Twentieth Century." In *Modern Chinese Religion: 1850 to the Present*, edited by Vincent Goossaert, Jan Kiely and John Lagerwey, 685–728. Leiden: E. J. Brill, 2015.

———. *Falun Gong and the Future of China*. Oxford: Oxford University Press, 2008.

———. "Approximations of Chinese Bandits: Perverse Rebels, Romantic Heroes, or Frustrated Bachelors?" In *Chinese Femininities/Chinese Masculinities: A Reader*, edited by Susan Brownell and Jeffery Wasserstrom, 226–250. Berkeley: University of California Press, 2002.

———. "Recent Chinese Scholarship on the History of Chinese Secret Societies." *Late Imperial China* 22, no. 1 (2001): 139–158.

———. *Brotherhoods and Secret Societies in Early and Mid-Qing China*. Stanford: Stanford University Press, 1996.

———. "The Heaven and Earth Society as Popular Religion." *Journal of Asian Studies* 54, no. 4 (1995): 1023–1046.

Paderni, Paola. "Between Constraints and Opportunities: Widows, Witches, and Shrews in Eighteenth-Century China." In *Chinese Women in the Imperial Past: New Perspectives*, edited by Harriet T. Zurndorfer, 258–285. Leiden: Brill, 1999.

———. "I Thought I Would Have Some Happy Days: Women Eloping in Eighteenth-Century China." *Late Imperial China* 16, no. 1 (1995): 1–32.

Palmer, David. "Heretical Doctrines, Reactionary Secret Societies, Evil Cults: Labeling Heterodoxy in Twentieth-Century China." In *Chinese Religiosities: The Vicissitudes of Modernity and State Formation*, edited by Mayfair Yang, 113–134. Berkeley: University of California Press, 2012.

———. *Qigong Fever: Body, Science and Utopia in China*. New York: Columbia University Press, 2007.

Pan Dinggui 潘鼎珪. *Annan jiyou* 安南紀遊 [*Travel record of Annam*]. In *Annan zhuan (ji qita erzhong)* 安南傳 (及其他二種) [Commentaries on Annan (and two additional sources)]. Preface dated 1689. Beijing: Shumu wenxian chubanshe, 1985.

Pang, Laikwan. "The State Against Ghosts: A Genealogy of China's Film Censorship Policy." *Screen* 52, no. 4 (2011): 461–476.

Panyu xianzhi 番禺縣志 [Gazetteer of Panyu county, Guangdong]. 1871 edition. Taibei: Chengwen chubanshe, 1967.

Park, Nancy. "Poverty, Privilege, and Power and Imperial Chinese Proverbs." *Proverbium* 15 (1998): 243–263.

Park, Nancy, and Robert Antony. "Archival Research in Qing Legal History." *Late Imperial China* 14, no. 1 (1993): 93–137.

Penny, Benjamin. "Falun Gong, Prophesy and Apocalypse." *East Asian History* 23 (2002): 149–168.

Perry, Elizabeth. *Challenging the Mandate of Heaven: Social Protest and State Power in China*. Armonk, NY: M. E. Sharpe, 2002.

———. "Social Banditry Revisited: The Case of Bai Lang, a Chinese Brigand." *Modern China* 9, no. 3 (1983): 355–382.

———. *Rebels and Revolutionaries in North China, 1845–1945*. Stanford: Stanford University Press, 1980.

———. "When Peasants Speak: Sources for the Study of Chinese Rebellions." *Modern China* 6, no. 1 (1980): 72–85.

Pham, Sherisse. "Singles Day: Alibaba sales blitz set for record haul as Chinese shake off Covid-19." *CNN Business*, November 11, 2020. https://www.cnn.com/2020/11/10/tech/singles-day-2020-alibaba-intl-hnk/index.html.

Pingyang xianzhi 平陽縣志 [Gazetteer of Pingyang county, Zhejiang]. Zhejiang Provincial Archives, dated 1925.

Pires, Benjamim Videra. "The Chinese Quarter One Hundred Years Ago." *Review of Culture* (English Edition), nos. 7–8. Accessed February 26, 2020. https://www.icm.gov.mo/rc/ viewer/20007.

Port, Andrew. "History from Below, the History of Everyday Life, and Microhistory." In *International Encyclopedia of the Social and Behavioral Sciences*, second edition, 11: 108–113. New York: Elsevier, 2015.

Porter, Jonathan. *Macau, the Imaginary City: Culture and Society, 1557 to the Present*. Boulder: Westview Press, 1996.

Potter, Jack. "Wind, Water, Bones and Souls: The Religious World of the Cantonese Peasant." *Journal of Oriental Studies* 3, no. 1 (1970): 139–153.

Pu Chaojun 蒲朝軍 et al. *Zhongguo Yaozu fengtu zhi* 中國瑤族風土志 [Records of customs of China's Yao minority]. Beijing: Beijing daxue chubanshe, 1992.

Qian Haiyue 錢海岳. *Nan Ming shi* 南明史 [History of the Southern Ming]. 14 vols. Beijing: Zhonghua shuju, 2006.

Qian Yikai 錢以塏. *Linghai jianwen* 嶺海見聞 [Things seen and heard in the mountains and seas]. First published eighteenth century. Guangzhou: Guangdong gaodeng jiaoyu chubanshe, 1992.

Qin, Amy. "Coronavirus Threatens China's Devotion to Chopsticks and Sharing Food." *New York Times*, May 25, 2020. https://www.nytimes.com/2020/05/25/world/asia/china-coronavirus-chopsticks.html.

Qin Baoqi 秦寶琦. *Qing qianqi tiandihui yanjiu* 清前期天地會研究 [A study of the Heaven and Earth Society in the early Qing period]. Beijing: Zhongguo renmin daxue chubanshe, 1988.

Qin xianzhi 欽縣志 [Gazetteer of Qin county, Guangdong]. Qinzhou Gazetteer Office, dated 1946.

Qin zhouzhi 欽州志 [Gazetteer of Qinzhou, Guangdong]. Ming Jiajing edition. Shanghai: Shanghai guji shudian, 1961.

Qing Gaozong shilu xuanji 清高宗實錄選輯 [Collection of the veritable records of the Gaozong reign]. Taibei: Taiwan yinhang, 1964.

Qing shilu Guangdong shiliao 清實錄廣東史料 [Historical sources for Guangdong from the Qing veritable records]. 6 vols. Compiled by the Guangdong Provincial Gazetteer Office and the Guangzhou City Gazetteer Office. Guangzhou: Guangdong sheng ditu chubanshe, 1995.

Qing shilu yu Qing dang'an zhong de Guangdong shaoshu minzu dang'an huibian 清實錄與清檔案中的廣東少數民族史料彙編 [A collection of historical documents about Guangdong minorities from the Qing veritable records and Qing archives]. Compiled by Lian Mingzhi 練銘志. Guangzhou: Guangdong renmin chubanshe, 2011.

Qingdai dang'an shiliao congbian 清代檔案史料叢編 [Compilation of historical documents from the Qing dynasty]. Beijing: Zhonghua shuju, 1980.

Qingdai mimi jieshe dang'an jiyin 清代秘密結社檔案輯印 [A collection of archival sources on secret societies in the Qing period]. 10 vols. Compiled by Li Qing黎青. Beijing, 1999.

"Qingmo Yuexi shuyi yu shuyi fangzhi zhuanzhu de bianzhuan" 清末粤西鼠疫与鼠疫防治專著的编撰 [Review of treatises on plagues and plague prevention in western Guangdong in the late Qing]. Accessed March 16, 2020. https://mp.weixin.qq.com/s/g87LsZCqZsp8_kQEzl-isQ.

Qingshi liezhuan 清史列傳 [Qing historical biographies]. 10 vols. Taibei: Zhonghua shuju, 1962.

Qiu shi da zongpu 邱氏大宗譜 [Genealogy of the Qiu family]. Lianzhou, dated 2007.

Qu Dajun 屈大均. *Guangdong xinyu* 廣東新語 [New discourses on Guangdong]. First published 1700. Beijing: Zhonghua shuju, 1985.

Quackenbush, Casey, and Aria Chen, "'Tasteless, Vulgar and Obscene:' China Just Banned Hip-Hop Culture and Tattoos from Television." *Time*, January 22, 2018. http://time.com/5112061/china-hip-hop-ban-tattoos-television.

Rao Zongyi 饒宗頤. "Taiguo 'Yaoren wenshu' de houji." 泰國'瑤人文書'的後記 [Later writings of the Yao people in Thailand]. In *Yaozu yanjiu lunwen ji: 1986 nian Yaozu yanjiu guoji yantaohui* 瑤族研究論文集: 1986年瑤族研究國際研討會 [Collected essays on the Yao from the 1986 international conference on Yao studies], edited by Qiao Jian 喬健, Xie Jian 謝劍, and Hu Qiwang 胡起望, 37–45. Beijing: Minzu chubanshe, 1988.

"Religious Faith Is Protected by Law." *Beijing Review* 26, no. 52 (December 26, 1983): 9.

Renjing huabao 人鏡畫報 [People's mirror pictorial journal]. Tianjin, 1907.

Robinson, Katherine. "Robert Frost: 'The Road Not Taken.'" Poetry Foundation, posted May 27, 2016. https://www.poetryfoundation.org/articles/89511/robert-frost-the-road-not-taken.

Ruhlmann, Robert. "Traditional Heroes in Chinese Popular Fiction." In *The Confucian Persuasion*, edited by Arthur F. Wright, 141–176. Stanford: Stanford University Press, 1960.

Sakura Magozō 佐倉孫三 [Dashan 達山]. *Minfeng zaji* 閩風雜記 [Miscellaneous jottings on the customs of Fujian]. Fuzhou: Meihua shuju, 1904.

Sakurai, Yumio. "Eighteenth-Century Chinese Pioneers on the Water Frontier of Indochina." In *Water Frontier: Commerce and the Chinese in the Lower Mekong Region, 1750–1880*, edited by Nola Cooke and Tana Li, 36–52. Lanham, MD: Rowman and Littlefield, 2004.

"Sandao de laili" 三島的來歷 [On the origins of the Three Islands]. In *Fangcheng xian minjian gushiji* 防城縣民間故事集 [Collection of folk stories from Fangcheng county, Guangxi], edited by Zhou Minsheng 周民生 et al., 311–313. Nanning: Fangcheng xian minjian wenxue, 1988.

Sandburg, Brian. "Beyond Encounters: Religion, Ethnicity, and Violence in the Early Modern Atlantic World, 1492–1700." *Journal of World History* 17, no. 1 (2006): 1–25.

Sangren, P. Steven. "Orthodoxy, Heterodoxy, and the Structure of Value in Chinese Rituals." *Modern China* 13, no. 1 (1987): 63–89.

———. "Female Gender in Chinese Religious Symbols: Kuan Yin, Ma Tsu, and the 'Eternal Mother.'" *Signs* 9, no. 1 (1983): 4–25.
Sanxing leitan 三星雷壇 [Handbook of amulets of the three stars and thunder altar]. Guangdong: handwritten copy, dated 1930.
Sasaki Masaya 佐々木正哉. *Shinmatsu no himitsu kessha, zempen: Tenchikai no seiritsu* 清末の秘密結社, 前篇: 天地會の成立 [Secret societies in the late Qing period, Part 1: The establishment of the Heaven and Earth Society]. Tokyo: Gannandō shoten, 1970.
Scarth, John. *Twelve Years in China: The People, the Rebels, and the Mandarins*. Edinburgh: T. Constable and Co., 1860.
Schafer, Edward H. *The Divine Woman: Dragon Ladies and Rain Maidens*. First published 1973. San Francisco: North Point Press, 1980.
Schaffer, Kay, and Xianlin Song. "Unruly Spaces: Gender, Women's Writing and Indigenous Feminism in China." *Journal of Gender Studies* 16, no. 1 (2007): 17–30.
Scheen, Lena. *Shanghai Literary Imaginings: A City in Transformation*. Amsterdam: Amsterdam University Press, 2015.
Schipper, Kristofer. *The Taoist Body*. Translated by Karen Duval. Berkeley: University of California Press, 1993.
———. "Vernacular and Classical Ritual in Taoism." *Journal of Asian Studies* 45, no. 1 (1985): 21–57.
———. "Démonologie chinoise." In *Génies, Anges et Demons*, edited by Dimitri Meeks et al., 405–427. Paris: Éditions du Seuil, 1971.
Schlegel, Gustave. *Thian Ti Hwui, The Hung League or Heaven-Earth League*. Batavia: Lang and Co., 1866.
Schneewind, Sarah. "Competing Institutions: Community Schools and 'Improper Shrines' in Sixteenth-Century China." *Late Imperial China* 20, no. 1 (1999): 85–106.
Schoenhals, Michael. "Demonizing Discourse in Mao Zedong's China: People vs Non-People." *Totalitarian Movements and Political Religions* 8, nos. 3–4 (2007): 465–482.
Scott, Beresford. *An Account of the Destruction of the Fleets of the Celebrated Pirate Chieftains Chui-Apoo and Shap-ng Tsai, on the coast of China, in September and October, 1849*. London: Savill and Edwards, 1851.
Scott, James C. *The Art of not Being Governed: An Anarchist History of Upland Southeast Asia*. New Haven: Yale University Press, 2009.
Seal, Graham. "The Robin Hood Principle: Folklore, History and the Social Bandit." *Journal of Folklore Research* 46, no. 1 (2009): 67–89.
Seidel, Anna. "Imperial Treasures and Taoist Sacraments: Taoist Roots in the Apocrypha." In *Tantric and Taoist Studies in Honour of R. A. Stein*, edited by Michel Strickmann, 2: 291–371. Bruxelles: Institut Belge des Hautes Etudes Chinoises, 1983.
Seiwert, Hubert, with Ma Xisha. *Popular Religious Movements and Heterodox Sects in Chinese History*. Leiden: Brill, 2003.
Shahar, Meir. *The Shaolin Monastery: History, Religion, and the Chinese Martial Arts*. Honolulu: University of Hawai'i Press, 2008.
Shangyudang 上諭檔 [Record book of imperial edicts]. Palace Museum, Taibei.

Sharpe, Jim. "History from Below." In *New Perspectives on Historical Writing*, second edition, edited by Peter Burke, 25–42. University Park: Pennsylvania State University Press, 2001.

Shen, Fu. *Six Records of a Floating Life*. Translated by Leonard Pratt and Chiang Su-hui. London: Penguin Books, 1983.

Shepherd, John R. "Taiwan Prefecture in the Eighteenth Century." In *The Cambridge History of China, Vol. 9, The Ch'ing Dynasty to 1800, Part 2*, edited by Willard J. Peterson, 77–110. Cambridge: Cambridge University Press, 2016.

———. *Statecraft and Political Economy on the Taiwan Frontier, 1600–1800*. Stanford: Stanford University Press, 1993.

Shih, Patricia Feng-Yu. "Female Pollution in Chinese Society." MA thesis, McMaster University, 1978.

Shiliao xunkan 史料旬刊 [Collections of historical materials], *tian* 天 and *di* 地 series. Taibei: Guofeng chubanshi, 1963.

Shin, Leo K. *The Making of the Chinese State: Ethnicity and Expansion in the Ming Borderlands*. Cambridge: Cambridge University Press, 2006.

Sihui xianzhi 四會縣志 [Gazetteer of Sihui county, Guangdong]. 1896 edition. Taibei: Chengwen chubanshe, 1967.

Sivelle, Kristina. "Chinese Women and Their Contraceptive Choices." *China Daily*, January 18, 2005. https://www.chinadaily.com.cn/english/doc/2005-01/18/content_410003.htm.

Sivin, Nathan. "State, Cosmos, and Body in the Last Three Centuries B.C." *Harvard Journal of Asiatic Studies* 55, no. 1 (1995): 5–37.

Siu, Helen. *Agents and Victims in South China: Accomplices in Rural Revolution*. New Haven: Yale University Press, 1989.

Siu, Helen, and Liu Zhiwei. "Lineage, Market, Pirate, and Dan: Ethnicity in the Pearl River Delta of South China." In *Empire at the Margins*, edited by Pamela Crossley, Helen Siu, and Donald Sutton, 285–310. Berkeley: University of California Press, 2006.

Skinner, G. William. "Cities and the Hierarchy of Local Systems." In *The City in Late Imperial China*, edited by G. William Skinner, 275–352. Stanford: Stanford University Press, 1977.

Slade, John. *Notices on the British Trade to the Port of Canton, with Some Translations of Chinese Official Papers Relative to that Trade, etc.* London: Smith, Elder, and Co., 1830.

Smith, Paul Jakov. "'Shuihu zhuan' and the Military Subculture of the Northern Song, 960–1127." *Harvard Journal of Asiatic Studies* 66, no. 2 (2006): 363–422.

Smith, Steve. "Fear and Rumour in the People's Republic of China in the 1950s." *Cultural and Social History* 5, no. 3 (2008): 269–288.

Snowden, Lisa R. "Chinese Déjà Vu: Parallels Between the Urban Popular Cultures of Republican and Post Mao China." MA thesis, University of Kansas, 2009.

Sommer, Matthew. *Polyandry and Wife-Selling in Qing Dynasty China: Survival Strategies and Judicial Interventions*. Berkeley: University of California Press, 2015.

———. "Dangerous Males, Vulnerable Males, and Polluted Males: The Regulation of Masculinity in Qing Dynasty Law." In *Chinese Femininities, Chinese Masculinities: A Reader*, edited by Susan Brownell and Jeffrey Wasserstrom, 67–88. Berkeley: University of California Press, 2002.

———. *Sex, Law, and Society in Late Imperial China*. Stanford: Stanford University Press, 2000.

Song, Geng. "Masculinizing Jianghu Spaces in the Past and Present: Homosociality, Nationalism and Chineseness." *Nan Nü* 21 (2019): 107–129.

Song, Weijie. "Space, Swordsmen and Utopia: The Dualistic Imagination in Jin Yong's Narratives." In *The Jin Yong Phenomenon: Chinese Martial Arts Fiction and Modern Chinese Literary History*, edited by Ann Huss and Jianmei Liu, 155–178. Youngstown: Cambria Press, 2007.

Spence, Jonathan. *Treason by the Book*. New York: Penguin, 2001.

———. *God's Chinese Son: The Taiping Heavenly Kingdom of Hong Xiuchuan*. New York: W. W. Norton, 1996.

Stanton, William. *The Triad Society or Heaven and Earth Association*. Shanghai: Kelly and Walsh, 1900.

Stein, Rolf. "Religious Taoism and Popular Religion from the Second to Seventh Centuries." In *Facets of Taoism: Essays in Chinese Religion*, edited by Holmes Welch and Anna Seidel, 62–66. New Haven: Yale University Press 1979.

Stevens, Keith. "The Popular Religion Gods of the Hainanese." *Journal of the Hong Kong Branch of the Royal Asiatic Society* 41 (2001): 43–93.

Stewart, Douglas. *The Brutal Seas: Organized Crime at Work*. Bloomington: Author House, 2006.

Sterckx, Roel. *The Animal and the Daemon in Early China*. Albany: State University of New York Press, 2002.

Strassberg, Richard, ed. and trans. *A Chinese Bestiary: Strange Creatures from the Guideways Through Mountains and Seas*. Berkeley: University of California Press, 2002.

Strickmann, Michel. *Chinese Magical Medicine*. Edited by Bernard Faure. Stanford: Stanford University Press, 2002.

Stübel, Hans. "The Yao of the Province of Kuangtung." *Monumenta Serica* 3, no. 2 (1938): 345–431.

Struve, Lynn. *Voices from the Ming-Qing Cataclysm: China in Tigers Jaws*. New Haven: Yale University Press, 1998.

———. "The Southern Ming, 1644–1662." In *The Cambridge History of China, Vol. 7, The Ming Dynasty, 1368–1644, Part 1*, edited by Frederick Mote and Denis Twitchett, 641–725. Cambridge: Cambridge University Press, 1988.

———. *The Southern Ming, 1644–1662*. New Haven: Yale University Press, 1984.

Suleski, Ronald. *Daily Life for the Common People of China, 1850 to 1950: Understanding Chaoben Culture*. Leiden: Brill, 2018.

Sutton, Donald. "Violence and Ethnicity on a Qing Colonial Frontier: Customary and Statutory Law in the Eighteenth-Century Miao Pale." *Modern Asian Studies* 37 (2003): 41–80.

———. "From Credulity to Scorn: Confucians Confront the Spirit Mediums in Late Imperial China." *Late Imperial China* 21, no. 2 (2000): 1–39.

Suzuki Chusei 鈴木中正. "Shincho chuki ni okeru minkan shukyo kessha to sono sennen okoku undo e no keisha" 清朝中期における民間宗教結社とその千年王国運動への傾斜 [Popular religious societies in the mid-Qing and their tendencies towards millenarianism]. In *Sennen okokuteki minshu undo no kenkyu* 千年王国的民衆運動の研究 [Studies on millenarian popular movements], edited by Suzuki Chusei, 151–312. Tokyo: Tokyo daigaku shuppankai, 1982.

Swope, Kenneth M. "The Legend of Tang Saier." In *The Ming World*, edited by Kenneth Swope, 311–321. Abingdon: Routledge, 2019.

———. *On the Trail of the Yellow Tiger: War, Trauma, and Social Dislocation in Southwest China during the Ming-Qing Transition*. Lincoln: University of Nebraska Press, 2018.

Szonyi, Michael. "Making Claims about Standardization and Orthopraxy in Late Imperial China." *Modern China* 33, no. 1 (2007): 47–71.

Taiwan tongzhi 台灣同志 [Gazetteer of Taiwan province]. Taibei: Datong shuju, 1984.

Tang Ruiyu 唐瑞裕. *Qingdai lizhi tanwei* 清代吏治探微 [An investigation of government administration in the Qing period]. Taibei: Wenshizhi chubanshe, 1991.

Theiss, Janet M. *Disgraceful Matters: The Politics of Chastity in Eighteenth-Century China*. Berkeley: University of California Press, 2004.

Thwing, E. W. "A Legend of the Ius, Translated from the Chinese." *The China Review* 22, no. 6 (1897): 781–782.

Tiandihui 天地會 [The Heaven and Earth Society]. 7 vols. Compiled by the First Historical Archives and the Institute of Qing History at People's University. Beijing: Zhongguo renmin daxue chubanshe, 1980–1988.

Van Dyke, Paul. *Whampoa and the Canton Trade: Life and Death in a Chinese Port, 1700–1842*. Hong Kong: Hong Kong University Press, 2020.

———. "Floating Brothels and the Canton Flower Boats, 1750–1930." *Review of Culture* 37 (2011): 112–142.

Waijidang 外纪檔 [Outer court record books of palace memorials]. Palace Museum, Taibei.

Wakeman, Frederic. *The Shanghai Badlands: Wartime Terrorism and Urban Crime, 1937–1941*. New York: Cambridge University Press, 1996.

———. *The Great Enterprise: The Manchu Reconstruction of Imperial Order in Seventeenth-Century China*. 2 vols. Berkeley: University of California Press, 1985.

———. "Romantics, Stoics, and Martyrs in Seventeenth-Century China." *Journal of Asian Studies* 43, no. 4 (1984): 631–665.

———. *Strangers at the Gate: Social Disorder in South China, 1839–1861*. Berkeley: University of California Press, 1966.

Wang, Di. *The Teahouse: Small Business, Everyday Culture, and Public Politics in Chengdu, 1900–1950*. Stanford: Stanford University Press, 2008.

———. *Street Culture in Chengdu: Public Space, Urban Commoners, and Local Politics, 1870–1930*. Stanford: Stanford University Press, 2003.

Wang Jianchuan 王見川. *Taiwan de zhaijiao yu luantang* 台灣的齋教與鸞堂 [Vegetarian sects and recitation halls in Taiwan]. Taibei: Nantian shuju, 1996.

Wang Mingke 王明珂. *Fansi shixue yu shixue fansi: wenben yu biaozheng fenxi* 反思史學與史學反思: 文本與表征分析 [Reflections on history and historical reflections: Analysis of texts and representations]. Shanghai: Shanghai renmin chubanshe, 2016.

Wang, Q. Edward. *Chopsticks: A Cultural and Culinary History*. New York: Cambridge University Press, 2015.

Wang, Shuo. *Please Don't Call Me Human*. Translated by Howard Goldblatt. New York: Hyperion, 2000.

———. *Playing for Thrills: A Mystery*. Translated by Howard Goldblatt. New York: William Morrow, 1997.

Wang Xuetai 王學泰. *Shuihu jianghu: lijue Zhongguo shehui de ling yitiao xiansuo* 水滸江湖:理解中國社會的另一條綫索 [Water Margin, rivers and lakes: Another clue to understanding Chinese society]. Xi'an: Shaanxi renmin chubanshe, 2011.

Wang, Y. Yvon. "Heroes, Hooligans, and Knights-Errant: Masculinities and Popular Media in the Early People's Republic of China." *Nan Nü* 19 (2017): 316–356.

Wang, Yuanfei. *Writing Pirates: Vernacular Fiction and Oceans in Late Ming China*. Ann Arbor: University of Michigan Press, 2021.

Ward, Barbara. "Regional Operas and Their Audiences: Evidence from Hong Kong." In *Popular Culture in Late Imperial China*, edited by David Johnson, Andrew Nathan, and Evelyn Rawski, 161–187. Berkeley: University of California Press, 1985.

Watson, James. "Hereditary Tenancy and Corporate Landlordism in Traditional China: A Case Study." In *Village Life in Hong Kong: Politics, Gender, and Ritual in the New Territories*, edited by James Watson and Rubie Watson, 145–166. Hong Kong: Chinese University Press, 2004.

———. "Self Defense Corps, Violence, and the Bachelor Sub-Culture in South China: Two Case Studies." In *Village Life in Hong Kong: Politics, Gender, and Ritual in the New Territories*, edited by James Watson and Rubie Watson, 251–265. Hong Kong: Chinese University Press, 2004.

———. "Of Flesh and Bones: The Management of Death Pollution in Cantonese Society." In *Village Life in Hong Kong: Politics, Gender, and Ritual in the New Territories*, edited by James Watson and Rubie Watson, 355–389. Hong Kong: Chinese University Press, 2004.

———. "Waking the Dragon: Visions of the Chinese Imperial State in Local Myth." In *Village Life in Hong Kong: Politics, Gender, and Ritual in the New Territories*, edited by James Watson and Rubie Watson, 423–441. Hong Kong: Chinese University Press, 2004.

———. "Living Ghosts: Long-Haired Destitutes in Colonial Hong Kong." In *Village Life in Hong Kong: Politics, Gender, and Ritual in the New Territories*, edited by James Watson and Rubie Watson, 453–469. Hong Kong: Chinese University Press, 2004.

———. "Standardizing the Gods: The Promotion of T'ien Hou ('Empress of Heaven') Along the South China Coast, 960–1960." In *Popular Culture in Late Imperial*

China, edited by David Johnson, Andrew Nathan, and Evelyn Rawski, 292–324. Berkeley: University of California Press, 1985.

Wei Yuan 魏源. *Shengwu ji* 聖武記 [Record of imperial military campaigns]. First published 1842. Beijing: Zhonghua shuju, 1984.

Weller, Robert P. "Matricidal Magistrates and Gambling Gods: Weak States and Strong Spirits in China." *Australian Journal of Chinese Affairs* 33 (January 1995): 107–124.

———. "Bandits, Beggars and Ghosts: The Failure of State Control over Religious Interpretation in Taiwan." *American Ethnologist* 12 (1985): 46–61.

Weng Kuan 翁寬. "Qinzhou Sanniang wan shihua" 欽州三娘灣史話 [Historical tales about Qinzhou's Sanniang Bay]. In *Wenshi Chunqiu* 文史春秋 (January 27, 2015). http://www.fx361.com/page/2015/0127/1414132.shtml.

Weng Liehui 翁烈輝. "Zheng Chenggong zai Shanwei de shishi he chuanshuo" 鄭成功在汕尾的事實和傳説 [History and legends about Zheng Chenggong in Shanwei]. *Shanwei chengqu wenshi* 汕尾城區文史 6 (2012): 52–56.

Weng Tongwen 翁同文. "Tiandihui yinyu 'mulidoushi' xinyi" 天地會陰語 '木立斗世' 新議 [A new explanation of the tiandihui secret slogan 'mulidoushi']. *Shixue huikan* 史學彙刊 7 (1976): 167–189.

White, Hayden. *The Practical Past*. Evanston: Northwestern University Press, 2014.

———. *Tropics of Discourse: Essays in Cultural Criticism*. Baltimore: Johns Hopkins University Press, 1978.

White, Richard. *The Middle Ground: Indians, Empires, and Republics in the Great Lakes Region, 1650–1815*. Cambridge: Cambridge University Press, 2011.

Williams, C. A. S. *Outlines of Chinese Symbolism and Art Motives*, third edition. Shanghai: Kelly and Walsh, 1941.

Williams, S. Wells. *The Middle Kingdom: A Survey of the Geography, Government, Literature, Social Life, Arts, and History of the Chinese Empire and Its Inhabitants*. 2 vols. New York: C. Scribner's Sons, 1899.

Willoughby-Meade, Gerald. *Chinese Ghouls and Goblins*. London: Constable and Co., 1928.

Wise, Michael, ed. *Travellers Tales of the South China Coast: Hong Kong, Canton, Macao*. Singapore: Times Books International, 1986.

Wolf, Margery. "Women and Suicide in China." In *Women in Chinese Society*, edited by Margery Wolf and Roxane Witke, 111–141. Stanford: Stanford University Press, 1975.

Wong, Sik-ling. "More Notes on the Ruler of the Yao of Loh-Fah Mountains." *Lingnan Science Journal* 18 (1939): 123–125.

———. "In Search of a Forgotten Tribe: The Yao People of the Mountains." *Lingnan Science Journal* 17 (1938): 477–481.

Wordie, Jason. "Lai Choi San, All Woman, All Pirate." *Hong Kong Sunday Morning Post*, October 8, 2000.

Wu Gaozi 吳高梓. "Fuzhou Danmin diaocha" 福州蛋民調查 [Investigation of the Danmin of Fuzhou]. *Shehui xuejie* 社會學界 4 (1930): 141–155.

BIBLIOGRAPHY

Wu, Helena Yuen Wai. "A Journey across Rivers and Lakes: A Look at the Untranslatable 'Jianghu' in Chinese Culture and Literature." *452° F, Electronic Journal of Theory of Literature and Comparative Literature* 7 (2012): 58–71.

Wu, Junqing. *Mandarins and Heretics: The Construction of Heresy in Chinese State Discourse*. Leiden: Brill, 2017.

Wu, Pei-Yi. "Yang Miaozhen: A Woman Warrior in Thirteenth-Century China." *Nan Nü* 4 (2002): 137–169.

Wu Ruilin 伍銳麟. *Sanshui Danmin diaocha* 三水蛋民調查 [Study of Sanshui Danmin]. Taipei: Dongfang wenhua shuju, 1971.

Wu, Yiching. *The Cultural Revolution at the Margins: Chinese Socialism in Crisis*. Cambridge, MA: Harvard University Press, 2014.

Xi Jinping 習近平. "Zai quanguo minzu tuanjie jinbu biaozhang dahuishang de jianghua" 在全國民族團結進步表彰大會上的講話 [Speech given at the National Ethnic Unity Advancement Commendation Conference], Beijing, September 27, 2019. https://www.xinhuanet.com/politics/leaders/2019-09/27/c_1125049000.htm.

Xiangshan xianzhi 香山縣志 [Gazetteer of Xiangshan county, Guangdong]. 1879 edition. Taibei: Taiwan xuesheng shuju, 1968.

Xiao Yishan 蕭一山. *Jindai mimi shehui shiliao* 近代秘密社會史料 [Historical materials on modern secret societies]. 4 vols. Beiping: Guoli Beiping yanjiuyuan zongban shichu chubanshe, 1935.

Xiao, Zhiwen, Purnima Mehrotra, and Rick Zimmerman. "Sexual Revolution in China: Implications for Chinese Women and Society." *AIDS Care* 23, supplement 1 (June 2011): 105–112.

Xingke tiben 刑科題本 (*daoan* 盜案 category). First Historical Archives, Beijing.

Xinning xianzhi 新寧縣志 [Gazetteer of Xinning county, Guangdong]. 1869.

Xu Anqi 徐安琪. "Beidongxing juezequan he di manyidu" 被動性抉擇全和底滿意度 [Passivity, power to choose, and low satisfaction]. *Shehuixue yanjiu* 社會學研究 3 (1990): 105–108.

Xu Wenqing 許文清. "Lun Liannan Pai Yao de shenhua gushi" 論連南排瑤的神話故事 [Myths and stories of the Liannan Pai Yao]. In *Yaozu yanjiu lunwen ji: 1986 nian Yaozu yanjiu guoji yantaohui* 瑤族研究論文集: 1986年瑤族研究國際研討會 [Collected essays on the Yao from the 1986 international conference on Yao studies], edited by Qiao Jian 喬健, Xie Jian 謝劍, and Hu Qiwang 胡起望, 177–188. Beijing: Minzu chubanshe, 1988.

Xu Wentang 許文堂 and Xie Qiyi 謝奇懿, eds. *Da Nan shilu Qing Yue guanxi shiliao huibian* 大南實錄清越關係史料彙編 [Collection of historical materials on Qing-Vietnam relations from Vietnam's Veritable Records]. Taibei: Academia Sinica, 2000.

Xu Xiu Siku Quanshu 續修四庫全書 [New revised complete books of the four treasuries]. Compiled by Gu Tinglong 顧廷龍. Shanghai: Shanghai guji chubanshe, 1995.

Xu Zhenghong 許正鴻. *Fuzhou mixin fengyun* 符咒祕辛風雲 [On popular charms and incantations]. Tainan: Daxing chubanshe, 1993.

Yai zhouzhi 崖州志 [Gazetteer of Yai department]. Qing Guangxu edition. Guangzhou, 1988.

Bibliography

Yang Xiguang 楊曦光. *Niugui sheshen lu: wenge qiujin zhong de jingling* 牛鬼蛇神錄: 文革囚禁中的精靈 [Anecdotes about ox-demons and snake-spirits: The vitality of Cultural Revolution prisoners]. Hong Kong: Niujin daxue chubanshe, 1994.

Yang Yiqing 楊奕青. "Guanyu Zhao Jinlong qiyi jige wenti de shangque" 關於趙金龍起義幾個問題的商榷 [Re-examining some problems about the righteous uprising led by Zhao Jinlong]. *Minzu yanjiu* 民族研究 1 (1985): 34–38.

Yangshan xianzhi 陽山縣志 [Gazetteer of Yangshan county, Guangdong]. First published 1938. Taibei: Chengwen chubanshe, 1974.

Yao Shun'an 姚舜安. "Zhao Jinlong lingdao de Yaomin qiyi" 趙金龍領導的瑤民起義 [The Yao uprising led by Zhao Jinlong]. *Guangxi minzu daxue xuebao* 廣西民族大學學報 2 (1983): 62–67.

Yao, Yusheng. "The Elite Class Background of Wang Shuo and His Hooligan Characters." *Modern China* 30, no. 4 (2004): 431–469.

Yates, M. T. "Ancestral Worship and Fung-Shuy." *China Recorder and Missionary Journal* 1, no. 3 (1868): 37–43.

Yongan xian sanzhi 永安縣三志 [Gazetteer of Yongan county, Guangdong]. 1822 edition. Taibei: Chengwen chubanshe, 1974.

Yongzheng zhupi yuzhi 雍正硃批諭旨 [Published edicts and palace memorials of the Yongzheng reign]. Taibei: Wenhai chubanshe, 1965.

You, Ziying. *Folk Literati, Contested Tradition, and Heritage in Contemporary China: Incense Is Kept Burning*. Bloomington: Indiana University Press, 2020.

Yu Yingshi 余英時. *Shi yu Zhongguo wenhua* 士與中國文化 [Warriors and Chinese culture]. Shanghai: Shanghai renmin chubanshe, 1987.

Yuan Yonglun 袁永綸. *Jing haifen ji* 靖海氛記 [A record of pacification of the seas]. 1830 edition. Accessed June 5, 2019. https://www.shuge.org/ebook/jing-hai-quan-tu.

Zeng, Huijuan. "From Sheds to Houses: A Dan Village in the Pearl River Delta in the Twentieth Century." In *The Fisher Folk of Late Imperial and Modern China: An Historical Anthropology of Boat-and-Shed Living*, edited by He Xi and David Faure, 159–172. London and New York: Routledge, 2016.

Zhang, Juwen. *Oral Traditions in Contemporary China: Healing a Nation*. Lanham, MD: Lexington Books, 2022.

Zhang Qu 張渠. *Yuedong wenjianlu* 粵東聞見錄 [Record of things seen and heard in Guangdong]. Preface dated 1738. Guangzhou: Guangdong gaodeng jiaoyu chubanshe, 1990.

Zhang, Yingjin. *The City in Modern Chinese Literature and Film: Configurations of Space, Time, and Gender*. Stanford: Stanford University Press, 1996.

Zhang, Yingyu. *The Book of Swindles: Selections from a Late Ming Collection*. Translated by Christopher Rea and Bruce Rusk. New York: Columbia University Press, 2017.

Zhanghua xianzhi 彰化縣志 [Gazetteer of Zhanghua county, Taiwan]. First published 1836. Taibei: Chengwen chubanshe, 1983.

Zhao, C. "From Punk to Environmentalist: The Return of Chun Shu." In *Women of China*, July 30, 2010. https://www.womenofchina.cn/womenofchina/html1/people/writers/10/8535-1.htm.

Bibliography

Zheng Dehua 鄭德華. "Guangdong zhonglu tuke xiedou yanjiu" 廣東中路土客械鬥研究 [A study of armed conflicts between the Punti and the Hakka in central Guangdong, 1856–1867]. PhD diss., University of Hong Kong, 1989.

Zheng Guangnan 鄭廣南 et al. *Xinbian Zhongguo haidao shi* 新編中國海盜史 [Revised history of Chinese pirates]. Shanghai: Zhongguo dabaike quanshu chubanshe, 2014.

Zheng Hui 郑慧. *Yaozu wenshu dang'an yanjiu* 瑤族文書檔案研究 [A study of Yao literary documents]. Beijing: Minzu chubanshe, 2011.

Zhong Jingwen 鍾敬文. *Dan ge* 蛋歌 [Dan folksongs]. First published 1927. Taibei: Dongfang wenhua gongying she, 1970.

Zhou Bei 周蓓. "Songdai fengshui yanjiu" 宋代風水研究 [A study of geomancy in the Song period]. MA thesis, Shanghai Normal University, 2003. http://t.docin.com/p-752900546.html?docfrom=rrela.

Zhou Qufei 周去非. *Lingwai daida* 嶺外代答 [Representative answers from the region beyond the mountains]. Song dynasty edition. Accessed March 26, 2012. http://www4.webng.com/khcjhk/ song/lwdd1a.htm#_Toc128805855.

Zhu, Yujie. *Heritage and Romantic Consumption in China*. Amsterdam: Amsterdam University Press, 2018.

Zhuang Jifa 莊吉發. "Gugong dang'an yu Qingdai minsu" 故宮檔案與清代民俗 [Palace Museum archives and folk customs in the Qing period]. In *Qingshi suibi* 清史隨筆 [Musings on Qing history], edited by Zhuang Jifa, 54–63. Taibei: Boyang wenhua shiye youxian gongsi, 1996.

———. *Qingdai mimi huidang shi yanjiu* 清代秘密會黨史研究 [A study of secret societies in the Qing period]. Taibei: Wenshizhi chubanshe, 1994.

———. *Qingdai tiandihui yuanliu kao* 清代天地會源流考 [On the origins of the Heaven and Earth Society in the Qing period]. Taibei: Gugong bowuyuan chubanshe, 1981.

Zhupi zouzhe 硃批奏摺 [Unpublished palace memorials]. First Historical Archives, Beijing.

"Zongju tichu jiemu jiabin biaozhun: ge tiaodi wenshen xiha wenhua buyong" 總局提出節目嘉賓標準:格調低紋身嘻哈文化不用 [The central office announces behavioral standards for guests: no more hip-hop or tattoos]. *Sinlang yule* 新浪娛樂, January 19, 2018. http://ent.sina.com.cn/tv/zy/2018-01-19/doc-ifyquptv7935320.shtml.

Index

altars (Triad), 102, 116–17
alternative culture, 239
Amoy (Xiamen), 68–69, 111, 116, 207
amulets, 5, 11–14, 64, 92, 113–17, 122, 154, 208, 232, 304n72; as heavenly signs, 113, 115; as protection from apocalypse, 5, 50, 108, 125, 134, 150; as protection from robberies, 115; handbooks of, 14, 113, 115, 122; jade, 113, 116, 119; laws prohibiting, 113, 232; peach wood, 111, 116; sale of, 5, 34, 113–14, 125–26, 152; to cure illness, 5, 115, 124, 145; to expel demons, 114–15, 117; to improve livelihoods, 145, 124; used by messianic groups, 142, 146–47, 150; used by ritual specialists, 113, 184; used by Triads, 115, 142–44, 153, 304n72; with cat images, 92
Annan. *See* Vietnam.
apocalypse, 5, 50, 108–12, 118, 125, 128, 135, 142–51, 153, 235–36
arhats, 148–50
armed feuds (*xiedou*), 56, 80, 103, 106, 124, 126, 131, 135, 139, 151, 160, 162, 164, 180
authenticity, 6, 42, 97, 236, 247
azure tiger, 94, 97. *See also fengshui*.

Badlands (Shanghai), 26
Bai Lang, 36–37
baleful stars. *See* comets.
banditry/bandits, 3, 11, 23–37, 54–56, 60, 65–66, 82–93, 100, 119, 152, 180–81; and beggars, 5, 134–35; and cannibalism, 37; and marginalization, 29, 31, 73; and Robin Hood idealism, 36–37; and secret societies, 102, 105, 125, 135, 138; and social banditry, 65; and social disorder, 44, 47, 51–52, 55–56, 162, 167–68, 186–87; and socioeconomic equality, 34, 99; as heroes, 23, 27, 29, 35–36, 40; as symptom of cosmic disruption, 49–50; collusion with local notables, 87–88; geomantic explanations of, 93, 97–99; government suppression, 78, 88; lairs, 23–24, 26, 83–86, 131, 134; occasional, 8; official collusion, 84; social backgrounds, 86–87; supernatural protection against, 115; survival strategy, 8, 105; urban refuges, 24, 26
banners (flags), 1, 11, 34, 118–20, 124–25, 134, 136–39, 142, 144–46, 155, 164, 209; and sedition, 4, 118, 134; as

talismans, 5, 34, 115; Manchu armies, 52; in Yao rebellion, 183, 185; in pirate fleets, 203, 204; marked with names of saviors, 1, 5, 111–12, 118, 142; representing divine generals/armies, 109–10, 112, 120; sacrifices to, 138, 142, 156; used by Triads, 116, 137, 143, 150, 153
barbarians, 108–9, 118, 170, 229, 244–46, 248
bare sticks (*guanggun*), 22, 28–29, 37, 41–42, 56, 87, 287n37
Barrow, John, 194–95
Bayansan, 84, 88
beggars, 5, 8, 29, 31, 33, 51, 73, 76, 86, 216, 232, 243
Beijing Doll (*Beijing wawa*), 242
Bezos, Jeff, 230
Biên Hòa, 53
Black Bones Mai. *See* Mai Yarong.
blood, 47–48, 95, 120, 193, 245; in medicine, 92, 120, 193; menstrual, 241–42; oaths, 16, 20, 32, 104–8, 118–22, 125–27, 186; of cocks, 120–21; sacrifice, 119–20, 245; ritual use of, 120, 245
boat women, 9, 191–97, 200–5, 210, 212–13, 239, 245, 311n2
Book of Changes (*Yijing*), 236
Book of Documents (*Shujing*), 48
Book of Rites (*Lijing*), 91
boxers/boxing. *See* martial arts.
Boxers (revolt), 31, 33, 35, 242
Brando, Marlon, 206

Broken Shoes Chen the Fourth. *See* Chen Lanjisi.
brothels, 20, 24–26. *See also* floating brothels; flower boats; prostitutes/prostitution.
Buddha of the Future. *See* Maitreya.
Buddhism, 7, 91, 99, 108, 123, 131, 149, 151, 219, 234–35. *See also* lay Buddhist groups.
bushel, 110, 116–17

Cai Buyun, 136, 152
Cai Qian, 205
Cai Qian Ma, 203, 205, 206. *See also* women, pirates.
Candy (*Tang*), 33, 238–40
cannibalism, 40, 47. *See also* human sacrifice.
Canton delta, x, 78–80, 99, 101, 197–99, 214, 224, 297n66; and banditry, 24, 83–86, 88, 96, 125; and Dan, 32, 192, 197, 199, 219; and hired laborers, 81; and lineages, 80–82; and messianic groups, 112, 124; and piracy, 67, 202, 204, 224, 227; and sand fields, 79–82; and tenancy, 81; as core area, 79; famine, 204; in Ming–Qing dynastic wars, 54, 68; Red Turban revolt, 164
cats, 6, 89–92, 97, 100–101
celestial armies. *See* divine armies.
Celestial Masters, 177, 182
celestial soldiers. *See* divine soldiers.
Celestial Wolf Star, 34
Chao Gai, 30

Index

Chaozhou, 34, 52, 102, 105–6, 110, 115, 122, 135, 161, 198
charms. *See* amulets.
Charter from Emperor Ping (Pinghuang quandie), 174
Chashan, 132, 134
Chen Biao, 102, 135
Chen Fangqi, 164
Chen Jiaxun, 158
Chen Jingang, 162–64, 166, 306n22. *See also* Chen Lanjisi.
Chen Jinjiang. *See* Chen Lanjisi.
Chen Lanjisi, 7, 10, 131–33, 136–48, 140, 144, 148, 150, 152–53, 155–66, 305n20
Chen Maosheng, 73
Chen Shangchuan, 53, 57, 67
Chen Shizhuang, 138, 155, 157–58
Chen Shunxi, 44, 46, 48–51, 54, 56, 59
Chen Weiyan, 161
Chen Xingcai. *See* Chen Lanjisi.
Chen Yaben, 136
Chen Zhongru, 158
Chengdu, 26, 32, 238
China Youth Daily, 37–39, 240
Chinese Bazaar (Macau), 26, 204
Chun Shu, 242
City of Willows, 117–18, 147. *See also* Cloud City.
Classic of Mountains and Seas (Shanhaijing), 109, 298n16
Cloud City, 118, 147. *See also* City of Willows.
cocks (chickens), 120–21
comets, 46–51, 66, 286n1
community pacts (*xiangyue*), 133

Confucianism, 8, 35–37, 52, 97, 99–100, 122, 196, 213, 238, 247; filiality, 35–36; loyalty, 35–36; popular cynicism about, 14; revival of (PRC), 230–31, 234–35; righteousness, 35–36; social harmony, 37; underworld attitudes about, 37; virtues, 35–36
consumer culture, 43, 230, 238, 242, 287n37
covenants, 104–5, 107–8, 118–22, 126, 146, 148, 150. *See also* blood, oaths.
Cui Jian, 239
Cultural Revolution, 32, 40, 43, 74, 222, 230–32, 314n20

Dachengjiao, 130, 139–41, 143–46, 149–54, 235–36, 303n38
Dan (minority), 9, 12, 17, 57, 217–19, 222, 224, 226, 244, 285n19; discrimination against, 29, 81–82, 87, 192, 222; ethnic profiling, 217; ferrying, 82, 195, 198; fishers, 12, 80, 82, 195, 214, 219–20; pearl gathering, 216–17; pirates, 83, 210, 214; prominent families, 82; prostitution, 197–200; tenant farmers, 82. *See also* boat women.
Dan females. *See* boat women.
Daoguang emperor, 182, 184
Daoism, 7, 21, 94, 104, 108–10, 117, 131, 144, 150, 181–82, 184, 219, 234–35

demonology, 104–5, 107–8, 113–14, 118, 126, 150–51, 232
demons, 47, 50, 72, 74, 90–92, 108–18, 120, 125–28, 145, 152, 207–9, 212, 222, 231–34, 243–44. *See also* evil spirits; ghosts.
Deng Xiaoping, 229, 234
Deng Yao, 49, 52–54, 57, 59, 66
Ding Bogui, 209
divine armies, 64, 108–10, 112, 116, 150, 231
divine generals, 110, 111, 120
divine soldiers, 5, 64, 103, 108–9, 111, 116, 118, 125, 134, 184, 189
Divine Woman of Meizhou (Meizhou shennü). *See* Empress of Heaven.
Dog of Heaven (Tiangou), 47
Donghai Ba, 220
Doufu Bagui, 183, 190
Dragon Flower Scripture (*Longhua jing*), 149–50
Dragon Ladies, 206, 209
droughts, 47–50, 54, 111, 131, 186
Du Guoxiang, 30, 123
Du Qi, 119, 123, 126
Du Shiming, 142, 145, 147–48, 152–53
Du Yonghe, 53

Empress of Heaven, 69, 73–76, 191, 208–9, 214, 217–22, 224–28, 237
Empress Wu Zetian, 92
Endicott, James, 203

epidemics, 49–51, 90, 108, 113, 116, 120, 126. *See also* plagues.
ethnic: classification (PRC), 169, 246, 311n4; conflict, 54, 133, 135, 151, 153, 163–64, 168, 172, 180; diversity, 245, 246; fusion (*minzu ronghua*), 246; groups, x, 9, 29, 153, 160, 172, 189, 200, 244–49; identity, x, 9, 133, 153, 168–75, 188–89, 200, 244, 247; profiling, 217; tourism, 247–48. *See also* Dan; Hakka; Jing; Yao.
evil spirits, 47, 74, 91–92, 109, 116–17, 236, 241, 243. *See also* demons; ghosts.
exorcism, 5, 47, 104, 108–22, 126, 142, 144, 182, 186, 207–8, 212, 222, 231–32

famines, 47–51, 118, 131, 134–35, 149, 186, 204
fan Qing fu Ming. See slogans.
Father and Mother Society (Fumuhui), 107
Fei Xiaotong, 246
females. *See* women.
feminism, 238, 240
Feng Heng, 116, 122
Fengshan, 1, 3–4, 106, 111
fengshui, 14, 78, 88–89, 93–101, 186, 273
feuds. *See* armed feuds.
Five Ancestors (*wuzu*), 30–31
Five Banner Calvary, 183–84, 189
Five Emperors (Wudi), 234, 237
Five Encampments (*wuying*), 109–10

Five Houses (*wufang*), 110
Five Vessels Teaching (Wupanjiao), 140, 143, 146, 236, 303n44
floating brothels, 82, 198, 200, 203, 210. *See also* prostitutes/prostitution.
Flower boats, 198. *See also* prostitutes/prostitution.
folk religion. *See* popular religion.
folklore, 10, 12, 14, 42, 61, 66, 78, 83, 89, 97, 100–101, 183, 188, 231, 247
fortune telling/fortune tellers, 8, 12, 26, 34, 41, 123, 127, 134, 232
Fuzhou, 192, 195, 198, 200–201, 209, 237

gambling/gamblers, 15, 22, 24–26, 29–30, 32, 76, 102, 108, 124–25, 158, 204
gangsterism/gangsters, 26, 28, 40, 76, 102, 104, 108, 124–27
geomancy. *See fengshui*.
ghost altars, 72
ghosts, 5, 9, 16, 71–73, 76–77, 91, 96, 108–9, 112, 115–16, 207, 232, 242. *See also* demons; evil spirits.
Girl of the Modern Age (*Shidai guniang*), 239
Goat Dung Mountain (Yangshishan), 137, 148
God of War (Guandi), 110, 122
God of Money, 230
Goddess of Mercy (Guanyin), 5, 50, 139, 219, 237
Goddess of Wealth, 70, 77

Gowned Brothers (Paoge), 32
Great Clearance, 51, 54–55
Great Hong Kingdom (Taihongguo), 162, 165
great peace (*taiping*), 110, 116, 150, 154, 236
Great Proletarian Cultural Revolution. *See* Cultural Revolution.
Gu Long, 21, 31, 36
Guan Yuelong, 138, 144
guanggun. *See* bare sticks.
guardsmen, 82, 86–87, 100. *See also* sandsmen.
Gulf of Tonkin, 45–46, 50, 52–53, 56–59, 65–66, 208, 214, 217–21, 224, 227, 243–44
Guo Fei, 215
Guo Podai, 204, 220

Hải Nha, 57
Hailing'a, 185
Hainan, 47, 49, 52–54, 57–58, 60, 63, 105, 209–10, 214, 224
Hakka, 9, 23, 129, 131–36, 145, 151–52, 154, 161–64, 226; communal organization, 133; discrimination against, 132–34; females, 195; feuds, 160–61, 163–64; heartland, 129–30, 140; identity, 153; on Yao frontier, 178–79, 186; sectarianism, 140–44; social disorder, 129, 134–35, 140, 153, 180, 184–85, 224; Triad uprising, 135–39, 155–57
Hakka–Punti War, 163–64, 224

Index

Han dynasty, 120, 122, 169, 215
Han Youxian, 60
haohan, 22, 24, 27–28
He Deguang, 32
Heaven (*tian*), 36–37, 49, 64, 66, 76, 115–16, 119, 148, 150, 154, 183, 189
Heaven and Earth Society (Tiandihui). *See* Triads.
heroes, 7, 9–10, 23, 27–28, 33, 36, 40–41, 66, 68, 161, 165–66, 183
hip-hop (*xiha*), 21, 28, 32, 41
Holy Mother of Shuiwei (Shuiwei shengmu), 210
Holy Mother of the Yellow Lotus (Huanglian shengmu), 33
Hong Kong, 195–96, 200–201, 203–6, 209, 219–20, 226
Hong Xiuquan, 23, 162
Hongxing Society (Hongxingshe), 32, 288n48
Hooligan Yan, 239
hooligans. *See liumang*.
Hu Jintao, 230, 234
Hu Sanniang, 33, 42
Huang Dawan, 148
Huang Dehui, 146, 147, 149
Huang Hairu, 52, 56
Huang Kaiguang, 224–25, 227
Huang Liuhong, 21, 32, 36–37
Huang Tingchen. *See* Huang Dehui.
human sacrifice, 119, 138, 243. *See also* cannibalism.

imperial treasures, 64, 119. *See also* national treasures.

incantations, 11, 50, 64, 90–92, 112–16, 124, 148–50, 184, 208, 232
iron, 92–93, 115–16, 232
Iron Cat, 78, 88–89, 92–93, 96–99
Iron Ruler Society (Tiechihui), 30–31, 114, 119–20, 123, 126

jade, 64, 113, 116, 119
Jade Emperor, 64, 112, 127, 219
Jiang Zemin, 236
jianghu. *See* rivers and lakes.
Jiangping (Giang Bình), 218–19, 244
Jiaqing emperor, 40, 138, 161
Jin Yong, 21, 24, 31, 36, 38, 42
Jing (Kinh), 243–46, 248
Jinggangshan, 23
Journey to the West (Xiyouji), 7
Jueluo Jiqing, 135, 138–39, 158

Kang Youwei, 230
Kangxi emperor, 21, 55–56, 103, 177, 208
knights-errant, 21–22, 27–28, 30, 33, 35, 41–42, 141, 238
Koxinga. *See* Zheng Chenggong.
kungfu. *See* martial arts.

Lady of the Golden Flower (Jinhua furen), 234, 237
Lady of the Seventh Star (Qixing Niangniang), 209–10
Lai Choi San, 203, 205–6. *See also* women, pirates.
Lai Dongbao, 138, 144
Lan Xiuwen, 138
Laozi, 213

lay Buddhist groups, 8, 17, 108, 123, 131, 139–45, 148, 151–53, 233. *See also* Buddhism.
legends, 10, 14, 34–35, 42, 44, 52, 61, 63–65, 67, 69–71, 103–4, 166, 184, 204–5, 207, 215, 219, 225, 243–44. *See also* mythology.
legitimacy/legitimation, 60, 65, 97, 110, 119, 183, 206, 226. *See also* Mandate of Heaven.
Leizhou, 45, 49, 52–58, 60–61, 105, 208–9, 214, 217–18, 221–28, 232, 240
Li Awan, 110, 114, 122, 124
Li Chengdong, 52
Li Deming, 181–82
Li Dingguo, 54
Li Hongzhi, 235–36
Li Jiukui, 111–12, 125
Li Kaihua, 111–12, 115, 118, 122, 134, 142, 147, 151, 153
Li Lingkui, 140–43, 145, 147–48, 150, 152–53
Li Mei, 112–14, 116, 118–19, 122, 124–25
Li Shimin, 7
Li Taohong, 111, 150
Li Tianbao, 111–12, 116, 119
Li Weifeng, 96
Li Wenmao, 31, 288n41
Li Yinhe, 238
Li Zhong, 31
Liang Qichao, 40
Liang Yaxiang, 83–84, 86–88, 98, 125
Liangshan. *See* Mount Liang.
Lianshan, 167, 177–79, 181, 185

Lianzhou, 157–58, 160–62, 164–66, 177, 182, 185–86, 290n6
Liao Ganzhou, 142, 147, 152
Liars' Square (Chengdu), 26
Lienzhou, 47, 50, 52, 54–55, 214, 218–19, 226, 290n6
Lin Daoqian, 67, 70–71, 191
Lin Guniang. *See* Lin Jinlian.
Lin Jinlian, 70–71
Lin Moniang. *See* Empress of Heaven.
Lin Shuangwen, 102, 105, 115, 123, 139
lineages, 13, 80–83, 87–88, 94, 99–100, 103, 133, 153, 158–60
liquor, 24, 113, 119–20, 198
Liu Zaifu, 40
liumang, 8, 21–22, 26–28, 32, 35, 37–39, 41–42, 240
Lob Lob Creek, 198
Lockhart, J. H. Stewart, 96
Longmen county, 132, 136, 138, 148
Longmen island, 52–53, 57–60, 63–64
Loviot, Fanny, 202
lower-body literature, 239. *See also* Chun Shu; Mian Mian; Wei Hui.
Lu Dian, 91
Luo Qi, 239, 243
Luo Teaching (Luojiao), 123, 139–40, 145–46, 303n38
Luoxiying, 137, 156–57

Macau, 26, 54, 197–200, 202, 204–6, 210, 219, 221, 224, 226
macho. *See haohan*.
Madam Big Foot (Da Jiao Sao), 203

magic/magicians, 5, 8–9, 29, 33–34, 64, 69–70, 72, 77, 92–93, 102, 107, 113, 116–17, 122, 134, 172, 182–84, 186, 207–8, 219, 232, 242. *See also* ritual specialists.
Mai Yarong, 83, 86–87
Maitreya, 123–24, 140, 142, 144, 146–47, 149–51, 236
Mandate of Heaven, 36, 119. *See also* legitimacy/legitimation.
Mao Zedong, 7, 23, 40, 231
martial arts, 20–24, 26–27, 29–31, 33–38, 41–42, 69, 74, 123, 141, 151, 182
Mazu. *See* Empress of Heaven.
Mazu gales (Mazu *ju*), 209
mean people (*jianmin*), 29
messianism, 104–8, 110–11, 114–20, 122–27, 134, 147, 150, 169, 180, 187, 236. *See also* millenarianism.
Mian Mian, 33, 238–42
militias (*tuanlian*), 29, 47, 55–56, 133, 136, 138–39, 148, 157, 160, 162, 164, 168, 185–88
Milk Ladies (Nainiang), 210
millenarianism, 7, 108, 117, 140, 146, 148–50, 235, 237. *See also* messianism.
Ming loyalism, 3, 45, 51–53, 56, 59–61, 63, 68, 73. *See also* Southern Ming.
Ministry of Culture (PRC), 41
Ministry of Public Security (PRC), 21, 27, 32, 38
Monk Hong Er. *See* Tixi.

monks (Buddhist), 5, 8, 30–31, 102, 122–23, 140, 142, 148, 151–52. *See also* ritual specialists.
Morrison, Jim, 239
Mother of Typhoons (Jumu), 209
Mother of Winds (Fengmu), 209
Mount Liang, 23, 29–31, 36, 40
multiculturalism, 231, 245, 247
mutual support, 32, 103–4, 129, 145
Muzimei, 239–41, 243
Mỹ Tho, 45, 58
mythohistory, 14, 68, 169, 182, 188–89, 249
mythology, 9–10, 14, 42, 103–4, 111, 113, 117, 147, 166, 169, 173, 188–89, 193. *See also* legends.

National Learning (*Guoxue*), 236
national treasures, 115. *See also* imperial treasures.
natural disasters, 10, 46, 48–50, 68, 131, 135, 152
Nayancheng, 138
New Cultural Revolution, 238–39
Nezha (Nocha), 111
Ng Akew (Wu Ajiao), 203
Nine Lotus Scripture (*Jiulian jing*), 146–47, 149

Old Official Vegetarian Hall (Laoguan zhaitang), 139
omens, 46–48, 66, 90, 119, 209, 236
opium, 26, 188, 198, 203–5
ox-demons and snake-spirits, 231–33
Ox Head Society, 134, 138. *See also* Punti.

Panda Sex (*Xiongmao*), 242
Panhu, 9, 169–75, 181–84, 186, 188–89
peach/peach wood, 111–12, 115–16
Pearl River delta. *See* Canton delta.
Phan Phú Quốc, 57–59
piracy/pirates, 8–9, 32–33, 44–46, 51–63, 73, 83, 119, 125, 162, 214–15, 224–27; and cannibalism, 37; as good outlaws, 36, 63–64; as heroes, 44, 66; as rebels, 34, 52–53, 58, 60, 66, 68, 73; collusion with officials, 65; Dan, 82–83, 217–19; deification, 67, 76, 191; lairs, 53, 215–16, 220, 247; occasional, 8; predictions of decline, 46–47; survival strategy, 8, 224; treasure, 64, 69–72, 77; women, 33, 201–7, 212–13
Pissing Woman, 207–8, 242
plagues, 90–91, 108–9, 112, 115, 125, 149, 231. *See also* epidemics.
Polders. *See* sand fields.
pollution, 38, 71, 234, 241–42, 245
popular religion, x–xi, 74, 104, 116–17, 126, 131, 232, 234, 237, 248
portents. *See* omens.
Powdered Lady (Huafen furen), 210–11
Practice of the Wheel of Law (Falungong), 235–36
priests (Daoist), 5, 29–30, 47, 91, 110, 112–13, 115–16, 120–23, 144. *See also* ritual specialists.
primordial energy. *See qi*.

Proclamation of [the right to] cross the mountains (*Guoshan bang*), 174
prostitutes/prostitution, 8, 22, 24–26, 28, 32–33, 41, 76, 192, 194–95, 197–200, 203, 210, 213, 239, 241, 246, 295n17. *See also* brothels; floating brothels; flower boats.
Pugnacious youths (*dazai*), 87. *See also* bare sticks.
punk (*pengke*), 21, 41, 239
Punti, 131–39, 153, 159–61, 163–64, 224

qi, 92–95, 99, 293n1
Qianlong emperor, 40, 86, 88, 107, 133, 161
Qin dynasty, 41
Qin Liangyu, 33
Qinghui. *See* Third Old Lady.
Qinzhou, 45–49, 52–53, 58–61, 66, 217–19
Qiongzhou. *See* Hainan.
Qiu Yajiang, 161
Qu Dajun, 80, 94–95, 111, 171, 192–93, 209
Quanzhou, 106, 311n5
Queen Mother of the West (Xiwangmu), 94

racketeering, 26, 29, 32, 105, 205–6, 295n17
Rat Hill (Laoshushan), 23, 78, 83–89, 93, 96–101, 125
rats, 6, 32, 78, 83, 89–93, 96, 100–101
Rebellion of the Three Feudatories, 48, 51, 55–56, 59

red (color), 112, 144
Red Guards, 231
Red Lanterns, 33, 242
Red Turban Revolt, 31, 157, 161–64, 224
righteous armies (*yijun*), 60–61, 165
righteous uprisings (*qiyi*), 50, 52, 59, 165
Righteous Yang. *See* Yang Yandi.
righteousness, 1, 23, 35–36, 61, 63–66, 69, 92, 150, 219
Riley, Lucky Jack, 26. *See also* Badlands.
ritual space, 5
ritual specialists, xi, 5, 8, 113, 115, 120, 176, 182–84, 189. *See also* magic/magicians; monks; priests; shamans; sorcery/sorcerers; spirit mediums; wizards.
rivers and lakes, 8, 21–23, 27, 32–34, 43, 127, 234, 249
rob the rich to aid the poor (*jiefu jipin*). *See* slogans.
rogues, 8–9, 20, 25, 90–91, 96, 100, 124–25, 134, 249
rotten lads (*lanzai*), 56, 87. *See also* bare sticks.

Sakura Magozō, 200
saltwater girls, 194, 198. *See also* floating brothels; prostitutes/prostitution.
saltwater songs (*xianshuige*), 197
sand fields (*shatian*), 79–83, 87–88, 97, 192, 197
sands people (*shamin*), 81–82

sands sticks (*shagun*), 82. *See also* bare sticks.
Sandsmen (*shafu*), 82. *See also* guardsmen.
Sanpo. *See* Third Old Lady.
Santaizi. *See* Nezha.
saviors, 5, 7, 10, 108–12, 115, 118–19, 134, 142, 144–51, 153, 169, 182–83, 189
Scarth, John, 161
Scripture of the Five Lords (*Wugong jing*), 149–50
Scripture on the Great Precepts of the Great Vehicle (*Dacheng dajie jing*), 140, 143, 147
Scripture on the Roots of Benevolence (*Enben jing*), 140, 143, 147
seals, 11, 55, 113–15, 119, 134, 139, 144, 146, 148, 186
secret societies, x, 8, 11, 31–32, 35, 102–4, 108, 126–27, 129, 145, 151–54, 162, 168, 180, 233–35. *See also* Triads.
See, C. S., 194
serve the people (*wei renmin fuwu*). *See* slogans.
Seventy-two Passages, 53
sex work. *See* prostitutes/prostitution.
shamans, xi, 5, 8, 34, 47, 107, 109, 115, 120, 123, 144. *See also* ritual specialists.
Shang Kexi, 52–53, 55–57, 60
Shang Zhixin, 55
Shanghai, 26, 197, 238–39
Shanghai Baby (*Shanghai baobei*), 238
Shaolin, 30–31, 103, 110

Shap-ng-tsai (Shiwuzai), 203, 224
Shi En, 24–25
Shi Xianggu. *See* Zheng Yi Sao.
Shuihu zhuan. *See* Water Margin.
shuntian xingdao. *See* slogans.
Shunzhi emperor, 177
Sister Furong, 239, 243
Sky Spirit, 182
slogans: *dajie fuhu* (rob rich households), 34; *fan Qing fu Ming* (oppose the Qing, restore the Ming), 31, 59, 63; *jiefu jipin* (rob the rich to aid the poor), 36, 125, 165; *jingshen wenming* (spiritual civilization), 231, 234; *jingshen wuran* (spiritual pollution), 234, 241; *shuntian* (follow Heaven), 119; *shuntian xingdao* (follow Heaven to carry out the Way), 136, 137, 142, 155; *titian xingdao* (on behalf of Heaven carry out the Way), 34, 35, 119; *wei renmin fuwu* (serve the people), 37, 229, 241
Small Knives Society (Xiaodaohui), 107, 111, 119, 123, 125–26
Song dynasty, 21, 23, 33, 42, 91, 97, 192, 217, 221, 225, 227
sorcery/sorcerers, xi, 5, 8, 34, 50, 69, 74, 90, 92, 120, 123, 144, 159, 222, 235, 245. *See also* ritual specialists.
Southern Efflorescent King (*Nanxingwang*). *See* Chen Lanjisi.
Southern Ming, 51, 54, 56, 59–61, 63–65, 68. *See also* Ming loyalism.

specter gates (*guimen*), 109
spectral kings (*guiwang*), 109
spectral warriors (*guibing*). *See* divine soldiers.
Spells. *See* incantations.
spirit armies. *See* divine armies.
spirit generals. *See* divine generals.
spirit mediums, xi, 8, 34, 73, 111, 122–24, 144, 208, 222–23, 234. *See also* ritual specialists.
Spirit soldiers. *See* divine soldiers.
spiritual pollution (*jingshen wuran*). *See* slogans.
steles, 12, 18, 73–74, 92, 177, 217–18, 221, 224
stone inscriptions. *See* steles.
Stübel, Hans, 182
Su Guansheng, 217
substitution (*dingxiong*), 160–61
Sui dynasty, 34, 92

Taiping Rebellion, 23, 162, 224
Taiwan, 1–5, 45, 55, 58–60, 63, 65, 67, 70–71, 102–3, 105–6, 111, 119, 126, 139, 209, 235
talismans. *See* amulets.
Tang dynasty, 7, 28, 91–92, 109–10, 120, 147, 153, 171, 174
Tang Saier, 34
Tanka. *See* Dan.
Ten Feet of Steel (Yizhangqing). *See* Hu Sanniang.
Third Old Lady, 191, 214–28, 234, 236–37, 314n14
Thistle Mountains, 23
Thousand Family Grotto (Qianjiadong), 170, 175, 182, 184, 189

361

Three Kingdoms, 31, 39, 288n41
Tiandihui. *See* Triads.
Tianhou. *See* Empress of Heaven.
Titian xingdao. *See* slogans.
Tixi, 103, 123, 147
Toothless Man (*wuchifu*), 4–5, 11, 106, 111, 115
treason, 59
Triads, x, 31, 102–5, 111, 129, 145; initiations, 35; lore, 31; members, 127, 142; rebellion, 135–39, 162, 168, 224; rituals, 115; slogans, 119, 139. *See also* secret societies.
Tuxi. *See* Tixi.
typhoons, 47, 49, 54, 209

vegetarian sects. *See* lay Buddhist groups.
Venerable Cat (*maolaoye*), 92
Vietnam, 23, 44–46, 53, 57–61, 65–66, 70–71, 109, 112, 217–19, 224, 243–44, 290n5
vital force. *See qi*.

Wang Atong, 34–35, 115–16, 122, 124
Wang Conger, 33
Wang Liangchen, 134, 153
Wang Shuo, 21–22, 28, 32, 36–37, 42
Wang Tianzu, 142, 147, 153
Wang Xuetai, 22
Wang Yue, 239
Wang Zheng, 125
Wang Zhihan, 53–54, 57
Wangye (Royal Lords), 126
Warrior Mazu. *See* Zheng Zuxi.

Water Margin, 21, 23–24, 29–30, 33, 35–37, 39–40, 42
Way of Former Heaven (Xiantiandao), 146–47, 235
Way of Pervading Unity (Yiguandao), 146, 235
Wei Hui, 238–40, 242
Weizhou, 57, 214–25, 227, 306n23, 314n14, 315n27
Wen Dengyuan, 138
white (color), 144
White Dragon Tail (Bailongwei), 243–44
white horse, 7, 164, 166, 236
White Lotus Teaching, 131, 144, 237
white tiger, 94, 97. *See also fengshui*.
White Wolf. *See* Bai Lang.
wizards, xi, 8, 34, 64, 109, 116, 122, 127. *See also* ritual specialists.
women, 9, 20, 32, 40, 92, 184; and pollution, 241–42; and power, 201, 242; as denizens of the underworld, 8, 27, 29, 32; as the essence of *yin*, 193, 213; consumerism, 238, 240, 242; deities, 34, 67, 71, 207–12, 214, 217–28; ethnic minorities, 245–46; gender equality, 238; in messianic groups, 123–24; New Cultural Revolution, 238; pirates, 201–7; sexual revolution, 238–40; victims, 41, 56–58, 180; warriors, 33, 185. *See also* boat women; prostitutes/prostitution.
Wu Fusheng, 3, 106
Wu Gaozi, 201

Wu Ping, 70
Wu Ping's Sister, 70
Wu Qingyuan, 143, 303n44
Wu Ruilin, 197
Wu Sangui, 55, 60, 291n44
Wu Tao, 31, 35, 141, 152
Wu Wenchun, 142–43, 153
Wu Zixiang, 140–43, 145–49, 303n38
Wuchuan, 44, 46, 48–49, 52–54, 56
Wushi Er, 215, 220, 314n14, 315n27

Xi Jinping, 41, 230, 234, 241, 246
xia. See knights-errant
Xian Biao, 59
Xiao Liangdi, 92
Xie Huoying, 83
Xu Guodong, 52
Xu Kun (literary critic), 242
Xu Kun (Qing poet), 195
Xu Qianjin, 143, 145, 148–50, 153–54
Xue Youlian, 109

Yan Yan, 102–3, 127
Yang Er. *See* Yang Yandi.
Yang Er Sanpo, 71, 77, 227
Yang Miaozhen, 33, 42
Yang Yandi, 10, 44, 46, 48–49, 53, 56–66, 68, 71, 215, 249, 293n79
Yangpan Teaching, 141
Yao, 9, 29, 162, 167–90, 195, 245–46
Yao charters (*die*), 169, 173–75, 189
Yao King, 169, 182–83, 187, 189–90
Year Star (Taisui), 20, 32, 47–48, 110, 286n1

yin and *yang*, 193, 213, 238
Yinpan Teaching, 141
Yongli emperor, 51–54, 63. *See also* Southern Ming.
Yongzheng emperor, 29, 73–74, 107, 198
You Lihe, 143
Youling, 173–74
youths (male), 21–22, 27–28, 32, 37, 41, 87, 111–12
youxia. *See* knights-errant
Yuan dynasty, 40, 192, 216
Yuan Yonglun, 220, 314n15
Yunxiao, 125, 200

Zeng Qinghao, 138
Zhang Baozai, 10, 36, 67, 73, 204, 220–21, 293n1
Zhang Che, 21, 30, 42
Zhang Fei, 31, 42, 288n41
Zhang Fengjie, 111
Zhang Juzheng, 171
Zhang Polian'gou, 125
Zhang Yingyu, 25, 29
Zhanghua, 106, 126
Zhangzhou, 102–3, 106, 135, 311n5
Zhao Fucai, 181, 185–86
Zhao Jinlong, 169, 182–87, 189–90, 246
Zhao Wenfeng, 185–86
Zhao Zaiqing, 182, 186
Zheng Chenggong, 1, 10, 34, 54, 59, 67–69, 72–73, 103
Zheng Jing, 59–60
Zheng Yi, 203, 215, 220
Zheng Yi Sao, 36, 203–6. *See also* women, pirates.
Zheng Zhilong, 68

Zheng Zuxi, 10, 34, 67–69, 71–75, 77, 208, 221–22, 228, 237, 249
Zhou Caixiong, 217
Zhou Shounan, 32
Zhou Yan, 28
Zhu Ajiang, 115–16
Zhu Fen, 202
Zhu Hongzhu, 110–11, 119, 142, 147, 151, 153
Zhu Santaizi, 111–12, 118, 125, 300n64
Zhu Sitaizi, 1, 4–5, 111, 118
Zhu Yajin, 143–44, 148
Zhu Yigui, 3, 106, 119
Zhuangzi, 21
Zhuluo, 1, 3–5, 106
Zu Zeqing, 50, 55–56, 59–60